Becoming Turkish

Modern Intellectual and Political History of the Middle East
Mehrzad Boroujerdi, *Series Editor*

BECOMING TURKISH

Nationalist Reforms and Cultural Negotiations in Early Republican Turkey, 1923–1945

HALE YILMAZ

Syracuse University Press

Portions of chapter 3 were previously published in "Learning to Read (again): The Social Experiences of Turkey's 1928 Alphabet Reform," Hale Yılmaz, *International Journal of Middle East Studies* 43, no. 4 (2011): 677–97.

∞ The paper used in this publication meets the minimum requirements of the American National Standard for Information Sciences—Permanence of Paper for Printed Library Materials, ANSI Z39.48-1992.

For a listing of books published and distributed by Syracuse University Press, visit our website at SyracuseUniversityPress.syr.edu.

ISBN: 978-0-8156-3317-4

Library of Congress Cataloging-in-Publication Data
Yilmaz, Hale.
Becoming Turkish : nationalist reforms and cultural negotiations in early republican Turkey, 1923–1945 / Hale Yilmaz. — First Edition.
pages cm. — (Modern intellectual and political history of the Middle East)
Includes bibliographical references and index.
ISBN 978-0-8156-3317-4 (cloth : alk. paper) 1. Turkey—Politics and government—1918–1960. 2. Kemalism. 3. Nationalism—Turkey—History—20th century. 4. National characteristics, Turkish. 5. Clothing and dress—Political aspects—Turkey—History—20th century. 6. Turkish language—Political aspects—History—20th century. 7. Turkish language—Orthography and spelling. I. Title.
DR590.Y54 2013
956.1'024—dc23   2013013639

Contents

Illustrations

Acknowledgments

This book would not have been possible without the generous support of many individuals and institutions since I first began work on this project as a doctoral dissertation at the University of Utah more than a decade ago. It is a pleasure to have an opportunity to recognize at least some of the assistance I have received in the course of the research and writing of this book.

I owe the greatest debt to my advisor Byron Cannon for his constant encouragement, intellectual guidance, and moral support from my first days of graduate school at Utah through the completion of my dissertation. Byron had faith in me and was confident that this particular project offered something new, exciting, and important. He deeply appreciated my search for a more inclusive history and was tremendously supportive of my attempt at blending archival historical research with oral histories and interdisciplinary approaches. I sincerely hope that he will be pleased with this final product. Peter Sluglett, too, has been a constant source of intellectual inspiration, encouragement, and support from the initial days of my graduate studies through the research and writing of this book. I am especially grateful to Peter for encouraging me to consider Syracuse University Press as a possible venue for this book. I would also like to thank Ibrahim Karawan, Jim Lehning, and Roberta Micallef for their insightful feedback on the dissertation. The kind reassurance from my committee that this was a project worthy of publication as a book has been critical in sustaining the research and writing beyond the dissertation.

In the early years of my graduate studies at Utah, the teaching and mentoring of Jim Kelly, Bernard Weiss, and Hanna Freij were indispensable for my scholarly development. In yet earlier stages of my education at Marmara University in İstanbul, Mensur Akgün, Ayhan Aktar, Fulya Atacan, Günay

Göksu Özdoğan, and Şule Kut were inspirational teachers and scholars who deserve much credit for nourishing my scholarly interests and for preparing me for an academic career.

During my graduate studies at the University of Utah I was fortunate to receive generous institutional support from the Middle East Center, the Department of History, the Graduate School and the Tanner Humanities Center. A Tanner dissertation fellowship provided invaluable writing time and a wonderful intellectual environment in the critical early stages of writing this project. At Utah, I would also like to thank staff at Marriott Library's Middle East and Interlibrary Loans divisions.

My research in Turkey drew on sources in a number of archives and libraries, and was facilitated by the generous support of a number of individuals including family, friends, and interviewees. I would like to thank the following institutions for allowing me access to their resources: Başbakanlık Cumhuriyet Arşivi, İçişleri Bakanlığı Emniyet Genel Müdürlüğü Arşivi, Türkiye Büyük Millet Meclisi Arşivi, TBMM Kütüphanesi, Milli Kütüphane, Türk Tarih Kurumu, Beyazıt Devlet Kütüphanesi, Taksim Atatürk Kitaplığı, Basın Müzesi, Trabzon İl Halk Kütüphanesi, and Karadeniz Teknik Üniversitesi Kütüphanesi. I am especially grateful to the Turkish Ministry of the Interior for a rare research permit to its archive. The new data collected from the EGM archive has been essential for the arguments made in this book. I would also like to recognize the hospitality extended to me by the EGM staff during the months of research there. In Ankara, Meliha Baka, a true friend, and my uncle Nurettin Yılmaz and his family welcomed me warmly, making my extended stays there pleasant and comfortable. Mustafa Özgüler, Hüseyin Albayrak, Defne Karaosmanoğlu, Ali Taşıgüzel, and İsmail Hacıfettahoğlu offered help at different moments of research in Ankara. In Trabzon, Veysel Usta, Ömer Güner, Pınar Güner, and Mesut Çapa offered hospitality and assistance. I am grateful to Michael Meeker not only for his exemplary scholarship, to which I am intellectually indebted, but also for the initial Trabzon contacts when I first began research on this project.

The oral histories I conducted were no doubt the most exciting and rewarding part of this research. My interviewees and their families welcomed me warmly and generously shared with me their memories of childhood and youth. Meliha Tanyeli, Neriman Tanyolaç, Ömer Güner, Avni Yurdabayrak, Yusuf Altınkaya, Mehmet Baltacı, and Recep Göksoy were particularly generous in sharing memories and (when available) family albums and private documents. I regret that most of my interviewees passed away between the 2002 and 2003 interviews and the writing of these lines. It was certainly a privilege to hear them and to record their memories. In addition to the interviews I conducted, I drew on an oral historical study by Sevil Atauz. I am grateful to Professor Atauz for allowing me to quote from her work on Antep. Parts of Chapter Three appeared in the November 2011 issue of the *International Journal of Middle East Studies*. I would like to thank *IJMES* editors and the Cambridge University Press for the opportunity to reprint material from that article here.

At Syracuse University Press, Mary Selden Evans invited the manuscript with great enthusiasm for this particular research and guided me through the review process. I am grateful to her and to Mehrzad Boroujerdi, the series editor, for making it possible to share this research with readers through Syracuse University Press. I would like to thank the entire staff at Syracuse University Press, and especially Deanna McCay for her professionalism in embracing a project she inherited half-finished when Mary retired. I benefitted immensely from the thoughtful feedback provided by two outside reviewers for the press. I am grateful to both reviewers for their careful reading of an earlier draft and for their constructive feedback. I think this is a better book thanks to their insightful criticism and feedback. I would also like to thank Maria Hosmer-Briggs for her careful copy-editing.

A number of colleagues and friends provided invaluable advice and assistance along the way. At MESA, AHA and other venues, Gavin Brockett, Faith Childress, Emine Evered, Behrooz Ghamari, Kathy Libal, June Marvel, Sultan Tepe, Meltem Türköz, and Murat Yüksel offered sincere feedback and fresh ideas, or simply friendly conversation and encouragement. I am especially grateful to Gavin for reading and commenting on the entire manuscript more than once. My colleagues in the History department of Southern Illinois University, Carbondale and my former colleagues at the University of Montana deserve thanks for providing a supportive work environment. I am most grateful to Kay Carr, Holly Hurlburt, and Robbie Lieberman for the generous help they have given me since my employment at SIU. I am also happy to record the contribution of my graduate students, particularly those in my *Nationalism in the Middle East* colloquium where our discussions helped me rethink the broader context of the Turkish case. Ümit Kartal did an excellent job in transcribing several of the interviews I conducted for this project. Andrew Bynom was generous with his time in the careful and meticulous editing assistance he provided. Paul Sloboda prepared the map with utmost care and attention to detail, and patiently and diligently prepared all the images in this book. I am grateful to Paul for his patience with my many queries and requests with the images. Nancy Deal was a wonderful friend who supported me from the early days of my graduate studies; I regret that she will not see the culmination of this project as a book. Ervin Deal kindly read several chapters to see if this book would make any sense to a mathematician with no expertise in Turkish studies. Roger Deal has contributed to this project in so many ways that I cannot possibly record them all. I am forever grateful to him for his patient support over the years.

My family in Turkey has been the greatest source of support and encouragement throughout this intellectual journey. For more than a decade now, this book has become a way of reconnecting with family and friends in Turkey. My search for a better understanding of the national past led to a renewed interest in family history as well. My grandfather Mustafa Bayındırlı lovingly and joyfully recounted memories and stories of his childhood and youth. Other family members contributed to this project in many different ways. I am grateful to my uncle Memiş Bayındırlı for an initial contact that proved to be crucial for research in Ankara. My sister Fatma and my brother Mustafa have over the years patiently and tirelessly supplied the books and other materials I requested from Turkey for this project. My brother-in-law Hüseyin Kaptan has been generous in his assistance with computers to a very low-tech historian. My nephew Deniz joined our family during the writing of this book and has been a very special source of inspiration and optimism. My niece Defne Ece was born days before the writing of these lines, bringing joy and renewed inspiration as I bring this project to a close. My parents Makbule and Cemaleddin Yılmaz deserve very special thanks for their loving and unconditional support of me and my work. They have patiently and quietly tolerated the long periods of my absence as my studies and this book have dragged on. This book is dedicated to them with gratitude for their loving care, support, and understanding; and to Deniz and Defne Ece, in celebration of childhood.

İstanbul
August 2012

A Note on Spelling and Pronunciation

Throughout this book I have used standard modern Turkish spellings for Turkish and Ottoman names and terms. Modern Turkish uses a modified Latin alphabet, adopted in 1928. Each letter of the alphabet represents a single sound. Most consonants are pronounced essentially the same as in English. The exceptions and ambiguities are:

c is pronounced as *j* in *John* (*hoca*). (Thus *hoca* is often written in English as *hoja* or *hodja*.)

ç is pronounced as *ch* in *chair* (*peçe*).

ş is pronounced as *sh* in *shoe* (*şapka*). (Thus *paşa* is often written in English as *pasha*.)

j is pronounced as in French or as *s* in *measure*.

ğ has various values, but most often it merely serves to lengthen the previous vowel (*oğlu*).

Modern Turkish has eight vowels:

a is pronounced as in German or as *a* in *father* (*kalpak*).

e is pronounced as *e* in *pet* (*peştemal*).

ı represents a sound that does not exist in English, but is pronounced similar to the *e* in *happen*. (It represents an unrounded version of the *oo* in *good*.) (*Bayındırlı*)

i is pronounced somewhere between *i* in *ship* and *ee* in *sheep* (*imam*).

(The letter i carries a dot even when it is capitalized, as in İstanbul or İzmir.)

o is pronounced as *o* in *open* (*manto*).

ö is pronounced as in German ö or French eu (*Gökalp*).

u is pronounced as *oo* in *room* (*Mustafa*).

ü is pronounced as German ü or French u (*Türk*).

BECOMING TURKISH

TURKEY circa 1940

BULGARIA
GREECE

BLACK SEA

USSR

IRAN

IRAQ

SYRIA

MEDITERRANEAN SEA

CYPRUS

Edirne
Kırklareli
Tekirdağ
İstanbul
Çanakkale
Kocaeli
Bilecik
Bursa
Balıkesir
Kütahya
Eskişehir
Manisa
İzmir
Aydın
Denizli
Muğla
Burdur
Isparta
Afyon
Antalya

Zonguldak
Kastamonu
Bolu
Çankırı
ANKARA
Konya
İçel (Mersin)

Sinop
Samsun
Amasya
Tokat
Çorum
Yozgat
Kırşehir
Niğde
Kayseri
Sivas

Ordu
Giresun
Trabzon
Rize
Çoruh (Artvin)
Kars
Ağrı
Van
Hakkari

Gümüşhane
Erzurum
Erzincan
Tunceli
Elazığ
Bingöl
Muş
Bitlis
Siirt

Malatya
Diyarbakır
Mardin
Urfa
Maraş
Seyhan (Adana)
Gazi]Antep
Hatay (Antakya)

0 100 200 300 Kilometers
0 100 200 Miles

Hatay (Alexandretta) joined Turkey in 1939.
Rize and Artvin were merged as Çoruh province 1933-1936.
Tunceli was created as a province in 1935.

Hakkari was part of Van province 1933-1936.
Bitlis was part of Muş province 1929-1935.
Bingöl was created as a province in 1936.

Map of Turkey circa 1940. Map by Paul Sloboda.

Introduction

In 1923 the Republic of Turkey was proclaimed, following the breakup of the Ottoman Empire at the end of World War I and a War of Liberation against Greece and other victorious Entente Powers. The proclamation of the Republic was accompanied by a sweeping series of modernizing reforms covering all aspects of life. Historical and political studies of early Republican Turkey tend to emphasize the elitist and the statist aspects of the Republican project of modernization. Yet to attain a better understanding of early Republican Turkish society, culture, and politics, it is critical to study the societal aspects of the reform process. The experience of the early Republican, or what came to be known as Kemalist, reforms became part of the larger social process of various local communities coming to terms with what they had lived through during a decade of wars and destruction. How did ordinary people experience the process of Kemalist reforms? How did they receive and react to the state-initiated changes? This process involved a plethora of responses between the two extremes of passive reception and outright rejection. This book explores the ways in which the meaning of the Kemalist reforms was negotiated between individuals, communities, and the state.

This study focuses on the period from 1923, the formation of the Republic, to 1945, the beginning of multi-party politics with the foundation of the Democrat Party. During these two decades Turkey was ruled by a radical single-party regime, the Republican People's Party (RPP), which was presided over by a charismatic revolutionary leader, Mustafa Kemal Atatürk, until his death in 1938. Drawing on the legitimacy of the success in the War of Liberation, the revolutionary leadership of post-Ottoman Turkey embarked upon an ambitious project of modernization and secular nation-building. The aim of this project was summarized as elevating the Turkish nation to the level of contemporary civilization. The sphere of the reforms extended from the abolition of the Caliphate to the adoption of the Latin alphabet and to the declaration of Sunday as the new day of rest. Traditionally, historical narratives of this period have been told from the point of view of the modernizing state. The main exception to this trend has been the histories of violent resistance to the reforms and of the ensuing clashes and suppression. I argue that neither the histories that focus on the state nor those that focus on opposition and resistance capture the complexity and richness of social and cultural life in Turkey in the 1920s and 1930s. I argue, following the path that has been suggested by Joel Migdal,[1] that we can arrive at a more comprehensive understanding of social and cultural life by focusing on the meeting grounds of and the dialogue between the state and the society.

This book examines state-society relations in Turkey in the context of the nationalizing and modernizing reforms of the early Republic. It tries to provide a better understanding of the Turkish nation-building process by focusing on four specific sites of the state's attempt to produce a new Turk and a modern Turkish nation. The sites or areas of Kemalist reform that I examine are men's clothing, women's clothing, language, and national celebrations. I do not claim that these were the only or even necessarily the most important aspects of the Kemalist nation-building process. My choice of these areas of reform in part reflects my consideration of these sites as significant elements of the process that will reveal more about the overall process, beyond the issues specific to each particular reform area. The selection of the themes, naturally, also reflects my own interests as a historian in the politics and culture of language, dress, and celebrations. I treat men's and women's dress issues separately to demonstrate how (and why) the state and society dealt with the male and female dress differently in nationalizing and modernizing/Westernizing dress, and to better incorporate women and their experiences in the history of the early Republic. Language was a crucial site of the new state's nationalizing, secularizing, and modernizing policies. Turkish nationalists, both ideologues such as Ziya Gökalp and statesmen such as Şükrü Kaya, emphasized the Turkish language as a fundamental element of Turkishness. In the early years of the Republic, the state pursued a wide range of language policies aimed at building a homogeneous nation. By 1923, the foundation of the Republic, the religious diversity of the population had been heavily curtailed, but the population left within the boundaries of the new state was still ethnically and linguistically diverse. Officially, every Turkish citizen was considered a Turk regardless of religion, race, ethnicity, or gender. However, the abstract concept of citizenship did not provide the ideological bond necessary to create a sense of belonging to a new Turkish nation. The early Republican state tried to create a sense of Turkishness among the population in part through the regulation of written and spoken language. In this book I focus on the 1928 alphabet reform and its social experiences as a part of the state's language policies that aimed at modernizing and nationalizing simultaneously. I include national celebrations as a site that is not explicitly political (hence is not always recognized as part of the process of reforms) but one that was nevertheless crucial for the political socialization and nation-building processes in potentially more inclusive ways.

My goal in this book is not to provide an exhaustive survey of, or to examine all aspects of, the Turkish nation-building process. There is a rich and growing body of literature on Turkish nationalism that deals well with the ideological and institutional aspects of that particular nationalism.[2] Works such as Soner Çağaptay's *Islam, Secularism, and Nationalism in Modern Turkey*, for example, have revealed how religion (Islam) continued to play a fundamental role alongside language and ethnicity (Turkishness) in the shaping of nationalist policies of the Kemalist state in the 1920s and 1930s.[3] Drawing on an impressive body of archival sources, Çağaptay's work provides us with a better understanding of the nature of Turkish nationalism by studying state policies dealing with citizenship, immigration and settlement, language, and the overall state policies toward non-Muslim (especially Jewish) and non-Turkish Muslim (particularly Kurdish) communities. While it makes an important contribution to the historiography of Turkish nationalism, Çağaptay's work nevertheless remains concerned with the state and the politics of the nation-building process. It does not take into account the social and cultural processes of nation building, nor does it deal with the responses of those who were targets of the state's nationalizing policies.

My main goal here is to provide a better understanding of the practice of the Turkish nation-building process by focusing on certain aspects of the state-initiated reforms that aimed at creating a new national culture, modern and secular. In doing that I hope to shed light on how the process was experienced, promoted, contested, and negotiated by those who were targets of the reforms, not only in the major cities such as İstanbul and Ankara but also in the provinces. In the process I also hope to contribute to a better understanding of the nature of the early Republican state.

Much of the scholarship on recent Turkish history has been written from a perspective of the modernization paradigm, as best exemplified by the seminal work of Bernard Lewis.[4] From this point of view, the Republican Revolution is seen to be the culmination of a long period of Ottoman reforms. Nationalist histories, including official histories as best represented by the textbooks written for the *History of the Turkish Revolution* courses, have also generally worked within the framework of modernization theory.[5] These histories mostly begin with the outbreak of World War I, present Ottoman participation and defeat in the War, and provide a detailed account of the War of Liberation as an anti-imperialist nationalist struggle for independence. They discuss in detail the foundation of the Republic, the policies of the new regime and especially the reforms, and the principles of Kemalist ideology. These works emphasize the break from the Ottoman past and identify the first two decades of the Republic as a new revolutionary era with universal implications. Turkish nationalist historiography (produced mainly in Turkey and by Turkish scholars) by and large continues to be written in defense of the secular Republic, manifesting concerns over the future of the Republic.[6]

In the last two decades the broader Turkish historiography has moved away from the narrative of a radical and revolutionary break after 1922, emphasizing instead the continuities between the late Ottoman and early Republican eras. Erik Zürcher's work has pioneered and best examplifies this historiographical shift. Zürcher locates more continuity than rupture between the Young Turk or the Second Constitutional and the early Republican or Republican People's Party periods in terms of institutions, ideology, political outlook, and nationalist and secularist policies, including the treatment of minorities and demographic engineering.[7] In his most recent work, Zürcher elaborates on these themes, particulary on the demographic policies of the Young Turks and the RPP.[8]

This line of scholarhip has important implications for understanding and writing modern Turkish history. It suggests a new periodization of modern Turkish history and the possibility of moving the dividing line from

1923, a symbolic date marking the proclamation of the Turkish Republic (or 1922–1924, referring collectively to the years of key institutional changes from the abolition of the Sultanate in 1922 through the secularizing legislation of 1924, which included the abolition of the Caliphate), to somewhere around 1908. This rethinking of periodization is reflected in a recent volume edited by Zürcher.[9]

I have focused in this book on the post-1922 period, in part because of the nature of the questions I explore: the implementation and the experiences of the secular modernist, nationalist reforms of the RPP era. This is also because I see not a total break, as the Turkish revolutionaries desired and insisted on, but at least a partial break or rupture after 1922. This was a consequence in part of the radical acts and aspirations of the early republican regime, but the break was also due to the impact of World War I and the War of Liberation, and the social, demographic, economic, and psychological changes created by the wars and by government policies. Taking 1923 as an important historical moment does not necessarily mean taking an uncritical stance toward modern Turkish history, or uncritically accepting the Republican claims that a profound rupture from the nation's imperial past had taken place in 1923. In exploring the social experiences of the Kemalist reforms, I look for and take into account the Ottoman background and Ottoman origins in each area of reform I address, including the culture of national holidays.

Zürcher's line of scholarship also introduces a powerful new criticism of the historiographical paradigm that the Turkish experiment in the first decades of the Republic constituted a revolution. Scholars have for some time debated whether the Turkish experiment was indeed a revolution. As Şerif Mardin pointed out some years ago, the Turkish experience of the 1920s and 1930s cannot be considered a revolution in the conventional sense of the term used to refer to the French, Russian, and more recently, Iranian Islamic revolutions. According to one of the widely known definitions, provided by Samuel Huntington, a revolution is a "rapid, fundamental, and violent domestic change in the dominant values and myths of a society, in its political institutions, social structure, leadership, and governmental activity and policies."[10] Accordingly, revolutions are different from rebellions, revolts, coups, and wars of independence. Mardin noted (with reference to Alexis de Tocqueville's discussion of the French Revolution) that the Turkish experiment lacked some of the fundamental criteria of a revolution, such as violence and a revolutionary theory. But where Mardin did locate a powerful revolutionary aspect in the Turkish case was in the commitment of the Turkish revolutionaries to change the values of the society.[11] In other words, it was in the sphere of culture, rather than social structure, that the Turkish Revolution was truly revolutionary. When we consider the opinions of those involved in the process, not only the leading statesmen such as Atatürk and İsmet İnönü but also the parliamentarians, governors, journalists, teachers, and People's Houses activists, it is clear that they thought they were indeed experiencing or leading a cultural revolution. This is abundantly evident in the contemporary speeches, Parliamentary and party debates (as we will see in the RPP Congressional debate over banning the *peçe* and *çarşaf*), memoirs, and press debates. A perusal of the titles of contemporary works such as Recep Peker's *İnkılâp Dersleri* (*Lessons in the Revolution*), Peyami Safa's *Türk İnkılâbına Bakışlar* (*Perspectives on the Turkish Revolution*), and Celal Nuri İleri's *Türk İnkılâbı* (*The Turkish Revolution*) also reveals a contemporary political and intellectual perspective that regarded this experiment as a revolution.[12]

My goal here is not to resolve this difficult question of whether this experiment can still be called a revolution, but to contribute to the debate indirectly by exploring the social experiences of the Kemalist reforms. Cognizant of the ambiguities, uncertainty, and disagreement over the meaning and use of the term revolution in this particular historical context, I have chosen to use the term "reforms" rather than "revolution" throughout the book. I am more concerned with how this process of making (and becoming) a modern Turkish nation worked, and how it appeared to those targeted by the process, than with whether we should or should not call it a revolution.

Drawing on a textual analysis of documents such as Atatürk's speeches and the Republican People's Party programs, political scientists Taha Parla and Andrew Davison characterize the Kemalist ideology and political system as a form of "nationalist, laicist and solidaristic corporatism" that at times incorporated characteristic elements of fascism.[13] Disagreeing with the observers of the Kemalist era who see in authoritarian modernist Kemalism a potential for democratic development, Parla and Davison maintain that despite its progressive tendencies, Kemalism remained an anti-liberal and anti-democratic ideology at its core. While the authors' critical assessment of the Kemalist ideology and its relation to present day questions of democratic consolidation can help expand the debate on the ideological aspects of modern Turkish history, their work is not particularly helpful in understanding how that ideology translated into policy and how those policies affected the lives of Turkish citizens.

A commonly accepted view of the Kemalist period (a view which I question) is that the state-initiated reforms did not reach or affect the lives of the majority of the population. This assumption tends to make the questions of reception, reaction, and resistance to the reforms less relevant for understanding this period. Zürcher has expressed this view in the following words:

> The reforms hardly influenced the life of the villagers who made up the great mass of the Turkish population. A farmer or shepherd from Anatolia had never worn a fez, so he was not especially bothered about its abolition. His wife wore no veil anyway, so the fact that its use was discouraged did not mean anything to him or her. He could not read and write, so the nature of the script was in a sense immaterial to him, although the fact that the only man in the village who was able to read and write was the local imam tended to strengthen the religious connotation of the Arabic alphabet. He had to take a family name in 1934, but the whole village would continue to use first names (as is still the case) and the family names remained for official use only. The new family law made polygamy illegal, but those farmers who could afford it would still quite often take into the house a second woman, without marrying her, ascribing her children to his legal wife, if need be.[14]

While Zürcher is right in his analysis that the rural residents of Anatolia were less directly and less frequently affected by the reforms, this book will demonstrate that the early republican state's modernizing and nationalizing reforms targeted, and reached sometimes in unexpected ways, even the illiterate peasant who had never worn a fez. This was in large measure because the state's modernizing and homogenizing interests were not confined to the removal of the fez, as the conventional scholarship has argued, but extended to other symbols of his ethnic, religious, local, and tribal identities as well. The reach of the state in the lives of small town and village communities was uneven, irregular, and incomplete, but it was not nonexistent.

Of the works dealing with the political history of the early Republican period, Hakkı Uyar's study on the Republican People's Party and the Single-Party Era, in addition to being one of the most comprehensive accounts of the RPP also expands our understanding of opposition to the RPP regime.[15] Uyar's treatment of opposition between 1923 and 1950 includes not only organized opposition through legal and illegal political parties but also "unorganized" opposition in the press, opposition from outside the country, particularly by the "150'likler,"[16] and opposition and debates over the question of democracy within the ruling RPP at the center and at the provincial level. While Uyar's widening of the term "opposition" beyond political parties is useful, his central concern is on the analysis of the Turkish political system during the RPP years and his treatment of opposition remains largely limited to political and ideological opposition mostly by the elites. Uyar's work does not deal with the questions of opposition and reaction from various segments of the society in response to the actual policies of the RPP regime.

One study that departs from the mainstream literature in its treatment of opposition in the formative period of Turkey is Ceylan Tokluoğlu's dissertation on the role of resistance in the formation of the Turkish state.[17] Tokluoğlu conceptualizes resistance as a category distinct from organized political opposition. She examines resistance movements against the state from 1919 until the mid-1930s in two periods: during the War of Liberation, and in the decade following the formation of the Republic. Tokluoğlu studies different forms of collective and individual resistance, including social banditry, military desertion, ethnically and religiously based uprisings (especially the Kurdish uprisings), and popular resistance against a number of the state-initiated reforms. Tokluoğlu's focus is on demonstrating how the processes of state- and nation-building provoked resistance and how in turn resistance and state responses to resistance influenced the process of state formation. While helpful in conceptualizing Turkish state formation as a political and cultural process that evolved in part in response to resistance, Tokluoğlu's analysis is rather limited in explaining the process of reforms in the decade following independence. Tokluoğlu relies almost exclusively on secondary sources for her rather brief accounts of resistance to a number of the state-initiated reforms; hence, our knowledge of the actual processes and lived experiences of reform is not furthered by her research. Furthermore, since her emphasis is on the impact of resistance on state formation, the social process and the everyday experience of reforms are not of primary concern in her work.

The subject of this work is not organized opposition, collective resistance, or moments of violent reaction. Rather than focusing on the state or the moments of conflict and violent rebellion, such as the Sheikh Said rebellion, on which there is a rich literature,[18] I am interested in understanding the Kemalist modernization and nation-building process as a social and cultural as well as a political process. I examine how Republican reforms were implemented and how they affected social and cultural change. I study how individuals and communities received, reacted to, negotiated, and experienced reforms in their everyday lives, and how and by whom those policies were mediated on the ground. I look at different forms and degrees of acceptance, accommodation, negotiation, and resistance, such as voluntary change, forced compliance, and petitions to the authorities. If individuals were discontented with the new laws, were their positions based on religious, traditional, local, ethnic, class, gender, or other interpretations? I study the ways in which individuals negotiated the meaning of the reforms with the state authorities, for instance through the creation of new public and private spheres and the assumption of different identities in different spheres. This work also takes into account mediating institutions and individuals such as governors, courts and judges, the People's Houses, The Directorate of Religious Affairs and the imams, and schools. It was through such agencies that the state and the citizens communicated at the local level.

Sociologist Şerif Mardin has criticized "Kemalist" and "Marxisant" Turkish scholars of modern Turkey for "their inability to acknowledge a 'micro' component of social dynamics" due to their focus on the state and "macro" models and structures.[19] Mardin asserts that while selectively attending to the "macro" social dynamics, these scholars systematically neglect "micro"-dimensions of social life, or "life-worlds." Due to their narrow focus on the "macro" social structure as the subject of inquiry and the level of analysis, Mardin argues, this approach does not explore "micro" social relations: processes of identity formation, personal histories, or "the resources of the dominated, or their 'discourse'."[20] Mardin invites Turkish scholars to pay more attention to the "life-worlds" and to the "everyday," and to link the macro- and micro-levels of social change and analysis to achieve a deeper understanding of Turkish modernity.

Mardin's work on the life and ideas and followers of Bediüzzaman Said Nursi (1876–1960), the radical Islamist thinker and founder of the Nur movement, exemplifies the approach he has proposed to the scholars of modern Turkey.[21] Mardin explains the case of Said Nursi in the social and cultural context of the nineteenth century Ottoman, Young Turk, and early Republican secular reforms. Mardin asserts that these reforms, beginning with the Tanzimat era and intensifying under the Republic, disrupted the "everyday" world of the average Ottoman/Turk by eliminating "the discourse . . . which gave life to interpersonal relations for the average Ottoman."[22] For Mardin, it was the language of Islam that provided Anatolian Muslims with the norms of everyday conduct. Said Nursi's ideas developed during a time in which Islam as social practice came under attack by reforms that promoted a different view of social relations. In Mardin's words,

> Bediüzzaman's struggle against materialism emerges as a stand taken against a new image of social relations and a protest against the practices linked to this image. The novel concept of social relations which came with reform was one which ignored a code of conduct drawn from Islam and the personal relations which formed around this code, and superceded them with an understanding of society as an impersonal machine.[23]

Mardin explains that Said Nursi's ideas appealed to many in this context as he presented the norms of Islam "in such a way as to re-introduce the traditional Muslim idiom of conduct and of personal relations into an emerging society of industry and mass communications."[24]

Mardin persuasively argues for the role of Islam as "life-world" and as the language of the dominated in the development and appeal of Said Nursi's ideas and movement. While Mardin's call for investigating "life-worlds" opens up exciting possibilities of new research, taking religion as "life-world" too far would eliminate the exploration of other possible "life-worlds" such as class, ethnicity, gender, regional and local specificities, and individual choice. While Mardin may be justified in criticizing Turkish social scientists for their "inability to understand the power of Islam,"[25] assuming the primacy of Islam as the dominant ideology guiding the lives of Anatolian men and women may well mean replacing the focus on the state with a new focus on religion at the expense of explorations of other "life-worlds."

More recently, Mardin reiterated his call to Turkish historians and social scientists to pay closer attention to the linkages between macro-politics/macrostructures and the "micro" social worlds/local cultural parameters. He continues to consider religion as key to understanding the micro-cultural worlds of Turkish modernity, but now acknowledges that Turkish social scientists, including himself, have not sufficiently considered "the role of subaltern elements as independent force" in the evolution of Turkish modernity and its contradictions.[26] This book, too, is interested in understanding how women, peasants, and other subaltern groups experienced the nationalizing reforms of the early Republican era without the assumption that religion was necessarily the principal factor shaping their social and cultural worlds and everyday acts and decisions.

Although the bulk of the existing literature on the history of the Republic focuses on the state, some recent works (for instance, by Bozdoğan, Brockett, Öztürkmen, Libal, and Türköz) expand the history of this period beyond the state and open the door for more inclusive and more complicated interpretations.[27] The present study contributes to, and seeks to further, this emerging scholarship on the social history of the early republican period by drawing on new written, oral, and visual evidence to deepen the analysis in several specific sites of nationalist reforms, and also by placing the Turkish modernist-nationalist experience in its broader regional context.

Of these recent works, Faith Childress's dissertation on early Republican education examined the role of education in the creation of a Turkish national identity by examining how Turkish national identity was represented in textbooks.[28] While a number of earlier works had dealt with the same question,[29] Childress expanded the scope of analysis in two ways. She first incorporated the process of transforming ideology to educational policy by studying the activities and decisions of the Instruction and Pedagogy Committee, or *Talim ve Terbiye Heyeti*, the body responsible for setting education goals, pedagogies, and curriculum, and examining and commissioning textbooks. Then she analyzed and compared the nationalist ideology presented in music, geography, reading, history, and civics textbooks from the 1930s to the evolving Kemalist ideology and rhetoric. Her argument is that there are significant differences between the evolving Kemalist ideology (as expressed, for instance, in Republican People's Party programs) and the Kemalist message communicated to students in textbooks. Childress drew attention to the gap betweeen Kemalist ideology and Kemalist policy by demonstrating that differences emerged in the process of translating ideology into curriculum and textbooks. She also placed emphasis on the role of bureaucrats in turning ideology into policy and in contributing to the articulation of that ideology in the process.

Among the most insightful recent works on the social history of the early Republican era is Meltem Türköz's study on the implementation of the 1934 Surname Legislation.[30] Drawing on a variety of sources including oral historical interviews, archival documents such as population registry records, and coverage in the popular press, Türköz explored how the state-imposed reform was mediated between government officials and citizens and among families. She discovered that the experiences of surname adoption varied depending on factors such as the relationship between the official and the citizen, and the citizen's social, educational, and minority status. While some citizens were simply given or assigned a surname by an official, other citizens chose a surname for themselves and negotiated with the government official to register the name of their own choice. Türköz also noted that not only citizens but also population officials interpreted the law in multiple ways. Government officials were not always in agreement with one another, for instance, on the criteria for acceptable Turkish surnames. Türköz also studied one aspect of what happened to surnames after the initial adoption: namely, the process of surname changes initiated by citizens dissatisfied with their registered surname or citizens who wished to return to the family names that they had before the Surname Law and by which they were socially known. That surname change petitions followed shortly after the adoption of surnames is indicative of how the state-imposed measures are subject to negotiation and modification by citizens affected by those measures. A related research topic that would be even more revealing in terms of understanding social consequences of surname adoptions is the process of actual use of surnames, once adopted. Türköz's concern with aspects of the Surname Law as it was actually experienced, with the process between rationalizing and nationalizing legislation and its consequences, and with contact between citizens and state officials, deserves attention in the study of other areas of Kemalist reforms, as well. I seek to further this line of historical analysis by exploring similar issues in several other areas of reform.

This book examines the everyday experience of Kemalist reforms, considering a wide range of state and non-state agencies in the implementation of Kemalist policies, as well as the range of reactions and responses that included a broad spectrum of everyday forms of resistance, accommodation, coping with change (or "muddling through"), or active or passive support that fell between the two extremes of violent resistance and passive submission. Unlike what happened in other contemporary Muslim contexts, such as Afghanistan and the Soviet Union in Central Asia, Kemalist reforms were not imposed on society by a colonial state, or by a very narrow modernist political elite that did not command much support or sympathy among the general population outside of the capital city. Despite the Republican rhetoric to the contrary, Kemalist reforms rested—at least in part—on the political, ideological, cultural, and institutional legacies of the post-Tanzimat Ottoman state.

The experiences of and devastation caused by a decade of wars, from the Balkan wars through the War of Liberation, too, were crucial in creating a social and psychological environment that was conducive to the creation of a new regime and contributed to the profound social and cultural transformations that regime led. The failure of the Ottoman state in World War I for all practical purposes put an end to the Ottoman order and discredited the institutions of the old regime, making possible the abolition of some institutions such as the Sultanate and the Caliphate. At the same time, the military and diplomatic victories of Mustafa Kemal and the nationalist forces in 1922 gave the new leadership credibility and legitimacy. The experiences and the consequences of war created a set of social, psychological, demographic, and economic circumstances that made the society more receptive to radical change.

This process of modernization and nation-building was not entirely determined, controlled, or experienced by men only, even though those in positions of political authority were nearly exclusively male. This book brings women into the historical narrative of the Kemalist era, not only as objects of the Kemalist reforms and a site of contestation between a modernist state and a patriarchal society and traditional culture, but as subjects of and active participants in a crucial period of social and cultural change. I have tried to avoid a tendency of feminist historians to write women's history separately from the mainstream history. Following the example of scholars such as Beth Baron (in the Egyptian context) and Afsaneh Najmabadi (in the Iranian context), I try to incorporate women's experiences in the overall process of Turkish modernization and nation-building. Several influential gender scholars, such as Deniz Kandiyoti, Nilüfer Göle, and Yeşim Arat, have written on women and gender in the Republican era from sociological and political science perspectives. While they have produced valuable research on women in modern Turkey, the field of modern Turkish history is still dominated by male scholarship that still tends to overlook the categories of women and gender.[31]

Like women, children and youth were very much part of this process. This book brings children and youth into the general narrative of the Kemalist era, not only as targets and recipients of state initiated processes but also as eyewitnesses and active participants of a society in rapid transformation. I also draw attention to the importance of age and generations as explanatory factors in understanding the transformations of the early Republican era.

The book is organized around four thematic chapters following the introduction. Chapter One focuses on the social experiences of men's clothing reforms in the early Republic. It argues that dress was significant for the new Turkish regime in the early decades of the Republic for its symbolic and transformative functions in making a modern, Western, secular nation. Dress was equally significant for individuals and communities as an important aspect of their ethnic, tribal, religious, or occupational identities, as they responded to the state-imposed regulations. Dress for the new Turkish regime meant much more than has been described in the conventional accounts of the "hat reform" of 1925. The "hat reform," which proclaimed the European style hat as the Turkish national headgear and prohibited others, had both symbolic and transformative functions to simultaneously modernize and nationalize the citizens. Although headgear continued to be the most closely regulated aspect of men's appearance, other elements of male clothing, such as European style trousers, shirts, and ties, were also important in making a unified, modern nation by eliminating visible markers of ethnic, religious, regional, occupational, and other differences. The new dress would help create secular, modern, European-looking citizens whose uniform appearance would suggest common membership in a new national community. I argue here that the commonly accepted model of a zealous Kemalist elite forcing its will upon the silent masses is not entirely justified. Rather, there was tension between the judiciary and the administration, and between central government and government officials in the provinces, regarding the implementation of the Law. Reactions were diverse, and depended on a number of factors, including tradition, class, and economics; hence 'Islam' does not appear to be the only or even the main relevant factor. There was indeed a segment of society that welcomed and actively supported the hat reform. Open opposition and protest were rare, yet there was resentment, and men resorted to what James C. Scott has called the "weapons of the weak."[32] This chapter concludes by arguing that even though the hat reform was intended as a homogenizing measure, it actually led to new class distinctions based on headgear.

Chapter Two turns to women and the politics and culture of their dress in making a new Turkish nation. While traditional histories of the dress reforms have focused almost exclusively on male dress, gender scholars (including leading scholars such as Nilüfer Göle and Yeşim Arat) have not challenged that focus, nor have they investigated male dress reforms from a gender perspective. By drawing on sources including party, ministerial, and police records, interviews, and local and national newspapers, I revise the standard account of the early Republican dress reforms depicted as pertaining to men only. Contrary to the official rhetoric that women's dress issues were left to the forces of fashion, modernization, and urbanization, the Turkish state indeed tried to regulate women's clothing, as did a number of other modernizing or colonial states in the contemporary Muslim world, from French Algeria to Iran, Afghanistan, and the Soviet Union in Central Asia. However, the inability to form a consensus on the issue within the ruling Republican People's Party, coupled with the fear of hostile reaction, led the Party to delegate the responsibility of regulating women's dress to the provincial governors. Women's reactions to the unveiling campaigns were varied, and depended on economic, social, class, cultural, and educational factors. Civil servants, especially female teachers, were both the objects and the agents of the new dress regulations. The majority of urban, educated, upper class, already-modernized women embraced and promoted the new dress. The Westernized upper classes not only provided a support base for the regime, but were also crucial in the long term, as their dress and life styles provided a model for the lower and the middle classes to emulate. While a segment of urban women actively supported the new dress regulations, many people, male and female, resented those regulations. Women coped with the new situation by resorting to creative solutions such as adding umbrellas to their new outdoors outfit. Women also resorted to various "weapons of the weak" such as avoiding the public sphere by secluding themselves in their homes: acts that avoided defiance and sanctions, yet expressed their resentment. Men raised their voices over women's dress in the name of tradition and honor, and women had to accommodate simultaneously to the demands of an authoritarian state and the demands of a male-dominant culture. This chapter concludes by emphasizing that dress continued to be, and remains, a major site of cultural contestation, domination, and resistance between the state and the society, between men and women, and between women of different class, status, religious, and ideological backgrounds.

Chapter Three addresses the questions of alphabet and language in Turkish nation building. Language, both written and spoken, is an important aspect of both individual and collective identity. A shared language makes it possible to imagine a national community rather than an Islamic, ethnic, or tribal community. The literature is rich on the institutional aspects of the language reform, including the alphabet reform, the Turkification policies of the Turkish Language Association, and the Sun Language Theory, yet the actual practice of language reform has been much less studied. This chapter considers the implementation of and responses to those language policies. I look specifically at the transition to and use of the new Latin-based Turkish alphabet, which replaced the Ottoman alphabet based on Arabic/Persian letters, including the continuing use of the old script in private, and occasionally in the public sphere. I also explore the connections between the alphabet reform and other nationalizing language policies such as "Citizen, Speak Turkish!" campaigns and the Surname Law of 1934, which required all citizens to adopt a Turkish family name. This chapter locates the alphabet reform simultaneously in the secular nationalist context and the modernist context of the early Republican era and tries to understand how this dual nature of the alphabet change (language and nationalism on the one hand, literacy and modernization on the other) influenced the implementation and the long term impact of this law. Rather than assuming an obedient and indifferent public silently following the decrees of an authoritarian and repressive regime, this chapter explores the actual processes, institutions, and lived experiences of the alphabet reform by drawing on a variety of sources including unpublished archival evidence and personal narratives collected through oral interviews. It draws attention to the multiplicity of experiences of learning to read the new letters, as well as to the persistence of Ottoman script and the state authorities' ways of dealing with this persistence. The chapter concludes with an assessment of the impact of alphabet change and related language policies on the emergence of a nationalist culture in the early Republican era.

Chapter Four explores the emergence of a culture of national celebrations as a key component of creating a collective national memory and a common national identity. The new regime "invented" a number of national holidays that were celebrated repeatedly and became institutionalized over time. I see these celebrations as another rich site of the state's encounters with its citizens that has been largely ignored by the historians of Republican Turkey. For the state, national holidays were an instrument of political socialization and mobilization. These holidays celebrated the new regime and its accomplishments with the help of its citizens. On this site the encounters were less confrontational and were potentially more participatory and inclusive. This chapter looks at how these holidays were celebrated, who mediated these celebrations, who was included, and who was excluded. Newspapers, detailed celebration reports sent from the provinces complete with photographs, and oral historical data provide rich insights into how these special days were celebrated not only in İstanbul and Ankara, but in the smaller and more remote towns of Anatolia. By focusing on a number of specific instances of national celebrations, this chapter investigates what the collective experience of these celebrations meant for the organizers, participants, and audiences in terms of their social, cultural, and political identities, as well as how they interacted with and reinforced the reforms.

Although the main chapters focus on four distinct areas of the social, political, and cultural processes of making and becoming a modern Turkish nation, issues and arguments fundamental to understanding that process recur in the different chapters throughout the book. Keeping in mind throughout that we recognize the category of social and culture change at a personal level, potentially falling outside of ideologically or politically oriented forms of opposition and resistance, my discussion focuses on the following major themes and arguments. I consider the importance of childhood and youth and the related phenomenon of generations (whether in abandoning established linguistic or sartorial habits or learning a new script or language). I emphasize the role of women and gender, and highlight the importance of individual and collective memory. I recognize the role of the education system, the press, and, if not civil society per se, associations such as the People's Houses and Children's Protection Society. I draw attention to the importance of understanding the different levels of the state's involvement in the everyday lives of Turkish citizens (from the Republican People's Party central government and the Directorate of Religious Affairs to the provincial governors, *kaymakam*s, gendarmerie, and teachers). I acknowledge the role of religion, not only as an element of identity and ideological source of resistance, but also as an instrument of secular nation building. I consider the broad range of responses to the modernist nationalist reforms, from active support and promotion to everyday forms of individual and collective resistance. Finally, I note the role of class, urban-versus-rural, and regional differences throughout the book.

For practical and analytical reasons this book focuses its attention on specific areas of reform. Naturally, in people's experiences, these changes did not occur in isolation, but were part and parcel of a broader process of social and cultural change affecting different aspects of their lives, their daily habits, and even the physical environment. As Anatolian men and women were adjusting their appearance, moving to literacy or learning to read and write in a new alphabet, and celebrating new national holidays, they were also adapting to a number of other innovations: a new calendar, a new weekly day of rest (Sunday rather than Friday), a new clock (*alafranga* time measurement replacing the *alaturka* time), co-education in classrooms, adopting and using family names, and learning and speaking Turkish, to name just a few. As I will demonstrate, the novelty of such changes varied considerably for different social groups, and the reach and effectiveness of these reforms were uneven and often incomplete. Nevertheless, it is important to keep in mind this broader context of the reforms. We should also note that the experiences of these social, cultural, and legal changes were accompanied by material changes such as the diffusion of radios, the expansion of roads and railroads, the (re)establishment of state control after the wars, the institution of a state-led industrialization program, and the expansion of the school system.

Sources: Archives and Interviews

I have relied on a wide variety of primary and secondary sources for this book, including archival data, oral histories, contemporary newspapers and magazines, memoirs, and contemporary travelers' accounts. Government archives proved to be an extremely helpful resource for this study. The majority of my primary sources came from the Prime Minister's Archive of the Republic (BCA) in Ankara, and the Archive of the Ministry of the Interior (EGM), also in Ankara. Most of the archival data presented and analyzed in this book, particularly the evidence gathered from the Archive of the Ministry of the Interior, is new to the scholarship.[33]

This is the first book to make extensive use of the Archive of the Ministry of the Interior for a social history of the Kemalist reforms in the foundational decades of the Republic. The only other scholarly monograph thus far to utilize the Archive of the Ministry of the Interior is Soner Çağaptay's already mentioned *Islam, Secularism, and Nationalism in Modern Turkey.* Çağaptay's interest is in understanding the evolution of Turkish nationalism by charting state policies in areas such as citizenship and ethnic and religious minorities. Taking a different perspective and going a step further, I have utilized the Archive of the Ministry of the Interior and the Republic Archives not only in trying to better understand the goals of the RPP regime, but in order to trace the social and cultural processes of making a modern Turkish nation and to capture the reactions and responses of those targeted by the Kemalist reforms. Voices and perspectives of the state authorities may dominate government archives, but these archives also contain glimpses into the lives and voices of ordinary citizens in the form of documents such as letters and petitions. Even documents produced by government officals, such as governors, party inspectors, police officers, and RPP officials, or what I have called official mediators, provide a wealth of information into the implementation and social experiences of the Kemalist reforms throughout the country.

Interviews

Oral historical methodology proved to be particularly fruitful for this study.[34] In 2002 and 2003 I conducted a series of in-depth interviews with elderly men and women who had lived through and remembered the 1920s, 1930s, and 1940s. Although most of the interviews took place in İstanbul, Kastamonu, and Trabzon (a reflection of my personal connections and my original research plan to focus on Trabzon when I began working on this project in 2002), my informants came from a variety of social backgrounds and geographic origins. They included men and women, the educated and the illiterate, individuals with urban and rural backgrounds, the urban elite, professionals such as teachers, and peasants. Because of the large-scale immigrations in the late nineteenth century and at the end of the Ottoman era, and the rural-to-urban migration in the past half century, my informants often traced their family origins, and in some instances their childhood and youth, to a different city or region. None of the individuals I interviewed in İstanbul were originally from that city. Therefore, these oral historical narratives reflect a broader and more complicated picture than one might assume by considering that they were collected in a small number of cities. All of my informants were Muslim (albeit of varying degrees of religiosity or commitment to secularism) and all of them considered themselves Turkish (although in some cases, of a non-Turkish ethnic background).

The use of oral interviews as evidence about past events provides rich possibilities, as well as possibly raising potential concerns about how memory is constructed and how that process might distort what is remembered. Personal memory, like collective memory, is shaped not only by one's past experiences, but also by a person's present circumstances and the dominant (and sometimes oppositional) political and ideological contexts. In the interviews I conducted, I asked my elderly informants about their childhood, their youth, and their families. Their unique personal and family narratives indeed reflect their real experiences of life in the 1920s and 1930s, even if some of these stories were framed and colored by "nostalgia for the modern"[35] or other ideological considerations. As Marianne Kamp argues in her analysis of oral interviews with elderly Uzbek women, "while each subject's interpretation of her life changes over time, her remembrance of particular events generally remains stable and does reflect what she experienced decades ago."[36] I use these oral interview narratives in combination with other historical sources such as visual images/photographs, memoirs, travelers' accounts, inspectors' reports, police reports, petitions, and national celebration reports to gain a better understanding of the social experiences of Kemalist reforms and of becoming Turkish throughout Anatolia.

1

Dressing the Nation's Citizens

Men's Clothing Reforms in the Early Republic

The Ottoman Background

The clothing of urban and upper class Ottoman men went through a significant transformation in the nineteenth century. As modernization spread from the military, legal, administrative, and political to the social and cultural spheres, Ottoman elites began to adopt European habits, manners, and ways of life. Speaking French, using European style furniture, and wearing European style clothes became symbols of modernity.[1] Ottoman bureaucrats, soldiers, diplomats, intellectuals, and more generally the educated urban upper classes employed by the expanding state or the growing modern economy adopted Western style suits and ties. These cultural changes were in part a consequence of increasing contact with the European culture, and in part they were initiated and promoted directly by the state, to be reinforced by increasing interactions with Europe.

When the Hat Law of 1925 mandated the European hat and prohibited the fez and all other ethnic, traditional, or religious forms of headgear, it had not yet been a full century since the introduction of the fez as the national headgear for all Ottoman men. Even though the fez was defended and the hat resisted in part in the name of Islamic and national tradition in 1925, the fez was in fact a relatively recent Ottoman innovation, or an "invented tradition,"[2] and had initially met with popular resistance. Like rulers in other European, Asian, or American contexts, since the early days of the state Ottoman sultans had used clothing laws for a range of social, economic, cultural, and political purposes. In Ottoman society, clothes, and particularly headgear,

22

were important markers of ethnic, religious, and other communal identities as well as of social class and rank. In traditional societies clothing regulations generally served to reinforce or maintain existing ethnic, religious, gender, or social distinctions by making those differences visible in dress. Modernizing or revolutionary states, on the other hand, have used clothing regulations to erode old social and communal distinctions and to create and promote new social distinctions and new identities. The importance of clothing laws lies in the fact that they are never simply about the clothes the subjects or the citizens wear, but rather they are reflections of the broader cultural, political, social, or economic concerns and changes. They serve as "instruments of negotiation" between states and ethnic, religious, or other communities, between elites and other social classes. Their enforcement, social meanings, and eventual success or failure are not determined by the state alone but are shaped in large part through these negotiations.

The Ottoman state mandated the fez as the common headgear for all Ottoman men in what Donald Quataert has called "the clothing revolution of Sultan Mahmud II."[3] The Sultan had first introduced the fez to the new Ottoman army, Asakir-i Mansure-i Muhammediyye (The Victorious Soldiers of Muhammed), a year after the destruction of the Janissaries. An 1827 imperial decree adopted the fez as the common headgear for the new army, to complement the pantaloons, boots, and other articles of the Europeanized Ottoman military uniform.[4] In an effort to expand the power of the state and to create a new basis of legitimacy, Mahmud II extended the clothing regulations beyond the military. An 1829 law specified the clothing and headgear of all ranks of Ottoman civil and religious officials, mandating the fez as the uniform headgear for all. The law attempted to homogenize and unify Ottoman subjects by eliminating visible differences of dress between Muslims and non-Muslims, between government officials and subjects, and between different social classes on terms determined by the state alone. The fez would symbolize the equality of all Ottoman subjects before the Sultan, while reminding the fez-wearing subjects of their common identity as Ottomans. Hence, the Sultan was offering equal citizenship to all his subjects on the basis of a common secular Ottoman identity, a full decade before the Gülhane Imperial Rescript formally established the principles of equality and the rule of law.[5]

The fez indeed became a symbol of a common Ottoman identity in the 19th century, but it was a symbol whose meaning was contested and changed over time. While some Ottoman subjects responded to the 1829 law positively and embraced the fez, others rejected or modified it. There is some disagreement in the field as to who rejected the fez and why. The scholarship has generally assumed that the non-Muslims embraced the fez as a symbol of equality, while some Ottoman Muslims rejected it on religious grounds.[6] Quataert, on the other hand, has suggested class consciousness and solidarity as key factors in the resistance to the fez.[7] Accordingly, while upper- and upper-middle-class Muslim and non-Muslim Ottomans responded positively to the introduction of the fez, Ottoman artisans and workers rejected the new headgear. According to Quataert's thesis, the rejection of the plain fez by Ottoman workers, Muslim and non-Muslim, and the popular resistance to the fez in İstanbul and the provinces, was an expression of the workers' discontent with Mahmud II's policies, such as the destruction of the Janissaries and the liberal economic policies that destroyed state protections. The Sultan backed down on his clothing legislation in response to this resistance and given the economic and military weakness of the Empire in the face of the Greek and Egyptian threats. Ottoman artisans and workers modified the fez by wrapping a turban around it to distinguish themselves from the officials and upper class urban Ottoman men, hence preserving a visible symbol of their class distinctions. Thus, it appears that the use of the fez never became universal, despite Mahmud II's intentions to make it a marker of a common Ottoman citizenship based on equality and homogeneity. Quataert notes (in part on the basis of visual evidence) that many Ottoman artisans continued to wear the fez wrapped in various fabrics throughout the 19th century. Outside the cities, especially in the tribal and more remote areas of the empire, ethnic and local clothing and headgear persisted throughout the final decades of the empire and into the republican years.[8] Not only did Ottoman subjects, Muslim and non-Muslim, continue to wear *kalpaks*,[9] *takkes*,[10] and other forms of headgear, but when they wore the fez, it did not necessarily conform to the standard fez of the Ottoman bureaucrats, and reflected social, ethnic, regional, and even climatic differences in its shape and wrapping.

Despite the persistence of other forms of headgear and the modified uses of the fez by artisans and others, the plain fez had indeed become a symbol of a common Ottoman identity sometime in the mid-nineteenth century, well before the reign of Abdülhamid II. During his long reign (1876–1909), Sultan Abdülhamid defended the fez in the name of national and Islamic tradition. While the diversity of ethnic and tribal clothes did not necessarily or directly challenge the official Ottoman identity and its symbolic manifestations, a limited trend toward the adoption of the European hat near the end of the century signaled a challenge to the fez and the identity it represented. Some of the Ottoman officials employed in Europe, particularly in the consulates, began to wear the hat to express their European identity and equality with the Europeans. Within the Empire, some among the non-Muslim subjects donned the brimmed European hat, much as they wore fashionable European clothes and rode in fancy carriages, as markers of their (often recently acquired) wealth and social status, as well as to exhibit their difference from (and perhaps superiority over) the Ottoman-Muslim subjects.[11]

For late nineteenth century Ottoman intellectuals and bureaucrats who supported Westernization, the hat served as an embodiment of European modernity to which the Ottoman state aspired. Ottoman subjects working for European companies that operated within the Empire came under the conflicting demands of the foreign employer and the Ottoman state as to what kind of headgear to wear.[12]

Sultan Abdülhamid attempted to preserve the uniformity of Ottoman national headwear by banning the European hat in 1877 and ordering Ottoman subjects to continue to wear the fez as a symbol of the common Ottoman identity.[13] The Ottoman government prescribed sanctions including termination of employment and imprisonment for government officials who violated the fez requirement by wearing the European hat.[14] The 1925 Hat Law, which reversed the relationship between the fez and the European hat, drew upon this nineteenth century Ottoman state tradition of imposing and defending a common national headgear through state mandate and control, in the cultivation of a new Turkish identity.

At the end of Abdülhamid II's reign, the return to a constitutional regime and the Ottoman boycott of Austrian goods in 1908 did not displace the fez immediately, but ushered in new headgear practices and new debates about appropriate Ottoman-Turkish headgear. During the 1908 boycott of Austrian imports in response to the annexation of Bosnia-Herzegovina by

Austria-Hungary, the refusal to buy Austrian fezzes and particularly the public spectacle of demonstrators rending fezzes in the streets of İstanbul and other Ottoman cities came to symbolize the whole boycott movement.[15] In fact, it led not only to an effort to expand the domestic (Hereke and İstanbul) supply of fezzes, but the boycott movement also triggered a debate and a search for an alternative national headgear. The protestors in Ottoman cities began donning *kalpak*s, *külah*s,[16] and other forms of headgear to express their support for the boycott effort.[17]

While the fez continued to be regarded as a marker of Ottoman and Ottoman/Islamic identity throughout the CUP (Committee of Union and Progress) period, the search for an alternative headgear continued. This was also a reflection of the intellectual transformations during the Second Constitutional period to redefine Ottoman/Turkish national identity. In 1909 the CUP regime adopted the khaki *kalpak* as official headgear for the army—not only for the officer class but also for the common soldiers, students of military schools, and civilians working in the military. At that point the *kalpak* was not intended to completely replace the fez, but was used alongside it.[18] During World War I, Enver Pasha introduced a new headgear to the army, the *kabalak*, essentially a brimless sun helmet.[19] Later during the War of Liberation years, the *kalpak* increasingly served as the common headgear of the Young Turk officers and was transformed into one of the most visible symbols of the nationalist resistance in Anatolia, distinguishing the nationalist leadership from the fez-wearing Ottoman officials. After independence, it was eventually the European hat, not the *kalpak*, which the Republican leadership adopted and mandated as national headgear for Turkish men. The *kalpak* would have revealed Turkey's difference from Europe as well as the continuity with the final years of the Empire and particularly with the CUP regime. The European hat, on the other hand, expressed visually Turkey's determination to adopt European modernity in its entirety and its aspirations for equality with the European nations, as well as the new regime's desire for a total break from the nation's recent past. Ironically, the war years may have bolstered the fez as a symbol of Ottoman (national) and religious (Islamic) unity for segments of the Anatolian population, even as those years witnessed the transformation of the *kalpak* into a symbol of nationalist resistance, particularly in provinces that came under Russian, French, or

Greek occupation during or after the World War I years. By 1923 there was no consensus on a national headgear, and Turkish citizens continued to wear a variety of hats as well as clothes. The CUP rule and the war years had further politicized headgear and created new attitudes toward fezzes, *kalpaks*, and European hats. On the one hand, the debates over and the search for an alternative national headgear, coupled with the rapid changes in headgear practices during the CUP and War of Liberation years, meant that the appropriateness of the fez as national headgear had already been questioned and its authority challenged by 1923. Those involved in the resistance movement, and many of their supporters, had already moved from the fez to another type of headgear (the *kalpak*) in a very short span of time. Their identification with and loyalty to the fez must have been weakened in that process. Such factors presumably facilitated the transition to the European hat at a personal level, in the sense that clothing changes require changes to one's established habits. Conversely, for those who came to associate the European hat with European colonialism and with the Christian populations of Anatolia—increasingly perceived as potential enemies during World War I and the War of Liberation years—the fez had gained renewed significance as a marker of their Muslim Ottoman/Turkish identities.

In European eyes, the fez had become a primary and most visible marker of Ottoman (and Muslim) identity by the late nineteenth century. Europeans associated the fez primarily, but not exclusively, with the Ottoman nationals. Upper-class Muslim men in colonial contexts such as India and Egypt—which although nominally part of the Ottoman Empire had evolved autonomously under Mehmed Ali Pasha and his successors and had come under British occupation in 1882—had also adopted the fez.[20] In fact, for Ottoman diplomats and educated upper- and upper-middle-class Ottoman (and post-1922 Turkish) men travelling to Europe, the fez was the principal, if not only, external symbol of their difference, revealing them as Ottoman and non-European.[21] (This is, of course, leaving aside their Turkish-accented French and German, and the differences in physical attributes such as skin color, height, and facial features. Obviously such physical and genetic characteristics could not be easily corrected by state intervention, making it all the more important for late modernizing states in non-Western contexts to control the clothing of their citizens.)

Other sartorial aspects of the upper class urban Ottoman men, such as shoes, pantaloons, shirts, and coats, conformed to European fashions, as we can see in the image below of Ali Salim (Peker), a Trabzon merchant whom we will meet again in the following pages and chapters. Their carefully trimmed beards and mustaches also followed European practices. Beards became shorter and eventually disappeared altogether, while the mustache did not disappear entirely, owing its survival arguably to serving as a symbol of masculinity.

For the Republican leaders after 1923, the fez stood as a symbol marking Turkey's difference (perceived as inferiority) from Europe even as it revealed

1. Ali Salim Peker (1881–1953), a Trabzon resident, in 1923. Note the fully Westernized clothing, with the exception of the fez. Photograph from the family album of Meliha Tanyeli.

the continuity between the nation's Ottoman Muslim past and its present. The adoption of the European hat as national headgear would eliminate that visible marker of Turkish Muslim difference and inferiority and would symbolize Turkey's (aspirations for) modernity and inclusion in the "civilized world," while simultaneously serving as a powerful symbol of its break from the Ottoman era and a harbinger of the coming of a new era.[22] Some of the major institutional changes, such as the abolition of the Caliphate in 1924 (which was crucial because of its implications for the place of religion in the new political and social order), did not require individual citizens to make adjustments in their personal lives and daily habits. The Hat Law and the attendant expectation of the adoption of European clothes, however, meant that the state demanded of Turkish men that they make adjustments at a personal level. The degree of required changes and the attitudes toward them depended on a variety of social, economic, cultural, and individual (such as generational) factors.

The images in figure 2, of four of Ali Salim Peker's brothers, demonstrate the shift from the fez to the *kalpak* and then to the European hat in the transition from the Empire to the Republic. It is noteworthy that in each instance, the headgear did not challenge or modify but complemented the essentially European outfit of an upper- or upper-middle-class, educated urban (Ottoman) Turkish citizen.

The 1925 Hat Law and Its Consequent Social Experiences

The Law on the Wearing of the Hat (Şapka İktisâsı Hakkında Kanun, "The Hat Law") was passed on 25 November 1925. It declared "the common headgear of the Turkish nation is the [European style] hat[23] and that any practice contrary to that is prohibited by the government."[24] The Hat Law was a key component of Turkey's effort to modernize. However, it was also a part of the project of building a Turkish nation. Indeed, Sami Efendi, the Party's Inspector General for the fifth region, reporting a few months after the law's promulgation, explicitly stated the nation-building dimension of the law, and argued on that basis for the extension of the Hat Law into a more general clothing law.

Reporting from Van, Sami Efendi wrote that a clothing law was "needed not only for Westernization and modernization, but also to facilitate our

2. Ali Salim's brothers. Top left, Şükrü wearing a fez; top right, Şevki, and bottom left, Kazım, both wearing *kalpak*s; and bottom right, Sami wearing a bowler hat and a bow tie. Photograph from the family album of Meliha Tanyeli.

policy of assuring that the other nations [in Turkey] wear the same modern clothes as Turks do and of gradually Turkifying them."[25] He argued that "the Kurds have generally maintained their national clothing" even though they had pretended to comply with the Hat Law, describing how the Kurds in his region would roll up the ends of their conical hats when they came to the administrative centers, only to roll them back down again when they returned to their villages, thus going back to their traditional appearance and identities.

In the 1920s and 1930s, government officials like Sami Efendi not only recognized the transformative functions of clothes in nationalizing and modernizing society, but they were also keenly aware of the importance of appearance as an external manifestation of Turkish modernity and national unity, or the lack thereof. In 1937, a police inspector wrote a detailed report on the general state of the Tokat province, covering issues ranging from the state of the economy and the Party to the minorities and foreigners in the province.[26] For the cultivation of a national culture in the province, particularly in the Yerköy district, the inspector recommended policies such as prohibiting the use of any languages other than Turkish, distancing Kurdish children from their traditions through education, and the dispersion of the dense Kurdish communities in some of the villages through resettlement in Turkish villages. Writing about the town of Turhal, the inspector said he noticed some men at the train station wearing strange clothes that had no relation whatsoever to Turkish clothing. They were dressed in white pants that had turned black from dirt, and shirts of the same color that hung down to their knees. He was concerned that they were wandering around in that state in full view of the public and the foreigners. He said he knew they were Kurdish from their speech. They had been dispersed throughout the province to nullify any political threat, but he observed no change in their clothing. The police inspector expressed concern that men in such strange clothing along the railway and in front of the foreigners in the town could lead to foreign propaganda against Turkey.[27] He was confident that this clothing issue could be solved by local measures, recommending that the clothing of these men should be put in order, that at the very least they should be made to tuck their shirts in.[28]

The police inspector's report may be an extreme example, but it reveals what was at stake for the new state with the clothing laws. Turkish citizens should look European, especially in the presence of foreigners. Dress reforms were a part of the wholesale effort to modernize in the 1920s and the 1930s. For the new regime, culture and civilization were inseparable, and borrowing European civilization meant borrowing European culture as well, including its dress. As had been the case in the Ottoman period, clothes were powerful external symbols of modernity. This was true of articles of clothing such as European-style trousers and jackets, but most importantly of headgear.

Initial responses to the Hat Law were characterized by a wide range of individual and collective actions ranging from the quick adoption of the hat, pro-hat rallies and demonstrations, and fez rending celebrations to anti-hat demonstrations and riots in towns such as Rize, Erzurum, Sivas and Maraş. My goal here is not to focus on the brief episode of collective resistance to the hat and its rapid and brutal suppression. That episode has already received considerable attention. As scholars have already shown, regional cultural differences (particularly different types of encounters and varying degrees of familiarity with Western culture and civilization in different parts of the country), religious opposition, and the local meanings ascribed to the fez and the hat as a result of a town's recent history were some of the key factors in bringing about collective responses to the hat in several Anatolian cities. [29]

While this initial urban collective reaction to the hat and state responses to it must be acknowledged, we should bear in mind that the initial popular reaction was both limited and suppressed decisively. Rather than focusing on the short-lived period of urban collective reaction to the hat reform, which would be to misconstrue the experiences of men's clothing reforms by effectively reducing them to those moments of collective or violent reaction, this chapter aims at understanding the application of the Hat Law as part of a broader process of socialization into a national culture. I will do this by linking the role of political and cultural institutions (such as schools, governors, police, and the Directorate of Religious Affairs) and sociological factors (such as class and regional factors) with individual, family, local, and everyday (i.e. subaltern) responses and experiences. Responses the Hat Law elicited were by no means limited to resistance, and resistance, though no longer a possibility as a form of collective action after the harsh punishments passed by the Independence Tribunals, could be expressed in other ways as well. As James C. Scott has argued, with specific reference to peasant struggles, it is more important to understand "everyday forms of peasant resistance" than to focus on peasant rebellions.[30] He has suggested that when "outright collective defiance" and rebellion are not possible, people resort to everyday forms of resistance. This involves what Scott has termed "weapons of the weak" such as "foot dragging," "false compliance," and "feigned ignorance." These acts require little or no planning, tend to be individual acts of self-help, and avoid direct confrontation with authority.[31]

One of the forms of individual reaction to the hat reform was to avoid the use of the hat by avoiding the public sphere altogether. In an extreme example of this kind in Antalya province in the South, Hamdi Yazır never left his house from the passing of the Hat Law in 1925 until his death in May 1942.[32] Often the initial anger and the attempt to seclude oneself in the private sphere eased with time. When Mustafa Kemal first introduced the hat on 24 August 1925 on his trip to Kastamonu, the Turkish Hearths branch in Konya asked its members to wear the hat, and one of them, Numan Efendi, became the first man to wear the hat in Konya. The elderly townsmen, including Numan Efendi's father Hacı Yusuf Efendi, were much angered by this act. Hacı Yusuf Efendi was so embarrassed at the sight of his son wearing a hat that he refused to appear in public for several days, secluding himself in his house.[33]

In a similar case, initial open defiance of the Hat Law quickly shifted to silent protest in the form of avoiding the public sphere altogether. This ended in obedience of the new law, albeit resentfully. In her travel accounts, Lilo Linke, a German journalist and opponent of the Nazi regime, told the story of an old peasant she met in the village of Ulaş, in Sivas, in 1935.[34] Linke reported that this man had first tried to disobey the law, but he was fined by the *muhtar*, the village headman. Then he had stayed indoors for a week or two. Having come to the conclusion that he could not live indoors all his life, he ordered his son to buy a cap (*kasket*) in Sivas. Once the cap arrived, it took him some time to resign himself to actually wearing it. According to Linke, seeing that all the villagers were wearing similar headgear helped him to resign himself to wearing it.[35] Linke observed that at the time of her visit the old man was wearing a woolen cap, but still with resentment, and with the hope to return to the fez one day.

Abdullah Eltan related that in Trabzon, his father, Ömer Efendi, insisted at the time of the reform that he would not wear a hat.[36] Ömer Efendi left his shop to his son and stayed home. This was not a viable solution in the long term. Yet he could not go out in the street wearing a fez, since policemen were not letting men wear prohibited headgear in the streets. Ömer Efendi eventually convinced himself to wear a cap. He had a cap made with a brim as narrow as the width of a finger. Eltan says that his father was conservative and had an Ottoman mindset. However, Ömer Efendi was also a maker of silk thread used in the fez industry, and thus the hat reform clearly was threatening his own craft. This suggests that economic reasons, often in conjunction with personal, emotional, generational, social, cultural, or other factors, helped determine one's reaction to the new clothing regulations.

When a group of weavers from Maraş petitioned the authorities, they were concerned, like Ömer Efendi, that their craft would collapse because of the new clothing regulations.[37] These men were weavers of the cloth used for making the local baggy pants called *karadon*, and the sleeveless summer top *aba*, worn with the *karadon*. When the local government prohibited the wearing of the *karadon*, their trade was jeopardized. The Maraş weavers resorted to a well-established form of expressing discontent and raising demands by writing petitions to the provincial government, and to the RPP and central government authorities. Since Ottoman times, such petitions had provided a channel for the masses to communicate directly with the government. İstanbul artisans had also resorted to petitions when the Ottoman government prohibited the women's *çarşaf* in the 1880s.[38] In the case of the Maraş weavers, the party did not back down from the local clothing decree, calling the weavers "men who did not want to follow the requirements of the time and did not understand their own interests," but it did make recommendations to the petitioners to alleviate their economic distress. The party suggested that they shift production to making cloth that could be used for making *setre* pants.[39] It also promised to help form a cooperative among the Maraş weavers. As we will see, particularly in the context of responses to the state's attempts to regulate women's dress, petitions, although not always effective, provided a rare form of collective (as well as individual) action that Turkish citizens employed in their dealings with the new state.

It is difficult to establish with any certainty what percentage of the population supported the hat reform, and what percentage opposed it, resented it, or simply did not care. A recent study on the Kırşehir province in Central

Anatolia explored the level of support and opposition to the Hat Law in that province by drawing on oral interviews. 14 percent of the elderly informants who participated in the survey reported they had been against the dress reforms at the time, and 5 percent reported they had not had an opinion.[40] Those who had been against the reforms did not specify whether they had expressed their opinion in any way. It seems the majority of the male population readily agreed to wear a form of headgear that was acceptable to the local enforcement authorities.

Cultural resentment against the hat was often worsened by economic conditions. Poverty and lack of supplies were also emphasized by the governors in their reports from the provinces. In January 1926, governors throughout the country reported to the Ministry of the Interior on the progress made in the application of the Hat Law. While the majority of these reports confirmed that "the Hat Law [was] being fully enforced" or that "[t]here is not a single man left in the province not wearing the hat," a number of them distinguished between its application in cities and in rural areas, and mentioned that hats were not yet worn universally in some villages. They attributed the slower adoption of the hat in the villages entirely to economic reasons. According to Sinop governor Nizameddin, men in the towns, as well as villagers who traveled to the towns, had put on hats, and it was only in very distant villages that there were men who had not been able to obtain hats. Elaziz (Elazığ) governor Ali Rıza informed the ministry that the townsmen in the province had adopted the hat, and argued specifically that it was not conservatism or opposition but economic reasons that accounted for the small numbers of villagers following suit.

Many could not afford to buy a hat, so they bought caps instead. Often people had cap-like headgear made at home. Some would wear the cap with the brim on the side or on the back as an expression of discontent or indifference. Often people came up with creative solutions such as adding a brim to their locally produced conical hats (*külah*s).[41] Such practices constantly brought up the problem of supplies and raised the question of what qualified as a hat. State authorities attempted to ameliorate the problem of supplies first through the foundation of a hat factory in Karamürsel, and later by shipping Sümerbank-produced caps (*kasket*s) to the provinces as needed, particularly later during the World War II years. As they tried to manage the supply side of the issue, the real concern of the government authorities centered on the motivation behind citizens' making peculiar forms of headgear that gave the appearance of a hat or cap, but were versatile enough to be worn as *külah*s or *kalpak*s when so desired. Officials worried that in this way citizens were in reality evading the law, while pretending to conform to it. The Ministry of the Interior reminded governors repeatedly that neither the peculiar forms of headgear nor the ludicrous styles of wearing caps by bringing the brim over the ear were permissible. In one such communication, the minister informed the provincial governors that citizens had been turning *kalpak*-like headgear into caps by adding narrow visors to the front, but that these hats were sometimes worn as *kalpak*s by folding back the brim and attaching it to the interior of the *kalpak* with a snap fastener. Defining civilized headgear ("*medeni serpuş*") as derby (bowler), felt, or cap (*melon, fötr, veya kasket*), the minister asked the governors to communicate to their fellow citizens that other forms of headgear were prohibited and would not be tolerated.[42] As visual evidence from the 1930s, such as the photograph below, indicates, the cap indeed became quite common for the peasants and the popular classes of Anatolian towns, yet Turkish citizens did not necessarily conform to the proper style of wearing caps as designated by the government, and some continued to wear their caps with the brim on the side or on the back.

Local, tribal, or regional forms of headgear and dress often coexisted with the brimmed hat. In parts of southeast Anatolia, clothing of the tribal communities closely resembled the clothing of the Arab tribes south of the French Syrian border. Photographs from the 1930s, such as those in People's Houses publications showing People's Houses representatives with the male residents of rural communities in Mardin province, attest to the mixing of old and new, traditional and modern forms of clothing. In his memoirs, Cemal Madanoğlu writes about his service as an officer with the gendarmerie forces in Urfa province around 1933, and comments on the persistence of the "*kefye-agel* and *maşlah*"[43] among the tribesmen along the Syrian border and the selective use of the hat and other European forms of clothing. He observes that when a tribal member needed to go to Urfa, the provincial center, he would borrow the "community" cap, pants, and jacket before going into town, but would put on the *kefiye* and *agel* when he returned from the city to the desert.[44] It appears that this separation between the city and the

3. Prisoners, prison employees, and guard, at the Akçaabat prison, Trabzon, 1930s.
Note that most prisoners were either wearing a cap or holding one in their hands or
on their knees. Note also that one of the men in the back right was wearing his cap
with the brim turned to the side. Only one had a felt hat. Most conformed to a basic
European-style dress with European-style jackets and pants. Photograph from the
collection of Atilla Bölükbaşı.

country, which corresponds to the distinction between public and private
for urban residents, was a practical solution for all parties involved (rather
than an act of opposition to the state): it satisfied the official clothing requirements in case the tribesman came into contact with state authorities in the
town, without giving up traditional clothes that were familiar and perhaps
also more functional in the desert.[45] Moreover, by dressing differently when
visiting the city, the tribesmen in Urfa were in fact also following a traditional
social practice of dressing according to context. The Kurdish villagers from
Van, discussed above, were essentially following the same traditional social
practice by rolling up their conical hats (*külahs*) when they travelled to the
city, making them look like caps. Popular recognition that different contexts

such as village and town had different clothing conventions, and the resulting social practice of changing dress according to context (rather than insisting on uniformity and homogeneity), contributed to the modernist nation-building process by facilitating accomodation between local norms, older conventions, and the newly mandated sartorial requirements.

At the same time, by wearing a cap when travelling to the city or by making their conical hats look like caps, these rural and tribal populations were not only adjusting to the established city conventions but also recognizing that the rules of the city had changed: the new rules now required the wearing of a European style hat or a cap rather than a fez. Another factor that facilitated accomodation to the new dress codes during travel to the city was that the temporary nature of adapting to the city norms meant it did not challenge or threaten the local, tribal, or ethnic identities of the wearers, at least not immediately. However, as inspector Sami Efendi's letter from Van makes abundantly clear, the government authorities were aware of the importance of clothes for the maintenance of ethnic and other collective identities. By the same token, the erasure of sartorial distinctions that marked group identities and the homogenization of appearance were perceived to be crucial for creating a sense of identification with the national community. For that reason, the Republican state's sartorial demands from its citizens extended to the rural and local contexts as well, although in practice the government had far too limited resources to fully dominate those social spaces.

The state had disarmed these tribes along the Syrian border, but changing their clothing habits, like changing their linguistic habits, was in some ways more difficult to accomplish. In the 1920s and 1930s, the language question, or the question of Arabic, also occupied a prominent place in the state efforts to fully integrate Urfa and the other southern provinces into the national culture. In the neighboring Mardin province, for example, state authorities encouraged the voluntary adoption of Turkish through education and propaganda, as well as by instituting monetary fines, following the example of a number of other towns in the 1930s that instituted fines for speaking a language other than Turkish in public. Through its publications the local Halkevi encouraged the residents of Mardin to learn Turkish and to speak Turkish only. Using arguments similar to those on the foreignness of men's *agel* and *kefiye* and—as we will see—women's *peçe* and *çarşaf* and the Arabic script, Halkevi authors called on the citizens to abandon the habit of speaking this foreign language, Arabic, and to return to their own pure national tongue. While the propaganda campaign targeted all age groups, as with most other reform measures, it was particularly important to ensure that children grew up speaking Turkish.[46] It would be through closer educational, cultural, economic, and social contact with the urban and national life, along with accompanying changes in social life and cultural attitudes, that linguistic and clothing changes would be more genuine and meaningful.[47]

The task of enforcing dress codes belonged to government officials including governors, *kaymakams*, judges, and policemen. Despite the general tendency to avoid any confrontation with these authorities, citizens often had to encounter government officials. Before turning to such encounters I will discuss some of the other agencies involved in the enforcement of dress codes.

Directorate of Religious Affairs

The newly founded Directorate of Religious Affairs (Diyanet İşleri Riyaseti) proved to be a useful instrument in implementing the male dress reform.[48] Through the Directorate, the state attempted to co-opt a group that it feared might act as potential leaders of opposition to its modernizing and secularizing reforms, turning them into allies who would support the new state's reforms, including its attempt to modernize male dress. Some Islamic scholars had opposed attempts to modernize and secularize society, including the adoption of outward symbols of the West such as clothes, since the nineteenth century.[49] Such opposition was based on interpretations of Islamic doctrine, but was also concerned with the social and political impact of secularizing trends for the society in general, and especially for the place of religious scholars within that society. In 1924, an Islamic scholar, İskilipli Âtıf Efendi, published a book decrying the borrowing of the hat as an imitation of the infidels, declaring that it was not acceptable according to the Quran and the *hadith*, and that wearing the hat would cause one to lose one's Islamic identity.[50] Âtıf Efendi was tried by the Independence Tribunals and executed in February 1926 for his involvement in anti-hat protests in Rize, Giresun, Erzurum and Sivas.[51] A number of other *hocas* were also involved in these protests.

One aspect of the co-optation and control of religious leaders during the early decades of the Republic involved regulating their clothing. As civil servants, they would retain a distinctive, and distinctly religious, form of dress, but one defined and mandated by the state. The early Republican state's attempts to regulate the outward appearance of the men of religion should also be seen as part of the overall process of secularization through professionalization of religious services. This, in turn, was a part of the process of building a modern state, which during the early years of the Republic was evolving parallel to a process of nation-building. Very much like the Janissaries who ran shops and coffee houses (before 1826), or like the members of the newly created Ottoman police who continued to run barber or coffee shops in nineteenth century İstanbul, Muslim prayer leaders were often involved in economic activities alongside their religious duties. Just as reformist Ottoman authorities in the second half of the nineteenth century insisted on policemen wearing their uniforms (and wearing them on duty only) and quitting their other economic activities, the Republican state demanded from men of religion that they wear their robes and turbans while providing religious services only and not at any other time. Ideally, the provision of religious services would be an imam's main income-generating activity, for which he would depend on the state as employer through the Directorate. The previous porous and undefined boundary between religious services and other work would be replaced by a more rigid separation between religious services and secular work. Men of religion would function as professionals whose status as such would be visibly marked by their robes and turbans: articles of clothing reserved as a uniform for Muslim prayer leaders and therefore rendered inaccessible for other Muslim citizens.

In September 1925, the turban (*sarık*) was decreed to be reserved specifically for imams (Islamic prayer leaders, who were technically government employees). The Decree on the Religious Class and the Religious Garb specified that the distinguishing feature of the garb for the members of the religious class was the white turban and the black gown.[52] Membership in the religious class was mainly determined by one's connection to the Directorate, and included all levels from the President of the Directorate to the *müfti*s and *müsevvid*s[53] in provincial and district centers, to imams and preachers salaried by the Directorate, and to village *hoca*s (imams) appointed by the

Directorate. Only those prayer leaders with a valid permit could wear the turban. Any imam who continued to wear the turban and continued to preach without a permit would be brought before the court to face legal charges.[54] Although it appears that there was no organized or collective resistance on the part of the imams to the regulation of religious garb, there was a degree of non-compliance. While some men made an active effort to prove that they qualified for a permit to wear an imam's turban,[55] it appears that others continued to wear the turban, at least in the first several months after the regulation, in defiance of the permit requirement. It is difficult to establish if, and to what degree, such noncompliance may have been an act of resistance and opposition, and to what degree it was due to other motives. Correspondence between the *kaymakam* of Ödemiş in İzmir province and the town's *müfti* suggests that the administration perceived such noncompliance as oppositional and dangerous. The *kaymakam* provided a list of men from Ödemiş who reportedly continued to wear the religious garb without a permit to do so.[56] Most of the ten men on the list had titles such as *hoca*, *hocazade*, imam, *hafız*, and *hacı*, suggesting that these men had some locally recognized religious position due to their religious learning, their past or present religious function in the community, or their having been to Mecca on a pilgrimage. Hence we can assume that they had long been wearing the turban as their everyday headgear. Their reluctance to either obtain a permit or wear a hat may have reflected the power of long-established habits as much as it may have been an expression of discontent and resentment.

A bigger problem with the religious garb was the imams' failure to wear a proper turban and gown. In an effort to enforce the religious garb, the Directorate informed the *müfti*s in May 1926 that the permits of those prayer leaders who continued to wear "strange and ridiculous" clothes would be cancelled.[57] The Directorate specifically mentioned jackets and overcoats (*pardesü*) and turbans worn over a fez with half of the turban wrapped inside the fez. The Directorate was clearly concerned with the visibility of the fez despite its partial concealment under the imam's turban. It was no coincidence that the Sinop Parliamentarian Recep Zühtü Bey submitted a bill recommending that religious functionaries wear their turbans over proper headgear made of cloth, hence bringing an end to the visibility of the fez under the imam's turban and thus totally eliminating the fez.[58] It is not clear if or how commonly imams chose to make their fezzes visible under their turbans to make a political statement. Evidence from official correspondence suggests the interplay of a number of factors. Reports, for instance, on village imams strolling in town markets with "*çarık*[59] on their feet and a piece of cloth resembling anything but a turban on their dirty fezzes,"[60] or imams wearing a military jacket over *şalvar* (baggy pants),[61] hint not so much at any acts of opposition but at prevailing economic circumstances and local clothing customs. If village imams came to the town wearing *çarık*s, it was most likely because they were no better off than their fellow villagers, and were not that different from them socially and culturally. It should be emphasized that official statements were concerned with more than the basic requirement of a turban and a robe. They dealt with the full outfit of the imams, from headgear and pants to shoes, and with the cleanliness and orderliness of those outfits. As civil servants, prayer leaders were expected to look "civilized" and lead their fellow countrymen by way of example. When a decree authorized to civil servants an advance cash payment equaling one month's salary for the purchase of hats and clothes, *müfti*s and *müsevvid*s were included among those eligible for this payment.[62]

A letter from the *kaymakam* of Kula to the town's *müfti* sheds further light on the regulation of religious clothing.[63] After stating that the purpose of the religious garb was to maintain the honor of the religious functionaries and their designated dress, he wrote that he had seen that many of the imams, both in the town and in the villages, did not follow the ordinances concerning religious clothing, and wore jackets and different-colored clothing. The *kaymakam* also pointed out that he had witnessed imams wearing their turbans while performing other duties, such as running a shop or working in the fields. This, he observed, was disrespectful to the religious clothing as a symbol of a title and a profession. The *kaymakam* had a specific concern regarding the village imams under his jurisdiction. He reported that some villages obtained imams' certificates by claiming extra *masjid*s. In one such case, he noted, the village had gotten certificates for two masjids in addition to the one mosque. He wrote that none of these buildings were used, except for the mosque in the month of Ramazan. Moreover, the two masjid buildings were in ruins and looked like stables. He had seen one of the masjid imams working as a tinsmith with a turban on his head, and the other one hoeing the fields. The *kaymakam* asked the *müfti* to bring such unacceptable behavior to an end, stressing that this was a convenient time to do so. He demanded the revocation of permits improperly obtained, or issued to unqualified persons, and asked that imams should not wear religious clothing during personal or other transactions outside their duties as religious functionaries. Finally, he announced that after a fifteen-day grace period those wearing a turban in public without the black robe and those who wore religious clothing while performing other jobs would be detained by the gendarmerie and taken before the courts for breaking the religious clothing ordinances.

This *kaymakam*'s observation of the widespread lack of conformity in religious clothing in his district is in line with other reports and correspondence on the issue. His observation regarding village imams raises some interesting questions and possibilities. If the governor was right that some villages were indeed obtaining imams' permits for unused masjids, how are we to interpret the motivations behind such requests? It may have been a way of giving those with some unofficial or occasional religious function in the village community the legal ability to maintain their position, including the right to wear their turban. Such a possibility suggests that this was an example of individuals and communities developing mechanisms to cope with the new demands and regulations of the state, while avoiding direct confrontation. It should also be noted that such coping mechanisms were not necessarily liberating for the whole community, or for all the individual members, and may often have reflected existing hierarchies of power.

The *kaymakam*'s observation that the imams performed other tasks, such as running a shop or working in the fields, points to a major problem in the enforcement of religious clothing ordinances. As clearly expressed in the governor's letter, from the point of view of the administration imams only had the privilege of wearing the religious clothing in their capacity as religious functionaries. However, in reality, prayer leaders often combined their religious functions with another occupation. While village imams often worked the land like their fellow villagers, many imams in the towns were shopkeepers or artisans, or were otherwise involved in some economic activity. The imams' continued use of the turban while performing duties as shopkeepers and artisans ran counter to the state's effort to eliminate the everyday use of the turban by making it the official clothing, and a symbol, of Islamic religious functionaries. In October 1928, the Ministry of the Interior informed the governors and the Directorate that religious functionaries with a permit to wear the turban who ran coffeehouses, *aktariyes*, tobacco shops, or grocery stores, or who were involved in other trades, had to wear the hat while functioning in their non-liturgical occupations.[64] The same circular also banned foreign nationals (specifically mentioned were Iranian "*menla*s and *seyyid*s") from wearing the turban and the fez.[65]

The ban on wearing religious clothing while performing other duties did not always work as intended. It led to confusion and different interpretations, and complicated the implementation of the ban at the local level, as illustrated in correspondence from Kula in 1928. The *müfti* of Kula complained to the *kaymakam* that some of the "men in turbans" who did not have other jobs were taken to the police station and their turbans confiscated. He requested that the *kaymakam* give the necessary orders to prevent a reoccurrence of such events.[66] The *kaymakam* responded that it was not possible for the gendarmerie to distinguish between those permit holders who had another job and those who did not. He argued that the gendarmerie had to first assume that a man wearing a turban in public was acting against government orders, and the officer was therefore obligated to take the man to the nearest police station. For the *kaymakam* it was the responsibility of the turban-wearer to prove that he was not acting against government orders. He suggested to the *müfti* that he issue papers to those who did not have an external job, saying that they were authorized to wear the turban at all times. Clearly the *müfti* and the *kaymakam* interpreted the 1928 circular very differently, with the governor favoring more a rigid interpretation and implementation. It is also important to note that the *müfti* made an effort to obtain better treatment for the men of religion in his district when he felt that the gendarmes were exceeding their authority in enforcing religious clothing. Individual imams may not have been in a position to appeal to the district governor directly, but they were often able to find support within the administrative hierarchy, from the town's *müfti* in this case. It appears that the *müfti* saw his role to be more than the unilateral transmission of orders from higher authorities to the men of religion, and at times acted to defend these men's rights against higher government authorities.

In 1934, the state attempted to put an end to confusing and conflicting interpretations in the implementation of the law by further limiting the use of the turban to the mosques. "The Law Relating to [the Requirement] that Certain Clothes May Not Be Worn" stated that "[m]en of religion, of whatever religion or sect they may be, are forbidden to wear the religious clothing outside of places of worship and prayer."[67] The law allowed for the government to approve only one member of the clergy per religion and sect to wear religious clothing outside of places of worship and prayer.[68] Correspondence from the Ministry of the Interior shows that the 1934 law led to practices that avoided insistence on the turban but fell short of the desired compliance, the adoption of the hat. The minister complained that some religious officials, when faced with the prospect of taking off their turbans, began to go out bareheaded or to wear berets and *takkes* (skullcaps), while still carrying their gowns.[69] He argued that wearing berets and *takkes* was not as bad as going out bareheaded, yet it still meant a refusal to adopt modern clothing. Although the Minister's statement suggests that wearing headgear outdoors was still the norm, the fact that some men of religion would go outdoors bareheaded implies that social practices were beginning to change from headgear to no headgear. While men in 1925 rushed to buy hats and caps partly because appearing in public bareheaded was not socially acceptable, a decade later some men of religion chose to appear in public with no headgear rather than to wear a hat when the turban was banned. That other men of religion adopted berets and *takkes* implies that they were part of a shift towards alternative headgear in the 1930s. The fact that some prayer leaders chose to wear berets or *takkes*, or to go bareheaded instead of wearing the hat, also suggests the persistence of an anti-hat reform sentiment among some men of religion, a full decade after the initial Hat Law.

In addition to helping the state eliminate the turban as headwear for the average male citizen by making it solely a part of the imams' official clothing, the Directorate provided a channel for the state to transmit its ideas on dress to large masses of Muslim men. The government's answers to questions such as whether wearing a hat conformed with Islamic law (Sharia) were transmitted to the masses with the help of the Directorate. Mosques and imams provided a pre-existing network throughout the country to reach adult Muslim men, regardless of literacy, both in urban and in rural areas.[70] The task assigned to men of religion regarding the clothing of male Muslim citizens focused on the proper headwear to be worn in the mosque. The question of the compatibility of the hat with Islam was bound to emerge in the physical setting of the mosque, and was complicated by the practical problems involved in substituting the hat for the fez during prayers. As part of the set rituals, the individual's forehead has to touch the ground several times during each of the five daily prayers, a process that would be unwieldy to anyone wearing a hat.[71] On the other hand, if the perception of the hat as Christian and un-Islamic could be overcome in the mosque, the hat could more easily be worn elsewhere.

In November 1925, shortly after the passage of the Hat Law, and drawing on a report from the İstanbul province, the Minister of the Interior described the state of headgear worn in mosques and the proposed action regarding the same.[72] He wrote that although the majority of men had adopted the hat, some of those praying in the mosques were making a rather peculiar scene by wearing fezzes, *kalpaks*, or *takkes*, or by wrapping handkerchiefs around their heads. He considered that the most important reason for this was the failure of those in charge of "sermons and guidance" (that is, men of religion appointed by the Directorate of Religious Affairs as prayer leaders). It was the task of prayer leaders "to explain [to the public] in suitable language that headgear has no special place in the performance of prayers (*namaz*), and that there is morally no difference in performing prayers bare-headed or wearing a hat, and that on the contrary, praying bare-headed would express respect."[73] Their failure to fulfill this task would encourage reactionaries to pursue anti-hat action. Based on this assessment, İstanbul province had already asked the *müfti* of İstanbul to instruct his personnel to take the necessary action. Anticipating that the situation would be much the same in other parts of the country, the minister asked the prime ministry for authority to request the Directorate to "guide and enlighten" the citizenry throughout the country that it was acceptable to wear a hat while praying.

In early January 1926, the Directorate responded to this request by issuing a circular to the *müftis'* offices in the provinces asking that the preachers (*vaiz*) enlighten the public regarding appropriate headgear inside mosques along the lines recommended by the executive.[74] The circular suggests that the opinion of the presidency of the Directorate was in full conformity with that of the Ministry of the Interior on this particular issue. The circular invoked two reasons why the hat could be and should be worn in mosques. First, the hat had been adopted by the Parliament and henceforth it was essential to accept it as the modern and the national headgear. Second, it confirmed that no objections could be found in the Sharia to wearing a hat in a mosque. Therefore, there was no justification for the disorderly state of dress within mosques, with men wearing *takke*s or praying bare headed. Preachers should inform the public accordingly in order to maintain uniformity of appearance in mosques.

It was not uncommon for the Directorate to supply prayer leaders with the actual texts of sermons to be delivered in the mosques. The Directorate also tried to keep an eye on the actions of its members by requesting prayer leaders to submit regular activity reports. There are, however, signs that the regime's control over the mosques was not absolute.[75] One case from Bursa suggests that individual prayer leaders may have acted contrary to their assigned mission by encouraging the turban well after the initial stages of the hat reform. The governor of Bursa province informed the Ministry of the Interior that it had received intelligence that some men had been wearing kerchiefs or shawls over skullcaps when they went to the Yıldırım mosque for prayers. Following this tip, authorities found two men who were wearing articles resembling a turban over a felt conical hat and a skullcap during morning prayers. A case had already been filed with the prosecutor's office about these men. As discussed later in this chapter, the diversity in men's headwear continued well into the 1930s. What is significant in this report is that it blamed the mosque imam Gürcü Baltacı Mehmet Hoca for inciting "ignorant people" to unlawful behavior. The governor argued on the basis of the ongoing investigation that Mehmet Hoca encouraged men to wear the turban by reciting some Quranic passages and the Prophet's sayings and preaching that a prayer performed with a turban on one's head was equal to seventy without wearing a turban.[76] Although we do not yet know the extent of such incidents, the Bursa case suggests that prayer leaders did not uniformly follow the Directorate's orders to promote the hat.

We need to be aware that not all imams followed the orders of the Directorate. Nevertheless, many prayer leaders probably discussed the issue of headgear in the mosque by elaborating on the circular described above, although most likely there were also sermons prepared on that topic by the Directorate itself.[77]

Hat Sermons and Public Opinion beyond the Directorate

Muallim Hüseyin Refik in Konya

While the Directorate typically provided the texts of mosque sermons, sermons may have come out of local initiatives as well. In one such case that crossed the boundaries of public and private, in the fall of 1925 a schoolteacher in Konya prepared a sermon for the local mosques, advocating modern dress, including hats, arguing that it was not against Islam to wear clothes identified with (Christian) Europeans. At some point that same fall, while the hat campaign led by the President himself was going on but before the Hat Law, a group of the town's residents including several *hocas* visited Hüseyin Refik (Kırış), a mathematics and literature teacher in Konya İmam Hatip High School, in order to learn his opinion on the use of hats from an Islamic point of view.[78]

An 1887 graduate of the Darüşşafaka[79] in İstanbul, Hüseyin Refik had previously worked as a teacher and educational admininistrator in Ottoman Damascus, Latakia, Baghdad, Van, Konya, and İstanbul. Prior to his tenure at Konya İmam Hatip Lisesi (High School), Muallim Hüseyin Refik had been a director of the constitutional era Konya Law School, upon whose closure in 1919 he had been appointed as a teacher in the Konya Darülhilafetilaliyye Medresesi. Hence, he was presumably a well-known and respectable public figure in Konya, whose opinions the local community trusted and sought after. According to Fuad Arın, Hüseyin Refik's son and biographer, who was present at this fall 1925 meeting, his father explained to his guests that there were no objections to the hat from an Islamic point of view, given that the fez and the *kalpak* had also been originally borrowed from foreigners. Apparently, Hüseyin Refik went beyond an abstract verbal explanation, displaying to his guests a Borsalino felt hat he had recently purchased from a Chevrolet dealer in town who had brought a small supply of Italian hats. Hüseyin Refik put the hat on his head and informed his guests that he would wear it once the law approved it.[80] By the end of this meeting, the group decided that the opinions expressed in the press to promote the hat should also be explained to the public in Konya through sermons in the mosques.

Following this event, Hüseyin Refik wrote a sermon justifying and promoting the hat, invoking the authority of both the Qur'an and the hadith as well as the requirements of national progress. He argued that, since it has been established by the hadith and by numerous *fetvas* that outward appearance cannot affect the spirit, it would be a mistake to consider it sinful for a Muslim to wear clothes used by non-Muslims, such as pants, jackets, hats, and caps. In fact, he likened the refusal to wear the types of clothes that Christians wear to practices such as not eating food prepared by a Christian or refusing to touch the hand of a Christian, behavior which he argued may on the surface seem Islamic, but in fact were a result of ignorance and fanaticism.

While stressing that there are no religious objections to the hat (hence challenging the opponents of the hat with the very language they used to attack the hat), he also addressed the issue in a broader national context. Hüseyin Refik reminded his potential audiences of the backward state of the nation, and highlighted the need to work hard and to live in line with the advancements and requirements of the times, suggesting the need to embrace change. He encouraged citizens to adopt the modern clothes ("*kisveyi medeniye*": i.e., clothing such as the European style hat) that the elected officials of "our Republican government" have found "compatible with the modern needs of our country and with the four fundamentals of our religion."[81] Hüseyin Refik was thus presenting the state as the ultimate authority not only in identifying what constituted modern attire and in deciding what clothes Turkish citizens should wear, but also in deciding what was compatible with the fundamentals of Islamic law. He advised every Turk and Muslim to remain loyal to the Republican government, going so far as cautioning them that refusal to wear the modern clothing designated by the government as suitable for the modern needs of the nation would invite reproach and punishment as a deterrent to others. The sermon ended with prayers for the well-being of the nation, its parliament, its government, and the leader.[82] In an effort to encourage a favorable public reception of the Hat Law, this sermon, which employed religious rhetoric in the service of the modernist-nationalist cause, was recited to the public in the mosques in Konya in November and December of 1925.[83]

Regardless of the effectiveness of Hüseyin Refik Kırış's sermon among the residents of Konya, it is evident from photographs taken in the years following the passage of the Hat Law, such as the picture on his teachers' identification card issued in 1926, that Muallim Hüseyin Refik indeed adopted the European hat, just as he had promised his guests in the fall of 1925.

Interestingly, in a lecture delivered in the Konya Darülhilafetilaliyye Medresesi a few years earlier, Hüseyin Refik had criticized those who confused Westernization with wearing ties and starched shirts, dancing, and the adoption of European morality and customs. Westernization, Hüseyin Refik had told his audience, rather meant building factories and businesses, flying in the air and travelling under the seas, and the acquisition of Western science and knowledge.[84] He had thus maintained a careful distinction between culture and civilization, in the fashion defended by the sociologist Ziya Gökalp, the ideologue of Turkish nationalism whose passing Hüseyin Refik would lament in his poetry two years after this 1922 talk.[85] In practice, however, the boundaries between culture and civilization, Western and modern were blurred, if they existed at all.

It is evident from the available biographical information as well as the pictures taken as early as the 1890s that Hüseyin Refik himself pursued a life that blended traditional or Islamic ways of life with modern and Western habits and practices. An Ottoman Turkish nationalist and a devout Muslim who always performed his daily prayers, he was also a teacher and administrator who had received his formal education in a modern Ottoman school, the Darüşşafaka. Fluent in Arabic, Persian, and French, Hüseyin Refik enjoyed translating works from the French as well as reading poetry in Persian. In his private life he was a monogamous father and husband whose second marriage took place only several years after his first wife's death. In public, Hüseyin Refik was an Ottoman Turkish citizen whose plain fez complemented his European style shirt, jacket, and tie for most of his adult life, until 1925. (Since he had already been dressing in an essentially European style, the Republican regime's promotion of Western style clothing did not require changes to his sartorial habits, with the exception of the hat.) We should interpret his 1922 speech as a criticism of excessive or superficial Westernization, rather than as a rejection of all values and practices Western. By 1925 he appeared more willing to embrace measures that he may have criticized earlier as excessive Westernization. His open and active public support for the reformist measures of the new republic (such as the hat and the new alphabet) likely derived from his modernist belief—which he shared with the Kemalist reformers—in the ability of the state to lead a war-torn and impoverished nation on its way to progress and modernity, rather than from a fundamental change in his ideological positions.[86]

The Press

The hat campaign of 1925, led by the President himself, was accompanied by massive propaganda in the press. Newspapers, both national (based in İstanbul and Ankara) and local, promoted and advocated the new hat. The Law on the Maintenance of Order (Takrir-i Sükûn Kanunu), passed by the Parliament in March 1925 in response to the Sheikh Said Rebellion in Eastern Anatolia, authorized the government to close down any publication it deemed a threat to law and order for two years. Eight of the leading İstanbul newspapers and periodicals, and a number of provincial papers, were shut down under this law. Leading journalists from İstanbul were also arrested and brought before the Independence Tribunals. They were eventually released but not allowed to go back to journalism. The law remained in force for four years, significantly reducing the expression of anti-hat opinion in the press in the first few years following the Hat Law.

Newspapers advocating reform discussed the benefits of the hat reform, helping to form pro-hat public opinion among the literate public.[87] The national press continued to promote modern dress in the 1930s, even when direct discussions of men's clothing issues had slowed down, by disseminating images of modern men, women, and families in photographs, and especially in advertisements. By the late 1940s and 1950s, both national and regional newspapers and magazines had become more diversified, and debates on "proper dress" resurfaced.[88]

Schools and the Education System

Education was one of the principal means of Kemalist nation building and modernization.[89] Early Republican leaders hoped to create loyal and productive citizens through secular public education. In a mostly illiterate, poor, peasant society, especially after the devastation wrought by nearly a decade of wars, the education of the masses was a basic requirement for rapid economic development. It was also a useful tool for a state that was trying to instill in its citizens a new cultural identity as well as loyalty to a new regime and its secular nationalist ideology. The foundations of a modern public education system had been laid during the Tanzimat era. Sultan Mahmut II declared primary schooling compulsory, and the subsequent Ottoman laws and regulations on education reaffirmed the Ottoman state's commitment to free mandatory primary education. In the final decades of the Empire, the Ottoman state tried to use public education as a means of creating loyal and productive Ottoman citizens. As the late Ottoman state expanded the public education system and employed it for its modernist and ideological projects, public education co-existed with traditional and other forms of education such as the *medrese* system and the missionary schools, which largely operated outside the supervision of the state.[90] Republican leaders were also amply aware of the importance of education as a basic requirement for rapid development and for building a new, secular Turkish nation. The 1924 constitution declared primary education compulsory and free of charge for all Turkish students in public schools. The 1924 Law on the Unification of Education eliminated religious schools and brought all education under the control of the Ministry of Education.[91] It created the legal framework for the establishment of a secular national education system. The state emphasized all levels of education, including vocational and adult education programs, yet the education of children and youth were most important for the modernist and nationalist goals of the early Republican state. Even as the education system struggled with major problems, such as financial constraints, shortages of teachers and teaching materials, and a mixed reception from the population, schools, especially primary schools, continued to function as crucial vehicles of socializing the youth into the new national culture.[92]

Schools were directly involved in the process of changing all clothing conventions, since both teachers and students had to follow specific dress codes. While teachers had to abide by the dress codes for civil servants, students had to wear a uniform, which at some levels included a hat. Hence, school was a place where students were socialized into modern dress. It was also through textbooks that students learned about modern dress and dress reforms. Textbook references to dress reforms presented the Hat Law to students not only as a law to be followed, but also within the context of requirements of civility: civilized people must appear and act in a civilized manner. Mitat Sadullah's *Yeni Yurt Bilgisi* (Knowledge of the Homeland) textbook for fourth grade students includes a set of "Civilized Rules Which Everybody Should Respect in Town and City Life." Regarding proper appearance in public, Sadullah argued:

> The problem of appearance in the street is very important. Civilized people can go out in the street only with a civilized appearance.
>
> The Republican Government which has changed everything bad in the country has also taken appearance under some regulation and has adopted the hat for the headdress. There is no possibility hereafter of walking in the streets with a gown and ketchekula [bowl-shaped cap].[93]

In her research on early Republican education, Faith Childress has shown that textbooks, especially reading and geography books, reinforced the state's promotion of Western dress for both men and women.[94] According to Childress, in some cases texts and illustrations advocated Western dress and dress reforms directly, but more often it was done in more subtle ways, such as the addition of illustrations and photographs to texts not directly concerned with dress issues. In fact, the introduction and promotion of the new dress in textbooks preceded legislation on dress. This must be seen within the context of efforts to create a favorable public opinion before the passing of the Hat Law. Textbooks were not standardized until 1936, yet the state tried to impose some control and uniformity through standardized curriculum and textbook commissioning and authorization by the Committee on Education and Instruction. Therefore, textbooks at times communicated messages that did not fully conform to the regime's principals or ideals. However, it appears from recent scholarship on early Republican textbooks that they generally contributed to the promotion of "modern" dress for Turkish men and women. Textbook images and illustrations changed after 1925 to reflect not just the Hat Law but also the state encouragement of Western clothes for both men and women. In one such example, the same illustration in the 1925 and 1928 editions of the same first grade reading book portrayed men and women dressed differently. In the 1928 edition, women's head scarves disappeared and the female teacher in the illustration appeared in a short sleeve dress and high heeled shoes.[95]

In another instance, when the publisher and the author of the *Kolay Kıraat* (Easy Reader) series for primary schools wrote to the Committee on Education and Instruction in 1926 asking for approval of the new edition for classroom use, they promised compliance not only with the new orthographic conventions, but also with the new Hat Law. The publisher Hilmi (İbrahim Hilmi Çığıraçan) and the author Seraceddin (Seraceddin Hasırcıoğlu) stressed that hats had replaced fezzes in the images found throughout the entire series.[96]

Here we find a convergence of the economic motivations of the publisher (and to a degree of the author), with the ideology and demands of the state (and particularly of the Ministry of Education). No doubt the publisher was concerned with the marketability of the classroom readers, and therefore with the Committee's approval of the series for classroom use. It would have been evident that textbooks containing images of men wearing fezzes would not get a favorable review from the Ministry of Education. Nevertheless, it appears to have been the case that rather than the reforms forcing the publisher and the author to make changes, the publisher and the author were themselves a part of the overall modernist intellectual camp in the late Ottoman Empire and the early Turkish Republic and were indeed supportive of the modernist reforms of the Republic.

This is particularly evident in the case of *Kolay Kıraat*'s author Seraceddin, a teacher, writer, translator, and poet who in his youth under Sultan Abdülhamid's regime had fled to Europe and studied natural sciences, botany, and anatomy at the University of Geneva in the 1890s. During the Second Constitutional Period he worked as a teacher in several prominent high schools in İstanbul, such as the Kabataş, Vefa, Üsküdar and İstanbul Girls High Schools, while also writing and publishing books for children. Seraceddin moved to Ankara shortly after the establishment of the Republic, assuming a position at the Ministry of Education as a member of the Publishing and Translations Committee (Telif ve Tercüme Heyeti), a position he retained until 1930. Afterwards he continued to teach, translate, and publish in İstanbul until his death in 1938.[97] Financial and marketing considerations must have had some effect on the content of Seraceddin Hasırcıoğlu's books, as indicated by his quick addition of images of hats to his easy reader series. Yet Hasırcıoğlu's record, particularly his voluntary acceptance of a position in the Ministry of Education, points to a more complicated relationship between authors, publishers and the state. As a writer, translator, teacher, and educational bureucrat, Hasırcıoğlu was involved in nearly all levels of choosing, creating, shaping, and transmitting to the youth reading and teaching materials that were intended to instill in their readers values associated with modernity.

Similarly, the life and works of İbrahim Hilmi Çığıraçan (1879–1963), the publisher of *Kolay Kıraat* as well as more than one thousand textbooks, literary, cultural, religious and military works, and translations, suggest that economic gain was not necessarily his only or primary motivation in publishing.[98] İbrahim Hilmi was a member of the RPP and was actively involved in the activities of the Yeşilköy People's House in İstanbul, where on national days he delivered speeches (which like his other writings and the writings of many of his peers, were composed in Ottoman letters).[99] More importantly, he had been an ardent supporter of Westernization well before the declaration of the Republic. In his writings during the Second Constitutional Period, he had advocated Westernization, which he equated with modernization and progress, as the only way for the rejuvenation of the Ottoman nation. Son of an immigrant family from Rumania, İbrahim Hilmi was a self-made man who lacked the formal academic training of the period's intellectuals. He was nevertheless knowledgeable, well travelled, and familiar with contemporary European practices, and was driven by a desire to help remedy the backwardness of the nation. He considered Westernization to be the adoption of European ways in education, politics, economy, work ethic, hygiene, clothing, and social manners, all without losing one's religion and national customs.[100] Although he may not have been in full agreement with the post-1922 regime concerning the boundaries of Westernization, as a major publisher of textbooks and other popular literary works İbrahim Hilmi contributed to the early Republican era culture of reading and education. Çığıraçan's support for the new regime through the publication of textbooks that complied with the clothing and other reforms, as well as his publication of readers and alphabet books that targeted the illiterate and newly literate adult population, should be seen in part as the contributions of a modernist publisher to the process of Turkish nation building, rather than as a purely financially motivated enterprise.

Following a commonly used strategy similar to RPP propaganda materials in the 1920s and 1930s, textbook images and illustrations encouraged Western clothes for Turkish men and women through "old vs. new" constructs. The promotion of European dress took place in some textbooks in the larger context of demonstrating the superiority of the new Turkish schools and teachers over the old Ottoman education system.[101] In textbook illustrations, the fez and the turban were associated with the traditional style Ottoman school, the bearded, frightening *hoca* in his turban, and with physical punishment, especially the infamous *falaka*, or bastinado. On the other hand, the new, modern Turkish teacher, depicted in his European style suit or in her modern dress, was more approachable and friendly, and did not use physical punishment.[102]

Republican leaders' preoccupation with appearance had much to do with external/foreign as well as internal/self-perceptions of Turkey's place among the community of nations. Textbook images also revealed perceived connections between outward appearance and Turkey's place between the East and the West. An early example of this was a chart showing the population of Turkey and its neighbors in a 1926 geography textbook.[103] Turkey had the largest population, with 13.5 million (followed by Iran, with a population of 9.5 million). Population sizes were represented by a drawing of men of different heights in proportion to the size of the population of each country. Not only was the man representing Turkey the tallest, due to the relative size of Turkey's population, but, interestingly, he was also the only one dressed in Western style clothes, wearing a suit, tie, and fedora style hat, while all the men representing the other countries were dressed in traditional clothes. As in other measures of progress, modernity, and Westernization, and as we shall later see in the question of a Latin based alphabet and literacy, this illustration was to reaffirm to Turkish students that not only did their country have the greatest population in the region—by itself a sign of Turkey's greatness, especially after massive population losses during the recent wars—but it was also the only nation in the Middle East that belonged to the contemporary Western civilization, as indicated by the clothes its members wore.[104] Such illustrations often conveyed more the aspirations than the accomplishments of the

Republican state. In another example of textbooks communicating to students the importance of outward appearance as a symbol of Turkish modernity to the outside world, a fifth grade history textbook described the veil as "unhealthy" and called the fez "a ridiculous accessory with no religious or national significance," telling students that the clothing of Turkish men and women could no longer be an object of ridicule as it had been previously.[105]

There is also information to suggest that schools may have been more actively involved in the transformation of dress. For example, during Mustafa Kemal's visit to Konya on 17–19 October 1925, the Konya High School organized a "fez-rending celebration" about two months after the hat was introduced by the President, but before the Parliament had passed any laws on it.[106] It appears that schools, teachers, and students were often involved in pro-hat lectures and demonstrations in partnership with the local branches of the Turkish Hearths. This is not surprising, given the modernist nationalist stance of the Turkish Hearths, and given also that the rank and file membership of the Turkish Hearths drew heavily on professionals including teachers, doctors, and the educated urban youth. In the 1920s, the Turkish Hearths, like the People's Houses that essentially replaced them in the early 1930s, provided a limited but active urban support base for the new Republican regime and its reforms. In fact, the Hearths appear to have begun a pro-hat public campaign immediately after Mustafa Kemal signaled the adoption of the European hat in his famous Kastamonu speech delivered at the İnebolu Turkish Hearths in August 1925. In the Grand National Assembly, several of the parliamentary delegates who spoke passionately on 25 November in favor of passing a Hat Law were members of the Turkish Hearths. In Trabzon province, the propaganda (*Tenvir ve İrşad*, or Enlightenment and Inculcation) committees of the Turkish Hearths and the Teachers' Union toured the provincial districts and villages promoting the hat. According to Mustafa Reşit Tarakçıoğlu, a high school teacher and the president of the Trabzon branches of both associations at the time, the program given to the "enlightenment" committees in the fall of 1925 emphasized that Islam was a modern (*asrî*) religion and that the adoption of the hat was not against the principles of religion. Thus, like the Directorate of Religious Affairs and like Muallim Hüseyin Refik in Konya, by using the very language that the opponents of the hat used, the Turkish Hearths and the Teachers' Union in Trabzon encouraged the residents of small provincial towns and villages to wear the hat and support the revolution. Apparently, in Maçka, Tonya, Arsin, and other towns and villages, the doctors and the teachers on the propaganda committees not only advised the public about the reforms and revolutionary ideals (which included the advice that they should not speak Greek [Rumca]), but they also provided tangible assistance such as free medical examinations and free medication.[107]

In another example (which took place even before the passage of the Law) of the Turkish Hearths and teachers cooperating locally in promoting the hat, a middle school principle delivered a pro-hat talk during the Republic Day celebration program hosted by the Turkish Hearths in Niğde province in central Anatolia. At the end of the talk, those present expressed their rejection of the fez by throwing away their fezzes en masse.[108] Through such symbolic collective action in Anatolian towns, the Hearths and the schools encouraged the public, and especially the youth, to adopt the European hat as a powerful symbol of modernity.

In addition to socializing students into the culture of Western style dress during their years of education, schools, especially after the elementary level, were crucial in shaping life styles, including norms of dress, by preparing students for employment. The early Republican state, with its expanding bureaucracy and services, was the principal employer. Employment with the state, as a teacher, doctor, nurse, or engineer, as a low level civil servant or as a high level bureaucrat, all required the adoption of external symbols of the life styles promoted by the state. Civil servants and all state employees, including teachers, were required to conform to a dress code that included modern Western clothes.

Private Citizens as Agents of Dress Change

The interest in, and commitment to, modernization of dress and appearance in general was not limited to governors, kaymakams and other party officials, teachers, or policemen. There are indications that some private individuals may have gone beyond changing their own dress, to actively promoting or enforcing the new dress.

İsmail Engin, owner of a rice factory in Finike, a town on the Mediterranean coast, acted as a self-appointed promoter of modern dress. In a letter dated 11 July 1935, Engin informed the RPP general secretary in Ankara that he had "opened a war on mustaches in Finike." He wrote:

> The clothing and appearance of the hundreds of people who came to see Antalya governor Mr. Sahip [sic] Örge during his visit to Finike was striking. I said perhaps their shortcomings in hats, dresses, and shoes can be tolerated as this depends on their material wealth. But I could not stand the one thousand and one varieties of mustaches and beards of the public and private individuals who appeared before the clean-shaven President and the governor. Starting the next day I opened a war on mustaches in Finike. I had to come up with convincing answers to my fellow countrymen's objections arising from their conservatism. When I saw that this issue, which has not been taken seriously, can be valuable for our national existence, I began to collect my notes with the intention of reading them collectively to my acquaintances. Around that time I went to İzmir on business. When a printer I saw said he would print a few hundred copies for five or ten liras I had my notes printed. After taking care of the legal procedures I brought them to Finike and mailed some of them to our President Kemal Atatürk and to some of the People's Houses. The following day I remembered it would have been more appropriate to send them to the Secretary General of our party. I am presenting the remaining copies in order to rectify the error.[109]

Engin's letter suggests that his dress booklet was a personal initiative undertaken at his own cost. He says he produced this pamphlet because he felt an obligation to encourage men in this port town to dress in a way that best represents the Turkish nation at a time when "our women have discarded their *çarşafs* and *peçes* until not a single one remained." Engin was probably a member of the RPP and of the local branch of the People's Houses, but there is no indication that he had prepared his booklet at the request of the Party or the People's House. Engin's case lends support to the argument that the rise of a new Turkish middle class was an important factor in building a pro-reform constituency.[110] Engin, a factory owner in Finike, was actively involved in the process of modernizing and harmonizing outward appearance. This may have been a form of voluntary activism out of an ideological commitment. It is almost certain that Engin was also motivated by the possibility of individual gains such as tax credits or other political favors that he might attract by acting as a good Kemalist.

Much like the Young Turk regime that had tried to build a Muslim Ottoman bourgeoisie after 1908, the early Republican state supported the creation of a national Turkish bourgeoisie. State support to the emerging industrialists continued after the regime turned from a liberal economy to a more planned economy following the global depression, when state involvement in the economy increased but did not replace capitalist investment.[111] For a small factory owner, a close relationship with the higher officials of the ruling party would no doubt have increased his chances of government favors in the form of credit or other economic incentives. But this would not have required quite the degree of individual action İsmail Engin took by writing, printing, and distributing a pamphlet on appropriate grooming and appearance.

Even if not as thoroughly Westernized as, and smaller in numbers than, the non-Muslim commercial bourgeoisie of the late Ottoman era (the vast majority of whom left Anatolia or died during the war years), the emerging (Muslim) Turkish capitalist middle class—at least segments of it—also enjoyed Westernized life styles.[112] We would expect the influence of the emerging middle classes on the rest of the society to be more in the form of a gradual cultural emulation of middle class tastes and habits rather than direct action aimed at changing public opinion and behavior. Yet Engin's attempt to directly influence local public opinion on appropriate dress in a small town like Finike followed a pattern of behavior that supporters of the reforms were frequently engaged in. Advocates of the reforms, whether they were genuinely supportive of the regime or felt obliged to express their commitment to the regime for economic or other personal gains, were quite often involved in symbolic acts or cultural activities demonstrating their support. Publishing a pamphlet on modern dress, or writing poetry dedicated to the hat,[113] however ineffective these efforts may have been in influencing public behavior, belonged to this category of symbolic acts and cultural activities. Participation in activities such as writing for People's Houses magazines was crucial for maintaining a support base for the regime, because it gave the participants the sense that they were indeed contributing to the making of a modern nation, even though the impact of such activities over the general population was rather limited.

Engin's use of language is also worth noting here. Not only does it suggest that the primary audience of his pamphlet was the higher RPP officials, but it also attests to how, through actions such as Engin's, the advocates of reform were first and foremost transforming their own habits and identities. In line with the language purification policies of the 1930s, Engin used a number of recently invented or rediscovered Turkish words in his letter, demonstrating his support for the language policies of the new regime. For example, while referring to Antalya Governor Sâib İhsan Örge, Engin wrote "Antalya ilbayı Bay Sahip [sic] Örge," preferring "*ilbay*" over "*vali*," and using the new title "*Bay*," which the state promoted as a male title of respect to be used regardless of class, education, or family status after the abolition of titles such as "*paşa*" and "*bey*."[114] Engin also observed the new Surname Law,[115] referring to the governor with his full name, including his recently acquired surname Örge, and by signing the letter with his own full name.

Another incident, related by Malik Aksel, suggests that there may have been cases of individuals acting locally to make sure that their fellow citizens complied with the dress code not only in the months and years following the Hat Law but as late as at the end of the RPP era. One day in 1950, Saip Mualla, a well-known painter of the early Republican era whose works included portraits of Atatürk, was in the İstanbul Patisserie in Ankara. There he saw a ragged middle-aged man with a turban on his head greeting people strangely and laughing mockingly. Aksel notes that the turban the man was wearing was not the kind worn by the men of religion, but was a beggar's (*goygoycu*) turban. Aksel writes that Saip Mualla saw it as a challenge to the Hat Law and as an insult to the headgear of the men of religion. Suddenly he stood up, declaring to the people in the coffee house, "In this country either there is law or there isn't." Mualla ran out of the patisserie leaving behind his painting canvas, returning in ten minutes with a policeman.[116] Aksel does not tell what happened next, but we can assume that at the very least the man was asked by the policeman to take off his turban. He may also have had his turban confiscated or may have been taken to the police station to have an official report made.

The fact that Mualla was infuriated by a man wearing a turban in a coffee house suggests that the turban was no longer commonly seen in public places. It also seems that Mualla was the only person in the coffeehouse who would not tolerate the presence of a man defying the dress code. His reaction was probably in part due to his commitment to the project of cultural modernization that the RPP regime had advocated at a time when the party had lost elections, and when some of its policies were beginning to be questioned and reversed. It may also have had a class aspect. A ragged man with a *goygoycu* type turban probably did not look very respectable to Saip Mualla, who was a leading artist of the time.

Headgear and Turkish Identity
in Re-making National Boundaries

In the 1920s and 1930s, hats and fezzes served as visible symbols of alternative conceptions of Turkish identity among Turkish and Muslim communities even beyond the frontiers of Turkey. The boundaries established in 1923 left significant Turkish minorities in the neighboring countries. (The terms Turk and Muslim were often used interchangeably, particularly in the Balkans). In the disputed *sanjak* of Alexandretta, an eastern Mediterranean province that was claimed by both Turkey and Syria and administered as an autonomous province within the French mandate of Syria, the brimmed European hat became the most visible symbol of the Turkish nationalists in the province, who agitated for unification with Turkey.

In 1936, French officials reported that "hundreds of local young men began to wear brimmed hats, and some young women began to abandon the veil." [117] (Indeed, the French officials referred to these Turkish nationalists as the "*chapiste.*") Meanwhile, Turkish Muslims who were not supportive of the Kemalist policies in Turkey along with other Muslim residents of Alexandretta who opposed unification with Turkey continued to wear the fez, whereas the Arab nationalists donned the *sedara*, or *faysaliyye*, a hat that was introduced by Iraq's King Faysal as a distinctive national headgear, as a sign of their commitment to Arab nationalism. In the 1930s, hats and fezzes became very much a part of the rhetorical as well as literal battles over the province's collective identity and future status, with demonstrators trampling on or throwing into the river the "wrong" hat.

France recognized the independence of the province in 1938 and the *sanjak* joined Turkey in 1939 as the province of Hatay. Interestingly, government correspondence from the 1940s reported instances of citizens, many of them older men, still refusing to wear the hat in Hatay. Whereas such violations often appeared to have been unintentional, what is notable in the nearly two dozen cases reported from Hatay in 1946 is the perception that these were acts of opposition to the hat, and to the regime. The governor's report described Murtaza Tırabzon, like the majority of the other men accused, as "an opponent of the hat ever since the accession of Hatay" and noted that "[h]e [did] not wear a [European style] hat unless he is forced to do so (*mecbur olmadıkça*)."[118] These new citizens had missed the collective experiences of the early stages of the Hat Law, from the propaganda campaign in the press and through the Directorate, to police and gendarme enforcement on the ground, to the Independence Tribunals, and thus had not been socialized into the nationalist culture of wearing hats and speaking Turkish.[119] Moreover, their anti-hat sentiment had been, if anything, hardened through the polarization of the mandate years.

These individual acts of resistance in Hatay in the 1940s were in a sense comparable to some of the early reactions to the Hat Law in 1925 and 1926, but the context was somewhat different: the regime felt more secure than it had in the mid-1920s and no longer resorted to measures such as the Independence Tribunals. Moreover, the Republican regime and its reforms had a powerful support base within the province.

In the case of neighboring Bulgaria, home to a considerable Muslim Turkish minority in the post-Ottoman era, as Mary Neuburger argues, the fez served as a symbol of the backwardness of the Muslim (Turkish and Pomak) internal "other" for the Bulgarian nationalists in their effort to create a new Bulgarian identity and a modern Bulgarian nation.[120]

Official Mediators: Governors, *Kaymakam*s, Policemen

Governors and other government officials were expected to lead the Turkish public by way of providing role models of the ideal Turkish man, woman, and family for the ordinary citizens to emulate. In their public behavior, from their modern but modest appearance to the ways they socialized as husband and wife and as families, government bureaucrats and their families were expected to lead by example in the transformation of society.

We can see an example of this in Figure 4, a 1935 portrait of Muhittin Tanyolaç, sub-district director (*nahiye müdürü*) of Midye/Kıyıköy, a small town on the western Black Sea coast of Kırklareli province, with his wife Azize and their son Kemal. Their appearance reflects the family's connection with the state, as well as their social and economic status. Unlike in earlier periods, the mother was no longer excluded from the family portrait, but in fact she now occupies the central location in it, evidence of the ongoing transformations in family and gender relations.

4. Muhittin, Azize, and Kemal Tanyolaç, Midye, 1935. Photograph from the family album of Neriman Tanyolaç.

Government bureaucrats were also directly involved in the process of reforming the habits and practices of the Anatolian population, including their sartorial habits. In a March 1939 cipher, the Ministry of the Interior informed the inspectors general and the governors that it had received intelligence that in some localities a number of men and women had abandoned the hat.[121] Instead, women had begun wearing headscarves and men were now wearing berets. With a view to understanding the scope of that trend, the ministry asked the governors and the inspectors to investigate and report back if such reactionary activities were going on in their regions.

The responses to the Ministry were generally along the lines of assuring Ankara that there were no reactionary trends, no opposition to the Hat Law, and that men did not wear berets. Yet several of the reports were quite informative on what the actual state of dress was and how the governors dealt with the issue at the local level.

The Governor of Sinop reported that the occasional incidents of defiance of the Hat Law were not intentional acts of opposition, but were a result of ignorance and poverty.[122] Çorum Governor Salih Kılıç wrote that unlike the backward state of the appearance of women, there was no such tendency among men. He added that all men wore hats and caps in the city and the towns, and all the villagers in the province wore caps.[123] Similarly, Kastamonu governor Avni Doğan expressed concern not over men's but women's clothing, although he reassured the ministry that the party and the People's Houses had been pursuing the matter throughout the province.[124]

Governor İ. Sabri Çıtak of Maraş, in the southeast, observed that "the ignorant masses" of the province were deeply conservative, but that they hid their conservatism. This he thought was due to the intense measures taken by the government after the hat incident, referring to the trials by the Independence Tribunals following the hat demonstrations in Maraş on 27 November 1925.[125] Çıtak wrote he was sure some men wore berets and skullcaps not in the streets but at home, in their back yards and in their fields, and he warned that even with a slight relaxation in implementation, berets and skullcaps would appear in the streets. Çıtak also observed that women in the province were more conservative than men, as townspeople were more conservative than the peasants. He expressed concern that there were individuals with reactionary tendencies in the town, who would attempt to "poison the pure and naive people" if the opportunity arose.[126]

Governor Cevat Ökmen of Mardin, also in the southeast, reported that there were no signs of reaction such as wearing berets instead of hats.[127] However, as in Maraş, the governor suggested that it was the force of the laws that ensured the wearing of hats, implying that people would not have done so in the absence of legal enforcement. Ökmen wrote that nationalist feelings in the province were rather weak, and expressed concern that relations between the people and the government were not good. He was especially worried because the province of Mardin was on the border with Syria.

Similarly, in a 1939 provincial inspection report, party inspector and Muğla parliamentarian Cemal Karamuğla expressed concern over the social state of Kars province on the Soviet border.[128] He observed a divide between locals and those who had come from territories lost to Russia. He noted that many villagers continued to wear the black *kalpak*, which was not considered a proper hat after the hat reform and may have been increasingly identified as Russian headgear.

Balıkesir Governor Etem Aykut informed the Ministry that no such reactionary acts had taken place against the hat, and that precautions had been taken to prevent such acts. He included an example of what measures were being taken locally. He wrote, "the other day at the station I saw a bearded man wearing a skullcap. I sent over a policeman at once, to have the man take off the skullcap and to advise him not to wear the skullcap again."[129]

Aykut's method of direct intervention on the ground via a policeman was apparently not uncommon. The majority of such interventions most likely ended simply with the policeman or the government official confiscating the headgear. In some cases the incident was reported to the judicial authorities. Then the public prosecutor could bring charges against the person involved for acting contrary to Law No. 671. For instance, on 19 January 1938, five men were seen strolling in Borçka, an eastern Black Sea town, wearing woolen *kalpaks*. The men, all peasants from nearby villages, were arrrested and taken to the judicial authorities in the town.[130] Similarly, according to a report from the Governor of Antalya, in the town of Elmalı, seventy-five-year-old Ali oğlu Rabıt Hoca (Rabıt Hoca, son of Ali), from the nearby Yuva village, was seen strolling in the street wearing a turban. He was taken to the

Public Prosecutor's office and was sentenced to two days' imprisonment by the court. His sentence was temporarily suspended.[131]

In another case, the prison sentence was overturned by the Council of Ministers. Seventy-two-year-old İsmail oğlu Ahmed (Ahmed, son of İsmail) was sentenced to one day's imprisonment on grounds of showing opposition to the government by not wearing the hat. On 5 October 1937, the Council of Ministers passed a decree pardoning Ahmed's one day imprisonment on health grounds.[132]

What these governors' reports and minor incidents tell us is that by the late 1930s, at least in urban public places, a majority of the male citizens were indeed wearing some type of headgear identifiable as a hat (*şapka*) or cap (*kasket*). The reports reveal a degree of disagreement as to how such widespread conformity with the Hat Law was accomplished. Some of the reports suggest that the hat (and the cap) had indeed become a "natural" or "normal" headgear for the male citizenry, whereas others imply that it was the actual enforcement of the Hat Law that ensured that men wore hats. As for reasons for the occasional defiance of the Hat Law, the governors explained it variously as an indication of ignorance, poverty, conservatism, or opposition. These explanations reflect the diverse circumstances the governors encountered within their respective jurisdictions, as well as the divergent opinions the governors themselves held as to the meaning and the application of the Hat Law and other reforms. It is hard for the historian to fully understand the motivations of those who defied the Hat Law. It is worth noting, however, that in the minor incidents discussed above, as well as the cases we will see shortly, none of the individuals caught in violation of the Hat Law was wearing a fez. It may well be that they had never worn the fez in the first place, that they had always worn other ethnic or regional headgear such as the *külah* or the *kalpak*. It no doubt also had to do with the unavailability of fezzes on the market after 1925. It also appears to be the case that the public clearly understood that the fez was no longer acceptable under the new regime: that the era of the fez, associated with the old regime, was over. It is noteworthy that in the transgressions discussed above, the men who defied the law in the late 1930s were old men in their seventies. I am not suggesting that it was only because of their age that these men violated the Hat Law. Nor am I arguing that it was only elderly citizens who defied the

Hat Law. (We will see cases involving younger men, as well.) However, as we saw with Numan Efendi's father (Hacı Yusuf Efendi) in Konya and Abdullah Eltan's father (Ömer Efendi) in Trabzon, who secluded themselves for a time in 1925, it must have been a more difficult transition for this generation of citizens to abandon a type of headgear that they had been using for a very long time and to adapt to the hat. Another example of the experience of the hat reform pitting elderly fathers against younger sons came in the memories of one of my informants. The late Avni Yurdabayrak (a retired judge and member of Parliament) recalled that a distant relative of his, a judge, had sentenced his own father to six months of imprisonment for failing to wear a hat.[133] Avni Bey could not remember any of the specifics of this instance, which he had heard from his father. He thought it had happened somewhere in eastern Anatolia; it may have been in Erzurum. It would have been interesting to know when and where this happened, if the sentence was actually applied or perhaps suspended or commuted, and more importantly, why the father and the son acted the way they did. Although we cannot fully capture their motivations, this case, like the examples above, nevertheless hints at a generational gap and tension between father and son in the reception and experience of the reforms.[134]

Public prosecutors, governors, and others responsible for the application of the Hat Law did not always agree on what the law meant and how to enforce it. A hat incident that took place in Trabzon in January 1939 shows not only how such small events could escalate, but also how the various branches of the government, local administration including the police, and individual citizens interpreted the Hat Law differently. A brief encounter at the city center between a police commissioner and Ahmet Tiryaki, a young villager in his early twenties from Yomra, was at the center of this minor but controversial incident. It is from the testimonies of Ahmet Tiryaki and Said Doru, another young man from Yomra about twenty years old and an eyewitness to the occurrence, that we get a detailed account of the incident.[135] (Despite their young age, both men were married and had children and were in town for business on 27 January, the day of the incident.) According to Ahmet Tiryaki's testimony, about a month earlier he, along with a group of men from his village, had come to the city to buy corn. Since his hat had worn out he had come to the city bare-headed with the intention of buying a new hat in the city. (He uses the word *şapka* (hat) and not *kasket* (cap), but he almost definitely means a cap rather than a full-brimmed European hat.) He had a shawl thrown around his neck. As he was walking through the municipal park, a police commissioner approached him and grabbed the shawl from his shoulders. The commissioner pulled his pocketknife, ripped up Ahmet's shawl with the knife, threw the shawl away and kicked Ahmet on the leg. At that moment a man entered the park and approached the commissioner and Ahmet, telling the latter to follow him. Ahmet would find out later that this man was a public prosecutor. As the public prosecutor was leaving the park with Ahmet behind him, they ran into a couple of police officers. The prosecutor ordered the policemen to go pick up the shawl on the ground and to bring the police commissioner and the shawl to the police station. The shawl was taken to the police station but the commissioner refused to go. Ahmet, on the other hand, followed the prosecutor to the police station, where an initial report was writtten. Then the prosecutor asked Ahmet to come and see him in the Courthouse in the afternoon. Ahmet went to the courthouse and found the prosecutor. There Ahmet told his story, which a clerk recorded on a form provided by the prosecutor. It appears that the prosecutor used this initial testimony to bring charges against the police commissioner for his misconduct: that is, for beating Ahmet Tiryaki.

Several weeks after the incident, at the beginning of his testimony at the Security Directorate in Trabzon, Ahmet said he had not made any complaints about the commissioner, apparently not considering the initial reports at the police station and the Courthouse to be complaints. At the end of his testimony when asked if he needed a medical examination due to his claims of having been beaten, Ahmet said he did not, for the pain where he was beaten had disappeared after a few days, but he said he wanted to file a complaint against the commissioner involved.

In his testimony, Ahmet Tiryaki argued that the reason he was not wearing a hat was because his hat was too old, and that he meant to buy a new one while in the city, clearly implying that he had not intended to defy the law. Tiryaki's account of the events in the park were largely corroborated by the testimony of an eyewitness, a man from Tiryaki's village who was also in Trabzon that day. Said Doru, the eyewitness, agreed with Tiryaki that he did not have his hat on that day, but was wearing a shawl on his head. Given that both the eyewitness and the police agree that Ahmet was wearing his shawl on his head, we can assume that this was the case, and that when Ahmet said it was around his neck, he was probably lying to avoid confrontation and punishment. Doru's account suggests that Ahmet initially, perhaps only for a moment, resisted the commissioner's attempt to take away his shawl, but that he quickly gave up, perhaps upon Doru's advice that it was not worth causing a scandal. At the same time, the police commissioner's act of removing the shawl from Ahmet's body and his kicking Ahmet on the leg followed a not uncommon pattern of state authorities' dealing with the peasants and other subaltern groups. There is nothing in Ahmet Tiryaki's testimony to suggest that he meant to oppose the Hat Law. He was ignoring, perhaps even evading the law, but it does not appear that he was consciously and intentionally defying, resisting, or opposing it.

For the local police and the administration, Tiryaki's intentions were irrelevant. From the point of view of the local police, commissioner Muhsin Öztürel had acted in accordance with the orders of the ministry when he saw a man strolling in the park acting against the Hat Law with a turban-like shawl on his head. Both Governor Refik Koraltan and Inspector-General Tahsin Uzel argued that the public prosecutor had interfered with a security official's effort to enforce civilized dress. Moreover, the prosecutor had incited the man involved to file a judicial complaint against the commissioner. Inspector-General Uzel complained to the Justice Ministry that while the public prosecutor had intervened to protect a citizen's rights, he had failed to fulfill his obligation by not bringing action against the man who had violated the Hat Law. The Ministry of Justice sided with the prosecutor and refused to terminate the case against the police commissioner.

In later correspondence with the Ministry of the Interior, Inspector-General Uzel commented that the Judiciary and the Administration had very different views on issues critical to the regime, and that existing legal sanctions against reactionaries were too weak. He stressed the need for stronger legal sanctions. Similarly, Governor Koraltan complained that the Judiciary was not sensitive enough to the regime issues. He suspected that there were reactionaries within the Judiciary who were not sincere about the reforms.

The statements by the Inspector General and the governor may have been exaggerated, yet they point to a real difference of opinion between the two branches of the government. The judiciary may have played a more restraining role on administrative action than is generally recognized.[136]

An incident that took place in a village in Kütahya province in the Aegean region suggests that the tension between the administration and the judiciary may also have existed to some degree within the ranks of the administration itself. In March 1936, Cemâl Yeğen, sub-district director (*nahiye müdürü*) of Aslanapa in Kütahya province, visited the village of Terziler. There he came across a young man aged eighteen or twenty wearing a cloth skullcap (*terlik*) decorated with beads.[137] Director Yeğen grabbed the man's cap, tore it apart, and threw it away. The young man, İsmail, picked up the torn cap and started to put it back on his head. Director Yeğen walked over to İsmail, ordering him to leave the cap on the ground. İsmail responded by pulling his knife and grabbing a rock. When the director called for help, the commander of the police, Corporal Abdullah, who was accompanying the director on the tour, attempted to arrest İsmail. At that moment another man from the village picked up an oak club and ran cursing towards the director with the intention of freeing İsmail. Two more villagers joined the attack against the director and set İsmail free. About fifteen others were also involved in the incident to a lesser degree.

Following an initial investigation in the village, Kütahya Governor Sedat Erim interpreted the incident first as an assault against a government representative, and second as a sign that many people were still prepared to act against the law and government orders. In a style very much reminiscent of the statements made following the Menemen incident, Erim argued for a swift and harsh government response in order to prevent a recurrence of such incidents. He reported that İsmail and his accomplices, who had run away to the nearby villages, had already been captured. The Public Prosecutor had already initiated the judicial process in the village.[138]

Governor Erim evaluated the incident exclusively from the point of view of the regime's security. He did not comment on the role and responsibility of the sub-district director in what had happened. He expected citizens to follow orders from government officials regardless of what the orders might be. He saw the sudden and unexpected reaction of the villagers as a sign that government authority may not have been firmly established. He wanted the government's response to serve as a lesson that its authority was to be respected.

Şükrü Kaya, Minister of the Interior, was also concerned about the implications the case had for political stability, but his assessment of the situation was different from that of the Kütahya governor. Kaya saw the real cause of the incident as the inappropriate action of the sub-district director. "The foolish and insulting action" of the director "would lead any honorable man to rebel."[139] Kaya informed the Kütahya governor that while the investigation of the villagers continued, the sub-district director should immediately be recalled to Ankara and brought before the court for "insulting and oppressing the people by misusing his authority." He warned that an administration treating people in this way would be preparing a rebellion with its own hands. A week later, in a second letter, Kaya informed the Prime Minister that an investigation of director Cemal Yeğen had been initiated, and that Yeğen had been recalled to Ankara.[140]

The available information on this case, though incomplete, suggests that there were differences of opinion in the RPP ranks that have not been recognized. All three administrators involved (the minister, the provincial governor, and the sub-district director) were probably equally committed to the enforcement of dress reform. The difference of opinion concerned implementation. Ministers and other party officials in Ankara could pass laws and regulations and ask the governors to enforce them. While officials in Ankara could make common-sense arguments without dealing with the specifics of implementation, it was the governors and lower level administrators in the provinces who had to act in the provincial cities to enforce the laws. While the center could maintain a degree of ambiguity about methods of enforcement, administrators at the local level had to take action, which must have resulted in a degree of tension between the central government and the provinces. Added to this were the professional ambitions of regional and local administrators. It seems that in an effort to be recognized by the party leadership, they often acted according to the letter of the law rather than the spirit, at times acting well beyond the intentions of the party and the central government. Sub-district director Yeğen's intervention with a young villager's bead-decorated skullcap may have been beyond the spirit of the Hat Law, but the act of intervention itself was not extreme or unusual. As indicated by the several cases above, it was a method employed occasionally, if not frequently, throughout the country.

In the popular imagination, Mustafa Kemal, as the hero of the War of Liberation and savior of the nation, appears to have firmly taken the place of the Ottoman Sultan.[141] Mustafa Kemal symbolized the ideal state, just and benevolent, whereas local government officials and especially the police and the gendarmerie came to represent the authoritarian and repressive aspects of state power. For the peasants the fear of the authoritarian state was first and foremost associated with the fear of physical violence from local government authorities, and especially from the gendarmerie. Personal narratives of peasants as well as bureaucrats attest to the fear of and actual use of physical violence as a factor in shaping citizens' actions.[142] It appears that the public generally maintained a careful distinction between the benevolent state epitomized by Mustafa Kemal and the local practices. Physical violence and other injustices committed at the local level were seen as excesses that Atatürk and the others at the head of the state did not authorize or condone.

For the ordinary Anatolian peasants, the gendarme, the policeman, the tax collector, and officials such as the public prosecutor represented the coercive power of the state in their everyday lives.[143] The fear of actual punishment in the form of monetary fines, verbal harrassment, or physical violence by a gendarme, policeman, or party official in the street, or by a prosecutor or other government official in a government office, was more real and immediate. As such, it was a more effective deterrent in shaping citizens' actions than the punishments prescibed by the legal system (or the knowledge and memory of the sentences passed by the Independence Tribunals after the hat riots in 1925). This fear, especially of physical violence, was implicit in the personal memories of my elderly informants of rural origins, as an important factor in the adoption of the hat.

In the childhood memories of Recep Göksoy, who grew up in a village in Kastamonu province in the 1920s, the fear of physical violence occupied a prominent place: "People could not wear the fez out of fear. The gendarme would tear them apart and issue a fine [to the wearer]. Once he [the gendarme] said 'you are being summoned to the *karakol* [police station],' you were finished, you could not get out of there without suffering a beating."[144] Another narrator, who lived in a nearby village in Kastamonu, emphasized the fear of the gendarme in connection with the economic circumstances of the times, including the problem of supplies—the difficulty of making and distributing reasonably priced hats (or caps) to the whole country. Mehmet Baltacı, who was fifteen years old when the Hat Law passed, identified the daily gendarme action of confiscating men's fezzes and passing out fines to the wearer as a key factor in men getting used to the hat. Baltacı also recalled that initially hats were not available in the local market and that people made their own hat-like headgear at home, out of whatever thick cloth they happened to have.[145] Other narrators and some written sources have also pointed out that many could not afford to buy hats even if they had been available.

In the memories of my respondents of rural backgrounds, the hat represented—more than any other meanings attached to it, such as a sign of the modern[146] or of the infidel—a government order that was closely associated with regime change. It was through the village headman or the sound of the town's crier (tellal) announcing that the fez had been banned, rather than the newspaper, the radio, or the school, that these peasants first heard of the institution of the hat. While in urban contexts the hat triggered some collective responses both by its supporters and by its opponents, for these peasants in small Black Sea communities the hat is remembered not so much as a change that threatened their local, religious, or other identities, but primarily as a requirement of the new regime that had to be observed despite the financial burdens it placed on already impoverished rural families. In rural Anatolia, ethnic, tribal, regional, religious, and other identities co-existed with official "national" identities; for peasants of small Black Sea villages and hamlets, the defense of the fez in the name of Ottoman or Islamic identity does not appear to have been a priority.

Conclusion

Reactions to the hat reform were varied. What we have is a much more complicated picture than either total compliance or total resistance. A combination of economic, cultural, and class factors determined one's attitude towards dress reforms, especially when it came to headwear.

Individuals generally avoided direct confrontation with the state, yet Anatolian villagers encountered the agents of the state more frequently than has been argued. A quick look at such encounters indicates that the mediators—local and regional administrators, judicial authorities, and policemen—played a significant role in the process. These encounters also reveal that there was tension within the government between the capital and the provinces, as well as between different branches of the government.

The hat reform was intended to be a homogenizing measure, but hats turned into new symbols of class distinctions. Peasants and workers wore the cap, whereas government officials and educated, well-to-do urban men wore European hats.

Visible aspects of modernity, including women's and men's outward appearance, continued to be an important symbol of Turkish modernity and its contradictions and contestations after the RPP era as well. The men's round hat gradually lost much of its significance, not so much because of its close association with the single party regime, but because in the mid-twentieth century, the use and cultural associations of the fedora style hat had changed enormously in Europe and elsewhere. As hats became unfashionable and men's use of headgear became much less common, they lost the importance attributed to them as primary markers of Western modernity in Turkey, the Middle East, and other late-modernizing or colonized parts of the world. At the same time it became inconceivable for the majority of Turkish men to contemplate a return to the fez or other forms of headgear and clothes associated with the nation's Ottoman past, or with the individual's traditional ethnic, tribal, or religious identities. For the vast majority of urban Turkish men, an essentially European outfit became the norm.

The cap survived for much longer than the fedora style hat, and longer for peasants than for urban workers, perhaps in part due to its not having the burden of close association with the RPP regime, but also because of its functionality, simplicity, and affordability, and because fashions and cultural changes penetrate the countryside much more slowly than the city. Until very recently, the cap continued to be a regular part of the typical outfit of rural Anatolian men and an important marker of urban-rural and class differences.

By the early 1970s, the cap as a marker of social class had gone through a partial transformation. Many writers, poets, and teachers, as well as the new leadership of the RPP, which now espoused a social democratic stance, adopted the cap. Other visible markers such as mustaches gained prominence in the

1970s as symbols of leftist, nationalist, or religious identities and ideological commitments of Turkish men, particularly among the university youth.

The diversity of ethnic, tribal, and regional headgear and clothes of the Anatolian population that had worried Turkish nationalists so much in the 1920s and 1930s (as a reflection of citizens' identities in competition with Turkish nationalism) did not entirely disappear, but continued to weaken after the RPP regime came to an end, not so much as a result of direct government interference after the 1940s, but as a consequence of several interrelated factors such as the loosening of tribal and other local controls, urbanization, education, greater economic integration, and the emergence of a mass consumption culture.[147] More recently, once a certain level of national cohesion and urban modernity was achieved, Turkish modernity has come to recognize and even celebrate diversity and difference (as may be seen from the proliferation of television programs featuring local and regional dialects and costumes, and from the increasing popularity of ethnic and local forms of music throughout the country), although that process is significantly circumscribed by the social and cultural polarization along secular versus Islamic lines, which demands new forms of homogeneity and conformity.

This chapter has focused on the practice of the early Republican state's attempts to regulate the clothing of its male citizens in its efforts to create a modern Turkish nation free from any visible markers of ethnic, religious, regional, class, or occupational differences. The RPP regime had as much of an interest in controlling and shaping the outward appearance of Turkish women as of Turkish men. Clothing laws of the Ottoman Empire, as was the case in other contexts in Europe and elsewhere, had often included gendered dimensions. Ottoman sartorial laws had attempted to regulate the appearance of Ottoman men and women on economic, political, social, and moral grounds. In the nineteenth century, as the "woman question" came to occupy a central place in the cultural debates between secular modernists and Islamists, and as Ottoman women came to represent alternative notions of Ottoman (Turkish) identity and culture, the control of women's appearance transformed into a matter of national importance. Such debates intensified during the Second Constitutional period. In the post-Ottoman era, women's issues, including their appearance, rapidly evolved into a fundamental concern for the new Turkish regime. Women came to symbolize the secular modernity of the new Turkish nation, and their inclusion in the emerging national community (through education, employment, and other forms of participation in public life) came to be seen as a requirement of national progress. The next chapter turns to the questions of women's dress in the process of making modern Turkish women through the early decades of the Republic.

2

Women, Politics, and the Culture of Dress in the Making of a New Turkish Nation

As with many late modernizers, the new Turkish state specifically emphasized visible aspects of modernity and national identity, such as architecture and dress. Dress was an important symbol of civility and modernity. It was also accorded a transformative function. It would help create modern and secular citizens. Arguably, it was the image of the new, Western-looking Turkish woman that symbolized Republican modernity more forcefully than any other image. This was in keeping with the early twentieth century trends from Egypt and Iran to Soviet Uzbekistan, where "the new woman" came to symbolize the new nation and its modernist and nationalist ideals.[1] The symbolic representation of the nation as a woman seldom culminated in women's full inclusion in the new national community with the full and equal rights of citizenship. Nevertheless, the image of the new woman served as a powerful symbol of each regime's aspirations for national unity, progress, and secular modernity. Recent scholarship has underscored that women's issues such as women's education, women's political participation, women's public visibility, and women's appearance were central to the Kemalist project of cultural transformation. Sociologist Nilüfer Göle has provided a compelling account of the pivotal role of women and their bodily visibility in Kemalism's "civilizing mission."[2]

Although scholars of Turkey have generally recognized the importance of women's appearance for the modernist nationalist program, the literature on clothing regulations in the early Turkish Republic has focused almost exclusively on men's clothing, which is often understood simply to mean the 1925

5. The new woman as the symbol of the nation on the fifth anniversary of the Republic. *Cumhuriyet*, 29 Teşrinievvel (October) 1928.

Hat Reform. For instance, in a recent article on the headscarf controversy Yeşim Arat wrote: "Within this particular trajectory of secularization, dress codes have always assumed an important role. Civil servants were expected to dress 'like their partners in civilized nations of the world.' Even though there had been state intervention in men's headgear (a 1925 law banned the traditional fez in favor of the Western-style hat), women's dress, outside public bureaucracy, was not regulated by the state."[3] Deniz Kandiyoti has also emphasized that Atatürk, unlike Reza Shah in Iran, never actually banned the veil; yet he was adamant about men's headgear as the European hat and tie served to eliminate ethnic, religious, and other social differences and came to signify loyalty to the Republican regime and its secular ideology.[4]

Recently there has been an increased awareness that women's dress issues were not totally left to the forces of modernization and fashion and that the state was indeed directly involved in regulating women's dress. The few works that have appeared on the regulation of women's clothing so far, however, do not go beyond establishing that there were attempts to regulate women's dress.[5]

Reflecting on the various histories of the modern Middle East, Albert Hourani once commented:

> They tell us what "modernizing" governments and elites wished to do and what they thought they had done, but what in fact was happening—how the process appeared to those whom the rulers were trying to change, or how they accepted the process but changed its direction—does not appear clearly; the "two rhythms of change" . . . are lacking.[6]

Keeping such comments in mind,[7] this chapter will discuss how dress regulations for women (such as *peçe* and *çarşaf* decrees)[8] were formulated and implemented, who was in charge of the process, how individuals came into contact with the agents of the state, and how men and women responded to and dealt with women's clothing regulations. Given the nature of the questions I have raised, this chapter will focus more on the social life of dress regulations as a political project, but it will at the same recognize the connections between politics, consumption, and culture in the changes to women's dress in the early Republican period. I begin the discussion with an introduction to the changes in Ottoman women's dress in the late Ottoman era.

The Ottoman Background

Late Ottoman and early Republican urban Muslim women wore the veil in varieties of ways reflecting their social class, economic means, cultural and ideological positions, fashion trends, and personal tastes. Peasant women of Anatolia were generally not veiled, in the sense that they did not wear the face veil, the *peçe*, but they generally covered their hair and would pull their headscarves over the mouth in the company of male strangers.[9] In nineteenth century İstanbul, the cosmopolitan capital that set fashion trends for other cities, urban women's dress had gone through a significant transformation as part of a general trend toward Westernization and paralleling changes in male attire. Despite the Ottoman state's efforts to control women's visibility, appearance, and public behavior, women's attire continued to change, reflecting European fashion and the ongoing process of Ottoman Westernization. In indoor clothing, there was a shift from the *şalvar* and *gömlek* to *entari*, a long dress that lent itself to adaptation of European dress styles, including the use of the corset. In outdoor clothing, increasingly at the center of cultural and political debates concerning women, and subject to state regulation and social control, urban Muslim women's *ferace* and *yaşmak*[10] continued to evolve, informed by European norms and fashions. The increased cultural and commercial contact with Europe (including the ever increasing availability of imported European goods such as clothes and fabrics, the opening of European style department stores, and advertisements of European products in the press) facilitated this process of borrowing European fashions.[11] Upper class urban women wore varieties of fashionable *ferace*s (some resembling the European-style coat) and thinner *yaşmak*s barely concealing their faces, with high heeled boots (which replaced the *terlik*, slippers) and a matching umbrella. Toward the end of the century, the *ferace* and *yaşmak* gave way to the *çarşaf* and *peçe*,[12] the primary target of the early republican state's efforts to modernize women's appearance in the 1920s and 1930s. Like the men's fez, the *çarşaf* and *peçe* would come to symbolize tradition and backwardness by the 1920s. Notably, the *çarşaf* and *peçe* emerged outside of the state control, and the women of the court, who in the nineteenth century were fashion leaders, were not involved in the process either. The *çarşaf*, originally a single piece of cloth that loosely covered a women's entire body hiding her feminine figure, would go through a rapid transformation allowing it to adapt to European fashions. As Nora Şeni has pointed out, once the *çarşaf* was cut in half to form a cape (that covered the head and the upper body) and a skirt that covered the lower body, the new two-piece *çarşaf* lent itself more readily to be worn in style. The skirt, which initially loosely covered the body from the waist to the ankles, would get shorter and narrower, eventually rising to the knee. The cape, which initially came down covering the fingers, would get shorter and smaller, with the accompanying *peçe* getting thinner and thinner, barely concealing the face. Eventually the cape was abandoned, replaced by an *eşarp* (scarf) to cover the head, and the transparent face veil disappeared. Later, the *eşarp* would also disappear, revealing the hair. By the final years of the Empire, at least in İstanbul, the *çarşaf* had evolved from its original *torba çarşaf* (sack *çarşaf*) to the fashionable *tango çarşaf* (*tango* was the shortest form of the cape). Although the vast majority of Ottoman women, whether in İstanbul or in other Ottoman cities, never made the transition all the way from *torba çarşaf* to the *tango çarşaf* (in fact the fully Westernized appearance of the *tango çarşaf* was subject not only to "playful" satire but also to angry social criticism),[13] Westernized Ottoman women in İstanbul and other major cities indeed began to wear the *çarşaf* fashionably and the two piece *çarşaf* formed the basis for the adoption of the two piece European suit.

The transformation of Ottoman women's clothing in the nineteenth century took place at varying rates and degrees for women of different social, economic, ethnic backgrounds. Nancy Micklewright has shown for nineteenth-century İstanbul that Christian Ottoman women (mostly Greek and Armenian) generally adopted the European styles of dress before their Jewish and Muslim counterparts did.[14] Upper class urban Ottoman Muslim women led the changes for other Muslim women. Rural and tribal women were affected the least, because of their limited contact with the market and the big cities and also the lack of economic resources. Moreover, village women's clothing styles were different from those of urban women, reflecting local, ethnic, and tribal styles as well as practical needs. It was, however, the changes in urban Muslim women's attire, such as their *yaşmak*s and *peçe*s becoming thinner, along with their increasing public visibility and mixing with men, that caused the highest concern for the Ottoman state and the opponents of Westernization. Sultan Abdülhamid issued several decrees during his reign (1876–1909), banning women from wearing styles of *çarşaf*s, *ferace*s, and *yaşmak*s that supposedly departed from the traditional ways and were not in line with the requirements of Islam. He called on Muslim women to dress and conduct themselves in accordance with the demands of religion and morality. In 1890 Sultan Abdülhamid issued a decree banning the *çarşaf* (because women of İstanbul had supposedly begun dressing immodestly, not covering themselves up properly).[15] A similar decree issued in 1900 asked the gendarmerie to prevent Ottoman Muslim women from "wandering around immodestly dressed and not taking into account the rules of *tesettür* (covering oneself according to Islam)."[16] Notably, it was not only the Ottoman sultan who attempted to control women's dress and public visibility. By the Young Turk era, marked by a CUP-led military coup in July 1908 and the proclamation of the Constitution, developments in the Westernized upper- and middle-class urban Muslim women's appearance and behavior (the transparency of their veils, with a small number of women even appearing in public unveiled; their increased public visibility; and husbands and wives appearing in public together) angered the conservatives, who perceived such changes to be a manifestation of moral corruption and social decay. Women's issues such as women's education, their dress, the regulation of their public visibility and interaction with men, and polygamy were at the core of the debates between Ottoman modernists and the opponents of Westernization during the Second Constitutional period. These debates continued to inform early republican ideology and policies, as well. Whereas the conservatives insisted on debating women's issues from within a strictly Islamic framework and continued to cherish polygamy, seclusion, and veiling as institutions vital for the preservation of public morality and social unity, the Westernizers, the nationalists, and the emerging feminists offered additional or alternative ideological possibilities. As Deniz Kandiyoti has remarked, this was a period "fraught with confusion and contradictions," and the CUP itself was divided and failed to pursue a radical or consistent set of policies concerning women.[17] The CUP nevertheless broadly promoted the ideal of a "new life" and a "new family" as the foundation for a national revival. The sociologist Ziya Gökalp (1876–1924) provided the ideological grounding for an emerging Young Turk nationalist vision concerning women and the family. According to Gökalp, as in the formulation of other early twentieth century modernists in other Middle Eastern contexts such as Iran and Egypt, the new or national family would be nuclear, monogamous, and democratic—based on the equality of husband and wife. Gökalp promoted the ideal of the new family as a revitalization of ancient Turkish values and customs, rather than as a borrowing of Western values and practices. Gökalp located an egalitarian gender system in the pre-Islamic ancient Turkish family in central Asia. Accordingly, the decline of women's status and the current sorry state of Ottoman/Turkish women were a result of the Turks' borrowing foreign, particularly Byzantine and Iranian, customs. Women's veiling, seclusion, and the neglect of their education had occurred due to such borrowing of alien customs. Gökalp was thus challenging veiling and seclusion not because they were Islamic practices (as some would have argued), but as alien customs. This argument presented an important shift in the terms of the debate. Gökalp's formulation did not preclude Islam from serving as a source of national culture and morality, but identified veiling and seclusion as foreign customs rather than as cultural practices required by Islam, thereby making it possible to reject those practices without denying Islam a role in the national culture. As we will see, in the post-1922 period as well, members of Parliament, governors, writers, journalists, and women themselves continued to challenge veiling and seclusion on the grounds that they were alien customs incompatible with the values and contemporary needs of the nation.

The cultural and ideological debates concerning appropriate dress for Ottoman Muslim women at times turned into an active effort to control what women wore and how they behaved in public. During the Second Constitutional period, the religious authorities apparently issued several warnings that women should avoid behaving in ways contradictory with "the national good morals and ethics" and that women should "dress according to 'the religious orders and national morals'."[18] As M. Şehmus Güzel has pointed out, in the relatively more Westernized major port cities of the Empire such as İzmir, İstanbul, Beirut, and Salonica, changes in Muslim women's public visibility, dress, and behavior alarmed the religious authorities. Muslim women began to appear in public with their faces barely covered behind a thin veil, or even unveiled, and they began to move about town in their carriages with their arms and legs not fully covered; some even dared to speak with unrelated men in public. Threatened by such trends, hocas encouraged the punishment of unveiled women by spitting on their faces and stoning their carriages, and beating them up when they were found alone, as if such acts of punishment were a religious duty.[19] In the Young-Turk-era journal Kadın, authors and readers alike complained that fashionably dressed Muslim women suffered from street harassment, even in a "civilized" (mütemeddin) city like Salonica. Women's adoption of Westernized clothing styles, the shortening of the çarşaf's skirt, and the discarding of the veil angered conservative men. Men harassed women who dressed immodestly, threatened them, intimidated them with a knife, or even attacked them.[20] It is not clear if these men were men of the lower classes, punishing upper and middle class women who they perceived as transgressing the requirements of Islamic covering, modesty, and privacy. Arguably, the imams' call on Muslim men to uphold the principles of *tesettür* did not create these male attitudes toward the fashionably dressed women, but they may have encouraged and legitimized men's taking action in the streets based on those attitudes.

Male patriarchal resistances to the evolution of women's appearance, in the form of street harassment, failed to fully arrest the radical changes that were occurring in Ottoman women's dress, public visibility, and social roles during the Young Turk era. It was the coalescence of the ongoing processes of Westernization with the relative political opening of the Second Constitutional period, the expansion of the ideological debates concerning women, state policies, and the circumstances of a series of devastating wars that shaped the course of changes in Ottoman women's appearance. The wars (the Balkan Wars and World War I) served as a catalyst of change by rapidly expanding women's participation in social and economic life.[21] Later, the War of Liberation further intensified those changes. Ottoman urban women had already been working as teachers, journalists, nurses, midwives, and factory workers since the nineteenth century. As in the other belligerent countries, the male labor shortage during the wars required tapping into women's labor. Between the labor shortage and the women's need to support their families, increasing numbers of urban Ottoman women were employed as bank tellers, post office clerks, factory workers, and (at least in İstanbul) as street sweepers, whereas peasant women had to assume greater responsibilities in working the fields. During World War I, women contributed to the war effort more directly as well, as orators giving public speeches, as nurses, and even as women's brigades providing support services.[22] The wars also made the work of women's associations, which expanded significantly during the CUP period, and the social services they provided, more relevant. It was during the years of World War I that urban women of İstanbul began to discard the veil. Women had already started wearing colorful or transparent veils and a small number of them even appeared in public with their husbands. During the war years some of them threw off the veil to one side or simply wore a scarf with no veil on their faces. It was also during wartime, in 1915, that an imperial decree allowed women to discard the veil during work hours.[23]

Population movements caused by the wars, including the massive flood of Muslim refugees into İstanbul and Anatolia, and the creation of internal refugees resulting from the allied invasion of parts of Anatolia (such as the Muslim populations of eastern Black Sea provinces when the region came under Russian occupation in the winter and spring of 1916), led to tremendous social upheavals as well as exposure to unexpected cultural contact. The arrival of about 200,000 White Russian refugees in İstanbul in the aftermath of the Bolshevik Revolution brought new cultural practices to the residents of İstanbul as well as exacerbating the ongoing social and moral crisis in the city. Upper-class Russian refugee women brought new fashions to the women of İstanbul, such as the Russian style headscarf and short hair styles.[24] The war's impact on women's comportment and social roles was presumably greater in cosmopolitan İstanbul than in the provinces, though in the provinces as well, local communities experienced varying degrees of encounters with the occupying forces and refugee conditions.

By the end of World War I, a majority of women of İstanbul, not only upper-class women but also many from the lower classes, had unveiled, despite an apparent lack of social consensus on proper dress for Ottoman Muslim women. During the Young Turk period, during and after World War I, one of the platforms where women's dress and other women's issues were debated was the press, including women's periodicals. İkbal Elif Mahir's research has demonstrated that there was no consensus in the İstanbul press over the meaning and necessity of veiling during the occupation years at the end of World War I. For some magazine authors the *çarşaf* and *peçe* symbolized Turkish nationalism and respect for religious values, whereas others saw the changes in women's clothing as a sign of progress.[25] Brummett has similarly noted that European or *alafranga* fashions were associated with progress in the press of the Second Constitutional period, at the same as they were portrayed as a manifestation of "subordination, consumption, and dishonor" as well as of "moral decline" in the satirical press.[26] Although women journalists did not agree on the necessity of the veil, some openly argued against it in women's magazines. In February 1919 in the journal *İnci*, Zehra Hakkı defended the modernization of women's dress as a social requirement: now that women were participating in social life alongside men, they had to modernize their dress just like men had done and just as they had to reform their mentalities. Zehra Hakkı argued against the *çarşaf* (like Ziya Gökalp and the post-1922 Republican reformers) as a foreign custom borrowed from the Iranians and Greeks which had nothing whatsoever to do with Islam. Citing numerous health and other disadvantages of the *çarşaf*, Zehra Hakkı proposed the adoption of *manto* and scarf as a modern alternative to the *çarşaf* that would perfectly fulfill the requirements of *tesettür*, or modesty. As for the *peçe*, she announced, "If you look around a little, you would understand that we have already abolished it."[27] In this way, the author was advocating a solution regarding women's dress that would evolve into the policies of the Republican state in the 1920s and 1930s. Here as in many other areas of reform, the Republican state's position (the effort to eliminate the *peçe* and the promotion of *manto* and scarf or hat as suitable alternatives to the *çarşaf*) was very much grounded in the ideas and debates as well as the social changes of the late Ottoman and particularly the Young Turk periods.

Modern Dress for Every Turkish Woman

Early Post-1922 Attempts to Regulate Women's Clothing

In the post-1922 period, the primary focus of the public debate on women's dress shifted to the abolition of primitive, foreign, and non-national (*gayrı milli*) clothes and the adoption of modern clothing. The public debate no longer centered on the interpretations of *tesettür* and the requirements of Islam concerning women and their dress. It was now a secular debate focused on the requirements of the nation's progress and modernity. But among large segments of the society, women's dress, their visibility, education, and employment, and the regulation of male-female relations continued to be perceived through local, tribal, and religious lenses.

The other major shift post-1922 was the Republican state's attempt to reach and reshape the entire population, including rural women, in its effort to create a modern and unified nation out of a diverse Anatolian population. The dress reforms aimed at the erasure of all signs of "backwardness" and difference, whether religious, tribal, ethnic, or local. Thus the early Republican state's clothing regulations targeted women outside of the major urban centers as well.

The 1925 Hat Law regulating the clothing of male citizens was not followed by a similar national law or decree concerning women's dress. Yet in the months and the years following the Hat Law, local authorities and organizations took the initiative to extend the issue of dress to the women through a combined effort of local decrees and a propaganda campaign in the local press. The new or modern dress essentially meant European style dress. Its exact meaning was open to interpretation and it had different implications in different social contexts. At a minimum, the modern dress implied unveiling or removing the face veil (the *peçe*) and the replacement of the *çarşaf*, the women's two piece outerwear that covered the entire body, with a *manto* or overcoat. The modern dress was in part defined by what it was not: clothes that were identified as or perceived to be ethnic, tribal, Islamic, or traditional did not qualify as civilized or national dress. The issue was more relevant in urban than in rural areas since peasant women did not cover their faces in their villages, but in the rural contexts, too, it implied the abandonment of clothes that marked ethnic, local, and tribal difference or "backwardness."

In Eskişehir in the Aegean interior, the mayor used the local newspaper to call on the townspeople to adopt the modern dress. The mayor contended that as the use of men's hats was spreading throughout the country, it was time women's *peştemal*s were also brought into conformity with modern dress.[28] He requested (*arz ve rica*) the town's residents to leave behind the "primitive" (*ilkel* [*ibtidai*]) and "uncivilized" (*gayrı medeni*) *peştemal*s and to adopt the civilized dress already worn by some of the town's women. The mayor saw the issue of *peştemal*s in the context of Turkish modernity and in connection with the male clothing. From a modernist point of view the traditional *peştemal* was a marker of backwardness, and the new dress a sign of Turkish modernity. Hence the elimination of *peştemal*s was perceived to be a requirement of national modernity. Although the mayor's main concern was the women's *peştemal*, perhaps because of his awareness of the necessity of male approval for such a change to take place and perhaps considering that the newspaper readers were mostly men, he appealed to both male and female residents of Eskişehir to voluntarily adopt the modern dress over a period of one month. Implicit in the mayor's statement is that some, perhaps a small number, of the town's women had already donned the new dress. He was inviting the rest to emulate the example of those women in modern dress.

Aware of the difficulty of accomplishing such an ambitious goal in such a short span of time, the mayor also advised the town's residents to modernize their *peştemals* by dying them in dark (*ağır*) and plain colors and hence getting rid of their "ugly" colors.[29]

In addition to the propaganda efforts for the voluntary adoption of the new dress (as in the example of Eskişehir), a number of local governments passed decrees on women's clothing in the years following the Hat Law. In Eskişehir, the mayor's call for the voluntary change of women's dress appears to have failed. By January 1927, the Eskişehir municipal council banned the

6. An idealized image of women wearing *peçe* and *çarşaf* (on the right), *yaşmak* (in the middle), and a peasant woman wearing a *peştemal*-style headscarf. From *Histoire de la Republique Turque*, Redige par la Societe pour l'etude de l'histoire Turque (Istanbul: Devlet Basımevi, 1935), 93.

peçe and the *peştemal* and the provincial parliament instituted monetary fines for noncompliance. It also authorized the police, the gendarmerie, and the municipal police to implement the decision.[30] The Aydın provincial parliament also passed a unanimous resolution in January 1927,[31] banning *peçe*, *çarşaf, üstlük*,[32] and *peştemal* as well as *zeybek* clothes.[33] Residents were given a grace period of three months to comply with the decision, after which time noncompliance would not be tolerated and would lead to legal measures. It should be noted that the decision targeted not only the *çarşaf* and the *peçe*, but also more local and traditional forms of clothing, both male and female. It seems that the motives underlying such decisions were complex, attempting to secularize, modernize, liberate, homogenize, and nationalize simultaneously. Although the Aydın decision was taken locally, it is not clear if it arose from local initiatives. Correspondence from the governor of Aydın to the Prime Minister suggests that the latter may have hinted at the need for such an action during his visit to Aydın the previous year, which implies a degree of coordination between central and local government on such decisions, if not incentives or orders from the central government or the leading statesmen.[34] That the Aydın provincial government passed various almost identical decisions in the mid-1930s[35] shows that the 1927 decision had had little effect.

Official correspondence from 1934 and early 1935 suggest that the fight against the *peçe* and the *çarşaf* had also had limited success and that some provincial officials were getting frustrated and impatient with their inability to solve this problem, and contemplated a more active struggle. In Iran, Reza Shah's initial unveiling campaign in 1935 (which was at least in part inspired by the Turkish example which he had observed during his official visit to Turkey the previous year)[36] focused on propaganda and voluntary unveiling. Arguably, it was Reza Shah's dissatisfaction with the results of the propaganda efforts that triggered his mandatory unveiling campaign in January 1936.[37] The governor of Antalya expressed his deep frustration in 1934 when he wrote "It has been proven by the struggle of many years that this condition that shows Turkish womanhood to foreigners in a primitive way cannot be eliminated through guidance (*irşat*)."[38] He asked the ministry if the central government had made a decision on this matter or if it was considering such a decision. If not, he asked for approval from the ministry to use the police (*zabıta*) to prevent women dressed in *peçe* and *çarşaf* from entering public places such as government offices, parks, and movie theaters. The ministry responded by disagreeing with the governor on the proper course of action. The minister disapproved intervention by the police and asked that efforts should be limited to propaganda and "inculcation" (*telkin*).[39] He also sent a circular to all the governors and inspectors general asking them to focus on propaganda and warning them to avoid excessive measures.

> At a time when our women are in fact following the requirements of our revolution, one should be wary of carrying this matter to excesses that might cause undesirable reactions. We should get the people to accept the requirements of the revolution not through police force but by way of well-managed inculcation. Therefore, it would be appropriate to be content with propaganda in the *peçe* and *çarşaf* matter as well.[40]

While the ministry recommended focusing on propaganda, provincial authorities continued to argue that such efforts were not sufficient. The governor of Sinop, for instance, explained that "encouragement, indoctrination, and propaganda" ("*teşvik, telkin, ve propaganda*") had produced some results, but that women could not totally abandon the *çarşaf* "due to the influence of good manners (*görgü*)." Many local women in Sinop who had previously adopted the overcoat (*manto*) had gone back to wearing the *çarşaf*.[41] The governor noted that the *peçe* issue had been solved with the help of a decree by the provincial council. He asked for the Ministry's opinion on passing a similar decree on the *çarşaf*, emphasizing that he had received requests from both the party and the municipality for the passing of a local decision to resolve the *çarşaf* problem.[42] As in the case of regulation of male clothing, especially in the example of İsmail Engin of Finike discussed in the previous chapter, the push for active regulations of women's appearance in part originated at the local level. Individuals and groups with a modernist outlook both within and from outside the ruling RPP put pressure on local administrators and party officials for the adoption of modern dress and for the eradication of the veil.

Debates on the proper measures needed to deal with the *peçe* and the *çarşaf* issue reached a climax at the Fourth Congress of the ruling Republican People's Party in May 1935. By that date, a number of legislative and other changes had been set in motion regarding women's social and political rights.

The new Civil Code of 1926, adapted from the Swiss Civil Code, was based on the principle of equality, giving women (relative) equality with men in matters of marriage, divorce, and inheritance.[43] Women had already been attending secular schools with men for a number of years, and by the end of 1934 women had full political rights. The state encouraged political participation and the public visibility of women. The RPP ran a campaign throughout the

7. "Reform in Clothing and Marriage." This RPP poster is reprinted from Lilo Linke, *Allah Dethroned: A Journey through Modern Turkey.* New York: Alfred A. Knopf, 1937.

country to increase party membership among women. Women were encouraged to participate actively in People's Houses and other national organizations, to take on professional jobs, and to run for political office both at the
local and at the national level. It was in this context of making a civilized
Turkish nation that the *peçe* and *çarşaf* issues were situated. Women in civilized dress would symbolize Turkish modernity while at the same time making it possible to build a new Turkish nation. Barriers to women's visibility
and participation in public life, whether through polygamy and seclusion in
the private sphere behind lattices (*kafes*) or through their clothes, were to be
eliminated.[44] RPP propaganda materials such as the poster shown in Figure 7
placed women's (and men's) dress issues in the larger context of the reforms.
In this poster, entitled "Reform in Clothing and Marriage" modernization
of women's clothing is merged with the modernization of men's clothing as
well as the expansion of women's rights in marriage and family through the
abolition of polygamy.

A Law on the *Peçe* and *Çarşaf*?

The Peçe-Çarşaf Debate at the 1935 RPP Congress

At the 1935 Congress, the RPP commission studying the various requests and
complaints received by the party from the provinces had prepared a report
on the *peçe* and *çarşaf* question in response to requests from Muğla and Sivas
for solutions to the problem. The commission's report first argued that this
was not an issue for the majority of women.[45] It pointed out that about two-
thirds of the Turkish population lived in the villages, where women did not
wear the *peçe* and *çarşaf*. Of the remaining third, the report claimed, a great
majority had left this tradition behind and those who had not were already in
the process of doing so without any legal measures. The report then raised the
question of whether it was necessary to take action on this matter. It asked:

> Should we leave this to our women's own tastes and to the progress in the
> social mentality of their husbands and fathers? Or, should we take them out
> of this outfit that is seen, here and there, as a disgrace on our women, by
> throwing out, with a small shaking of the center, this rotten fruit that has

been getting ready to fall down but is hanging on only out of respect for husbands and fathers?[46]

The commission's wording of both possibilities acknowledged implicitly that although the issue was women's dress, not men's, and that this was the party that recognized women's civil and political equality, the party's decision on what course of action to take had a great deal to do with men and their potential reactions. A minority of commission members had supported the second view, and proposed that the *peçe* be banned by the police laws. The "unanimous" recommendation of the commission, however, was that the issue should be resolved through the work of the party and the state institutions and without resort to a new law. The debate subsequent to the reading of the commission's report revealed disagreement within the party on how to deal with the *peçe* and *çarşaf* question. Although Şükrü Kaya, the minister of the interior, asked the delegates at the congress to endorse the recommendation of the commission, Hakkı Tarık Us, a member of Parliament from Giresun and a member and reporter of the commission, raised a number of objections.

Us made a distinction between the *çarşaf* and the *peçe* and focused his fiery comments on the latter. The *çarşaf*, Us argued, had an economic function and could be left to women's tastes and changing fashions. The *peçe*, on the other hand, was an entirely different matter. At a time when the party passed health laws for the banning of the *kafes*, or the wooden lattices in homes, he reminded the delegates, "What should we make of our tolerating our women's covering their faces?" ("*Kadınlarımızın yüzünü örtmesine göz yumar vaziyetimize ne demeli?*") He then asked rhetorically, "Why is it necessary to make a law for this?"[47] This, Us argued, was a natural consequence of the party's revolutionary principals, implicitly criticizing Minister of the Interior Şükrü Kaya for failing to uphold the revolutionary spirit of the regime by taking a gradualist approach to the *peçe* issue. He pointed to petitions to the party from various provinces, as well as to the provincial decisions banning the *peçe* in cities such as Adana and Trabzon, as evidence of strong support for the elimination of this practice. Ten years earlier in Trabzon, he had observed the effects of a provincial decree and had seen that women did indeed discard the veil. He was saddened to witness in a recent visit that the initial success of the ban had dwindled. Nevertheless, arguing that this might be a localized trend, Us agreed that a great number of cities had already passed decrees banning the *peçe* and that the institution of the *peçe* was indeed in decline and on its way to extinction. Yet he called for quick and complete eradication of the *peçe*, on the basis that even if it were used only by a small minority, it could still be construed as a symbol of a lack of trust: men's lack of trust of other men as well as men's distrust of women.[48] Us, and a few other delegates, also referred to health and security related reasons (that the *peçe* and *çarşaf* provided opportunities for crimes and criminals by concealing the identity of the wearer) for the banning of the *peçe*, but the bulk of the debate avoided the question at the heart of the *peçe* and *çarşaf* issue. Here Us acknowledged implicitly that getting rid of the veil involved a deeper change in existing gender relations, in the understandings of the appropriate place of men and women in society, including the norms of how unrelated women and men could interact in public. Reflecting the positivist outlook and optimism of the radical modernist reformers of the early twentieth century, Hakkı Tarık Us believed in the power of the law to effect social change in the issue of women's dress.[49]

Us criticized those who favored leaving the *peçe* issue to a natural process of change. "Why should we leave it to time?" he asked the delegates. The revolutionary spirit of the regime called for swift action to eradicate at once "this shameful [foreign] practice that somehow infected us" ("*Bize nasılsa geçmiş olan bu yüz karasını silip atmak*"), not for an evolutionary approach leaving it to time. With the same gradualist approach, Us remarked, other issues such as the land reform could also be left to time. He reminded the delegates that the adoption of the hat only took place through a great revolutionary move, a revolutionary law, and invited the delegates to consider the great leader's (i.e. Atatürk's) motivations in passing the Hat Law and to follow his example.[50]

In his travels in various parts of the country, Us had come to the conclusion that no woman wants to wear a veil on her face except to show respect for her husband and to maintain the peace and harmony in her family. Men do not want it either, Us remarked, referring again to the provincial resolutions and the views expressed at the Congress. "Women do not want it, men do not want it, why then does this *peçe* keep hanging on?"[51] He argued that this was essentially a psychological issue and all that the public needed was a signal from an authoritative place (such as the government) for the elimination of the *peçe* and *çarşaf*. If the issue were left to time, it would eventually be resolved, but perhaps in ten, twenty, or thirty years. The task of the party was to accelerate that process by making a revolutionary move.

Subsequent debates further revealed the division within the RPP between hardliners and softliners as to the significance and urgency of the *peçe* and *çarşaf* issue and the appropriate means of dealing with it. Us in his speech focused on the *peçe*, trying to maintain the distinction he had made between the *peçe* and the *çarşaf*. The speakers after Us were not as careful in separating the two and tended to treat the *peçe* and *çarşaf* as a single issue, as did many of the local government decrees before and after this RPP Congress. Two of the delegates expressed their firm opposition to passing a law on the *peçe* and *çarşaf*. Aka Gündüz, a delegate from Ankara, announced that "The Turkish Revolution [was] not a revolution undertaken for the *peçe* and *çarşaf*," and criticized Us for wasting the precious time of the congress with the *çarşaf* issue, which was essentially a matter for the police (*zabıta*) and gendarmerie. Dr. Muhtar (Berker),[52] a delegate from İçel, warned the Congress against passing laws on every small issue and spoke in favor of taking care of the *peçe* and *çarşaf* at the local and provincial level, giving the example of a recent party and municipality decision in İçel. General Kazım Sevüktekin, a delegate from Diyarbakır, spoke in favor of outlawing the *peçe* and *çarşaf* on the grounds of security, while Yusuf (Duygu), a delegate from Yozgat, expressed the most enthusiastic support for the position of Hakkı Tarık Us against a gradualist approach. "There is no room for gradualism in revolution" announced Yusuf Duygu, and reminded the delegates of the parallels with the hat issue. Earlier gradualist attempts, such as Enver Pasha's experience with the *enveriye* hat[53] in the Second Constitutional period, had not produced any results. Ultimately, Atatürk had resolved it by calling the hat the national headgear and saying "we will wear it" (thus making it mandatory). Without a national law, there would not be any legal basis to make provincial and municipal authorities pursue the *peçe* and *çarşaf* issue. Duygu therefore called for the passing of a general clothing law.

Duygu's comments also revealed some of the additional motivations and justifications for a clothing law. Concerning the argument that village women did not wear the *peçe*, Duygu highlighted the terrible state of village women's appearance, including the varieties of clothing such as the *şalvar*, a type of baggy pants. Duygu also hinted at other aspects of women's social status and gender relations that were in need of reform by mentioning the practice of women turning their backs when they encountered men in public places.[54] Worse yet was that foreigners visiting villages for various reasons, such as archeological excavations, witnessed this behaviour. "Would it be appropriate for them [foreigners] to continue to see this?" asked Duygu rhetorically and continued, "absolutely not."[55] Here the congressman was expressing a constant preoccupation of the Turkish reformers, the concern with the external perceptions of Turkey as a modern nation. Just as men in their fezzes or dirty shirts and baggy pants hurt the image of Turkey in the eyes of (Western) foreigners, so would women in their *şalvars*, as well as in their *peçes* and *çarşaf*s. Hence, the need was for modern clothes for Turkish men and women.[56] Finally, considering arguments against regulating women's dress on economic grounds, Duygu dismissed the claims that it would be necessary to provide village women with "modern" clothes if the *çarşaf* were outlawed because poor peasant women did not have the financial means to purchase new clothes from the market. He spoke with confidence that village women could make their own clothes, such as skirts and jackets, from wool, just as they made men's pants, jackets, and hats.[57]

This party congressional debate about what was essentially a women's issue (which had become as much an issue for men) took place almost exclusively among men. There were a small number of women delegates present at the Fourth RPP Congress, but the women were new to the political process. They did not have the political experience of their male colleagues and did not occupy key party positions such as ministerial posts. Nor is there any indication that the women members of the Congress advocated, or could have advocated, a different point of view on this issue. As feminist scholars have argued, professional women of the early Republic internalized the Kemalist project of modernization and worked in the service of the state to fulfill the modernizing nationalist mission. [58] Naciye Osman (Kozbek), a delegate from Niğde, the only woman to speak on the women's dress issue, called on her male colleagues to "outlaw the *peçe*" ("*Peçeyi yasaklayınız*") repeating in her brief remarks the argument that now that women had the right to vote, the veil had to be discarded to allow for the easy identification of voters in order to prevent duplicate voting.[59]

During the debates, Us and Sevüktegin submitted two separate proposals for the abolition of the *peçe*.[60] In his response to the debate as the minister of the interior, Şükrü Kaya dismissed the accusations of gradualism and failure to uphold the revolutionary principles of the regime, and expressed firmly his strong opinion in favor of dealing with this matter without resorting to any new laws. Kaya's remarks revealed his concern with implementation and the limits of law in bringing about social and cultural change.

Kaya called the *peçe* and *çarşaf* issue a "small task," and invoked Atatürk's authority on his behalf by hinting at Mustafa Kemal's views on the abolition of the veil. Kaya remarked, "If this were an issue, the one who made this revolution would have included this in his program and would have gotten from you the necessary decision." Kaya was correcting Hakkı Tarık Us and others on Atatürk's position on this matter by acknowledging implicitly that Atatürk did not favor the passage of a law similar to the Hat Law. He was also reminding the delegates of the limits of democracy within the party.

Atatürk championed women's rights, making this position a pillar of his cultural revolution. He personally pushed for women's civil, educational, and political equality. Recent feminist scholarship has criticized state feminism of the Kemalist era, arguing that the state used the issue of women's rights as an instrument of its modernist policies, and demonstrating the limits and constraints to women's rights and the persistence of gender inequality.[61] Despite these criticisms, scholars by and large agree that the secular reforms of the Republic had a positive impact on women's rights.

Atatürk demonstrated his commitment to women's rights in his personal life, for example by having daughters as adopted children in a society that traditionally favored boys over girls.[62] One of his adopted daughters, Sabiha Gökçen, Turkey's first female military pilot, served as an example of the ideal Turkish woman for a generation of urban Turkish women.[63] Mustafa Kemal wanted his own marriage to serve as a model for a companionate marriage and for the creation of a new family life. During his short-lived marriage to Latife Hanım (1923–1925), a young European-educated woman from a wealthy İzmir family and an advocate of women's rights, his wife Latife Hanım accompanied Mustafa Kemal on his tours of Anatolia, appearing in public before the gathered crowds alongside her husband, carefully dressed in riding gear or in other modest clothes, unveiled but with a covering on her head.[64] These public appearances of Latife Hanım were important for establishing the legitimacy of the women's public visibility and participation in the public eye. In his various public speeches in the first few years of the Republic, during and after his marriage and including his famous 1925 Kastamonu speech introducing the hat as a national headgear, Mustafa Kemal had referred to the necessity of reforming both men's and women's appearance.[65] He had apparently defended the necessity of unveiling and other rights for Ottoman women in his private letters as early as the 1910s.[66]

The passing of the Hat Law raised the possibility that a similar law would follow on women's dress. Yet no such laws followed suit. The following anecdote, related by journalist Ahmed Emin Yalman, although perhaps in a somewhat simplistic formulation, nevertheless offers a partial explanation of why women's dress was not regulated by law the way male dress was regulated. Yalman relates that after the Hat Law friends of his suggested to Atatürk that there was need for a new law to get rid of the women's veils. "Oh no," Atatürk responded. "You can't catch me doing that. When religious prejudice and men's jealousy over their women's faces being seen in public are coupled in this problem, it becomes most difficult to cope with. No legislation about veils! There is a natural law which will take care of it more easily than any written law. It is called 'fashion.'"[67]

Şükrü Kaya, one of the key statesmen involved in the formulation and implementation of the Kemalist reforms, agreed with Atatürk on the need to deal with the veil without resorting to legislation. Kaya asked the delegates at the RPP Congress:

Is there any national interest in presenting our women [as being] so dependent upon a piece of cloth? Our villagers don't wear it anyway. Their faces are uncovered. Some old women carry the *peçe* on their faces as a result of a bad habit. We should all implement this in our own districts [*muhit*, circle of friends and associates] and wherever your word is listened to. Promise you will do this, that is sufficient. (Applause and cries of "We promise.").....

The core of this issue has been resolved. Therefore, I reiterate, we should not turn the *çarşaf* and *peçe* into an issue and we should leave it to our women's own tastes and social understandings. The People's Houses of our party should carry out this task by enlightening the public.[68]

Kaya justified the state's attempt to eradicate the *çarşaf* and *peçe* by calling it a foreign custom. This was not an attack on national tradition, as some may have claimed, but an effort to liberate the nation from a backward and foreign tradition that embarrassed the nation and prevented its progress by stalling the progress of its women.[69] By highlighting the fact that peasant women did not wear the *peçe* and *çarşaf* and claiming that it was only "some old women" who covered their faces in public, Kaya tried to minimize the scale and the importance of this practice. While assigning the responsibility for dealing with the *peçe* and *çarşaf* to the party and the People's Houses, he allowed room for some flexibility as to when women might actually abandon the *peçe* and *çarşaf* by trusting it to "women's tastes and social mentality." While thus recognizing women's agency in choosing what they wore, unlike Hakkı Tarık Us, Kaya did not comment on how women's *peçe* may also relate to, and be circumscribed by, the men's culture and choices. Yet Kaya's relatively flexible attitude toward the dissolution of the institution of the *peçe* and *çarşaf* likely had to do with his consideration of potential male reactions to such attempts.

Kaya dismissed the accusations of gradualism and of failure to uphold the revolutionary principles of the party. Revolution was about the fundamentals. Its details should be left to time and would be implemented gradually. The Republic was a revolution, but once established, its implementation would take many years. It would take time for the Republic to take roots. Kaya considered the *çarşaf* one of these details that required time. One may have asked why the *peçe* and *çarşaf* were among the "details" and the men's hat among the fundamentals; or why the *peçe* and *çarşaf*, but not the hat, required the passage of time.

Kaya briefly acknowledged the economic consequences of discarding the *çarşaf* that could delay its dissolution. For many, the *çarşaf* served both as a dress and as an outer layer worn in public. Discarding the *çarşaf* raised the question of what to use in its place and how to afford that new item. The minister's final comments hinted at a fundamental concern of the government in dealing with the *peçe* and *çarşaf* question. Kaya, noting the Congress's inclination in debate, said the government would "take care of the *peçe* and *çarşaf* issue administratively and politically. But, passing a law [on the *peçe* and *çarşaf*] would put [the] party in a very difficult position." (The delegates applauded amid cries of "not worth it.")[70] Although the delegates never openly discussed the possibility of violent resistance to the banning of the *peçe* and *çarşaf*, Kaya's words revealed an unspoken fear of potential opposition and resistence to a law banning the *peçe* and *çarşaf*. It appears that Kaya, and Mustafa Kemal himself, anticipated, if not massive violent resistance, a considerable degree of opposition and further weakening of the RPP legitimacy and support base, if the state were to openly challenge the patriarchal social norms by telling women what not to wear.

While the party members did not make any explicit references to the Soviet experience in Central Asia, or to the Afghan case, it is likely that the Turkish politicians were aware of the Soviet experience. The *hujum*, the Soviet campaign launched in 1927 against women's veiling and seclusion in Muslim Central Asia, led to a tremendous amount of backlash and violent resistance, much of which was directed against women who had unveiled.[71] According to historian Douglas Northrop,

> Thousands of women and a smaller number of men were beaten to ensure their continued adherence to non-Soviet codes of female seclusion. Hundreds of unveiled and activist women had been killed in Uzbekistan by 1929, as retribution and to warn others contemplating the same path.
>
> Rape, murder, and the occasional mutilation of unveiled women and Zhenotdel activists occurred with regularity—by one estimate as many as 2,500 women in Uzbekistan had been killed by 1930—along with an apparently endless stream of cases involving polygyny, qalin, and forced veiling and seclusion.[72]

It is quite likely that the ongoing Soviet experience in Central Asia, especially in Uzbekistan, along with the deposition of Amanullah Khan in Afghanistan in part as a result of his policies concerning women,[73] led the RPP leaders to act with caution in assessing potential public reactions to legislation on women's clothing. At the end of the debates at the party Congress, Hakkı Tarık Us withrew his proposal to pass a law on the issue.

Local Decrees and Provincial Campaigns
for Modern Dress in the 1930s

In the absence of a national law, the party delegated the responsibility of modernizing and secularizing women's dress to the provincial and local authorities by sending confidential orders to the governors.[74] There were two main methods employed: A propaganda campaign was undertaken through the press, especially in local newspapers, People's Houses, and local party offices. The second strategy, often combined with the first, was to pass local decrees banning the *peçe* and the *çarşaf*:

> "Declaration to the Esteemed People of Aydın"
> Dress is an unerring measure of civilization. Therefore, in the Turkey of the Gazi, in the era of revolution and Republic there is no room for the custom of *peştemals*.
> The [provincial] government, having found justified the grievous sorrow and intense protests of the region against this backward and ugly piece of clothing that lowers the civilizational level of this town and which has no connection with the history of Turkish womanhood, had to take effective measures. While informing the esteemed Women of Aydın of this with the definitive voice of the [government of the] province, I request that our enlightened women help wholeheartedly the inculcation undertaken by neighborhood committees of the People's Houses.[75]

Contrary to the view commonly held in the scholarship that the decrees banning the *peçe* and *çarşaf* were limited to a relatively small number of localities,[76] such decisions were quite widespread throughout the country. From press and archival data, and in the absence of complete statistical data, it appears that such decisions were more common in the western cities and towns, as well as coastal and border towns. Presumably, the size, power, and pro-reform enthusiasm of the RPP support base in a particular town, the degree of urbanism, the relative conservatism of the town, and the current state of clothing norms, as well as who happened to be the governor or district governor, were important factors in the passing of local dress decrees. Most of the early Republican governors shared a common educational and social background and worldview and were committed to the Kemalist project of modernization,[77] yet there were some differences in their interpretations of how to realize the revolution on the ground in the provinces under their jurisdiction.

It appears that even in cities that passed decrees in the mid-1930s prohibiting the *peçe* and *çarşaf*, there may have been a lack of enthusiasm, reluctance, or even resistance within the local bodies who passed those decisions. In Trabzon, a city that had an active pro-reform constituency, a core group of modernist urban intellectuals, a pro-regime local press, and organizations such as the Teachers' Union, the Turkish Hearths, and after 1932, the People's House,[78] passing a municipal decree on the *peçe* and *çarşaf* was not an easy matter. The Trabzon Provincial Council had already banned the *peçe* in 1926,[79] and organizations such as the Turkish Hearths had been promoting modern dress through the local press and other activities,[80] but (as Hakkı Tarık Us explained at the 1935 RPP congressional debate) the effects of those efforts had been limited. In February 1935, when the local sports clubs introduced a municipal bill on the *peçe* and *çarşaf*, the municipal council delayed a decision for an entire year. Ultimately, it was the combined pressure from the governor and the RPP provincial office that ensured the passage, by majority vote, of a municipal decree in February 1936 that banned the *peçe* and *çarşaf*. This power struggle between the municipality (whose members were also RPP members) on the one hand, and the governor, the RPP provincial organization, the local press, and the organizations such as the local sports clubs, points to a lack of consensus at the local and provincial level over the desirability of such measures.[81] This tension also suggests that RPP membership in the provinces was not necessarily unified on all issues of importance to the center,[82] nor did the party have representation in all parts of Anatolia.

The regional variation in the existence and application of local *peçe* and *çarşaf* decrees can in part be explained by the limits of RPP penetration in Anatolia. In 1931 the RPP did not have any provincial organization in Beyazıt, Diyarbakır, Elazığ, Erzincan, Hakkari, Mardin, Siirt, and Urfa provinces, all in Eastern and Southeastern Anatolia. As late as 1936, the RPP did not have an organization in four more provinces, also in Eastern Anatolia: Bingöl, Bitlis, Tunceli, and Van[83]; and some of the most serious challenges to the Kemalist regime, such as the Sheikh Said rebellion, had come from the eastern provinces. Not surprisingly, social and cultural organizations such as the People's Houses had a limited presence in the region, and the support base of the regime remained narrow throughout the RPP period. It should, however, be noted that some of the eastern provincial cities, if not the smaller towns, did pass *peçe* and *çarşaf* decrees. For example, the municipality of Bitlis passed a decision in October 1935 banning the *peçe* and the *çarşaf*,[84] and the municipality of Siirt banned the *çarşaf* around the same time.[85] Hakkari, at the southeast corner of Turkey bordering Iran and Iraq, also banned the *peçe*, albeit at a later date than most towns, in November 1938, the month of Atatürk's death. The governor of Hakkari, Sadullah Kologlu, informed the ministry that the municipal council of Çölemerik, the provincial center of Hakkari, which now included a female member, had just passed a decision to ban the *peçe*.[86] The minister responded by cautioning the governor to avoid any use of police (*zabıta*) or other force or pressure, including verbal, at this time of reactionary provocations.[87] Unlike the usual response to governors in the *peçe* and *çarşaf* matters, the communication from the ministry fell short of advising the governor on the kinds of measures to take. It appears that at a critical transitional time following the death of the charismatic head of state, the survival of the regime became the key concern in Ankara.

A follow-up correspondence from Governor Kologlu provides a good view of the state of women's clothing in Hakkari in the late 1930s and what the Governor intended to do about it.[88] In reporting on women's dress in the province, the governor also commented on the progress made in women's participation in local social and political life. Kologlu announced the good news that for the first time women in Hakkari had participated in the municipal elections. He had observed that women voting at the polling stations were dressed in three different ways: A small number of women were in modern dress (*"asri kıyafet"*), presumably a *manto* and *eşarp*,[89] but these women were from families of civil servants who were not natives of Hakkari. The great majority of the women voting were in *peçe* and *çarşaf*. The last group the governor observed was women dressed neither in *peçe* and *çarşaf* nor modern dress, but in local clothing (which he did not describe). Following further investigation of the matter, including a personal visit to a number of districts and rural communuties in the province from Beytüşşebap to Yüksekova, the governor had determined that the population in the villages and the transhumant communities still lived a tribal life, with the women dressed not in the *peçe* and *çarşaf* but in local clothes (*"mahalli ve muhiti giyiniş"*). As for the town of Çölemerik, the provincial center, the governor reported two tendencies: The majority of the women of the popular classes did not wear the *peçe* and *çarşaf*, but were dressed in local clothes. On the other hand, the women of the well-to-do and notable (*eşraf*) families, as well as the women in families of local (native) civil servants, continued to wear the *peçe* and *çarşaf*. It is clear from the governor's statements that by 1938 the debate and the efforts to modernize and secularize women's dress had not had a major impact on the people of Hakkari beyond a small circle of civil servants. At that level, too, the impact was further limited to those civil servants who were not natives of Hakkari. The majority of the women in Hakkari continued to wear the *peçe* and *çarşaf* or other local, tribal, and traditional forms of clothing as they had done before. There is no indication in governor Koloğlu's report that the social and cultural expectations and constraints in the province had changed significantly to make unveiling and "civilized clothes" more meaningful for a majority of the women in the province. It was not clear how the municipal decree banning the veil would be enforced, especially given the warning from the Ministry of the Interior to avoid the use of any form of physical force or verbal pressure by the party or the police. It appears from the governor's correspondence that the focus was going to be on the persuasion of the civil servants and the town's notables, as husbands, fathers, brothers, and community leaders, that the *peçe* and *çarşaf* could not be considered civilized clothes and that it would not be in line with their social standing to allow their women to wear such clothes.[90]

Nationwide, responses to the women's dress regulations were varied, and depended on a number of factors including cultural, social, class, and economic concerns. Civil servants, especially teachers, were simultaneously the targets and the promoters of these regulations. The majority of the already modernized, urban, educated, upper class women and men embraced and promoted the new dress.[91] Both archival and oral historical evidence indicates that the Westernized local elites found many of the state-promoted reforms and lifestyles acceptable and even desirable. Existing lifestyles at the initiation of the reforms and previous contact with the outside world seem to have played an important role. The Westernized upper and upper-middle classes not only provided a support base for the RPP regime, but were also crucial for other reasons, especially as their dress and life styles furnished a model for the lower and middle classes to emulate. Segments of the upper classes in provincial towns had long been aware of the changing fashions and life styles of the Westernized men and women of İstanbul.[92] For women who had followed the changes in the İstanbul women's dress in the late Ottoman years, the banning of the *peçe* and *çarşaf* was not a radical act.

Figure 8 shows three generations of a Trabzon family after return from *muhacirlik* ("the refugee years" upon the Russian occupation of Trabzon in World War I): Hacı Hüseyin Bekaroğlu (Alemdaroğlu) with his wife, three daughters, four sons (Ali Salim Peker's brothers), and two grandchildren. While the wife or the mother was usually excluded from the late nineteenth-century family photographs of Ottoman Muslim families, by the early 1920s it had become acceptable for the entire family to pose together for a family photograph. Note that all the women's faces are uncovered, the women's scarves are loosely and partially covering the hair, and the younger daughters have no headscarves at all. The generational gap is also evident for the male members of the family; for example, in the contrast between the *medrese*-educated Hacı Hüseyin's traditional outfit (with the turban-wrapped fez complementing the

8. Three generations of a Trabzon family after World War I *muhacirlik*. Photograph from the family album of Meliha Tanyeli.

robe and the beard) and his sons' completely Westernized clothes (with the exception of the one plain fez).

Ethnographies of Dress and Provincial Modernity in the 1930s

One of my informants, Meliha (Peker) Tanyeli, recalled the ease with which her mother and the other women in her Trabzon family adopted the *manto*. "Everyone put on a *manto* right away. First they put a headscarf (*eşarp*) above it. Later hats become fashionable."[93] She recalled that her older sisters, students at the Trabzon Girls' Institute, made their own hats. Figures 9, 10, and 11 show Meliha Tanyeli's mother, Belkıs Peker, at three different moments in the

9. Belkıs Peker fashionably dressed in a *çarşaf*. Photograph from the family album of Meliha Tanyeli.

10. Belkıs Peker in a hat. Note that the scarf now served as an accessory. Photograph from the family album of Meliha Tanyeli.

1920s.[94] Peker's transition from the *çarşaf* to the hat and then to no head covering at all, while noticeable, does not appear to have been a radical change.

Meliha Hanım's narrative of her mother's quick and smooth transition from *çarşaf* to the *eşarp* and then to the hat captures well the connections between politics, consumption, and culture, and especially the social class dimension of consumption.

By the early 1930s, for many middle and upper class urban women, the hat had become a fashion item. Not only were government authorities encouraging women to discard the *çarşaf* and wear modern clothes including hats, but more importantly newspapers and magazines carried advertisements of imported hats, magazines published articles on European fashions, stores carried elegant hats, local tailors made elegant hats copying European styles, and young women learned how to make hats in class at the Girls' Institutes.[95] For urban women like Belkıs Hanım, hats, like literacy, the gramophone, the piano, and European style furniture, came to represent an element of the modern life and a symbol of modernity rather than a sartorial requirement of the state. Oral historical evidence from other regions of Anatolia also attests to an association of the hat with modernity in the memories of elderly urban

11. Belkıs Peker in a two-piece suit, with no scarf or hat.
Photograph from the family album of Meliha Tanyeli.

men and women. Arzu Öztürkmen has noted in her ethnographic research in Tirebolu, a Black Sea port town west of Trabzon, that her informants recollected the past modernity of their now "fallen town" through the image of "women wearing elegant hats in the streets of Tirebolu during the 1930s."[96] In the memories of the elderly townspeople Öztürkmen interviewed, Tirebolu of the 1930s and 1940s emerged as a town of "fine taste" (as opposed to the "vulgar" culture of some of the neighboring communities), where members of the local elite played the piano and the violin, made oil paintings for their homes, attended theatre performances, and enjoyed "garden parties" in the Republic Park.[97] Öztürkmen's research on Tirebolu attests to the presence of local elites who found the state-promoted reforms and lifestyles desirable and welcomed them and enjoyed republican modernity. Existing lifestyles at the initiation of the reforms and previous contact with the outside world appear to have played a role. Tirebolu was a vibrant port town connecting the inland trade from Anatolia and Iran to the Black Sea and Russian towns. Thus the town, with its diverse population of Muslims, Greeks, and Armenians, was well connected to the outside world, particularly Russian cities. Öztürkmen's research also suggests that the presence of the non-Muslim communities may have played a role in terms of previous familiarity with certain social and cultural practices that were promoted by the new regime.

Similarly, a multi-site study on elite families in provincial towns of Anatolia, conducted through oral interviews in Denizli, Aydın, Muğla, Gaziantep, and Maraş,[98] revealed a commonly perceived association between modernization and the adoption of Western life styles, manners, and consumption patterns. Durakbaşa, Karadağ and Özsan observed that wearing hats, like playing the piano, using European style furniture, and the adoption of *alafranga* eating habits, emerged as symbols of modernization in the oral narratives about older family members who lived through the early Republican reforms. Following Pierre Bourdieu and Deniz Kandiyoti's call for examining the local specificities of Turkish modernity, they emphasized the interplay between the construction of modernity and that of social class and status. From this perspective, modern dress, very much like going to concerts and women's participation in Republic balls and dance parties, emerged as a status symbol. Perhaps more importantly for the present study, they show that the provincial elites emulated the life styles of the bourgeoisie of İstanbul, İzmir, and Ankara, including their clothing fashions. Some of them travelled to these cities regularly to buy clothes; some even had a regular tailor in İstanbul. In addition, Durakbaşa, Özsan, and Karadağ have highlighted the close connection between local elites and government bureaucrats as another major source of change in habits and life styles.

The campaigns for unveiling and modern dress took place in an era of expansion of women's social, educational, legal, and political rights. Oral historical evidence attests to the gradual nature of the clothing changes and their embeddedness in the larger social context of increased opportunities (at least in the urban areas) for women's education and employment, and in an environment of changing notions of women, the family, and male-female sociability. Narratives of urban women discarding the *çarşaf* and removing the headscarf, or of young women not adopting it in the first place accompany the stories of going to school in co-educational schools, employment (as teachers or in other professional jobs), the support of modernist bureaucrat fathers as well as overcoming the resistance of conservative fathers, and marriage to "modern" husbands who were professionals or civil servants. While İsmail Efe, as we will see below, and many others resisted the state's efforts to change women's appearance in defense of women's rights and on cultural and moral grounds (and in defense of patriarchy), other male citizens acted as the ideal Turkish father supporting their daughters' becoming modern Turkish women.

In Meliha Tanyeli's memories of her childhood and youth spent in Trabzon, the *çarşaf* had no relevance to her life. In fact, the images she recollected of her home town did not contain images of *çarşaf*-wearing women. As she expressed it, "There were absolutely no *çarşafs* in Trabzon."[99] Meliha Hanım's life story illustrates aspects of the process of growing up as a "modern Turkish woman" in an Anatolian city in the 1920s and 1930s. If modern dress was the most visible symbol of the nation's "new woman," education was the key institution for women's socialization. Indeed, central to Meliha Hanım's recounting of her early life, in addition to her family, was her education from kindergarten through high school and university, which not only prepared her for a teaching career but also legitimized her public visibility and employment outside the home.

Meliha (Peker) Tanyeli was born in Trabzon in 1921 to an urban Muslim family for whom education of all children had already become common practice. As Benjamin Fortna has phrased it, by the final decades of the nineteenth century, reading was perceived as "both an indicator and a cause of modernity."[100] Such attitudes toward literacy, reading, and education appear to have been emulated by segments of urban society in major Anatolian cities as well. Meliha's parents, Belkıs (born in 1892) and Ali Salim Peker (born in 1881), whom we have already met, had both received primary school education. Meliha Hanım noted proudly that her maternal grandfather, Kitabi Hamdi Efendi, had made sure all of his children, including his two daughters, received formal education.[101] Therefore, it was only to be expected that Meliha and her three sisters would also attend school. In the early 1930s, there were no high schools for girls in Trabzon, other than the Trabzon Girls' Institute. After graduating from the Girls' Middle School, Meliha Peker became one of the first women to attend Trabzon High School when the school began admitting female students in 1935. This was narrated as a group of fourteen or fifteen girls determined to pursue their education beyond middle school, taking an oath to attend high school. Meliha Hanım also suggested that the father of one of her friends, Rıfat Danışman, may have used his influence in persuading school officials to admit female students.[102]

In this instance, the active support of a father for girls' admission to Trabzon High School (whether real or perceived) illustrates well the special connection scholars have identified between "Kemalist fathers and their modern daughters,"[103] or the phenomenon that Deniz Kandiyoti has described as "Men gave social birth to the new woman of the republic."[104] Progressive Turkish fathers, as best exemplified by Ziya Gökalp and Mustafa Kemal, valued their daughters (or adopted daughters), nurtured them, and supported their education, employment, and participation in social life. It was thanks to the support of these modernist fathers that a generation of educated and successful professional women emerged in the early decades of the Republic.[105]

Whether or not the intervention of one of the fathers was instrumental, ultimately Trabzon High School began admitting female students in 1935.[106] Meliha's family-she said "my family" rather than "my father"—had decided to send her to İstanbul Erenköy Girls' High School if necessary, but still Meliha Hanım considered it her great fortune that Trabzon High School opened its doors to female students just as she finished the Girls' Middle School. Her two older sisters as well as her younger sister attended the Trabzon Girls' Institute, apparently the younger sister with the intention of pursuing higher education at Ankara Yüksek Kız Enstitüsü (The Ankara Higher Institute for Girls), which did not materialize due to their father's illness at the time. Some of Meliha's classmates likely would not have had the resources to pursue high school education in another city had Trabzon High School not begun admitting female students that year. I should note, however, that Trabzon High School graduated no more than ninety-two students a year before the 1938–1939 school year, a modest number for a school that served an entire province.[107] Therefore, high school attendance was a rare privilege for the majority of the region's residents of both genders, and especially for women. While coeducation brought into action many of the desired effects of the unveiling policies such as changing the social norms concerning male-female interaction and encouraging and legitimizing women's participation in public life, we can discern from Meliha Hanım's narrative that the implementation and the initial experiences of coeducation, itself, involved a considerable degree of change in habits, perceptions, and expectations of teachers and administrators as well as of both male and female students. In Meliha Peker's first year in high school, the first academic year Trabzon High School enrolled female students, all the incoming female students were placed in one class (şube) along with the male boarding students from surrounding provinces such as Rize and Giresun. Thus initially, the female students, like the male boarding students, were separated from the male day students from the city, even when they were formally admitted as students.[108] It appears that either school officials or parents still found the mixing in classes of the local men and women inappropriate, even though the school had formally opened its doors to coeducation. Meliha Hanım remembered the feeling of that first year as one of deep unease, with the girls sitting in the front rows and keeping the interactions with the boys very limited and formal. That first year appears to have worked as a period for everyone to get accustomed to the new arrangement. Things would normalize the next year; several male students from local Trabzon families joined the class of girls and boarding students, and as Meliha Hanım put it, girls and boys got used to each other's presence at school and the teachers got accustomed to having female students in class. A graduation picture of the 1938 graduates of Trabzon High School with their teachers, as can be seen in Figure 12, indeed attests to the normalization—if still somewhat separated—of female students' presence at school and their integration as a group. (A 1942 graduation photograph of Meliha Peker with her classmates and professors at İstanbul University reveals a much more gender-integrated social environment.)

For Meliha and her sisters, modern dress was only one element of being modern, which both her family and her education encouraged. Neither the school (as we have seen) nor the home environment provided for complete gender equality, however. For Meliha Hanım this took the form, for instance, of socializing with girls only rather than in mixed gender groups during her high school years, or later giving up the administrative part of her assignment

12. Graduating seniors of Trabzon High School with their teachers, 1938. Meliha (Peker) Tanyeli is in the second row along with all the other female students; she is eighth from left. Note that both the students and their teachers, including the female teachers, are in fully Westernized attire. Photograph from the family album of Meliha Tanyeli.

due to her husband's "jealousy" when she returned to Trabzon High School as a geography teacher. Yet Meliha Hanım and her siblings benefitted from family and national aspirations for a modern life that was premised upon the inclusion of women and children. The social and economic status of the family provided for the material basis of the family's modernity, and in that process, the war years, the Russian occupation of Trabzon, and the loss of the province's Rum community in the post-war Turco-Greek population exchange led to enormous disruptions as well as new opportunities; the family house in Soğuksu, for example, was purchased from a certain Dr. Efremidi in the 1920s. However, it was in part the ongoing changes in family life, life styles, and attitudes toward children and spouses that shaped the specifics of what it meant to be modern. The social and cultural transformations scholars have observed for some time in the example mainly of late nineteenth- and early twentieth-century upper strata İstanbul families,[109] and particularly the rise of a child-centered society as part of the overall process of Westernization of life styles and tastes, had engulfed the emerging Muslim Turkish middle classes in Trabzon, as well. We saw that Meliha Hanım's mother Belkıs went from wearing fashionable *çarşafs* (and note that she was not wearing a *peçe* by the 1920s) to fashionable hats by the 1930s. In addition to child rearing and pursuing traditional hobbies such as embroidery, she was taking lute classes by the late 1920s and took part in charitable activities in Trabzon through the Red Crescent. We see the fathers and grandfathers (in this instance, Ali Salim Peker and Kitabi Hamdi Efendi) taking an active interest in the education and overall development of their children, including the daughters. From written and oral sources as well as family photographs, music appears to have been an important part of the family's enjoyment of modern life. On the way back from one of his business trips to İstanbul, Ali Salim had brought home a gramophone, which along with the phonograph records from İstanbul and Germany introduced the children to European and American forms of music and dance. He also bought a piano for his children, when the director of the Ottoman Bank in Trabzon was appointed elsewhere and did not want to take with him the family's imported Pleyel piano. Hence, Meliha and her sisters and brother Orhan learned to play the piano in their Trabzon home in the 1930s. Like European style furniture, European style clothing, education, and foreign language skills, the piano was a status symbol. But at the same time, Ali Salim Peker's purchase of a piano and gramophone, his bringing home a home movie projector, building a small trumpet for the family's youngest child Orhan so that he could play it at the Children's Day procession, and his support for his daughters' education, all point to a progressive father's genuine interest in the development of his children and their access to the means of modern life. Ali Salim Peker's (and Kitabi Hamdi Efendi's) acting as modernist fathers of the "new family" and the "new life" points to a convergence, or at least a close affinity, between the values and interests of an emerging local bourgeoisie in an Anatolian port town and the values and principles of the new republican regime.[110] Later, on one of his visits home during his Fine Arts Academy years in İstanbul, when Orhan expressed his desire to draw a portrait of a *Trabzonlu* in his local costume, a relative volunteered to pose for him, but the family had to borrow the outfit from the local Halkevi, where such costumes were used for theatrical performances.[111] By the 1940s, local and traditional clothing had indeed become an element of the past and of folklore for the family, if not uniformly so for the majority of their fellow citizens in the province.

A collection of narratives of urban women from Antep province ties together the multiple aspects of the unveiling process, connecting the removal of the *peçes* and *çarşafs* to state policies and education as well as fashion, to changing patterns of everyday habits and consumption and new forms of socialization, and to changes in gender relations. These narratives highlight the individual and family experiences of the unveiling processes, and particularly the ambiguous roles played by fathers and husbands within that process.[112]

Whereas Trabzon was a major port city with connections to İstanbul in the West and Russian cities to the East and North, Antep presents a case from the southern frontier of the Anatolian interior. Antep—Gaziantep after the Republic in recognition of the heroic defense of the city against the French—was not only in close geographic proximity to the Syrian cities to the south, but it had also been a part of the Ottoman province of Aleppo and was closely connected with Aleppo and other Syrian cities in its social practices (such as clothing habits) and cultural norms (such as the norms of appropriate male-female interaction). After 1922, the province's orientation was directed away from Aleppo towards Ankara and İstanbul, to which it was connected by rail. Nevertheless, Antep maintained a degree of economic and cultural contact with the Syrian cities.

For Antep, like Trabzon and much of Anatolia, the World War I years and the end of Empire had been a period of destruction and rapid demographic change with enormous social, economic, and psychological consequences. First the British and later the French occupation of the Cilicia region, anti-colonial resistance, intercommunal conflict, and the loss of Antep's sizeable Armenian community (estimated at around 45 percent of the city's pre–World War I population), created a social vacuum and new problems as well as new opportunities. Futhermore, the experiences and powerful memories of these events shaped the consciousness of the residents of Antep. In Atauz's research in Antep, her elderly interviewees emphasized these experiences in explaining why the residents of Antep supported or at least tolerated some of the changes of the early Republican period.

Concerning the clothing of the women of Antep, Atauz's informants agreed that in their childhood and youth (for many of them the 1920s), all the women were veiled and that women were segregated from the public lives of men.[113] They also agreed that there was a shift in women's clothing and public visibility around 1933–35. A primary source of that change was remembered as Atatürk's banning the *peçe* and *çarşaf*. Some referred to it as a ban during the time of Atatürk; other narrators recalled the local decrees banning the *peçe* and *çarşaf* as Atatürk's banning the *peçe*—although we may recall from RPP debates that Atatürk was against passing legislation on women's clothing. Individual memories of unveiling point to a gendered reception of the local ban and a period of tension within families between men and women. One narrator's account summarized concisely her positive assesment and appreciation of what she remembered as Atatürk's ban and her memory of the ensuing gendered tensions.[114]

> As long as I can remember, all the women were veiled. They would put the *peçe* on your face as soon as you were no longer a child. . . . Discarding the *peçe* started in 1933 and the *peçe* disappeared. The late Atatürk took care of it. We removed it gradually and slowly. First, the wives of civil servants began to uncover their faces. We were all thinking this is a good thing, but what if the men do not give their consent? With some the fathers and with others the husbands were not allowing it, making it impossible. In the end, they [men] understood that there was no way out of it and everyone uncovered their faces. The abolition of the *peçe* was the most important novelty of the Atatürk period. That's where civilization took off. . . .

Other narrators emphasized the role of fathers and husbands and identified their marriage as an important rite of passage in their individual experiences of unveiling and adoption of new life styles. The following account highlights the divergent understandings fathers and daughters, and fathers and husbands, held of the dress changes and the negotiations that resulted from those differences, pointing to gendered and generational differences.

> In those years, wedding ceremonies would begin at the girl's house. At my wedding, the mayor, witnesses, and so on were downstairs. Upstairs was

the religious wedding (*hoca nikâhı*). I was seventeen at the time; my father was very conservative and I wore the *çarşaf*. My father insisted that I should come down for the [civil] marriage wearing a *çarşaf*. Now up until that time I had never confronted him and hurt his feelings, I had done whatever he had said. But now I had had enough. I said how is it possible that I would appear before the groom in a *çarşaf* at my own wedding. If my father insists that I appear in a *çarşaf*, I said, then I've changed my mind about this wedding; I won't do it, I won't. This argument went on for a while, maybe one hour, two hours, anyway, they convinced my father, I put on a *manto*, a *sıkma baş* style scarf on my head and a single layer *peçe* on my face (just to say I had it), that's how our wedding was conducted. [So] I got married and came [to my husband's home]. My husband did not want me to cover up in any way. "It is impossible, *hanım*," he said. "I am willing to put up with anything, but not this attire; I am a civil servant (*ben memur bir insanım*)." He was a forward thinking gentleman for that time. A man everyone admired, with a rich social life. When we visited my father's house, I would leave home in elegant dress, my head uncovered. At my father's home, there was an entryway, where I would put the *peçe* on my face and the scarf (*eşarp*) in my bag, [then] I would appear before my father. The first couple of years were difficult. After that, we all relaxed and uncovered (*açıldık*), after 1934.[115]

Here the narrator's discarding of the *peçe* at her wedding is remembered as a moment of a woman's youthful rebellion against a conservative father that ended up in a compromise solution. (We may note that the wedding practices were also changing and that the wedding itself was a compromise: a civil as well as a religious ceremony.) In this instance, father and daughter clearly had different opinions about what was proper dress for the daughter. While the father resisted his daughter's unveiling, which the daughter attributed to his conservatism, the husband supported (maybe even encouraged) his wife's modern dress, which the narrator tied to his being a progressive man and a civil servant. Families of civil servants were expected to adopt modern dress and life styles and furnish a model for others to emulate.

These memories of unveiling run parallel to remembrances of other changes toward *asri hayat* or modern life such as women's education, the introduction of coeducation, women's increased public presence (women going shopping or going to the hairdresser), and transition to new forms of entertainment. Some of these changes, such as the introduction of the radio and the adoption of new furniture (such as sofas, dining tables, and chairs), did not have direct or overt effects on gender relations. Other changes, however, such as the transition from gender segregated forms of entertainment to new forms of socialization (including entertainment as a family, and husbands and wives attending balls and concerts together), involved important changes in the norms of male-female interaction and women's place in society.

In the provinces, governors, *kaymakam*s and People's Houses organized social activities that promoted women's participation in public life. Around the time Atauz's respondents discarded the *peçe* in Antep, the governor of neighboring Maraş embarked on a number of measures to encourage women's unveiling and public presence. One of these strategies was the persuasion of local civil servants to allow their wives to unveil and to bring them to social activities.[116] In November 1935, shortly after the passage of a municipal decree that prohibited the women's *peçe* and *çarşaf* as well as the men's *karadon* (the local baggy pants) and *aba* (men's sleeveless summer top),[117] the governor hosted a tea party at the local People's House, which apparently forty-one local civil servants attended along with their unveiled wives.[118] *Son Posta* reported that the attendees appauded these officials and their wives for having adopted modern dress.[119] By early 1936 the governor of Maraş reported success to the central government, although it is clear from later correspondence from the same province that this was a measured success and that the diffusion of the desired changes from the civil servants to other segments of provincial society was a more gradual and slower process than the governors anticipated. Press coverage and oral historical evidence indicate that similar social activities encouraging women's unveiling, public presence, and participation in new forms of social activities took place in other Anatolian town, as well. While the effectiveness of such activities appear to have been limited, oral narratives from Antep suggest that for at least a segment of the urban population, mixed gender forms of socialization and entertainment such as husbands and wives dancing together indeed became a part of their modern lifestyle.

A final oral account from Antep points to how unveiling and clothing changes involved a process of adaptation on an individual level and a period of tension within families, at the same time as they were part of a broader process of changing life styles, consumption, and fashion informed in part by one's social class.

> There was *peçe* at that time, women's faces were covered. The *peçe* was abandoned during Atatürk's time. At the time of the *peçe*, one would run away even from her own [male] cousins. I covered my head after grade school. When I finished grade school, they put the *peçe* on my face; they said you are now grown up. I was about thirteen or fourteen at the time; then Atatürk banned the *peçe* and we all discarded our *peçes*. It was difficult for us in the first days, but we quickly got used to it. Why should one always stay indoors as if in prison? My head was covered until I got married. I got married in 1933, in a wedding gown and tulle bridal veil decorated with silver thread; but when we visited my parents, I wore a *peçe*. When we went to İstanbul a year after our wedding, we bought hats and put them on our heads. Our hats had tulle on them, when we walked in the street in Antep, kids would shout after us "a bride is passing by." Every time I went to İstanbul, I would buy a few hats; I would lend them to others for wedding ceremonies and I did not ask for them back. An Armenian tailor made my dresses in İstanbul; we would also make sure to buy a hat.[120]

Similar to Durakbaşa, Özsan, and Karadağ's finding for elite families in provincial towns, and as we saw with Meliha Tanyeli's family in Trabzon, this oral account suggests that hats became fashionable symbols of modernity by the 1930s. This narrative also highlights the association women made between unveiling and the abolition of women's seclusion, as well as the gendered and generational tensions the process of adaptation created.

Men's and Women's Responses to the Local Decrees

There was almost no outright opposition to the local decrees banning the *çarşaf* and the *peçe*, yet there was resentment and discontent. As with men's reactions to the Hat Law, James Scott's notion of "weapons of the weak" is relevant here. When "neither outright collective defiance nor rebellion is likely or possible," people resort to individual acts of protest and resistance such as reluctant compliance, defiance, and gossip.[121] Such acts require little planning and organization and generally avoid direct confrontation with the state. One such response to which women resorted following the *çarşaf* and *peçe* regulations was secluding themselves in their houses.[122] Houchang Chehabi has shown that this was also a common response of Iranian women following the banning of the *chador* in Iran in the mid 1930s.[123] Women avoided open defiance and possible sanctions by avoiding the public sphere. This was combined with alternative solutions such as leaving the house only in the privacy of a carriage, or adding umbrellas to outdoors outfits.

Such responses took place, for example, in the town of Kilis in the province of Gaziantep. The town banned the *peçe* and the *çarşaf* in September 1935 with enforcement to begin on 15 September for the *peçe* and on 15 December for the *çarşaf*.[124] Failure to conform would result in monetary fines starting at one Lira and up to fifty Liras. Shortly after the enforcement on the *çarşaf* began, *Son Posta* reported the disappearance of the *peçe* and the *çarşaf* as well as the emergence of a new practice. The paper reported "A fashion of umbrellas has now begun here. No woman goes outdoors without an umbrella."[125] Just as it was not socially acceptable for men to appear bare-headed in public in the 1920s and the 1930s, the shift directly from the *çarşaf* to a complete lack of an outer layer in public seemed impossible for the majority of women. This was well understood by the state authorities, which promoted the *manto*, a long overcoat, as the preferred substitute for the *çarşaf* for women.[126]

A report by the governor of Maraş, Sabri Çıtak, provides an interesting description of such responses in Maraş.

As for the women: They are deeply conservative. There have been women who for years never stepped outside their houses when the *peçe* and the *çarşaf* were abolished. There have been some who went to visit their relatives in the city at night in carriages so that they would not have to wear an overcoat and go out without a *peçe*. Although time has more or less moderated these, umbrellas have taken the place of the *peçe*. Most of the local women go out with an umbrella when the weather is sunny or overcast, rainy or dry, and even at nights. While outwardly this purports to provide protection from the rain and the sun, in reality this is a sign of conservatism established due to the banning of the *peçe*. Almost none of the women wear a hat. Some of them wear a black scarf, while the more conservative ones wear *peştemal*s and other coverings in a way to cover half their bodies. Village people are more liberal and more free in that respect and are not involved

in any backward activity. However, there are people with backward tendencies in the towns and they would poison the naive and the pure people if the
opportunity is given.[127]

Whereas men's voluntary seclusion from the public sphere tended to be
short term, sources like the report by the governor of Maraş cited above indicate that some urban women were confined to their houses for years. It is
possible that it was the women themselves who decided to circumvent the
law by avoiding public places, but we must also question the role of men in
this process. Available sources such as the oral accounts we saw above from
Antep suggest that women often had to deal with two levels of domination in
this process: on the one hand, the demands of the state, and on the other, the
demands of the men in the family and the broader male-dominated culture.

Pressures on women to maintain the *peçe* and *çarşaf* must have begun at
the level of the family and the neighborhood, spheres that remained largely
outside the control of the state. As noted above, it was also at the level of
the family, in particular the families of government officials, that the state's
attempts to bring about the desired change in women's clothing began. Pressure on women in the private sphere or in the neighborhoods is extremely
difficult to document if such pressure did not involve violent acts leading to
injury or death, or did not somehow reach the police station or the courts.
Oral historical sources provide some hints at the local and family level controls on women's dress. Nuriye Güner, who attended elementary school in
Trabzon in the mid-1920s, remembered that some girls went to the school in
the *çarşaf*.[128] She also remembered a school teacher dressed in the *çarşaf*. She
recalled that at the time of the *çarşaf* issue,[129] that teacher quit her job and
many girls stopped coming to school. I do not know if these decisions were
reversed later. In terms of consequences, the act of a woman quitting her job
or school completely confounded the state's efforts to expand women's education and participation in social life. Such occurrences also tell us something
about the reactions of these girls' families. While it may be argued in the case
of the teacher that it was her decision to leave her post rather than give up on
"proper" dress, in the case of school girls, clearly it must have been the families who decided that their daughters must quit school rather than give up
the *çarşaf*.[130] The oral narratives Atauz collected in Antep also attest to social

pressure on families to stop sending their daughters to school when female students were asked to remove their *çarşafs* at school and when coeducation was introduced. These narratives point to fathers who made their daughters quit school rather than allowing them to study in the same classroom with male students; they also contain cherished memories of at least one father who resisted social pressures and supported his daughter's education, allowing her to become a teacher.[131]

There is some archival evidence to suggest that there was social pressure on women who unveiled, sometimes including verbal and physical harassment.[132] As we saw earlier, street harassment of women on the grounds of inappropriate dress was not a new phenomenon. Unveiled or fashionably dressed urban Ottoman women had faced harassment in the streets during the Young Turk era. Moreover, in the 1920s and 1930s, unveiled women encountered varying degrees of social pressure, street harassment, and physical violence in other Midde Eastern or Islamic contexts as well, such as Soviet Uzbekistan (as we have already seen), Iran, and French Syria and Lebanon.[133] In the Turkish context, one of the earliest documented incidents of men's harassment of women for not covering themselves sufficiently occurred in Yozgat province in Central Anatolia. Ethem Hoca, a mosque *vaiz* in the city of Yozgat, was taken before the court for calling women who dressed liberally ("*açık gezen*") whores and for making other reactionary comments.[134] This was apparently not the first time Ethem Hoca had been taken before the court on the same grounds. Although the state attempted to prevent such propaganda through the courts, it appears that the court's previous decision did not deter Ethem Hoca from continuing his verbal harassment of women.

A later and better documented case took place in Afyon province in the Aegean interior. One week after the prohibition of the *çarşaf* and the *peçe* in the province,[135] the Governor of Afyon reported first the good news that most women ("ninety percent") in the city had adopted "modern dress." Then he added that there were some malicious people who had verbally and physically assaulted the women with the intention of intimidating them and preventing them from wearing modern clothes. Upon learning this, he had warned the persons involved—although we don't know what kind of warning this was—and instigated police patrol in places frequented by women, such as the markets, bazaars, and the main streets. Although the governor did not specifically say that all the perpetrators were men, the language he used as well as the specific case he mentioned indicate that the attackers were male. In the specific case he reported, a certain city resident named Emine, married and about twenty years old, was attacked by Ahmet oğlu Abdurrahman while walking on İzmir İstasyon Street with her child. She was first verbally harassed by Abdurrahman. Then Abdurrahman grabbed Emine by the arm and began dragging her. The governor reported that Emine was rescued and the attacker was taken to court.[136] The Ministry responded by ordering that more rigorous measures be taken against men who attempted to harass women either verbally or physically for wearing modern clothes.[137]

One obvious implication of the correspondence between Afyon and the Ministry of the Interior is that the reported incident was not an isolated case of women's harassment in public on the grounds of inappropriate dress. Despite its brevity and limited content, the governor's letter offers us some insight into the motivations of the men who harassed women for failing to wear the *peçe* and *çarşaf*. We do not know for sure if the male perpetrators and the unveiled victims of harassment were from different social, economic, or educational backgrounds. But we know from the governor's report that men were shouting slurs at unveiled women, essentially calling them prostitutes. By shouting sexual slurs such as "what great local merchandise [i.e., prostitutes] we have," these men were questioning unveiled women's sexual morality and harassing women for inappropriate moral conduct. Women's discarding the *peçe* and *çarşaf* at the encouragement of the state challenged local, traditional, and patriarchal norms of morality. The state's intrusion in women's dress, along with the other changes it introduced such as coeducation and a new secular legal system, also challenged men's authority over women.

In Konya, Hüseyin oğlu Taşçı Ahmed was arrested for spreading rumors that policemen and gendarmes were killed for the tearing of *peçes* and *çarşafs* off women's bodies.[138] The governor insisted that such rumors were false propaganda. We cannot, however, rule out the possibility that Ahmed's words expressed the desired, if not realized, reaction of some who opposed the regulation of women's dress and the strict application of such regulations.

An incident mentioned by Michael Meeker reveals that public pressure over and control of women's appearance continued in small towns of

Anatolia as late as the 1960s. Meeker relates that "the wife of the only pharmacist in the town [of Of, in Trabzon province] was cursed and spat upon for leaving her hair uncovered during the weekly market."[139] Clearly some change had taken place in this conservative town and the *çarşaf* and the *peçe* were no longer the norm or the expected outfit. Yet, as this example shows, social pressure and sanctions on what was considered proper dress for women had not disappeared, and women were still expected to cover their hair. In his visit to Of two decades later, Meeker observed that old public sanctions (on women's appearance among other things) had lost their power. He saw women employees in the marketplace in short sleeves, which he says "would have been shocking two decades earlier." Meeker attributed the loosening of old social controls in Of mainly to the urbanization of the town and the anonymity that comes with urbanity, as well as changes in consumption patterns.[140]

Women resorted to other compromise solutions as well. One such solution, as British consular reports from Trabzon indicate, was that women treated the *çarşaf* and the *peçe* differently. Many urban women discarded the *peçe* following the local decrees, but continued to wear the *çarşaf* for a longer period.[141]

Economic factors were a part of the context within which women responded to the local decrees on dress. Poverty was both a reason and an excuse for failure to comply with the local decrees. Providing overcoats (*manto*) free of charge was an important part of the dress campaign carried out by the party, People's Houses, and women's organizations. Local and provincial decrees of the 1930s typically allowed for a transition period of one to three months so that families, particularly those with limited financial means, would have the time to acquire new outerwear (i.e. *mantos*) as replacement for their *çarşaf*s and *peştemal*s. When the effects of these decrees fell short of producing a rapid and complete transformation of adult women's clothing habits, government officials found themselves searching for answers. Economic reasons, along with cultural conservatism, the difficulty of changing established habits, and men's jealousy (which often amounted to or at least was blended with what we might call patriarchal social controls) were among the explanations offered. Differences of emphasis in provincial reports appear to reflect the diversity of prevailing social, economic, and cultural conditions in different regions, and urban and rural differences, as well as the governors' and party officials' own divergent expectations. Economic difficulties alone did not account for the delays in the transition from *çarşaf*s and *peştemal*s, but as in men's hats and caps, poverty and the lack of supplies were real obstacles in transforming women's dress. Similar to the mobilization of state resources for the provision of hats and caps[142] (albeit in a more limited way), some of the provincial governors tried to tap into Sümerbank production to provide overcoats at affordable prices, if not free of charge. In one such instance in 1939, the governor of Rize province along the eastern Black Sea coast wrote to the prime minister requesting permission for the production and shipment of inexpensive Sümerbank overcoats to the province.[143] (Sümerbank (Sumerian Bank) was a major state-owned economic enterprise that pioneered Turkey's industrial development, including its textile industry, which produced high quality, relatively inexpensive textiles for mass consumption.) According to the governor's report, nearly the entire population of the province, rural and urban alike, had failed to put on "civilized clothes": women were still wearing *peştemal*s, and the clothing of their male counterparts was marked by its diversity.[144] Arguing that both men and women in fact desired to wear civilized clothes, the governor underlined poverty as the fundamental cause of his fellow citizens' wretched state of appearance and their inability to conform to modern dress. He was therefore requesting approval for an initial shipment to Rize of one hundred Sümerbank *manto*s for women and one hundred Sümerbank suits for men (*erkek elbisesi*) with a view to lightening the economic burden of adopting what was perceived to be modern and national clothing. From a purely economic point of view, attempts to supply free or affordable *manto*s (through Sümerbank, People's Houses, or women's organizations) represented a minuscule effort, given the magnitude of the challenge. The governor may have been correct in his assessment that the residents of Rize were enthusiastic about wearing "civilized clothing," but we don't have much evidence to indicate that the women of Rize, particularly rural women (and their husbands and fathers), indeed wanted to replace their local *peştemal*s with European style overcoats.[145] Such changes would be more meaningful and consequential when combined with other changes such as urbanization and access to education and employment.

Petitions as Resistance: İsmail Efe of Ödemiş
and Dokumacı Şevki of Buldan

There were no specific guidelines on how to enforce the local decrees, and enforcement on the ground led to confrontations between local officials and the citizens as well as between local and central government, as clearly illustrated by the case of İsmail Efe, a leading citizen of the Aegean town of Ödemiş. İsmail Efe resorted to petitioning, an old instrument of political communication that subjects and citizens have used in traditional as well as modern societies in voicing their demands from the state.[146]

In a letter dated 18 December 1937, İsmail Efe of Ödemiş wrote:[147]

My Brother Hamdi Bey,

[. . .] The other day I went to Kahrat to see our Celal Bayar's school. . . . From there I went on to Tire. Our women's overcoat issue is still going on. But women have thrown away the *çarşaf*. [T]hose who find [something] put on something good or bad. There I saw with my own eyes the gendarmerie captain is out yelling "hey whores are you doing this out of spite" and tearing and throwing away their *yazma*s (scarves), no bigger than the palm of your hand. Later while sitting in a coffeehouse the captain came to the coffeehouse. Some old men [were] wearing the *takge* (skullcap) under their *kasket*s (caps). [H]e took them too together with their *kasket*s. A few gendarmes behind him with a bundle in each one's hand are taking the caps and wrapping them up in a bundle. Then he came and sat next to me. [I] asked [how he was], he said I am very much distressed today. So I told him you have found the easy way to get rid of distress. I said no more. According to what I heard from some good friends of mine from Tire, the commander of the gendarmerie is not on good terms with the justice officials. Apparently they complain about each other. If the justice inspector comes he defends the justice people, then the gendarmerie inspector comes and he defends the gendarmerie. Again it is the people who are squeezed in the middle. . . . If you ask our women of Ödemiş and the villages[,] they can't go out to the bazaars. Everyone down to even the drivers of the municipality is yelling in the middle of the streets sparing neither their dishonorableness nor their sluttishness. Relate this exactly like this to our Celal Bey. I told the *kaymakam* that the representatives [in the parliament] do not consent to this. He paid no attention. They should fulfill the promises they have made. Many greetings. Köse has worn the overcoat and the suit. He prays for you. Taking this opportunity we offer our respects.

Signed: Ismail Efe

İsmail Efe's observations expressed in this letter bear witness to the state of male and female dress at the time, as well as the enforcement of dress regulations on the ground in Tire and Ödemiş, towns in İzmir province. He witnessed that some old men in the coffeehouse were wearing the skullcap, but under their caps, which points to a compromise between maintaining old habits and the desire to avoid government sanctions for failing to comply with the Hat Law.[148] However, the statement "some old men" were wearing the skullcap also implies that a lot of the men were actually not wearing skullcaps and were probably wearing hats. He witnessed that the gendarmes intervened with the old men, removing the caps from their heads. İsmail Efe wrote about interventions by the local authorities on both male and female clothing, yet his real concern seems to have been "our women's overcoat issue."

Efe's observation that the women had given up the *çarşaf* was also confirmed by the provincial governor's reports at about the same time. On 24 November 1937, governor Fazlı Güleç reported to the minister of the interior that he had established that, thanks to the propaganda efforts in the last six months, in the city of İzmir with 170,000 inhabitants, only 600 women workers were wearing the *çarşaf*. He wrote he had ordered them to take off the *çarşaf* at once and had ensured the same in the districts, as well. He added that this has been achieved "with no mutterings of discontent and without reflection in the newspapers" ("*sızıltısız ve gazetelere aksetmeden*").[149] In a follow-up report to the Ministry on 9 December, Governor Güleç reported that there were absolutely no women wearing the *çarşaf* and the *peçe* in the province.[150]

Whereas the governor of İzmir did not specify how this was achieved (beyond mentioning propaganda), İsmail Efe's letter gives an insight into the implementation of women's dress regulations passed by the municipalities in the same province. Efe saw that the gendarmerie had taken up the task of ensuring that women did not wear the *çarşaf*. He argued that women had already complied with the law and were still being mistreated by the gendarmes and "everyone down to even the drivers of the municipality." Women were called prostitutes for wearing scarves, and their scarves were torn off and taken away. İsmail Efe seems to have interpreted this as a morally unacceptable situation which was the result of the local authorities exceeding their legitimate authority. He briefly refers to the tension between the gendarmerie and the judiciary in Tire, suggesting by implication that the conflict between rival local authorities may have contributed to misuse of authority. Efe wanted to speak to the higher authorities in Ankara, on behalf of what he saw as the mistreated men and women, assuming that the ministers and the members of the parliament in Ankara were of a different opinion than the local government officials. As Lex Heerma van Voss observed, "Petitions tried to use perceived fissures within ruling classes, for instance, by addressing a central authority with complaints about a local authority . . ."[151] This is the strategy that İsmail Efe was using when he tried to bring the authority of the ministers in Ankara to bear against the local administrative and military officials.

On 27 December 1937, nine days after the first letter, İsmail Efe wrote a second letter to Hamdi Bey:

My Brother Hamdi Bey,

We have already discussed the *çarşaf* [issue] in Prime Minister Celal [Bayar] Bey's house. That evening Celal Bey said that he had talked with Minister of the Interior Şükrü Kaya Bey [about the *çarşaf* issue] in Atatürk's house. He mentioned that no such orders were given to the governor of İzmir and even stated that Atatürk himself said the women's *çarşaf* should not be touched. I have already described in my previous letter the adventure unfolding in Tire. While talking with the commander of the gendarmerie in Tire, I said that Ankara did not know about it. Apparently the commander of the gendarmerie together with the *kaymakam* notifies the governor of İzmir of what I said. Then the governor orders the *kaymakam* of Ödemiş that they should take a statement from me or else I should be taken before the court. The *kaymakam* of Ödemiş summoned me and told me the order he had received from the governor. Please explain [the contents of] this letter to Prime Minister Celal Bey. If this matter is not resolved I will run away and come there. I send you my greetings and wish you good health.

Signed: Ismaıl [sic][152]

In this letter İsmail Efe spoke with more authority by arguing that the opinion of the key political leaders on the *çarşaf* issue was on his side. He had talked personally with Prime Minister Celal Bayar who had said, after consulting with the Minister of the Interior, that no such orders had been given to the governor of İzmir. Efe claimed Celal Bayar had also mentioned that Atatürk himself opposed interference with the *çarşaf.* Juxtaposed with the opinion of the president, prime minister, and the Minister of the Interior are the actions of the local leaders: the commander of the gendarmerie in Tire and the *kaymakam* had complained to the governor of İzmir in reaction to Efe's statement that the central government was unaware of the actions taken in Tire. Then the governor had threatened to bring him before the court. Efe once again appealed to the authority of the prime minister to put an end to this matter, writing another letter on 8 January 1938.

My brother Refik Bey,[153]
I talked to Prime Minister Celal Bayar regarding the women's *çarşaf.* He promised to order Şükrü Kaya Bey not to allow the governor of İzmir to misuse his authority, but nothing came out of it. Then I wrote to Ankara again. In a letter I received a week ago from Hamdi Bey in Ankara [Hamdi Bey] informed me that Prime Minister Celal Bayar has once again sent orders to the governor of İzmir via the Minister of the Interior. However, in Ödemiş, never mind wearing the *çarşaf,* neighbourhood watchmen ordered by the *kaymakam* are at street corners waiting to tear apart the covers on the heads of the women who are going for wood wearing a covering on their heads above their overcoats. Women cannot go out of their houses. As you are aware, this issue has become a matter of self-respect. I don't know if the governor does not give orders to the *kaymakam* of Ödemiş [on this issue], or the *kaymakam* does not give up. There is so much disgrace going on that cannot be described. I am tired of writing to Hamdi Bey. If possible, please see Celal Bey yourself and tell him thus. If you can resolve this issue as quickly as possible,

you will have freed the people and myself from this difficult situation. Please inform me by letter. Taking this opportunity I offer my respects and wish you good health.

Signed Ismaıl [sic][154]

In this letter, frustration has been added to İsmail Efe's familiar yet respectful tone. He argued that despite the promises made by the prime minister, the situation had not improved. He described another scene of the local authorities' intervention with the women's clothing. The pressure was such that women could not go out. He was again speaking on behalf of the mistreated women of the town, although he was also clearly speaking for himself: For him, this had become a matter of self-respect. He was frustrated but still sounded convinced that the authorities in Ankara could and would correct the situation.

Meanwhile, the first two letters written to Hamdi Bey were forwarded to Minister of the Interior Şükrü Kaya, as shown by handwritten marginal notes on both letters. The third letter to Refik Bey must also have been forwarded to the minister of the interior, because shortly after this third letter Şükrü Kaya wrote to Fazlı Güleç, the governor of İzmir, concerning Efe's letters, and because all three letters were filed together. In a letter dated 14 January 1938 and stamped "urgent," Kaya first stated that "it has been been established that in recent days İsmail Efe of Ödemiş has been sending letters to high authorities saying that the precautions taken by the local government in Ödemiş regarding women wearing the *çarşaf* and the *peçe* have saddened the people and himself alike."[155] Then he asked the governor to invite İsmail Efe to his office and to "inform him in a proper and firm manner that he should not occupy himself with such reactionary affairs (*irtica işleri*) in any way whatsoever." In addition, Kaya asked the governor to find out and report back on what İsmail Efe intended by these letters.

Clearly Kaya understood these letters in the context of reactionary opposition to the regime and its cultural project. That the letters focused on the local practices of dress regulations and not the reforms as such, and had no reference to religion, did not free İsmail Efe from being suspected of reaction. Kaya wanted to stop at once any further action by İsmail Efe, but also wanted to know more about what İsmail Efe himself meant by the letters.

Governor Fazlı Güleç responded the following day,[156] saying he was inviting İsmail Efe to tell him why he wrote these letters. The governor also provided a summary of his previous contacts with Efe on the issue. He wrote that Efe claimed that those in high authority (*büyükler*) had said "we haven't given such orders, we don't know about it, it is not right." The governor added that at that time he had refuted those claims, and had warned Efe via the *kaymakam* of Ödemiş not to make such statements and that he would be sued if it happened again.

The governor's meeting with İsmail Efe was delayed due to the latter's illness. The governor wrote that he did not object to waiting for Efe's recovery, since the illness was genuine.[157] On the second of February the governor reported back to the Ministry on his meeting with İsmail Efe.[158] According to the governor's letter, Efe repeated his argument that the Prime Minister had said, "They [women] may wear whatever they want. We haven't given such orders. I asked the minister of the interior. He said he hasn't given orders to the governor, either." Governor Güleç also noted that Efe said he did not oppose the women's taking off the *çarşaf*, he was in favor of women wearing modern clothes, but that the authorities should not put pressure on the poor (*fukara*). The governor summarized his response to Efe as: "Our leaders (*büyüklerimiz*) like you. Don't lose their favor, what we want from women is that they should take off not the overcoat (*manto*) but the *çarşaf* and that they should dress like human beings." Governor Güleç finished by noting "I cautioned him not to talk about these matters. We came to an agreement."

İsmail Efe's insistence, stated both in his letters and in the governor's correspondence with the Ministry of the Interior, that the ministers in Ankara had not ordered and did not know about what was going on in Ödemiş and Tire raises questions about the position of the central governmet on the *çarşaf* issue and how that position was communicated to and interpreted by the local governments. Petitions reflect the biases of the petitioner and might include "a certain element of fiction."[159] İsmail Efe's letters were clearly written from a particular point of view, yet there is no evidence to suggest that they were pure fiction. Information available on other cases suggests that İsmail Efe was telling a story which was true in essence if not in detail.

A 1935 police report from Kastamonu province in the western Black Sea region depicted a state of affairs in the town of Tosya not dissimilar to that described by İsmail Efe for Tire and Ödemiş.[160] The report first pointed out that the people of Tosya were conservative and did not adopt the clothing style of the families of civil servants. Hence, the municipality had passed a decision to ban the *peçe* and *çarşaf* and was trying to put it into practice with the help of the gendarmerie. Then he described how the gendarmes attempted to apply the municipal decision in the streets of Tosya.

> Upon receiving orders, the gendarmes have set out to pursue action. When they run into women dressed in the *peçe* and *çarşaf* in the streets, markets, and bazaars, they take off those women's *çarşafs* right there, leaving them in their underpants. The women in the villages and the town who have seen or heard of this situation do not go out.[161]

It is true that this police report may involve a degree of exaggeration, but oral historical evidence also points to intervention at the local level to dissuade women from wearing the *peçe* and the *çarşaf*. Nuriye Güner, for example, remembered distinctly that there was a time in Trabzon when policemen would take away women's *peçe*s and *çarşaf*s in the streets.[162]

The fact that the government took Efe's letters seriously also suggests that there was some truth in his account. Governor Güleç repudiated Efe's claims as to the "innocence" of the central authorities, but those authorities themselves did not dispute Efe's arguments. This may have been a reflection of a lack of consensus on women's dress at the ministerial level. As discussed earlier, the issue of reforming women's dress was debated in the 1935 Congress of the RPP, but no resolutions were passed on it.[163] This lack of consensus may have led to leaders with different views on the issue giving conflicting orders. A more plausible scenario, in light of the other available evidence combined with İsmail Efe's claims, is that the party leadership was committed to reforming women's dress, but was divided or undecided as to how to carry it out. Therefore, the orders given to the governors, *kaymakam*s, and other local authorities did not specify the means of implementation. The orders to employ "administrative methods" would give the local authorities wide discretionary powers in implementation with no clear boundaries to their authority. İsmail Efe may well have been right in arguing that the local officials were exceeding their authority. However, the Ministry of the

Interior's response to Efe's letters seems to imply that for the leadership in Ankara achieving the desired results was a more important consideration than how those ends were achieved.

Not long after the governor's conversation with İsmail Efe, on 17 February, the director of Security Affairs asked the Presidency of the National Security Agency (*Millî Em. H. Reisliği*) to "secretly" investigate İsmail Efe.[164] The response from the latter described him as a "virtuous and patriotic man" who had provided great services to the country during the War of Liberation.[165] The letter advised that İsmail Efe's letters concerning the *çarşaf* should be attributed to his good intentions.

The correspondence between the two security offices indicates that Efe's service to the country during the War of Liberation, while not entirely legitimizing his position, gave him the right and the authority to speak up. It seems that the boundaries of a citizen's right to criticize the government could in part depend on the role he or she played during the War of Liberation. İsmail Efe wrote his letters on "Farmer İsmail Efe" ("ÇİFÇİ [sic] İSMAİL EFE") letterhead stationery. However, as his surname indicates, he was an *efe*, or *zeybek*.[166] The Aegean region had a long tradition of *efe* culture, with both the public perception and the reality of *efe* actions ranging from popular heroism to banditry.[167] During the War of Liberation many *efes* supported and fought for the nationalist army. In fact, prime minister Celal Bayar, whom İsmail Efe referred to as "our Celal Bey" had been given protection by *efe* bands in İzmir and Aydın following the Greek occupation of the region and early in the war. Even though it was not openly stated in the letters, it is clear from Celal Bayar's own memoirs that İsmail Efe's acquaintance with Bayar went back to the War of Liberation.[168] This was the generation which had personally experienced the war, and the impact of that experience in the emergence of the Turkish state seems to have continued long after the war itself.

İsmail Efe's authority to speak up against local government action may have come in part from his social standing in the community as an *efe*. Even though no such titles were recognized by the new regime, and though the *efe* or *zeybek* culture was being relegated to the sphere of folklore, the social standing of individual *efes* was not to be eradicated overnight.[169]

On 21 October 1938 governor Güleç reported back to the Ministry of the Interior on the current state of İsmail Efe.[170] He reported that Efe was in

Gölcük, was not involved in any suspicious acts, and was being watched. In the absence of additional evidence, it seems that by that time, the İsmail Efe case was over.

When the municipality of Aydın passed a decision in August 1935, banning the *peçe, çarşaf, üstlük,* and *peştemal,*[171] Dokumacı (Weaver) Şevki of Buldan, a weaver of *peştemals,* evidently petitioned the provincial governor, arguing that the municipality had no legal authority to ban *peştemals,* a decision he feared would eliminate his craft. When the governor defended the legality of the ruling and advised Şevki to shift his production to *hamam peştemals,*[172] Dokumacı Şevki took his case directly to the top, sending a telegram to Mustafa Kemal.[173] In this telegram Şevki presented the ban not as a decision threatening his livelihood as a maker of *peştemals,* but as a matter of local authorities' violating rights: watchmen positioned in the streets to enforce the ban were trampling on individual rights by tearing off women's *peçes* and *çarşafs.* Interestingly, in this petition Dokumacı Şevki referred to *peçes* and *çarşafs,* and never mentioned *peştemals*—possibly because of the broad and overlapping definitions of these terms, but perhaps because he was primarily concerned with the gendarmes' interference with the women's *peçe* and *çarşaf.* Without further evidence, it is hard to tell with certainty to what degree Dokumacı Şevki's responses to the local decree were economically motivated and to what extent they reflected his moral and patriarchal concerns over the state's intrusion into what women wore. It would appear that Şevki's occupational and economic concerns were blended with moral and patriarchal anxieties and a resentment against the authoritarian methods of the application of these local decrees—as in the case of İsmail Efe.

Şevki's letter apparently resulted in a reply from Atatürk (which I did not see), which (according to the governor) Şevki was showing off around town as he tried to encourage others to join him against the ban. At the same time, Şevki's petition led to the Ministry of the Interior taking an interest in Şevki, with the fear of "reactionary intent" in Şevki's acts, and brought him under closer government scrutiny.[174] In responding to Minister Şükrü Kaya, the governor reassured the ministry that Dokumacı Şevki was mainly concerned with protecting his *peştemal* business and that the implementation of the local decision was progressing well.[175] In contrast to the case of İsmail Efe, in which everyone agreed that Efe was a respectable citizen who had contributed to the War of Liberation, in this instance the governor tried to diminish the credibility of Şevki's opinion by describing him as "half mad," a man with no social status, a man who had married a loose woman. In the end, as far as I can discern from the available documents, government officials carefully avoided giving an impression of compromise and Dokumacı Şevki's petitions failed to bring about any direct or visible change in the local decree on the *peçe, çarşaf,* and *peştemal.* But petitions from ordinary citizens had the effect of informing the central goverment of the local manifestations of dress regulations, resulting in frequent reminders to lower-level state authorities to avoid using police forces or any other excessive measures, even as they maintained a rhetoric of no compromise.

Provincial correspondence from Aydın about five years after Şevki's 1935 petitions suggests there had been some change, but not a complete transformation, in how the women of Aydın dressed. According to the new governor İ. Sabri Çıtak, a great majority ("90 percent") of the women in the province had discarded their *peçes, çarşafs,* and *peştemals.* Women still wore the *üstlük* shawls over their heads and shoulders, but their faces were uncovered. Village women wore these *üstlüks* only when they came to the town, but covered themselves less in their villages. (Village women's following different conventions in village and town was, of course, a very traditional social practice, as we saw with the men's attire as well.) Çıtak did not explain who (women from what social and economic groups) still wore the *çarşaf* and *peştemal* and why, but he asked provincial authorities under his jurisdiction to observe the following guidelines in pursuing the matter: no toleration for the *peçe* (for social and security reasons); an understanding that the *çarşaf* and *peştemal* cannot be considered modern dress that would allow Turkish women to participate in social life; and given that there was no legislation on women's dress, the focus should be on enlightening and persuading women through the People's Houses.[176]

Popular reactions such as İsmail Efe's and Dokumacı Şevki's letters did not lead to a fundamental change in government policies concerning unveiling, but they acted as constant reminders to the RPP regime of on-the-ground reverberations and the limitations of state policies. Even while government authorities carefully avoided giving an impression of compromise (which could be perceived as weakness) in responding to these letters and petitions, the RPP leadership constantly reminded provincial and local authorities to limit their efforts to propaganda (and to avoid the use of police forces). In that sense, petitions not only provided individual citizens with a traditional channel of (somewhat effective) communication with the government, but they also provided critical information and feedback to the government and contributed to a moderation of policies (or at least a moderation to the methods through which policies were implemented locally).

Conclusion

Regulations of women's dress in the early Republican decades was part of a broader process of making a modern nation and figuring out women's place in the new society. By the 1920s, unveiling and the adoption of European style clothes by urban Ottoman women were already under way, accompanied by important changes in family life, women's public visibility, and the norms of male-female interaction. In women's dress, as with the men's hats and with attitudes toward literacy, reading, and education, unveiling was not an innovation of the Republican period, but rather it was a modernist authoritarian state's measured acting on behalf of the modernist segments of the society, facilitating that process of change. Thus we see a considerable degree of convergence between the ideology and the policies of the regime and the social practices of segments of the population. Notably, in the 1920s and 1930s, unveiling took place not only in countries where the revolutionary or reformist states supported it (such as Iran, the Soviet Union, and Turkey), but also in colonized or recently decolonized Middle Eastern countries such as Syria and Egypt, where feminists called for unveiling and an end to gender segregation, and a growing number of Muslim women discarded the veil.

The information that emerges from the letters and petitions discussed here, such as the İsmail Efe and Dokumacı Şevki letters, official correspondence, and oral interviews, justifies a revision of the dominant view in the field that women's dress issues were not regulated by the Kemalist state. This chapter shows that there was not a fixed state policy on women's dress, but there were policies in the making. As in the previous chapter on the efforts to modernize and nationalize men's clothing, I question the assumption regarding the Republican state as a strong state and a unitary actor. I suggest that the multiple levels of the state, including the provincial and the local, be taken into consideration. It was through the regional and local agents of the state and the RPP that the citizens came into contact with the state.

As with men's reactions to the Hat Law, women's responses to the attempts to regulate dress were varied and depended on a variety of economic, social, class, cultural, educational, and generational factors. While a segment of urban women embraced and actively supported the new dress regulations, those who resented them avoided open resistance and conflict with the state. Women were the objects of dress regulations, but men and their (potential) reactions played a significant role in the formulation of and responses to such policies, especially as they affected women. Men raised their voices over women's dress in the name of tradition and honor, and women had to accommodate both the demands of an authoritarian state and the demands of a male-dominant culture simultaneously.

3

Language

A New Turkish Script for a New and Literate Turkish Nation

Language is an important aspect of both individual and collective identities. In Turkey, as in many other countries from the Soviet Union to Israel and Iran, it became a crucial site of the new state's nationalizing, secularizing, and modernizing policies. The language policies of the early Republican state ranged from the formation of the Linguistic Society, the invention of the Sun-Language Theory, and the purification of Turkish,[1] to the promotion of spoken Turkish as the national language,[2] the Surname Law,[3] and the renaming of places.[4] The majority of the existing literature on the language policies focuses on the ideological, institutional, or linguistic aspects of these reforms. A number of recent works, such as Aslan on the "'Citizen, Speak Turkish!' Campaigns" and Türköz on the acquisition of surnames, have begun to expand the scope of such studies to incorporate some of the societal aspects of these reforms as well as their implementation. This chapter examines the meaning and the implementation of the 1928 alphabet reform. It assumes that the alphabet reform, its implementation, and the reception of and responses to it should be seen in the broader context of the nationalist and modernist social and cultural transformations in which the Republican state and citizens were engulfed.

Scholars interested in the social, political, and cultural meaning of the alphabet change beyond its immediate linguistic consequences have generally viewed the alphabet reform either within a nationalist/ideological and disciplinary framework or a modernist developmentalist framework. Recent works such as Birol Caymaz and Emmanuel Szurek's article have provided a more theoretically grounded account of the alphabet reform as a political project aimed at establishing state authority through cultural domination, yet their analysis does not extend beyond the goals and the initial stages of the alphabet reform into the social life of the alphabet change as experienced by Turkish citizens in their everyday lives and in their encounters with the state authorities.[5] On the other hand, works such as Bilal Şimşir's *Türk Yazı Devrimi* have located the alphabet reform almost exclusively in the sphere of literacy and education, leaving aside the political and ideological nature of the alphabet change.

This chapter argues that the alphabet change should be understood both in the context of the early Republican state's nationalizing, secularizing language reforms, and in the context of its modernist, developmentalist goals, for which a literate society was a prerequisite. Through an exploration of archival evidence, published narratives, and oral interviews, it aims to discover how this political project of the Kemalist state initiated a process of cultural transformations whose terms were not entirely determined by the state, but shaped in part by the perceptions, decisions, and actions of Turkish citizens as well as the structural conditions of the times. This chapter strives to provide a more nuanced understanding of the social and cultural impact of the alphabet reform by paying attention to the everyday experiences of those who were targets of the reform. More broadly, it hopes to contribute to a better understanding of the social and cultural transformations of the early Republican era and of the consolidation of the Kemalist nation-state in that process.

The Alphabet Reform: A Brief Historical Overview

The alphabet reform debate emerged in the nineteenth century from within Ottoman intellectual and political debates about literacy and education. In the 1920s, alphabet reform increasingly became a part of the ideological project of Turkish nation building and a precursor to and facilitator of further language reforms. The new alphabet facilitated the standardization of Turkish grammar and spelling; it also eased the process of Turkish language purification (i.e., the purging of Arabic and Persian vocabulary and grammar from Turkish) and contributed to the vernacularization of Turkish. More broadly, it contributed to the building of a secular national language and culture.

The alphabet debates in Turkey go back to the Tanzimat period: Ottoman statesmen such as Ahmet Cevdet Paşa and Münif Paşa had raised the question of alphabet reform in the 1850s and 1860s.[6] The question revolved around the suitability of Arabic letters for Turkish and the difficulty of learning to read and write Turkish in Arabic letters. The Arabic alphabet, with only three vowels (a, u, i), does not have letters to express all of the vowel sounds of Turkish. Furthermore, it has a number of consonants that Turkish does not have and that were written in borrowed words only. All of this complicated both the reading and the writing of Ottoman Turkish.[7] The absence of punctuation marks in Arabic writing, the lack of standardized rules for the spelling of Turkish words, and the omission of short vowels led to additional difficulties and ambiguities. The early proposals for reform, such as the one by Azeri writer Mirza Fethali Ahundzâde, focused on bringing Arabic orthography and Turkish phonology into closer alignment by adding symbols to the alphabet to represent the Turkish vowels. The major argument for reform was that a modified writing system would help fight illiteracy, which was seen as a major barrier to progress. Of course, the problems of literacy were not simply a consequence of the difficulty or unsuitability of the Arabic script for Turkish, although scholars agree that the difficulty of a script can have an effect on the ease of learning to read and write. The scarcity of schools, cultural attitudes toward literacy and reading, methods of teaching literacy (memorization, particularly of the Qur'an), the content of reading materials (including the late introduction of Turkish language texts in the school system), and the gap between spoken and written Turkish all contributed to the literacy problem.[8] Nevertheless, the expansion of literacy was a genuine goal of the proponents of alphabet reform. A related argument for reform had to do with the unsuitability of the existing alphabet for printing presses, necessitating, as can be seen in Figure 13, more than 400 pieces of type (including various forms of all the letters and several letter combinations). A more functional and simpler alphabet would make printing more convenient and less expensive, thus contributing to increased literacy and readership.

By the 1870s the debates shifted from reforming the existing alphabet to adopting a Latin-based alphabet. By this time, Ottoman Albanian intellectuals were in the process of making Latin the shared alphabet for all Albanians.[9] The Muslim authorities in the Ottoman Empire refused to approve the

13. A Turkish type case using modified Arabic characters. *Histoire de la Republique Turque*, Redige par la Societe pour l'etude de l'histoire Turque (İstanbul: Devlet Basımevi, 1935), 255.

adoption of Latin letters by Muslim Albanian subjects on religious grounds, but the development of an Albanian language written in Latin characters continued hand-in-hand with the development of Albanian nationalism. Young Ottomans such as the poet and writer Namık Kemal tended to oppose the adoption of Latin letters due to the potential political consequences of such a move. Namık Kemal assigned the Arabic alphabet an important ideological function in maintaining the integrity of the Empire. He argued that it would be possible to teach Turkish to the non-Turkish Muslim elements of the Empire as long as it was in Arabic letters. As a result of this policy, he hoped, languages such as Lazuri and Albanian would be forgotten. He also believed that if the Latin alphabet were to be adopted, these languages too would develop separately as written languages, which could help light the fire of nationalism among these groups. Namık Kemal's other major concern was that the adoption of the Latin alphabet would separate the Ottoman Empire from the rest of the Islamic world and from its Islamic cultural heritage.[10]

The alphabet debate continued in the Young Turk period (1908–1918). The proponents of Westernizing reforms argued for the adoption of the Latin alphabet. The Association for the Reform of the Alphabet proposed a reform project, and the army experimented with a modified Arabic alphabet. In this period, Turkish nationalists such as Ziya Gökalp opposed the adoption of

Latin letters, arguing that abandoning Arabic letters would weaken the ties between Ottoman Turks and Arabs and other Muslims. Moreover, at this time Turks in Russia also used the Arabic alphabet: hence, the Arabic script could be useful in hiding differences among the different dialects of Turkish and in unifying them. However, with the adoption of the Latin alphabet by Azerbaijan in 1922, and with the decision of the First Turcology Congress in Baku in 1926 on the adoption of the Latin letters by all Turkish speakers in the Soviet Union, the pan-Turkist nationalist view shifted towards the adoption of Latin letters.[11] Dr. Kuhne, one of several foreign experts who were invited to Turkey in the 1920s for recommendations on reforming the education system, also recommended the abolition of the Ottoman alphabet and the adoption of a Latin alphabet to facilitate education and Westernization. Kuhne wrote:

> We are aware that it takes longer to read and write in Turkey. This is not only a problem of the alphabet, but it is a cultural and Westernization problem as well. If the Turks accept a transcription system similar to that of Hungarian and Finnish, languages which are related to Turkish, it will serve to bring them closer to Western civilization.[12]

Such a recommendation alone would not have been a determining factor, yet it must have re-affirmed and bolstered the opinion of Mustafa Kemal and the others who favored the adoption of a Latin-based alphabet.

Mustafa Kemal personally led the propaganda campaign for the new alphabet in the months leading up to the passage of the Alphabet Law by the Parliament on 1 November 1928.[13] On 9 August 1928 he made the first public announcement of the decision to adopt a new Turkish alphabet, in a speech he gave in Gülhane, the historical site where Mustafa Reşit Paşa had read the famous Tanzimat Fermanı in 1839. In the following days he participated in the debates among intellectuals, journalists, and politicians on the new alphabet. He attended the alphabet meetings in Dolmabahçe Palace that brought together the Alphabet Commission and some of the leading writers, poets, journalists, professors, and members of Parliament, including some who had objections to the reform. These meetings provided a forum for the teaching of and the debate on the new alphabet, and for building a consensus in its favor. The Dolmabahçe congresses served a similar function to the Sivas and Erzurum congresses at the beginning of the War of Liberation that had legitimized and provided support for the war effort led by Mustafa Kemal. On 29 August the congress in Dolmabahçe unanimously agreed that "in order to save the nation from illiteracy and ignorance[14] there is no solution other than to abandon the Arab letters that do not suit her language and to adopt Turkish letters taken from the Latin alphabet."[15] The assembly further agreed that "the alphabet proposed by the Commission [is] truly the Turkish alphabet and [is] definite. It [is] sufficient to meet all the needs of the Turkish nation."[16]

While thus working to build a consensus among the educated elites in İstanbul, Atatürk embarked on a tour in Anatolia in August and September to promote the new alphabet. In every town he visited he stood by a blackboard in the role of head teacher, demonstrating the new letters to the gathered crowd and testing administrators, teachers, and civil servants on the new alphabet. In acts approaching theatrical performances, he would ask the crowd "Have you learned the new Turkish letters?" Among the cries of "we have" and "we are" he would pick someone from the crowd—a butcher, a drayman, or a *hoca*—and ask him to write or read something on the board or teach him a few letters to demonstrate how easy they were to learn. He would encourage the crowd to learn the new letters and then to teach them to others. Mustafa Kemal clearly employed his personal charisma as the liberator of the nation in the service of the postindependence modernist, nationalist drive. This connection between Mustafa Kemal's use of his charismatic leadership and the nationalist reform program became most obvious in the alphabet reform. Mustafa Kemal characterized the alphabet reform as a war on ignorance, and predicted that the victory would be greater than previous victories won on the battlefields. The first leg of his alphabet tour included Tekirdağ, Bursa, Çanakkale, Maydos (Eceabat), and Gelibolu. Then he visited Sinop, Samsun, Amasya, Tokat, Sivas, and Kayseri, ending in Ankara.

Several of the towns he visited during the alphabet campaign had been the sites of critical moments in the recent history of the nation and occupied an important place in Mustafa Kemal's personal memory as well as the collective memory of the nation. Gelibolu (Gallipoli) represented a major victory, while Samsun, Amasya, and Sivas represented key moments in beginning the War of Liberation. Hence visiting these sites highlighted the similarities

14. The Atatürk Memorial, Kadıköy, on the Asian shore of İstanbul across from Gülhane. Modeled after a very well-known photograph from Mustafa Kemal's 1928 tour of Anatolia, this 1989 memorial by Haluk Tezonar commemorates Mustafa Kemal's teaching of the new letters to the Turkish nation. Photograph by Mustafa Yılmaz.

between the war on illiteracy and the War of Liberation, and gave Mustafa Kemal further legitimacy as the liberator of the nation.

Following this period of intense preparation in the summer and fall of 1928, the Parliament passed the Alphabet Law on 1 November 1928.[17] It declared the adoption of a new Turkish alphabet based on the Latin alphabet to replace the Arabic letters. After 1 December 1928, all newspapers, magazines, advertisements, film subtitles, and other signs had to be in the new letters. All government offices, banks, and other social and political associations and other institutions were required to use the new Turkish letters in all their transactions as of the first day of 1929. The public was allowed to use the old letters in their transactions with these institutions until the first day of June, 1929. All Turkish books had to be published using the new letters after the first day of 1929. The law asked all Turkish schools to begin educating students in the new Turkish letters immediately, and it explicitly forbade the use of textbooks in the old letters. The law set June 1930 as the absolute deadline for all public and private transactions, including all printed matter, such as laws and circulars, to be set in the new letters.

"Saving the Nation from Illiteracy and Ignorance"

Teaching and Learning the New Letters

The process of teaching and learning the new letters involved multiple channels, including the army, the education system, the Nation's Schools (Millet Mektepleri, a nationwide new alphabet and adult literacy program), and the press, as well as large-scale participation by members of the public as teachers and students. The success of state initiatives such as Millet Mektepleri depended on the voluntary participation of citizens. State propaganda focused on the benefits of literacy in the new letters in an attempt to persuade citizens to participate in the process.

Although the majority of the population did not have the means to do so, some were able to use their own financial or family resources to learn the new alphabet. As we saw in Chapter Two, Meliha (Peker) Tanyeli was born in the provincial center of Trabzon in 1921 to a comfortable urban family. Meliha Hanım and her siblings grew up and went to school in Trabzon. In our conversation, she recalled how everyone in her family learned the new alphabet quickly. Meliha Hanım and her sisters learned the new letters at school. She had already attended two years of preschool and the first year of elementary school by the fall of 1928. She had learned the Ottoman script, but had not had much time or experience reading and writing in Ottoman by the time she learned the new alphabet in her second year of grade school. Her father and mother, Ali Salim and Belkıs Peker, both of whom were literate in Ottoman, learned the new letters by taking alphabet lessons at home from Lütfi Bey, a teacher at Cudibey Elementary School in Trabzon.[18] Not only did the family have the financial means for private alphabet lessons, but their perception of themselves as a modern family demanded the skills of literacy and the practice of reading.

Mualla Eyuboğlu Anhegger also learned the new aphabet in Trabzon. Born in 1919, she was already in the third year of elementary school at the time of the alphabet reform. Her father Rahmi Eyuboğlu was a member of Parliament at the time. He was a graduate of the Mülkiye, the Civil Service School in İstanbul, and was fluent in French. He had served as a *mutasarrıf*[19] in a number of Anatolian towns during the War of Liberation, including Aegean towns in the war zone such as Afyon and Kütahya. Mualla Eyuboğlu Anhegger recalled her father as an ardent Kemalist,[20] and remembered that at the time of the alphabet reform her father brought home a blackboard on which he taught his children the new letters. She noted that her mother Lütfiye Hanım joined her children in these lessons and learned to read the new Turkish alphabet, even though she could not write it.[21] It appears that Rahmi Eyuboğlu fulfilled his task of promoting the new alphabet as a parliamentarian by teaching his immediate family, but it is not clear if his role as a teacher for the new Turkish alphabet extended beyond his wife and children to relatives, servants, or the residents of Trabzon.

Millet Mektepleri: The Nation's Schools

The majority of the population did not have the means to learn the new letters on their own. Given the high levels of illiteracy of the majority of the citizens, learning the new alphabet in fact meant learning to read and write for the first time. According to the 1927 census, only 8.16 percent of Turkey's total population of more than 13,600,000 were literate, including 12.99 percent of men and 3.67 percent of women.[22] While the regular school system had the task of teaching children the new alphabet, the government initiated a comprehensive education project for adult citizens, aimed at teaching them the new letters while simultaneously expanding literacy. Millet Mektepleri, or the Nation's Schools, became the symbols and the engines of the "mass mobilization for literacy" as well as functioning to speed the transition from Ottoman to the new Turkish letters among the public.[23] The overall literacy rate of the school age population of Turkey improved to 20.4 percent by 1935 (31 percent male, 10.5 percent female) and to 30.2 percent by 1945 (43.7 percent male and 16.8 percent female).[24]

The Nation's Schools were founded by a Council of Ministers decision on the Nation's Schools Regulation (*Millet Mektepleri Talimatnamesi*, hereafter Regulation) on 11 November 1928, only ten days after the Parliament passed the Alphabet Law, and the first schools opened on the first day of January, 1929.[25] The purpose of these schools, as stated in the Regulation, was to extend literacy to the masses quickly. Every Turkish citizen, male and female, was to be considered a member of the Nation's Schools, with Mustafa Kemal the head teacher. The Regulation called for the mandatory attendance in the Nation's Schools of all male and female citizens between the ages of sixteen and forty who could not read and write the new letters. There would be two types of schools: four-month schools for adult citizens who had never learned to read and write before, and two-month schools to teach the new letters to those who were literate in Ottoman. Citizens who claimed to have learned the new letters could be exempted from these classes by passing a literacy test.

The Millet Mektepleri were put under the general direction of the Ministry of Education, and the structure of these schools followed the hierarchy of the civilian administrative divisions. The Regulation called for the creation of Education Committees in all administrative units from provinces to villages. Administrations and elected officials, such as governors, *kaymakam*s, public prosecutors, health directors, heads of the gendarmerie, education directors, mayors, representatives from the provincial and district parliaments, and local heads of the RPP would participate in the literacy campaign through these committees. The Education Committees would have the authority as well as the responsibility for the organization and running of the literacy classes at the local level. The responsibilities of the committees included tasks such as determining the schedule of classes, finding classrooms, providing the necessary equipment, paying instructors' salaries, and ensuring regular attendance of the citizens registered in the courses. In addition to regular school buildings, a host of other public and private places such as mosques, government offices, coffeehouses, and clubs could be utilized as classrooms. The Regulation called on the Committees to mobilize the help of the police, the gendarmerie, employees of the municipalities, neighborhood heads (*muhtarlar*), and tradesmen's associations to regulate attendance in the courses. The main task of the actual teaching in the Nation's Schools mostly fell upon elementary school teachers. Secondary school teachers could be called upon when necessary. The Regulation authorized the Committees to gather the help of other intellectuals to teach in the second category classes (for those who could read and write Ottoman), but only in cases where the number of teachers in a district did not meet the demand for Nation's Schools teachers.

As a comprehensive educational project with the goal of including all citizens, the Regulation instituted a category of traveling teachers to reach remote villages that did not have a school. In a similar vein, prison directors were required to open literacy classes for prisoners (with a term of six months or longer) in coordination with Nation's Schools committees. The Regulation also assigned responsibility in teaching the new letters to public and private employers, such as farms, factories, municipalities, banks, ports and railroads, and other state-owned enterprises. The Regulation obliged all state employees to learn the new letters by attending the Nation's Schools by June 1929.

The effectiveness of the Nation's Schools depended on the participation by and cooperation of large segments of the society in the process: teachers, common citizens (as voluntary students),[26] the press, Education Committees, the Ministry of Education, and various other public and private agencies and individuals. The RPP propaganda campaign for the Nation's Schools focused on the need to combat illiteracy for the whole nation, and emphasized how easy it was to learn the new alphabet. The RPP poster below (Figure 15) highlighted the simplicity and ease of the new letters in contrast to the old letters, by illustrating how a single letter in the new alphabet represents several letters and their different forms in the old alphabet. The poster reads "The old writing was very difficult. The new writing made reading and writing easier. Everybody is learning to read." Frequent images of men and women reading in RPP propaganda materials, like the peasant couple reading the paper *Hakimiyet-i Milliye* in this poster, symbolized an invitation to all citizens, male and female, and from all backgrounds, to learn the new letters.

Halk, a weekly magazine published by the Ministry of Education shortly after the opening of the Nations' Schools, promoted the literacy campaign, and especially women's participation in it, not only through editorials and news, but also through frequent images of women reading, women learning to read, or women working using their reading and writing skills. These were images of ordinary women as mothers or as working women. Such images included an urban woman reading *Halk* while waiting for the ferry; a group

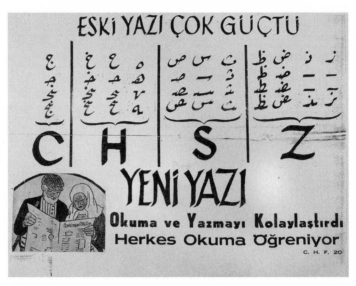

ESKİ YAZI ÇOK GÜÇTÜ

YENİ YAZI

Okuma ve Yazmayı Kolaylaştırdı
Herkes Okuma Öğreniyor

15. "Everyone Is Learning to Read." Başbakanlık Cumhuriyet Arşivi 030.10.198.352.13.

of women walking cheerfully to their Millet Mektebi class with books in hand despite the cold and the snow; female students in a literacy class, female secretaries working as productive citizens thanks to their ability to read, write and type; and, on the cover page of the very first issue of *Halk*, a mother learning to read while holding her small child in one arm, as seen in Figure 16.[27]

While government propaganda underscored the inclusive nature of a literacy campaign that embraced women and the rural population, both statistical and oral historical evidence reveal a more complicated picture of the reception and implementation of the Millet Mektepleri program. One of my informants, the late Mehmet Baltacı, recalled learning the new alphabet in a Millet Mektebi course.[28] Born in 1910 in a remote village in the Black Sea province of Kastamonu, Baltacı had had access to some schooling in Hanönü, a nearby village, before the Republic and before the Alphabet Law. He remembered that at the time of the alphabet reform a class was opened in the village mosque. A teacher was brought in "from outside." There may not have been anyone literate in the new alphabet in that region in the early phases of the reform. Baltacı's teacher at the school had been "Kürt İmam," not a graduate of one of the teacher training schools who may have been familiar with the Latin alphabet,

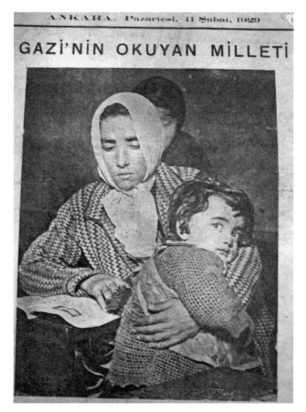

ANKARA. Pazartesi, 11 Şubat, 1929

GAZİ'NİN OKUYAN MİLLETİ

16. "The Gazi's Reading Nation." *Halk*, 11 February 1929.

but a mosque imam. The teacher for the alphabet class was probably sent by the Ministry of Education office in the province. Baltacı remembered attending the alphabet class with others old and young, and both literate and illiterate in the old letters.[29] Baltacı was not a privileged child; after his father's death at Gallipoli, he was raised by his mother under the difficult circumstances of the war years. It appears that this class may have been open to different groups as dictated by the Alphabet Law and the Regulations on the Nation's Schools, with one major exception. Asked specifically about women's participation in the alphabet school, Baltacı told me that women did not attend these classes: "In those days there were no women [in public], they could not even go outside."[30] Clearly the alphabet class in Hanönü was in no way sufficient in a region where the vast majority of the population had had no schooling, and the majority of both men and women remained illiterate for years to come. Women, however, were denied access to the class. Apparently the gender equality prescribed in the law did not always apply in practice. Government statistics also reveal the existence of significant urban/rural and gender differences in the accessibility and the success of the Millet Mektepleri despite the intention of the state to create a fully literate society. In the first five years of the Millet Mektepleri, between 1928–29 and 1933–34, 54,050 schools were opened. About 34.4 percent of them (18,589 schools) were in the cities and 65.6 of them (34.461 schools) in the villages.[31] In those first five years—a period by the end of which Turkey's population exceeded 15 million—of the 2.3 million adults who attended a literacy class, about 1.25 million graduated successfully. In the rural areas, only 35 percent of the female students successfully completed a literacy course, as opposed to 51 percent of their male counterparts.[32]

The main function of the Nation's Schools, and a primary goal of the alphabet reform, was to create a fully literate society, but it was hoped they would also indirectly contribute towards the larger goal of creation of a national culture. In addition to teaching reading and writing Turkish in the new alphabet, Millet Mektebi classes would teach participants about subjects such as history, geography, and citizenship. Moreover, increased literacy in the new alphabet, which was based on the İstanbul dialect, would work towards elimination of regional dialects and toward standardization and building of a shared colloquial Turkish. Millet Mektebi classes could also help toward the dissemination of Turkish as a spoken language among communities that did not speak Turkish. Through the expansion of the regular school system, especially of elementary schools and boarding schools, greater numbers of school-age citizens would go through a nationalist education program, a process that would for some students entail learning the national language. By the early 1930s the ability and willingness to speak Turkish become a key requirement of full acceptance as a member of the Turkish nation. This emphasis on learning and speaking Turkish in defining the boundaries of the nation found expression in speeches by the leading statesmen, in intellectual and political debates, and in the streets, through "Citizen, Speak Turkish!" ("*Vatandaş Türkçe Konuş*") campaigns.[33]

M. Şakir Ülkütaşır relates the memoirs of an elementary school teacher, M. Adil Özer, who witnessed such a case in a village in North East Anatolia on the Turkish-Soviet border.[34] The village where Özer taught a year after the alphabet reform was a community of "Acara"[35] speakers. Özer recalled teaching reading and writing to his first graders, who spoke very little Turkish. He also recalled that village women, who knew very little Turkish, learned the new letters in a matter of a few months in a Millet Mektebi taught by a traveling teacher (*seyyar muallim*). In this instance we do not know how many or what percent of the women in this village attended the class, but it is significant that women in a remote village who did not speak Turkish were learning the new Turkish alphabet. Özer's account focuses on the role of the new alphabet in facilitating literacy and the importance of the Nation's Schools and the teachers in expanding it, yet it also shows that the issues of learning to read and write and learning the national language were interrelated matters. Government officials in the provinces were well aware of the connections between literacy, language, and national identity. Soner Çağaptay mentions a 1939 communication from the governor of Hakkari, a province in the South East dominated by Kurdish speakers, to the Ministry of Interior, reporting that men and women in the province had registered for The Nation's Schools and were being taught the Turkish language and the Turkish letters.[36]

In the long run, the Millet Mektepleri program only had limited success in its goals of producing a fully literate, Turkish speaking citizenry with a strong Turkish nationalist feeling. As previous scholarship has correctly pointed out, economic reasons were crucial in limiting the reach of the Millet Mektepleri program. The Millet Mektepleri initiative coincided with the onset of the Global Depression. As the RPP government was struggling with financing the regular education system and paying teacher's salaries, from the beginning the financing of the Nation's Schools was left to the provinces. Not every province had the same level of financial resources, nor were they equally committed to this literacy program. This led to very uneven levels of financing and uneven results in different provinces.

Newspapers

For newspaper readers, seeing Latin letters in Turkish newspapers was not entirely new in 1928. İstanbul newspapers and magazines had used Latin characters in a limited way since the late nineteenth century. For example, newspaper advertisements of imported or upscale goods were often in two or three different languages and different alphabets. Companies advertising their products in newspapers and magazines used languages and scripts in addition to the Ottoman to increase the appeal of their goods. Sometimes picture captions in magazines appeared in Latin letters. Another instance of use of the Latin characters was with the rendering of foreign words: sometimes Western language, especially French, words appeared in the original orthography in late nineteenth century Ottoman books and magazines, in much the same way as classical Greek quotations appeared in the original in books in English in the nineteenth century. Proper names in particular were rarely transliterated into Ottoman script. By the early twentieth century newspapers such as *Sabah* and *İkdam* printed their masthead in both Ottoman and French.

At the time of the alphabet reform, newspapers contributed to the transition to the new script in a number of ways. For literate citizens with a habit of reading newspapers, the change to Latin letters in Turkish newspapers meant they had to learn the new alphabet in order to be able to continue reading the news. The shift to the Latin alphabet in newspapers and in other writing, such as books and magazines published in Turkey after 1928, street names, signs, and subtitles in foreign films, meant that people had to learn to read the new letters in order for their literacy to be meaningful and functional. Learning to read the new alphabet acquired significance beyond simply following a law: it was crucial to maintaining one's cultural contact in the national context through reading, which also facilitated the imagination of a Turkish nation.[37]

Newspapers also contributed to the transition by directly promoting the new letters in their pages. While a number of leading journalists, such as Celal Nuri (İleri) in *İkdam*, Hüseyin Cahit (Yalçın) in *Tanin*, Yunus Nadi (Abalıoğlu) in *Cumhuriyet*, and Falih Rıfkı (Atay) in *Hakimiyet-i Milliye*, enthusiastically advocated the adoption of the Latin alphabet, there was no consensus in the press on the alphabet question in the years *preceding* the alphabet reform. Journalists such as Halit Ziya and Ali Canip had opposed the adoption of the Latin letters, with the concern that it would lead to a break with the Ottoman past and Ottoman and Islamic cultural heritage, resulting in a cultural crisis. A main function of the "alphabet conferences" led by the language commission in İstanbul in August of 1928 was to build a consensus among Turkish statesmen, politicians, and intellectuals, including journalists, in support of the new alphabet. Several journalists who had opposed the adoption of the Latin alphabet were present on the last day of the Dolmabahçe conferences on August 29, when the congress unanimously accepted the new alphabet proposed by the Alphabet Commission.[38] In the following days İstanbul and İzmir newspapers began a transitional phase toward printing in the new letters. *Cumhuriyet*, for example, began publishing short pieces in Latin characters in big print on its front page. *Cumhuriyet* printed its masthead, date, and editorials in both Ottoman and Latin scripts. *Cumhuriyet* also contributed to the transition more directly by publishing alphabet lessons, introducing the new letters and providing explanations in Ottoman for reading and writing the new letters. The short readings in Latin characters accompanying the letters also served to promote different aspects of the new regime.[39]

Despite their efforts to accustom their readers to the new letters, when newspapers began printing completely in the new letters following the

A	B	C	Ç	D	E	F	'					
G	Ğ	H	İ	I	J	K						
L	M	N	O	P	R	S						
Ş	T	U	V	Y	Z							
Â	E	Î	Ô	Û	Ö	Ü						
Ş	/	*	?	!						0	9	8
« »	( )	[ ]	:	;	1	1	2	3	4	5	6	7

j	f	—	-	'		ö		ü		â		
ç	b	c	d	e	s	g	ş	ğ	h	î	û	
										3 Punto		
z	l	m	n	i	o	p	k	1 Punto	2 Punto			
								1,5 Punto	4 Punto			
y	v	u	t	6 Punto	a	r	.	,	Katrat			

17. The new type case after the Alphabet Law, "simple and uncomplicated." *Histoire de la Republique Turque*, Redige par la Societe pour l'etude de l'histoire Turque (İstanbul: Devlet Basımevi, 1935), 254. Compare to Figure 13.

passage of the law, readership dropped sharply. While some smaller newspapers and magazines did not survive the ensuing financial crisis,[40] the major papers survived, in part thanks to government subsidies.[41] In the long run, the press would benefit from both the expansion of a literate public and the efficiency of the Latin letters in printing (see Figure 17), important factors in persuading journalists to agree to the adoption of the new letters.

"The Army Is a People's School"

The army was one of the key institutions supporting the modernizing mission of the Kemalist state. The task of the army went beyond the protection of the country and extended to the education and disciplining of male citizens in line with the requirements of the new state.[42] As the RPP poster in Figure 18 declared, "The Army is a people's school."[43] The poster depicted the army as a place where young men would learn to read and write, would increase their love for the motherland, and would become healthy and disciplined soldiers. It also contrasted the old army with the new: in the old days of the Empire, men went to the army young and became old by the time they finished their service. Now men would go to the army young and inexperienced and return as mature, healthy, and modernized gentlemen.

The army was a high priority (second after the administrative bureaucracy) in İsmet İnönü's program of action for transition to the new alphabet.[44] İnönü assigned to the Ministry of Education the task of training officer-teachers who were then to teach the new alphabet in the army. During his visit to Tekirdağı (then Tekfurdağı) on 23 August 1928 as part of his alphabet campaign, Mustafa Kemal made a personal appeal to the officers asking them to actively participate in the teaching of the new letters:

> Dictated to the Brigade Commander of the Officers Barracks: Today I am very pleased to have visited my brother officers in Tekirdağı. Please convey my happiness to those not present. I especially request from them that they speedily teach the new Turkish letters to all their friends and associates.[45]

The army as an institution directly contributed to the dissemination of the new alphabet among the male population by offering literacy classes for

18. "The Army Is a People's School." This poster has been reproduced from an original deposited at BCA 030.10.198.352.13.

conscripts during their mandatory military service.[46] As Uygur Kocabaşoğlu has noted, while these classes had a positive impact on expanding literacy, their long-term effect on an individual soldier's maintaining his literacy depended on whether that person continued to be in contact with the written word after his military service.[47] Kocabaşoğlu suggested that a person who ceased to come into contact with books and newspapers after his military service could easily lose his literacy after a period of time. Personal narratives from my informants support Kocabaşoğlu's view that it was extremely difficult to maintain one's ability to read and write in the absence of mechanisms to reinforce literacy. My own grandfather, Mustafa Bayındırlı, for example, who had no access to schools during his youth in his remote Black Sea village, learned to read and write during his military service in the Kütahya and Denizli provinces in the early 1950s. With essentially no access to books, newspapers, or any other printed materials in his village to reinforce his literacy, and with limited contact with the city or with the government that would have necessitated literacy, over time he lost his ability to read and write.[48]

By 1935 the state also experimented with using the army to train teachers for a literacy campaign in rural areas, a program designed by Ismail Hakkı Tonguç, General Director for Elementary Education and one of the most committed educational reformers of the early Republic. In this program, young men who learned to read and write in the army were sent back to their villages as educators (*eğitmen*) after completing a six-month course.[49] This campaign, although limited in its impact, also shows the Republican state's attempt at mobilizing all segments of the society as agents of state-initiated developmental projects.

The promotion and the teaching of the new alphabet and the creation of a cultural and physical environment dominated by the new letters were at the core of the implementation of the alphabet reform. Another important dimension of this reform was the prevention of any acts of direct or indirect opposition to the new alphabet. There had been intense debates among the intellectuals and in the press between those who promoted the adoption of the Latin alphabet and those who opposed it. The passing of the Alphabet Law effectively ended such debates in the press. However, after the passing of the Law, the most vocal opposition came not from within Turkey, but from within the Turkish minority communities outside Turkey, especially in the Balkans. Opponents of the new Turkish alphabet in Bulgaria defended their position in the press and attempted to prevent the spread of the new letters among the Turkish community there, especially through the education system. Initially those opposed to the Latin-based alphabet, with the head *müfti* of Bulgaria at the fore, appeared to be winning the fight against it. By 1930, however, the proponents of the new alphabet, led by the Teachers' Union in Bulgaria and with the support of the Turkish state, persuaded the Bulgarian government to make the new Turkish letters mandatory for all Turkish schools and to ban those schools using Arabic letters.[50] This was a crucial point in maintaining cultural contact between Turkey and the Turkish minority in Bulgaria in the long term. Alphabet debates continued among the Turkish communities in the Soviet Union and China, but Turkey's ability to interfere in these cases was much more limited than in Bulgaria.

In explaining the enormous success the alphabet reform has achieved and the absence of any significant resistance to it, historian François Georgeon has also stressed the close link between the alphabet reform and literacy.[51] After citing the two commonly provided reasons for the lack of mass resistance to alphabet reform, namely, the repressive political environment of the times and fear of the Kemalist state, and secondly, the indifference of the majority of the population, Georgeon locates the alphabet reform in the larger cultural context of transition to mass literacy in the late Ottoman Empire and post-Ottoman Turkey. He makes a powerful argument that a process of cultural change concerning literacy (a change in cultural attitudes in the sense of the "civilizing process" as theorized by the sociologist Norbert Elias) was already underway in the late Ottoman period.[52] A long process of transformation to mass literacy had already taken off as a result of a multiplicity of factors that obtained in the nineteenth century, factors such as the post-Tanzimat expansion of the state education system, the expansion of other educational institutions such as missionary schools, "emulation" among the different communities (especially Muslims, both intellectuals and also ordinary people, who increasingly saw the high rates of Muslim illiteracy as a cause for their relative backwardness compared with the non-Muslim communities of the Empire), and the expansion of the written word (the printed word becoming more pervasive in the state's business or in the physical environment). Georgeon also notes the important category of those that fell in between the worlds of the literate and the illiterate: people who participated in the world of literacy in a limited way through practices such as the use of scribes (*arzuhalci*) and through collective reading in places such as cafés and coffee (or reading) houses. He estimates that around the end of the Empire the literacy rate of the Ottoman population was about 10–15 percent, up from about 1 percent in 1800. He stresses that by 1914, literacy was still rare, but it was no longer a privilege monopolized by a small minority consisting of intellectuals, state officials, and clergy. The end of Empire marked the beginning of a long period of transition from "restricted" literacy to mass literacy, with the Ottoman population, not only non-Muslim minorities, but more diverse sections of society, demanding literacy. One of Georgeon's key propositions is that the alphabet reform and its reception and implementation should be understood in this context of changing attitudes toward literacy. From this point of view, then, the alphabet reform is identified as a site where the demands of the population for learning to read and write converged with the interests of a modernist state. Alphabet change becomes, at least in part, the state's response to the growing desire and demand from the society for literacy, or at least an act by the state which is in line with the social needs and demands, rather than being a top-down reform instituted by the state despite the wishes of the population.

It is evident from personal recollections of learning to read and write the new alphabet, such as the narratives of the Peker and Eyüboğlu families that I related earlier, that there was indeed a positive cultural attitude toward literacy, at least among the urban population. Several of my informants told the story of their families (children and both parents) learning the new letters in a very matter-of-fact way. These narratives suggest that literacy and education were becoming a normal or expected way of life, at least for segments of urban society. It is difficult though, to generalize for the entire country. As we know, (and as Georgeon discusses in some detail) there were tremendous gaps in literacy rates between urban and rural populations, between the different regions (most notably along the east-west axis) and between genders. The literacy rate in many of the Eastern Anatolian provinces did not pass 4 percent in 1927, and was at 1.3 percent in Van, almost as low as the overall literacy rate of the Ottoman Empire in 1800.[53]

It is reasonable to expect that a literacy campaign would have found widespread support in a country with a very high level of illiteracy and recovering from a decade of wars with significant numbers of refugees, immigrants, veterans, and orphans. Compared with the new clothing regulations (the hat, for example, required making a personal change from the fez, turban, or other headgear to which one had been accustomed), moving from illiteracy to learning the new Turkish alphabet did not involve sacrificing a personal habit or practice that was part of one's identity. Becoming literate implied only a gain, rather than giving up something that was positively identified with one's identity. Furthermore, while the benefits of the European hat or the *manto* (women's overcoat) were not always obvious or immediate, literacy could be expected to bring material benefits under some circumstances. As Benjamin Fortna has explored in his insightful work on learning to read in the late Ottoman Empire and the early Republic, reading is an activity with enormous economic and potentially counterhegemonic political consequences. In his analysis of children's literature, including books, textbooks, and magazines, Fortna observed that the Republican state, like its late Ottoman counterpart, strove to use reading for the cultivation of loyal, economically productive, and civilized citizens. Such an observation is in line with the scholarly consensus on the education goals of the late Ottoman and early Republican regimes. Departing from the traditional state-centric approach (including his own earlier work on education), Fortna draws our attention to the market and commercial aspects of publishing and argues that the state was not able to fully control the messages children received through reading. Private publishers had their own commercial interests and priorities, which did not always match with the ideological goals of the state. This created a counterhegemonic potential, or the possibility of challenging the state's secular-nationalist, ideological project of reading/literacy.[54] Similarly, higher rates of literacy, combined with the expansion of the press, and especially with the proliferation of the provincial newspapers in the 1940s and 1950s, allowed for the inclusion of a broader base of authors and readers in debates of national importance. Gavin Brockett argues in his recent work that Turkish nationalist identity transformed and crystallized in a process in which those press debates played a key role.[55]

The consequences of failure to conform to the law were also different in the different areas of reform. A recent study in Kırşehir province in central Anatolia has found that 73 percent of those included in the survey had been in favor of the alphabet reform at the time of its enactment. Fourteen percent said they had not had an opinion, while 11 percent said they had been against it.[56] The study also noted the higher rates of "no opinion" among illiterate respondents. Despite the state's intention to make all citizens literate, geographical remoteness and other factors meant that significant segments of the population remained both beyond the reach of the alphabet mobilization and beyond the overall alphabet debate. For many of these people, the questions of approval of or resistance to the new alphabet were irrelevant.

Using the New Alphabet—Persistence of the Old Alphabet

In Kayıseri, Sivas, Şebin Karahisar, and the other district centers I visited, the civil servants have familiarized themselves with the [new] Turkish letters. Official correspondence is in Turkish letters. But it appears that it is not widely used among the people. Aside from the fact that the results of the

Nation's Schools are quite weak, those who can read and write lack the practice or are about to forget the new letters. All transactions amongst the most enlightened of the people are in Arabic letters. I also found reading and spelling in Turkish in high and middle schools to be very poor. I know that proficiency and skill will not be gained in a short period of time and that a long time is needed for it to become general among the people. However, I sensed that the impact and the power of the first attack have weakened. . . . [57]

In addition to expressing his concerns over the current quality and the future of teaching the new alphabet, Minister of the Interior Şükrü Kaya's June 1929 letter to Prime Minister İsmet İnönü highlights a critical dimension of the alphabet reform that went beyond simply learning the new alphabet, namely, that learning the new letters did not automatically entail using them. While those who had been illiterate prior to the alphabet classes faced the danger of forgetting and falling back to illiteracy, those who had been literate could continue to use the Arabic letters. The minister himself had observed during his travels in a number of central Anatolian provinces that the educated continued to use the Arabic letters. Contrary to the official rhetoric that did not tolerate any persistence of the old script, however, Kaya's words in this letter indicate a more realistic and accommodationist approach that acknowledged that it would take some time for the alphabet change to take effect in the everyday lives of most people.

Both archival and interview data demonstrate a degree of persistence of the Arabic alphabet and coexistence of the old and the new letters, not only in the months following the Alphabet Law but in the years to come. The argument here is not that this is the first work to note the persistence of the Arabic alphabet in private life; one finds casual references to this phenomenon in which it is taken as a given without any discussion of what it means. [58] My goal here is not only to document that persistence in private life, but to demonstrate that it also persisted to some extent in public life, as well as to place the issue of persistence in the context of social and cultural change and state-society relations in the early decades of the Republic.

This phenomenon can in part be explained in the context of "everyday forms of resistance," as I have discussed above in the chapters dealing with the attempts to regulate men's and women's clothing. However, I suggest that the persistence of the Arabic alphabet was not always a result of opposition or resistance. The conventional view concerning that group of citizens who could read and write in Arabic letters has been that the majority of them were also familiar with European languages, and thus, that the adoption of the Latin letters did not create a serious problem for them. While there is some validity to this view, the actual alphabet reform experiences of those who were literate prior to 1928 and their socialization into the culture of new Turkish script have not received much scholarly attention. Many of them were indeed already familiar with French or another European language and learned the new Turkish alphabet through the Millet Mektepleri or through other venues. But they did not necessarily abandon the habit of writing in the old letters entirely. A small number of them lost their functional literacy for anything published in Turkey after 1928, never learning the new letters.[59] My research did not find any significant resistance in the sense of a collective or violent sort, but I did observe numerous strategies Turkish citizens used in coping with change in their everyday lives. While some of these responses were likely ideologically oriented and should be seen as "everyday forms of resistance," many were simply coping mechanisms created to deal with social change on an individual level. The following pages pursue the multiplicity of experiences of transition to the new letters in the larger nationalist-modernist context of the early Republic and the Kemalist state's ways of dealing with those experiences in its formative decades.

A number of statesmen, journalists, and intellectuals may have personally devoted themselves to the promotion of the new alphabet and refused to use the Arabic letters. However, other Turkish citizens continued to make choices in their everyday lives as to which letters to use. One important factor in making such decisions was the division between the public and private spheres, although in practice the boundary between the two was often porous or blurred. Meliha Tanyeli's mother Belkıs and father Ali Salim, whom I mentioned earlier as learning the new alphabet on their own initiative in Trabzon, continued to use the Ottoman letters as needed in their private lives. Communication with the older members of the family, such as letters to Meliha Hanım's grandfather Kitabi Hamdi (Efendi) Başman (1862–1948), continued to be in Ottoman.[60] Kitabi Hamdi Efendi (see Figure 19), the first Muslim publisher in Trabzon, was sixty-six years old at the time of the Alphabet

Reform. As we saw when we first encountered him, Kitabi Hamdi Efendi contributed to the emergence of a culture of reading in Trabzon by publishing, selling, and renting books (including textbooks, alphabet books, easy readers, dictionaries, and works on geography, religion, and ethics, as well as novels) and newspapers from the 1880s.[61] In a very real sense, Kitabi Hamdi Efendi pursued a life as an ideal Ottoman/Turkish entrepreneur who supported the modernizing mission of the state in an Anatolian town. According to İhsan Hamamioğlu, author of a brief biography of Hamdi Efendi, as a seller of texbooks Kitabi Hamdi Efendi incurred a heavy financial loss after the passage of the Alphabet Law when the schools were required to adopt textbooks printed in the new Turkish alphabet.[62] Hamdi Efendi had rebuilt his publishing business when he returned from *muhacirlik* in 1918 and found his store had been plundered during the Russian occupation. This time, at a more advanced age, he retired, transforming his publishing and book business to focus on stationery and photography and transferring the business to his sons. But the memories his grandchildren had of him and his store as sources of inspiration for reading and arts suggest that he stayed connected to the business.[63]

Hamamioğlu's brief account does not address how Kitabi Hamdi Efendi experienced the alphabet change in his private life. He probably learned the new letters, but it is not clear if he ever made the transition to them in everyday usage in the last twenty years of his life. Interview data and other fragments of evidence suggest that he may not have. In 1940 Hamdi Efendi gave a photograph of himself to his close friend, writer İhsan Hamami (Figure 20). He added a personal note: "To the Esteemed Writer İhsan Hamami, İstanbul, 15 May 1940, Kitabi Hamdi Başman (signed) Hamdi"[64] This handwritten note is in Ottoman script, including the date, and only his signature is in the new letters. He wrote the note in old letters, but presented himself with his full new name including the name "Başman," which he had acquired after the 1934 Surname Law, although his signature consisted of his first name only. The portrait photograph depicts a gentleman with a carefully trimmed moustache and beard, very short hair, eyeglasses, and wearing a jacket, vest, shirt, and tie. Compared to another photograph taken in 1899, the most notable difference is the absence of the fez in the second. The clothing of urban, educated, upper class Ottoman men had gone through a significant degree

19. Kitabi Hamdi Efendi with his children, circa 1899. Belkıs, Hamdi Efendi's oldest child and Meliha Tanyeli's mother, is on the right. Photograph from the family album of Meliha Tanyeli.

of Westernization in the nineteenth century, to the extent that for some segments of society, men's clothing regulations were not radical reforms except for the symbolic value of the fez.[65] Kitabi Hamdi Efendi made the transition from Ottoman to Turkish in appearance by abandoning the fez, but his language habits proved to be harder to transform. Republican leaders insisted on an uncompromising attitude on the alphabet question and avoided any public acknowledgement of the difficulties involved in changing established habits. İsmet İnönü's memoirs suggest that while publicly pushing for rapid and complete transformation to the new letters using all means available at their disposal, Republican leaders privately acknowledged the difficulties involved in abandoning the letters one is comfortable with and getting used to a new alpbahet. These leaders themselves had first-hand experience of getting accustomed to the new letters. İnönü himself refused to use the Arabic script any more and forced himself to use the new letters, but acknowledged the difficulty in doing so, and recognized that many others failed to ever make that transition.[66]

In some instances, older citizens who were literate in Ottoman never learned the new letters, resulting in their functional or partial illiteracy for the rest of their lives. In Bursa, for example, the parents of Avni Yurdabayrak (1914–2010), who could read and write in Ottoman letters but were not familiar with any European languages, never learned the new alphabet. Avni Bey's family, of Muslim Georgian ancestry from Batum, now Batumi, in Georgia, had fled to Artvin in the late nineteenth century (probably following the 1877–78 Russian-Ottoman war). Avni Bey's father, Molla Ahmet, had

20. Kitabi Hamdi (Efendi) Başman, circa 1940. Photograph is from Hüseyin Albayrak, *Kuruluşunun 100. Yılında Cudibey İlkokulu*, Trabzon, 1988, 67.

immigrated first to İstanbul where he ran a couple of successful *muhallebici* businesses and eventually settled in the village of Odunlu near Bursa before World War I. Avni Bey's family had first-hand experience of the wars leading up the formation of the Republic. His father, Molla Ahmet, was involved in the nationalist resistance movement in Bursa after 1918 and was imprisoned for awhile by the occupation forces for his support to the resistance. Similarly, Avni Bey's older brother Abdullah, who was in the last year of military medical school when the resistance movement took off in Anatolia, had participated in the War of Liberation.[67]

Avni Bey recalled that at the time of the Alphabet Law his father hired a teacher, and Avni Bey and all four of his (older) sisters learned the new letters at home. Avni Bey was fourteen at the time and in the last year of middle school in Bursa. He had already received several years of education in Ottoman. During our conversation seventy five years later, after a successful career that involved public service as a judge, governor, and member of Parliament, Avni Bey said he was still at ease with the Arabic letters and that he could read the Qur'an comfortably. As for his parents, Avni Bey said "they did not learn the new letters; they did not find it necessary." Molla Ahmet had good relations with the high level republican officials in Bursa. Literacy in the new letters could have been useful in maintaining those relations, but it was apparently not essential. It does not appear that he failed to learn the new alphabet due to lack of financial means to hire an instructor or to buy books: Molla Ahmet could afford to hire a private teacher for his children to learn the new alphabet. Avni Bey also remembered fondly that his father always brought home newspapers and later made sure that his son received the best education available in the country. It is possible that the challenges of coping with a new writing system at an advanced age were a factor in Molla Ahmet's not learning the Latin script. It is also possible that Molla Ahmet felt some resentment toward the state for its abandonment of the Arabic script; his lack of interest in learning the new letters may have been an expression of such resentment. For Avni Yurdabayrak's parents, especially for his mother Havva, knowledge of the Ottoman letters was closely associated with the reading and teaching of the Qur'an. Molla Ahmet was, as his nickname suggests, a *molla* or a *hoca* who had studied the Qur'an and had taught in traditional mosque schools. The only context in which Avni Bey mentioned his mother's literacy was in connection with the reading of the Qur'an. She had received a traditional style religious education. (In fact, she had been Molla Ahmet's pupil in the Qur'an school.) She had not studied in a new style Ottoman state school. For the purpose of reading the Qur'an she did not need to learn the new alphabet. Yet they became functionally illiterate in relation to anything published in Turkey after the script reform. Avni Bey recalled that his parents had to rely on younger members of the family for access, for instance, to newspapers.[68] The generational gap is again evident here. For older citizens who were literate in Ottoman, learning the new alphabet was perhaps both a more challenging proposition (Ottoman script was a part of their cultural identity as they had read and written in those letters for decades) and a less pressing matter than for younger adults because they generally did not have to worry about obtaining or maintaining employment.

Scholars have noted similiar trends following alphabet changes in other contexts. During her research in Turkmenistan in the early 2000s on language and script changes, Victoria Clement observed that many (especially older) Turkmen continued the habit of using the Cyrillic alphabet several years after Turkmenistan had adopted a new Latin-based script in 1993. Some had learned the new Turkmen script, but continued to write in Cyrillic out of habit. Others, especially members of the older generation, had not learned the new alphabet and had no intention of learning it in the future.[69]

Some historians consider generations a useful concept in explaining historical change and causality. Martha C. Howell and Walter Prevenier have suggested some useful ways of thinking about generations in explaining historical change. They argue that "[t]here are moments, short periods of time, when events so encapsulating and so powerful engage so many members of a population at a key time in their lives that they thereafter regard themselves as, and behave as, a group."[70] The generation of the late sixties and the early seventies in the United States and the World War II generation are well-known examples. It might be useful to think of generations as a fruitful tool in understanding the formative period of post-Ottoman Turkey. It might be useful to argue that the traumatic collective experiences of war (The Balkan wars, World War I, allied occupation, and the War of Liberation), including fighting at the front, disability, death, the loss of loved ones, poverty, famine, hunger, disease, violence, displacement, deportations, and short- and long-term migration, along with the overall social, economic, and psychological impact of such experiences, created in Turkey a generation whose expectations from and responses to the new state were deeply influenced by these collective experiences. Undoubtedly, the suffering caused by the wars did not affect all groups equally, and such experiences did not eliminate class, educational, urban and rural, political, ideological, and other differences; yet they provided a shared social and psychological context and a common outlook that were more receptive to state-initiated changes than would otherwise have been the case.

Within this adult population of the period from World War I to the end of Empire, we might be able to discern two generations (sub-generations; or, to follow Karl Mannheim, "generational groups"): Those who were young adults or working age adults at the formation of the Republic, and those who had spent a good part of their adulthood as Ottomans and were at or approaching retirement age and did not have high expectations from the state for employment or had other, more personal motivations.

Those who experienced the end of Empire as small children, along with those who were born roughly in the first decade of the Republic, constituted the first "Republican" generation (popularly phrased as "*Cumhuriyet Çocukları*," or "Children of the Republic")[71] as they grew up, went to school, and were socialized into adulthood in an era of rapid social and cultural transformations engineered by the modernist Kemalist state in the founding decades of the Republic. This was the critical generation that the Republican regime and Republican reforms targeted.[72] It did not have any deep seated loyalties to a pre-republican regime or its cultural or political institutions or symbols. In the case of the alphabet reform, this new generation did not have the knowledge or the long practice of using the Arabic letters. Those who had a few years of elementary school in Ottoman letters had not yet formed the rigid habits of their elders, and transitioned to the new letters more easily than the adult population. It was therefore crucial to teach this new generation the new Turkish letters (and ideally prevent or at least discourage children from learning and using Arabic) as a starting point of their education and socialization into the new secular national culture. Hence the insistence of the state authorities that the traditional neighborhood Qur'an classes discontinue teaching children the Arabic letters, and their careful monitoring of such courses.

Even those actively involved in republican politics did not all make a quick transition to the new alphabet in their private lives. Parliamentarian Rahmi Eyuboğlu, whom I mentioned above as teaching the new alphabet to his family, appears to have continued to write in Ottoman script in his private life after the passage of the Alphabet Law. A letter Eyuboğlu wrote to his eldest son Sabahattin in April 1929, five months after the law, was in Ottoman.[73] At the time, Sabahattin was studying in France. It is possible that Rahmi Eyuboğlu wrote this letter in Ottoman so that Sabahattin, who may have been in France during the early months of the reform, would not have to struggle through a letter in the new Turkish. More likely, Rahmi Bey himself did not yet feel comfortable using the new letters to express himself in this long and very personal letter. There is nothing in the letter to suggest any sense of resentment or opposition to the adoption of the Latin letters. On the contrary, in the same letter Rahmi Bey mentioned reading Jean Jacques Rousseau, sent by Sabahattin presumably in its French original. Rahmi Bey also mentioned that he was taking English language classes and asked Sabahattin to send him a French-English grammar.

In other cases the distinction between the private and the public was blurred. Texts produced for public consumption were often first written in Ottoman, but then were transliterated into the new letters before becoming public. Cemal Rıza Osmanpaşaoğlu (1903–1989) was a leading journalist in Trabzon for decades, beginning in the 1920s.[74] In the 1930s and 1940s he wrote for the major Trabzon newspapers *Yeni Yol* and *Halk*, which strongly supported state-initiated reforms and tried to create a pro-RPP public opinion in the province. Cemal Rıza Bey would write his newspaper columns in Ottoman and his assistants would transliterate them into the new letters before going into print.[75] It is hard to explain Cemal Rıza Bey's continued use of the Ottoman script as a sign of resistance. In addition to writing for pro-regime newspapers, Cemal Rıza Bey exhibited a life style in line with that promoted by the state. He donned the hat, gave public speeches at the town's square during national celebrations, and participated actively in the Trabzon Halkevi, writing for the Halkevi publication *İnan* and acting in the plays staged by the Halkevi. Getting used to writing in the new alphabet involved change at a very personal level, while approving the ongoing reforms could be done at an intellectual and ideological level. A later decision of Cemal Rıza Bey's also hints at the difference between approving reforms at an abstract level and internalizing them at the individual level. After the surname law of 1934, Cemal Rıza Bey took the surname "Çınar," meaning a plane tree. He had been (and unofficially continued to be) known as "Osmanpaşazade" or "Son of Osman Pasha," after an ancestor who had been an Ottoman Pasha. One of the goals of the Surname Law was to erase distinctions among citizens based on titles such as *paşazade*. In line with that policy, Cemal Rıza Bey initially took a surname that indicated no status or relation to the family heritage. In later years he would change his surname, going back to an acceptably Turkified form of his earlier name, "Osmanpaşaoğlu."[76] In his own life, Cemal Rıza Bey failed to fully conform to the reforms (in this case both the Alphabet and the Surname Laws) that he approved and tried to promote.

Although there was often an effort to separate between the private and public spheres, and to limit the use of Ottoman letters to the private sphere, the use of Ottoman persisted (albeit to a smaller degree) even in the public sphere—for instance, in schools and in citizens' dealings with the state authorities. Schools had gone over to textbooks in Latin letters in the 1928–1929 education year, in line with the requirements of the Alphabet Law. For children and youth who had learned to read and write in Ottoman but were still continuing their education after the Alphabet Law, schools were of crucial importance for learning and getting used to reading and writing the new letters. In an April 1931 correspondence, Minister of the Interior Şükrü Kaya reported, based on "complaints and information from various places," that some high school and university students still took their class notes in Arabic letters and that their teachers and professors not only tolerated such practices but themselves wrote their notes and lectures in Arabic letters.[77] Given Kaya's stated source for this information, it appears that if some students or teachers continued to write in Ottoman, there were others who found it necessary to inform the authorities of such practices. Kaya wrote that he did not consider it likely that such acts "against the law and especially against the revolution" would take place in these revolutionary institutions of learning, and did not comment on the extent or the causes of such practices. Anecdotal evidence from memoirs and interviews also points to a degree of persistence of the old letters in the schools. The process of transition to the new letters at schools would only be completed with the graduation of the generation of students who had learned to read and write in Ottoman, and the emergence of a new generation of teachers and professors trained after 1928.

In dealing with the state and its officials, citizens were more careful to observe the new letters. Even here, however, Ottoman persisted alongside the new letters, at least throughout the 1930s and 1940s, but especially in the first few years following the Alphabet Law. Even the educated elite and those in positions of power found themselves struggling with the requirements of the Alphabet Law, and in need of re-learning to read and write Turkish properly and comfortably. In April 1931, Halil (Menteşe), a president of the former Committee of Union and Progress, an Ottoman parliamentarian, head of the Parliament and a minister during the Young Turk era,[78] sent a personal letter to Mustafa Kemal from his hometown, Milas. Menteşe had written the lengthy letter, a report on the state of the Turkish economy, in Ottoman letters, but submitted it with a cover letter in the new letters explaining why the report was in Ottoman. After apologizing for having written the attached report in the old letters Menteşe wrote, "and I have not, unfortunately, been able to get accustomed to the new letters enough to be able to write without error on a subject this long and important. I especially mix them up with the French letters."[79] Menteşe's cover letter may in part have been an attempt to protect himself against any potential recrimination for failing to follow the Alphabet Law, but beyond that, there does appear to be a degree of truth in his statement. Menteşe was not an opponent of the regime; in fact, he would become a member of Parliament from İzmir shortly after this correspondence. Yet, born in 1874, Menteşe was an Ottoman in his culture and habits. For Menteşe, Kitabi Hamdi Efendi of Trabzon, and others of that generation, the transition to the new letters was a part of the larger process of Ottomans becoming Turks, which involved making changes in one's personal habits and everyday practices. Menteşe's letter also highlights a point about the role of familiarity with French in the transition to the new alphabet. Menteşe complained that he mixed up the new Turkish letters with the French. While familiarity with French made it easier to learn the new Turkish alphabet, fluency in French was not the same as reading and writing Turkish in the new script and still involved a process of learning and habituation. Turkish reformers had, for practical and ideological reasons, insisted on creating a Latin-based Turkish alphabet rather than borrowing the French or another

European alphabet in its entirety.[80] Despite all the similarities, the new Turkish alphabet was indeed different from the French in a variety of ways. It had a number of new elements, such as ğ, ı, and ş. Many of the French and Turkish letters had different values and the two alphabets used different letters or combinations of letters to represent the same sound, as in the combinations eu for ö, u for ü, and ch for ş. For someone fluent in French, such variations likely made generating Turkish in the new script a conscious, careful, and slow process, whereas writing Turkish in the Arabic script would have required no conscious thought and would have been comfortable and quick. Furthermore, the change in the look of the language would have been an impediment for those used to reading and writing Turkish in Arabic letters. When Turkish was written in Latin characters, it no longer looked like Turkish. Getting accustomed to the new look of Turkish necessitated a process of adaptation for those literate in Turkish prior to 1928.

At the Directorate of Religous Affairs in the 1930s, some of the letters submitted by citizens as well as some of the internal correspondence continued to be in Ottoman characters. The government had to send orders repeatedly to the provinces and the ministries that citizens must use the new Turkish letters in conducting official business, and that government offices must not respond to any requests submitted in Ottoman. For example, in a July 1934 circular, the prime minister alerted the ministers that some government offices had been tolerant towards citizens' use of Arabic letters in official business and requested that any applications submitted to government offices in the old letters be destroyed without being read.[81] At the same time the Prime Minister's office issued a similar statement to the public through the Anatolian News Agency, announcing that any requests submitted in the old letters would be torn up and thrown away without consideration.[82] The government thus tried to eliminate the use of Ottoman letters by appealing to both the authorities and the public directly.

Despite the government's efforts to eliminate the citizens' use of the old letters in dealing with government authorities, Ottoman persisted into the 1940s. There is evidence that some citizens, among them some nationalist intellectuals and politicians, saw no contradiction between their commitment to the Republic and their work to promote the principles, ideals, and institutions of the Republic on the one hand, and their continuing use of the old letters on the other. There were even instances of Ottoman letters being used in texts written specifically for the promotion of a Republican institution or ideal. In 1943, when Vedat Ürfi Bengü[83] sent his short monograph on the People's Houses to RPP parliamentarian Nafi Atuf Kansu, requesting its consideration for publication by the government, Bengü saw no contradiction between the goal and the script of his text.[84] The handwritten monograph, a brief propaganda text on the goals, activities, and accomplishments of the People's Houses, was mostly in Ottoman letters, with the exception of the title, subtitles, and some individual words in the text. Bengü's cover note was an interesting combination of the old and new letters: after addressing Kansu in the new script, the text of the note itself was in Ottoman characters, and it was then signed in the new letters but dated in the old. From the text it appears that Bengü was still more comfortable writing in Ottoman than in the new Turkish letters, despite the passage of years since the Alphabet Law and his familiarity with French as a writer and translator. The fact that Bengü submitted his monograph in Ottoman script to a leading member of the RPP also suggests that he did not anticipate any negative reaction from the party for having written his text in Ottoman.[85]

Some archival documents relating to the well-known Menemen incident reveal that the use of Ottoman in government bureaucracy did not disappear totally with the Alphabet Law. Briefly, the incident was a series of events that took place in the small town of Menemen, in the province of İzmir, on 23 December 1930. On that morning, a group of six men entered the town, declaring their leader the Mahdi. Events turned violent, including the gruesome beheading of an officer, and resulted in the military intervening in armored vehicles. Government officials interpreted this event as a sign of the threat posed by Islamic reactionaries to the secular state.[86] The parliament declared martial law, and two hundred sixty people were brought before a military court in Menemen. While most of the documents relating to Menemen were in the new letters, there were exceptions. A detailed plan of Menemen's town center drawn to show where and how the events took place was labeled in Ottoman. More interestingly, the decisions of the Menemen military court kept by the Ministry of the Interior were also written in Ottoman. In this case, Ottoman persisted even at a time when the state was particularly worried about the forces of reaction. State employees saw no conflict between their continuing use of the old alphabet and the case at hand. Failure to live up to the ideals of the new Republic was not always a sign of opposition to the regime.

The Ministry of the Interior sent circulars to the provinces asking governors to make sure civil servants used the new letters. Such correspondence occurred not only in the months and years following the Alphabet Law, but continued in the 1930s, which clearly indicates that the Ottoman script persisted even in government use. In a January 1930 circular, Minister of the Interior Şükrü Kaya informed the ministers, governors, and the First Inspector General that the documents received in his Ministry from the provinces contained notes, drafts, and marginal notes written in the Arabic letters.[87] Kaya argued that civil servants, whose duty he described as leading the public in this revolutionary matter, could not be allowed to continue to use the old letters in official correspondence. The solution he recommended was that those in positions of authority would encourage subordinate civil servants to use the new letters by first ensuring that their own correspondences, including drafts, were written in the new script. Kaya specifically assigned the governors the task of occasional inspections in government offices to prevent noncompliance.

In another circular on the same matter nearly three years later, Kaya mentioned three areas of noncompliance with reference to the Prime Minister's observations during his recent visit to some of the provinces: there were notes written in Arabic letters among official documents, some high ranking civil servants continued to take notes in the old letters, and the correspondences of gendarmerie offices were still in Ottoman.[88] Kaya reiterated his request from the governors that they personally pursue this matter and explain to civil servants that all correspondence must be written in the new letters.

There was concern in the 1940s that the use of the old letters by older civil servants caused problems because the younger civil servants could not read them. There were even a few cases where the central goverment tolerated a civil servant's failure to learn the new letters, despite protests from the provincial governor. One such case involved a number of mosque employees in the Eastern Anatolian province of Elaziz (now Elazığ) in 1935. The Director General of Pious Foundations intervened on behalf of these employees by taking their case to Prime Minister İnönü. The Elaziz office had informed the Director General that the governor of Elaziz witheld the salaries of those mosque servants who could not read and write the new letters.[89] The correspondence did not specify how many employees were affected or if they were literate in Ottoman. From the correspondence it appears that the governor wanted these men to take a literacy test and instituted a financial punishment at his discretion when they either refused to take the test, or failed it. In his letter to Prime Minister İnönü, the Director defended the men's right to continue to receive their salaries and to maintain their jobs on several grounds.[90] He argued that most of those involved were old men in their fifties and sixties who (except for about ten of them) did not have the ability to learn the new alphabet. If they were fired, in addition to the problem of replacing them, such an act would lead these men to fall into destitution in their old age. The Director further argued that learning a new script was a matter of time and that these people at an advanced age would not be able to learn the new letters suddenly and would need time. After asking his advisor whether the governor had the right and the authority to act as he did, İnönü wrote to governor Ahmet Tevfik Sırrı Gür's office telling the governor to release the salaries of the affected mosque employees immediately.[91]

While the central government had repeatedly asked governors to encourage all citizens and especially civil servants within their jurisdiction to use the new script, such requests did not specify measures to be taken in cases of noncompliance. In this instance, in an effort to fully implement the alphabet reform the governor instituted an ad hoc policy of dealing with noncompliance. Incidences of provincial or local authorities exceeding the limits of their authority or instituting arbitrary policies of enforcement occurred especially in cases where the central government instructed provincial or local authorities to implement a law, a decree, or a policy but did not provide specific measures of enforcement. As I have discussed earlier, this practice was especially prevalent in the case of women's dress regulations. In the Elaziz instance, it is also important to note how the various agencies of the state interpreted the case differently and how the citizens involved were able to mobilize the support of one institution to present their case successfully to another insitution, the head of government in Ankara, to overturn the governor's decision. There is no indication in the documents that the men involved made any attempt at learning the new letters. It also appears that the Directorate of

Pious Foundations had made no effort to encourage these men to learn them. The Director says he "was about to propose" that the more able of the men involved be sent to an alphabet class when he found out about the governor's action. The Director did not see the situation in terms of opposition, reaction, or resistance, and not only tolerated it but also succesfully presented the case to the Prime Minister, justifying the failure of these men to learn the letters on the grounds of old age and the need for time to adapt to such major changes. İnönü sided with the Directorate, overruling the governor's decision to stop the salaries of the men involved, an action which the Prime Minister believed exceeded the legitimate authority of the governor. The central government policy was in fact more sensitive to individual circumstances and more tolerant toward noncompliance than its own rhetoric suggested, especially when noncompliance was not viewed as an act of opposition or reaction.

In the 1940s, Ottoman script was still occasionally used (for informal communication) within government bureaucracy.[92] Even at RPP headquarters Ottoman did not totally disappear in the 1940s, although by this time it tended to be in drafts and not the final versions. As late as the 1950s, Bahri Turgut, a member of Parliament, still wrote his speeches in Ottoman.[93] Halil İnalcık, a renowned Ottoman historian and first-generation republican who was in the fourth grade in 1928, acknowledged recently that out of habit he still sometimes takes notes in the old letters.[94]

Conclusion

The Alphabet Law was a comprehensive reform effort with multiple and overlapping goals, all directed toward the creation of a secular, literate, modern nation. However, in spite of being one of the most carefully planned and executed reform efforts of the early Republic, the central government was not able to fully control the process. On the literacy front, even though institutions such as the army, the Turkish Hearths, and the People's Houses, and groups such as teachers, cooperated with the state, the state's ability to reach all areas and all groups remained limited and a majority of the population remained largely outside the impact of alphabet reform throughout the RPP period. In addition to the question of finances, there was the problem of lack of interest, after the initial outburst of excitement and support for literacy. Adult citizens who needed literacy for pragmatic reasons, such as maintaining or finding employment, learned the new alphabet quickly. For a vast majority, especially for the rural population, literacy was not an urgent need. There had been a process of cultural change concerning literacy in the nineteenth century Ottoman Empire, and there was indeed a positive cultural attitude toward literacy and demand for education. But at the same time, this cultural change and the perception of a need for literacy were uneven across regional, urban and rural, and particularly gender lines. Perceptions toward women's literacy and education changed more slowly than perceptions toward male literacy and education. Some of the means of teaching literacy to adult citizens, such as the use of the army and compulsory military service, also inadvertently favored the literacy of male citizens. Economic and structural as well as cultural factors were important in shaping the outcome.

This chapter has emphasized that for those who had been literate in Ottoman the transition to the new alphabet in everyday use often proved to be difficult. People frequently distinguished between the public and private spheres, and the Ottoman script persisted in the latter. Such reactions to the alphabet reform may in some cases be explained as a form of resistance. However, in other instances, individuals who actively supported the new regime in their dress and actions continued to use Ottoman. I therefore suggest that individual reactions to reforms, in this case the change of the alphabet, had much to do with a cultural and habitual change at a very personal level that did not necessarily fit the categories of ideologically oriented resistance or opposition. This chapter has also shown that the Ottoman script long persisted and coexisted with the new alphabet even in the public sphere. The transformation to the new alphabet was in fact more gradual and the government policy toward noncompliance more accommodating than has often been assumed in the literature. In the long run, the new alphabet became an essential part of the Republican national culture even for those who continued to oppose or criticize the Republic on the grounds of its excessive secularism or anti-Islamic stance. Today nobody is contesting the Latin-based alphabet. The recent language-related challenges to Turkish nationalism mainly concern the right to use (to speak, to publish, to name, to broadcast, to educate in) languages other than Turkish, not a return to the old alphabet.

4

Celebrating National Holidays

National celebrations have been important instruments of political socialization, legitimacy, and mobilization in Turkey. Yet Turkish historians have
rarely studied the culture of national celebrations in Republican Turkey, nor
have they examined closely the emergence and functioning of that culture
in the early decades of the Republic.[1] While historians of the early Republic
focused on the more explicitly political "reforms," celebrations were largely
assumed to exist within the separate sphere of folklore despite the very political nature of these events.[2] I suggest that we study early Republican celebrations as "invented traditions," to borrow a term from Eric Hobsbawm,[3] in
the context of the formation of a Turkish national identity and the consolidation of the Republican state. While reforms, including those discussed in
the previous chapters, were potentially more confrontational and conflictual,
national celebrations constituted a less confrontational, and potentially more
participatory and inclusionary, path of social and cultural change.[4] In this
chapter, I first give an overview of national celebrations in Turkey. Then I
turn specifically to the 23rd of April, National Sovereignty and Children's
Day, and study how the 23rd of April was celebrated in the 1930s, what those
celebrations meant for those involved, which groups were included, which
were excluded, and how national celebrations contributed to the creation of a
collective national identity. I also examine how national days were related to
and reinforced the reforms discussed in the previous chapters.

Official celebrations in the Ottoman Empire revolved around Islam and
the Sultan and the royal family.[5] The Sultan's accession to the throne, his girding on of the Sword of Osman, and the oath of allegiance to the Sultan were
important moments that the Ottoman state celebrated with its subjects. For a
republic that claimed to derive its secular authority from the nation, however,

celebrations that helped legitimize the Ottoman monarch were clearly irrelevant. The new state needed celebrations that would help citizens imagine a Turkish nation of which they were members, rather than a sultan to whom they owed allegiance. As Arzu Öztürkmen has noted, there were in fact the beginnings of secular holidays in the late Ottoman period, such as the *Hürriyet Bayramı*, based on secular European and especially French national celebrations.[6] Celebrations in the Republican era were rooted in the Young Turk era celebrations, yet in an effort to distance itself from its Ottoman past, the Turkish Republic would de-emphasize any such connections between pre- and post-Republican celebrations.

What Is Worth Celebrating? The Range of Republican Holidays

National celebrations help with the creation and maintenance of a collective historical memory and a shared identity. By marking important moments in the recent, or distant, past of the nation, they provide an opportunity to remember those events collectively and interpret them in a national context. Major victories or accomplishments of the nation, as well as major calamities that the nation has survived, provide reference points for national holidays. In the post–World War I nation-building processes in the Middle East, nationalist movements and leaders under the British and French mandates, as well as the regimes in independent states, used ceremonies in their efforts to build a collective national memory and a shared national identity. In Mandatory Palestine and in Israel after 1948, the commemoration of events from the distant past such as the defense and fall of Masada (in 79 CE) and the unsuccessful Bar Kokhba Revolt against the Romans (in 132–135 CE), and the events from the recent past such as the defense of a Jewish settlement in the Battle of Tel Hai in 1920, helped with the creation of a collective Jewish/Israeli historical consciousness. The recovery and reinterpretation of these historical events that ended in defeat and death turned them into heroic myths and legends of national revival.[7] In Iran in the 1930s, the commemorations and celebrations of pre-modern Iranian poets such as Hafez, Sa'di, Omar Khayyam, and Ferdowsi as national poets, as well as the annual *nowruz* (new year) celebrations, and celebrations of the Shah's birthday, became an important part of Reza Shah's efforts to create a modern, secular national memory and identity for Iranians. By building mausoleums for these poets to function as "secular pilgrimage sites," and through public commemorations such as millennial celebrations of Ferdowsi, the Pahlavi regime tried to create a new secular national consciousness. The choice as national icons of these particular poets, known for "their earthly sensibilities," marked the Reza Shah regime's desire to create a secular national identity and culture distinct from the collective identity of the Qajar era, which was closely associated with Shi'a Islam. Official commemorations of Ferdowsi and the other poets, with an emphasis on their contributions to a shared world civilization, would also prove to the outside world, as well as to Iranians themselves, Iran's compatibility as a nation with modernity.[8]

In early Republican Turkey, the imagined ancient past of the Turks in Central Asia provided a rich source of national myths, such as the legend of Ergenekon and the myth of the Gray Wolf (*Bozkurt*), symbolizing re-birth after defeat and near-extinction. (Such cultural legends also provided historical justifications for secular and modernist conceptions of the Turkish family and the appropriate place of women in Turkish society.) While Central Asian epics and myths of origin helped establish the Turks as an ancient nation, building a collective historical memory and national identity within Turkey's present day boundaries necessitated inventing traditions that tied the nation and its history to its current homeland, Anatolia.[9] Nationalism requires forgetting, or what Anderson has called "collective amnesia," as much as it involves remembering.[10] For Turkish nationalist leadership after 1922, the recent Ottoman past was the past Turks needed to forget, due to its association with defeat, but also, and perhaps more importantly, due to the new regime's desire to break with its Ottoman past and Ottoman identity in its effort to create a new secular nation and state with its own legitimating ideology, traditions, and institutions. In Turkey, as in the context of the French and American revolutions, "the need to commemorate arose directly out of an ideologically driven desire to break with the past, to construct as great a distance as possible between the new age and the old."[11]

As Hobsbawm reminds us, "revolutions and 'progressive movements' which break with the past, by definition, have their own relevant past . . ."[12] For Turkish nationalists, the relevant past centered around the War of Liberation. The War of Liberation and its culmination in a republic provided the "*lieux de mémoire*"[13] for creating a collective national memory and historical consciousness through national celebrations. In fact, the very construction and collective remembrance of the war years (of the period of violent events and destruction between 1918 and 1922 that included anti-colonial fighting, but also violent inter-communal conflict and displacement of populations in Anatolia)[14] as the War of Liberation took place in part through the invention of national celebrations. National days that commemorated the selected events of the war years, along with the nationalist re-writing of recent history, helped define that period as the War of Liberation. The 19th of May, celebrating Mustafa Kemal's landing in Samsun on 19 May 1919, which marked the beginning of the War of Liberation, became Youth and Sports Day. After Atatürk's death in 1938, the 19th of May holiday also served as a day to commemorate Atatürk.[15] The 23rd of April marked the opening of the Grand National Assembly on 23 April 1920. It was celebrated as National Sovereignty Day in the 1920s, but by 1927 the 23rd of April had become National Sovereignty and Children's Day (*23 Nisan Ulusal Egemenlik ve Çocuk Bayramı*). 30 August 1922, marking the final victory of the nationalist forces in the War of Liberation, became the 30th of August Victory Day (*30 Ağustos Zafer Bayramı*). The signing of the Lausanne Treaty on 24 July 1923 marked the international recognition of Turkey's independence as a sovereign state and became Lausanne Day (*Lozan Günü*). Unlike the 23rd of April and the 19th of May, Lausanne Day did not become institutionalized and did not outlast the RPP period as a major national celebration. Finally, the declaration of the Republic on 29 October 1923 marked the birth of the new Republican state and became Republic Day (*Cumhuriyet Bayramı*). In 1935 the Grand National Assembly recognized Republic Day as the only national holiday to be celebrated in the name of the state, giving Republic Day a unique status that set it apart from all the others, although several other national holidays continued to be celebrated by the state.[16]

Another category of celebration that emerged in the early years of the Republic was the Liberation Days of individual towns and cities. In the Aegean provinces, cities began to celebrate their own liberation days at the end of the War of Liberation. This practice expanded to other parts of the country and helped towns place their local history firmly in the context of the national liberation.[17] The last addition to these liberation days was the "Accession of Hatay to Turkey," celebrating Hatay's joining Turkey in 1939.

The state continued to invent new holidays in the 1920s and 1930s that celebrated the achievements and the goals of the nation.[18] The People's Houses were founded in 1932 as a form of cultural center affiliated with the RPP to spread the cultural revolution of the new Republic. 19 February, the opening day of the first People's Houses, was made People's Houses Day and became one of the most enthusiastically celebrated holidays of the 1930s and 1940s. 26 September, marking the opening of the first Turkish Language Congress in 1932, became Language Day (*Dil Bayramı*), celebrating the language of the nation. Following the Montreux Convention of 20 July 1936, which the Turkish government considered a diplomatic victory as it finally established full Turkish sovereignty over the İstanbul and the Dardanelles straits, 24 July, Lausanne Day, was expanded to become a day of joint celebrations of the Lausanne and Montreux treaties. Most of the major national days evolved in the 1920s and early 1930s, yet the invention of the Soil Festival (*Toprak Bayramı*) came at the end of the RPP era, following the passage of the Land Distribution Law (*Çiftçiyi Topraklandırma Kanunu*) in 1945. The goal of the Soil Festival, in the words of the RPP Secretary General Nafi Kansu, was "to create a consciousness of national solidarity and agricultural development."[19]

The long list of secular national days also included a few commemorations. In the Menemen incident of 23 December 1930 (described in chapter 3), an officer-teacher by the name of Kubilay was killed brutally. In official historiography this event came to be known as the Kubilay incident. 23 December became Kubilay Day, commemorating Kubilay for his courageous defense against what was perceived as a major reactionary assault on the secular Republic. The most important day of commemoration in the Republican era marks the death of Atatürk on 10 November 1938. It continued to be observed after the RPP period and remains among the major national days in Turkey today.[20]

While expanding the repertoire of secular national celebrations, the state did not attempt to discontinue the two major Islamic celebrations: *Şeker* or *Ramazan Bayramı* at the end of Ramazan, the Islamic month of fasting, and *Kurban Bayramı*, the Sacrifice holiday, commemorating Abraham's offer to sacrifice his son at the command of God. It did not officially sanction them as national holidays celebrated by the state, but still recognized them as national holidays, allowing the coexistence of the two religious holidays with the new secular national holidays. Other important Islamic days such as the celebration of the birth of the Prophet Muhammad, and folk festivals such as *Hıdırellez*, the celebration of the coming of spring, were neither mandated nor prohibited by the state, allowing space for the maintenance of these cultural practices at the local and individual levels. This continuity in the culture of celebrations through the religious holidays and folk festivals would facilitate the reception of the new secular celebrations: the new national days replaced not the entire calendar of cultural celebrations, but the state celebrations of the old regime.[21]

Celebrating the 23rd of April

The 23rd of April evolved as National Sovereignty and Children's Day through the convergence of a state initiative to commemorate the opening of the first national assembly in Ankara, and the desire of the modernist, reformist cultural elites and associations, particularly the Children's Protection Society (CPS), to raise awareness of the child question, which was defined as a national issue in the 1920s and 1930s. The early celebrations of the 23rd of April marked the opening of the National Assembly in Ankara in 1920, symbolizing the birth of the new Turkish nation and its break from the Ottoman Empire. In the early years of the Republic there were in fact two separate national days celebrating national sovereignty: 23 April and 1 November. While 23 April celebrated national sovereignty implicitly by marking the opening of Parliament, 1 November marked the abolition of the Sultanate on 1 November 1922 and had official recognition as "Sovereignty Day."[22] The 23rd of April eventually gained legal confirmation as "National Sovereignty Day" in 1935.[23]

The evolution in the 1920s of the 23rd of April as Children's Day, a celebration of childhood, took place largely as a result of the Children's Protection Society's efforts to raise public awareness of the importance of children for the future of the nation, and of the massive problems Turkish children faced. These efforts were rooted in a long-term cultural transformation that had been going on since the Tanzimat times. As Duben and Behar have observed, cultural contact with Europe in the nineteenth century led to a new interest in children and to the beginnings of a change of mentality and new attitudes toward childhood and children among Ottoman intellectuals and the upper classes of the Ottoman capital.[24] This was a process similar to and connected with the changing attitudes toward literacy, education, and women's place in the family and society. During the Tanzimat era, children came to be recognized as "individuals,"[25] and as "persons to whom society is going to be entrusted."[26] The identification of children with the future of the Empire led to an increased interest in the connections between child-rearing, children's health, children's education, and social reforms. Changing attitudes toward children also influenced the debates about the role of women as mothers and the role of the family. In late Ottoman literature, children came to be equated with the family, and family with the nation. Because the nation's welfare depended on the welfare of its children, by the Young Turk era child-rearing came to be seen as an important national duty. The changing attitude toward childhood and children manifested itself not only in the intellectual debates and literature, but also in government policies such as the expansion of the public education system, building of children's hospitals, and the publication of books and magazines for children.

During the years of the Balkan Wars and World War I, as the suffering of the population through death, displacement, hunger, and illness reached new heights and as the future of the state looked increasingly uncertain, the child question gained new urgency. There was, on the one hand, the enormous task of dealing with the massive problems Ottoman children faced—the Children's Protection Society was founded in 1917 mainly to provide for orphaned children. On the other hand, there was the ideological work of raising a generation of nationalist citizens loyal to the Ottoman nation and the CUP regime, through education and other means. Cüneyd Okay notes that during the World War I years, the CUP regime created a Children's Day (*Çocuklar Bayramı*) and other holidays such as Tree Day (*Ağaç Bayramı*), Flower Day (*Çiçek Bayramı*), Students' Day (*Mektebliler Bayramı*) and Physical Education Day (*İdman Bayramı*) that placed children at the center of the celebration.[27] Although these holidays were short-lived (necessarily so with the defeat in World War I) and appear to have been limited to a city or region, they reflect an ongoing change in the culture of Ottoman holidays that shifted the focus away from the Sultan and toward the nation and its children and youth. Some of the common elements of these holidays, such as parades, recitation of poetry, singing of marches, and performance of athletic events, also appear, as we will see, in the post-1923 Republican celebrations. Although there is no evidence of a direct connection between the CUP era and post-1922 national holidays, these Young Turk era children's holidays appear to have been cultural precursors of the Republican era national celebrations, especially of the 23rd of April National Sovereignty and Children's Day and the 19th of May Youth and Sports Day.

The late Ottoman notion of the child as the future of the nation gained a renewed emphasis in the early years of the Republic in a country depopulated and impoverished by a decade of wars. Children became both vehicles and symbols of "national renewal and development."[28] Building a strong Turkish nation would be in part through repopulating the country, or giving birth to children (hence the pro-natalist government policies and the renewed interest on the role of women as mothers), and raising them as healthy, educated, loyal, and disciplined citizens. In the 1920s and 1930s, as the image of the robust child, or *gürbüz çocuk*, came to represent the ideal Turkish child, and became a powerful symbol of the nation itself,[29] Turkish children were in reality faced with massive problems. The major challenges included high rates of infant and child mortality, large numbers of orphans and abandoned children, poverty, malnutrition, homelessness, and begging.[30] Overburdened by the requirements of post-war construction and hit by the global economic crisis in 1929, the RPP government did not have the resources to deal with the massive problems Turkish children confronted. In the absence of a comprehensive state program, the Children's Protection Society and a host of other institutions such as the Red Crescent Society, the Turkish Women's Union (until it was disbanded in 1935), the Mother's Federation, local RPP branches, Turkish Hearths, and after 1932, the People's Houses worked to ameliorate children's problems. It was in this context that the Children's Protection Society, the principal association dedicated to children's issues in the 1920s and 1930s, led the efforts to establish a children's day. Initially, the Society's efforts focused on generating revenue on the 23rd of April through donations and the sale of Children's Protection Society stamps.[31] In 1927 the Society declared the 23rd of April as Children's Day, to be celebrated by activities such as parades, the performance of plays (for and by children), movies, conferences (for children and parents), and robust-child contests. By 1929 the Society expanded the celebration to a Children's Week (20–30 April), although the focus remained on 23 April.[32] The choice of 23 April as the date for the Children's Day appears to have been due to its readily conceivable symbolic association with children: The opening of the National Assembly on 23 April 1920 signified the birth of the nation. By the late 1920s, official celebrations of the 23rd of April holiday indeed focused on children. A national holiday commemorating the nation's recent past came to be redefined and merged with a key social and national concern, not through the imposition of the central government, but through the work of the Children's Protection Society. (Like many other associations in the corporatist structure of the 1930s, the Society received some income from the state and many of its founders and activists were Parliamentarians and bureaucrats. In that sense it is true that the Children's Protection Society was not an autonomous civil society organization. At the same time, it should be recognized that the CPS was not a state-run organization and that the initiatives and activities of the doctors, nurses, and other CPS activists were not entirely planned or controlled by the RPP.) This was an important factor in why the 23rd of April created a holiday tradition of its own and survived the transition to multiparty politics. Even though the full legal recognition of 23 April as Children's Day took place much later, coming only after the 1980 coup, in the 1930s, government authorities generally accepted and treated the 23rd of April as "National Sovereignty and Children's Day," as if that were the official designation.[33] In many towns, the local RPP office, Children's Protection Society, and People's Houses planned Children's Day programs jointly.

We see a similar pattern in the emergence of the 19th of May as a major national holiday. In the 1920s, residents of Samsun remembered Mustafa Kemal's landing in their town in an annual Gazi Day. In the late 1920s the Turkish Sports Association (TSA, *Türk Spor Kurumu*) and the major İstanbul sports clubs, Beşiktaş, Fenerbahçe, and Galatasaray, organized gymnastics or sports festivals in May (which had their precursors in the Young Turk era Physical Education holidays mentioned earlier). The 19th of May developed into a national youth and sports holiday in the 1930s, on the basis of Samsun's Gazi Day celebrations and the sports festivals celebrated in İstanbul.[34]

It evolved through a convergence of local (Samsun) and national (RPP, TSA) efforts to commemorate Mustafa Kemal's landing in Samsun, which marked the beginning of the War of Liberation, and the desire of the RPP, TSA, and the private gymnastics clubs to celebrate youth and to raise awaresness of the importance of youth and sports for the well-being of the nation. Preserving the collective memory of Mustafa Kemal's landing in Samsun by making the 19th of May an official national holiday gained new urgency as Atatürk's health deteriorated in 1938. Parliament recognized 19 May as "Youth and Sports Holiday" in June, and the 19th of May gained legal status as a national holiday in July 1938, several years after the date came to be celebrated widely throughout the country following a Turkish Sports Association decision declaring it a "Youth Holiday."[35]

Like children, the youth represented the future of the nation. Raising healthy, robust, and disciplined young men and women was essential for the overall health and productivity of the nation, for the defense of the country (which gained increased importance in the tense international climate of the late 1930s), and also for producing healthy future generations. Sports, as an instrument of physical health and moral regulation, was regarded as an important national duty. In the 1930s, Turkish debates and policies about youth, sports, and bodily health were informed in part by the dominant ideas about these issues in contemporary Europe, including the fascist ideologies and regimes in Germany and Italy.[36] Such influences were especially apparent in projects such as the compulsory Physical Training program for male and female citizens (*Beden Terbiyesi Mükellefiyeti*) initiated in 1938. Aspects of 19th of May celebrations such as the display of healthy and disciplined bodies through athletic performances and the partial shift from town squares and street celebrations to stadiums reveal some of these fascist influences.

As with the National Sovereignty and Children's Day, the 19th of May took on contradictory meanings. There was a tremendous gap between the robust Turkish youth envisioned and celebrated on Youth and Sports Day, on one hand, and the reality of the economic and health conditions of the majority of young people in Turkey on the other. Nevertheless, young men and women in İstanbul and Ankara, but also in Samsun and other Anatolian cities and towns, celebrated their youth and commemorated Mustafa Kemal's landing in Samsun through poems, speeches, plays, and athletic performances that were intended to remind them of their membership in the national community and of the nation's recent past. These celebrations were similar enough to the 23rd of April celebrations of their childhood, even if the focus on the love for the child, for Atatürk, and for the nation was now replaced by an emphasis on discipline and respect for authority.

In 1935, RPP and People's House offices in many cities and towns throughout the country abided by the party's request to report on the 23rd of April celebrations in their respective towns. The local RPP office, or the People's House, or both, sent a report detailing the celebration to the Party headquarters, some towns sent a celebration program and report, and several towns added photographs taken during the celebrations to their reports. These reports tell us much about the actual experiences of these national days in various Anatolian provinces. National day celebrations in different cities followed the same general guidelines provided by the RPP headquarters. Therefore, celebration reports sent from various parts of the country contain a large degree of overlap and describe many of the same activities. Yet there were also differences in the actual celebrations depending on factors such as the region, the presence or absence of the RPP and other institutions such as the People's Houses and Children's Protection Society, overall state control, the level of economic and cultural development of the province, and the local/regional RPP leadership. Here I will discuss two specific *bayram* reports to illustrate what it actually meant to celebrate Children's Day in the small towns of Anatolia, as conveyed to us by RPP or People's Houses officials.

According to the RPP office in the town of Boyabat, in the western Black Sea province of Sinop, the town celebrated the Sovereignty and Children's Day of 1935 in the following way:[37]

The town, including the government, municipality, RPP, and People's House buildings, as well as the town's market and the neighborhoods, had been decorated for the day with flags and flowers. At night the town was lit with lanterns. On the morning of the twenty-third, the ceremony began at Republic Square with the singing of the Independence March (the National Anthem) and the Tenth-Year March (*Onuncu Yıl Marşı*, the march written for the tenth anniversary of the foundation of the Republic). This was followed by two speeches from the party's People's Podium, one by People's House member, Head Teacher Mr. Ekrem Vural, and the other by the chairman of the Children's Protection Society, Mr. İhsan Özcan. The speeches were on national sovereignty and the meaning and the significance of the child in the Turkish Republic.

Two children were chosen, to be *kaymakam* (district governor) and mayor for a day. They were taken to their offices and congratulated. The group then reassembled in front of the Party/People's House building, where the party chairman, Mr. Refik Tuzlu, gave a speech about the history of the War of Liberation and the Republic. The People's House handed out candy to four hundred children. Then the children were taken to a picnic area where they engaged in athletics and national dances until evening.

On the evening of the twenty-fourth, the students of İnönü School performed a play, and a teacher, Mr. İsmail Öztürk, gave a speech on child discipline. Two hundred citizens attended the play. The next evening the students of another school put on a play, and another teacher, Miss Saime Bakla, gave a speech on the child in the current age. A hundred ninety citizens attended the play and the speech.

On the twenty-ninth, the party chairman gave a speech on the duties of mothers and fathers to raise children who respect government authority. The play that was to be performed had to be cancelled, because two of the female members suddenly became ill. In its place they performed the play *İstiklâl* (*Independence*). Two hundred sixteen citizens attended this program.

The report ended by reaffirming that the local government, the municipality, the party, and the People's House cooperated to put on an exciting celebration.

The town of Sandıklı, in Afyonkarahisar province in the Aegean interior, also sent a report of how they celebrated the 23rd of April.[38] According to the chairman of the local People's House, they had put on a play to raise money for new clothes for poor children, which the children wore for the celebrations. On the twenty-third, markets and official buildings were decorated with flags and placards. Children carrying flags and "We Want" ("*İsteriz*") signs (stating what children wanted from their parents and the nation) paraded with decorated automobiles, the city band, and the townspeople through the town to the Republic Square. At the square children recited poems and made speeches. From the square they went to the municipality, the Party headquarters, and the People's House. At the People's House they were given candy.

There were speeches by members of the People's House and a few children recited poems. Then the children were taken by automobiles and carts on an excursion around the city.

The People's House players performed the play *Beyaz Kahraman* (*The White Hero*) twice, in the afternoon for children and in the evening for their parents and the public. Children performed skits and sang songs accompanied by the People's House *saz* orchestra. Also during the evening there was a speech on nationalism and children. The next day students were taken on an excursion where they had races, games, and dances. The winners of the races were given awards.

These two reports reveal quite different understandings of the 23rd of April celebrations. In the Boyabat report, which focused on the formal and educational aspects of the celebrations, children were virtually absent as active participants in the celebration and appeared mainly as the targets of speeches given by party leaders, teachers and other adults. The Sandıklı report, on the other hand, focused on children and their participation in the festivities. The two reports were also quite different in the language they used. This was at the height of the purification movement to cleanse Turkish of Arabic and Persian words, and the Boyabat report clearly reflects that mood. Like a number of the other reports in 1935, it made an effort to employ pure Turkish words. Hence in the Boyabat report *mektepli/talebe* (student) became *okuyan*; *tarafından* (by) became *yönünden*; *belediye* (municipality) became *şarbaylık*; and *kaymakam* (district governor) became *ilçebay*, to give a few examples. The Sandıklı report, on the other hand, did not use any newly created Turkish words to replace established words of Arabic or Persian origin. Correspondence such as these celebration reports gave local party officers and adminsitrators an opportunity to prove to the party headquarters and the government in Ankara that they were in fact following the policies promoted by the center. The style and language of the Boyabat report may have been a consequence of such considerations. It could also have been a reflection of the enthusiasm of the local RPP officers for language reform as well as their understanding of what the 23rd of April meant and how it should be celebrated. Despite the differences in language, style and emphasis, these two reports reveal a basic pattern of 23rd of April celebrations that was repeated in towns throughout the country in the 1930s.

Ceremonies typically began in the morning in the town's Republic Square, bringing together the town's governor or the *kaymakam*, RPP officials, People's House representatives, local military commanders, representatives from the Children's Protection Society and other clubs and societies, civil servants, professionals such as bank managers, doctors and lawyers, schoolchildren, and the public. Some reports also mentioned groups such as artisans and shopkeepers. Reports generally did not give the number of attendees in these ceremonies, although often they referred to "a big crowd" or "thousands of citizens." These reports most likely involve some degree of exaggeration, but in some cases photographs taken at the ceremony (for example, several photographs taken in Trabzon in front of the municipality building) do indeed show very large crowds in attendance. The ceremony opened with the singing of the National Anthem. Often the *Onuncu Yıl Marşı* (Tenth Year March), *Andımız* (Oath to the Nation) or *Çocuk Marşı* (The Children's March) were also sung by the crowd. Then came the speeches on the significance of the day by the governor or the *kaymakam*, the local RPP chairman, the People's House representative, the Children's Protection Society Representative, or a teacher. Regardless of whether or not the children in attendance followed the contents of the speeches, the ceremony provided an opportunity for the representatives of the government, children, and adults to unite in celebration of childhood and nationhood. The photograph below (Figure 21) shows the RPP chairman in Maraş in the southeast giving a speech in front of the municipality building during the Children's Day ceremony in 1936.[39] As was typical at these ceremonies, local army commanders can be seen here in their uniforms, alongside government officials and representatives of civil associations, reminding the public of the role of the Army as the guardian of the Republic. Some small girls are seen standing in their white dresses between the male respresentatives of the state and the spectator public, as the link between the state and the nation, and between the nation's present and the future.

During the ceremonies children carried, along with Turkish flags, signs saying "We Want. . . ." These signs, as seen in Figures 21 and 22 from Maraş, were mentioned specifically in some of the celebration programs and reports, also appearing in photographs from several different towns. Therefore, they must have been a centrally planned element of 23rd of April celebrations.

21. Celebrating Children's Day in Maraş, 1936. Note the children's "İsteriz" ("We Want") sign. Photograph is reproduced from an original at BCA 490.01/18.95.2.

These signs expressed children's wishes, or rather what the Party, the Children's Protection Society, the People's House, or the teachers thought should be the children's wishes, for themselves and for the nation. Among these wishes were "We want clean and regular food," "We want kindness and compassion," "We want to bathe every day," "We want to sleep alone," "We want healthy mothers and fathers," "We want family doctors," "We want mother's milk," "We want nurse midwives," "We want good health for Atatürk," and "We want ascendancy for the nation." While some of these signs clearly had nationalist slogans, others carried messages that combined modernist and nationalist concerns. These were messages about improving a child's health through proper nutrition and hygiene, and better child and health care services. The child question in the early years of the Republic was understood to be a national question. Children were seen as a national resource, and raising children as a national duty.[40] For this reason, the "We Want" signs should be seen as part of a campaign promoted by the Children's Protection Society, and supported by the government, to raise awareness of the child question and childcare issues.

22. School children, male and female, celebrating 23 April with their teachers, Maraş, 1936. Note the "İsteriz" signs children are holding, declaring their wishes for themselves and for the nation. Note also other reminders of the nation, such as the flag and portraits of Atatürk. Photograph from BCA 490.01/18.95.2.

Poetry, Performance, and the Making of a Collective Historical Memory

Children gave speeches and recited poems at the ceremonies. It was in part through the repetition of these celebrations, several of them in each school year and repeated year after year, that their messages became instilled in children's minds. There was also a strong personal dimension to them. One's own performance made these celebrations memorable. It was not necessarily the content of what was performed, but the fact of a participant's performance with the group and in front of the group that made these events memorable. Meliha Tanyeli, whom we have met before, remembered the excitement and the joy of leading the other students of Trabzon High School in the collective reading of a 19th of May speech at Kavakmeydanı, one of the major squares in Trabzon, surrounded by a big crowd of spectators. She could not remember what the speech was about, but remembered very distinctly that she would read a line first, and the whole crowd would repeat after her.[41]

For other narrators, the memory of the content and the message of the poetry they memorized for national celebrations was more powerful and long-lasting. In 2003, when I asked eighty-three-year-old Recep Göksoy about national celebrations in his childhood, he remembered reciting poetry in primary school in his small Black Sea town and rose energetically to his feet to recite this poem:

Remember! We were no more than a handful of people
The world became our enemy and we were defeated
They know the old Turk has died
They assume that the old Turk has died
They took our cannons and our bayonets
They loosed the Greeks upon our land
The treacherous Greeks with their soldiers
They plunged a dagger into our back
The Gazi promised us in the Assembly
We will strangle drown the Greeks in our land
This promise spread from heart to heart
Every Turk fought, man, woman, and child
The Turk shattered the foes' steel with his breast
The Turk proved true to his character
One day like a volcano on the horizon
A man finally took flame
O Turkish daughter! O Turkish son!
Take a lesson from this
Don't let others touch your land
Don't let the feelings inside you be lulled to sleep
Don't forget this fight for liberation.[42]

Later I came across the same poem in the memoirs of Subutay Hikmet, who had spent his elementary school years in Trabzon, Şebinkarahisar, Zara, and Sinop in the 1930s.[43] Mustafa Kılıç recorded a slightly different version of the same poem as recited by his father Hacı Mehmet Kılıç in 2002. Kılıç says his father Hacı Mehmet, born in 1339 (1923), memorized this poem in elementary school in Malatya, sometime between 1933 and 1935.[44] Given that these men, who came from different social backgrounds and lived in different parts of the country, remembered the same poem suggests that this poem circulated quite widely in the 1930s. That these three men, all in their eighties at the turn of this century, remembered this poem from their elementary school years also suggests that nationalist poems memorized by schoolchildren helped create a shared cultural context and a shared collective memory for children with access to education. Memorization and recitation of poetry at school was not limited to the times of national celebrations, but celebrations provided a regular calendar during which such activities intensified and recitation of poetry became a public event.

Messages of nationalist poems such as this one must have resonated deeply with the personal experiences of Göksoy and many children and youth of his generation. Memories of war (of the Balkan Wars and the World War, as well as the War of Liberation) were fresh in their minds, and their impact was still felt in the children's everyday lives in the 1920s and 1930s. In 2003, I interviewed Recep Göksoy and two other elderly men who were born before 1923 in villages in the same rural district of Kastamonu province. All three had lost a father, a step-father, or a close relative to the war. Also common to their narratives of childhood was extreme poverty and material deprivation. Göksoy's father was a veteran of the War of Liberation. This was Göksoy's mother's second marriage. Her first husband had died in war. She married her brother-in-law upon the death of her husband, as was the custom when losing a husband. Mehmet Baltacı's father had died at Gallipoli and his mother never remarried, raising her children alone as a war widow.[45] Yusuf Altınkaya, the oldest in the group, was born in 1323 (1907/1908),[46] and was also raised by a widowed mother. His father had died in one of the wars, probably the Balkan wars. His mother married his uncle, again as custom dictated, but the uncle/step-father was also called up and went to the front. He returned from war ill and died at home, and the mother never married again after the death of her second husband. Narratives of war widows raising children as single mothers were neither extreme nor unusual in the 1920s. Demographic data, such as estimates of the percentage of widows in post-war Turkey, confirm that cases such as the ones above were not uncommon. According to the 1927 census, in parts of Anatolia, especially in the Aegean and Eastern Black Sea regions, thirty percent or more of the women above the age of twenty were widows.[47] Thinking of the war years as the War of Liberation helped to make sense of one's own (individual, family, and community) involvement, loss, and suffering during that period by identifying these sacrifices as part of a greater cause—that of the liberation of the nation.

RPP leaders were keenly aware of the potential the recitation of heroic poetry and speeches carried for the creation and maintenance of a collective historical memory. State authorities encouraged the production and public consumption of poetry and speeches, as well as other literary forms such as epics and short stories. Textbooks and children's books and magazines contained many examples of nationalist poetry, some of which were intended for memorization and recitation during the national holidays. Poems intended for the 23rd of April generally combined themes of childhood with those of nationhood. The RPP supported the publication of nationalist poetry, plays, and epics by commissioning such work directly or by purchasing copies of such works for distribution to schools, public libraries, and People's Houses libraries. Literary production was among the major activities of People's Houses. Poetry, as well as short stories and essays recounting the heroism of the War of Liberation and explaining the importance of the national holidays, featured prominently in People's Houses magazines. The impact of these magazines on the general population may have been quite limited due to their modest readerships. Perhaps the real impact of the People's Houses magazines was on those who produced these publications. The People's Houses' magazines and other literary and cultural activities provided an institutionalized, if not autonomous, venue for the urban educated youth and professionals in various cities and towns throughout Turkey to become actively involved in the nation-building process. Significant numbers of teachers, doctors, lawyers, writers, and others, the majority of them male, but also including women, took part in the organization and celebration of national holidays and other social, cultural, and literary activities of the People's Houses.

A number of renowned literary figures were also directly involved in the production of a collective historical memory through the culture of celebrations and commemorations. The celebrated poet Behçet Kemal Çağlar, for example, contributed to the process of Turkish nation-building, not only through his many nationalist poems (among them "The Tenth Anniversary March," which he co-authored with Faruk Nafız) and plays, but also as an activist for People's Houses, and by reciting his own work at public celebrations and commemorations. At the 1941 ceremonies at the Ulus square in Ankara, commemorating the Martyrs of the Airforce (*Hava Şehitlerini Anma Günü*), Behçet Kemal Çağlar read a very emotional and exuberant poem and speech he had written specifically for the occasion. The poem called out to the unknown martyr on behalf of the whole nation, expressing the deep gratitude of the entire "seventeen million" and their pledge to make a homeland befitting its exalted martyrs. The speech addressed the "veterans (*gazi*) of the old wars," and "those who were looking for an opportunity to become martyrs," even as it continued to speak to the martyrs as if the dead and the living were sharing the same physical space. In the context of World War II, as Turkey's involvement appeared to be a real possibility despite the government's careful policy of neutrality, the collective memory of the War of Liberation gained a new urgency.[48] Behçet Kemal reminded his audience, the dead (including Atatürk) and the living ("the children of Atatürk and the soldiers of İnönü"), of the success of the War of Liberation and how that war set a great example to the oppressed nations of the world: as proved by the War of Liberation, no nation on earth could be "as brave, as obstinate, as determined, and as firm as the Turkish nation." He reiterated the nation's pledge to the martyrs and to Atatürk to defend the homeland, by fighting a new War of Liberation if necessary. As the government prepared for entanglement in a total war, delving into the collective memory of the War of Liberation became a useful means of raising nationalist consciousness. The RPP Secretary General distributed copies of Behçet Kemal's poem and speech to a host of government and affiliated institutions, including governors, RPP provincial and district offices, People's Houses, and People's Rooms (Halk Odaları), asking them to make sure the poem and the speech were read by as many people as possible.[49]

National Holidays in Schools and Textbooks

Schools were crucial in the building of a culture of national celebrations. Children's Day, as well as Youth and Sports Day, Republic Day, and a number of other national holidays, were an integral part of the regular school curriculum, and schools and teachers played key roles in planning, organization, and actual performance of these celebrations. Instructions issued for the elementary school teachers by the Ministry of Education (*İlkmektepler*

Talimatnamesi) acknowledged the role of national days in the creation of a patriotic feeling among students, saying, "Celebration of the National Holidays mentioned in the program is a source of love for the school, and later it develops into love for the community."[50] The *Talimatname* further emphasized, as Allen observed, the connection between education, creation of a Turkish national feeling, and national celebrations:

> The Turkish cause and Turkey will be the fundamental axle of training. The national feelings of the students should be strengthened at every chance. The significance and bountiful gifts of this Revolution must be explained thoroughly. Ceremonies and other exercises carried out on the anniversary of the Proclamation of the Republic [29 October][51] and the Bayram of 23 April give a chance to increase the national feeling of the children.[52]

What was performed in actual celebrations could be complemented and reinforced in textbooks, in the same way as clothing reforms were promoted in school books. Textbooks provided stories on the origins and significance of major national holidays. They also contained poems about national days for students to memorize and recite during the celebrations. In her examination of elementary school textbooks between 1923 and 1938, Tiregöl observed that textbooks in the early years of the Republic included references to major religious events and days such as Ramazan, the Islamic month of fasting, and the *bayram* at the end of Ramazan, while later textbooks covered only secular national days.[53] This was in keeping with the state's intensification of secularizing policies in the 1930s.

National holidays were also occasions for remembering, teaching, and celebrating the accomplishments of the new state and the nation. In a 1939 issue dedicated to the 23rd of April, *Birinci Sınıf Dergisi*, a children's magazine intended as a supplementary reading for first graders, celebrated the Children's Holiday with poems, images featuring children in action during 23rd of April celebrations, stories about, and illustrations from actual 23rd of April ceremonies, a history of the War of Liberation, and a brief illustrated essay on the accomplishments of the nation. The essay "What Have We Accomplished?" proudly recounted the major cultural, economic, and military accomplishments of the nation under the leadership of Atatürk, as well as its major goals and aspirations as envisioned by the RPP regime. It expressed these successes as "our accomplishments" in order to instill in children a feeling of belonging and a sense of pride in the collective achievements of the nation, which it summarized in seven clauses. These were:

1. The whole nation lives with the security of life and property.

2. The army is the guardian of our country. Today we have the greatest airplanes, war ships such as Yavuz, Saldıray, Yıldıray, and Batıray, cannons, rifles, and tanks. Our army is like steel. No one can look upon our country with evil intent.

3. Girls study in the same schools with boys.

4. With the recent revolution, we put the hat on our heads. The new revolution gave us these letters. Today the whole nation is reading.

5. The whole nation is one in the eyes of the state. There is no distinction between rich and poor, villager and townsman.

6. We have opened new schools in place of the old. Hundreds of thousands of Turkish children are studying at these schools.

7. Our homeland has been knit together with a web of iron and filled with factories.[54]

Through such narratives, *Birinci Sınıf Dergisi* communicated to school children in a clear and simple language some of the fundamental principles of the RPP ideology as well as some of the broader values and institutions central to the modernist nationalism of the Republican regime. Hence the essay's listing of the principles of equality and the rule of law, the army, literacy and education, women's education, the importance of the visible aspects of modernity, and economic development. The images accompanying the text (as can be seen in Figure 23) reinforced these messages visually: The soldier and the airplane would remind children of the importance of the army. The newspaper-reading peasant couple signaled the importance to the nation of literacy, education, and reading, as well as the significance of women and peasants. The scary old *hoca*, fez on his head and stick in his hand, reinforced the idea of a revolutionary break, and the superiority of the new education system of the revolutionary order. Finally, the girl, reading, dressed in her school uniform, like the child reading the essay in the picture on the 23rd of April, represented the nation itself and the importance of girls' education for the future of the nation.[55]

23. "What Have We Accomplished?" *Birinci Sınıf Dergisi*, 23 Nisan (April) 1939.

While the 23rd of April celebrated childhood and nationhood on the anniversaries of the opening of the Parliament in Ankara, the 19th of May celebrated youth and sports while commemorating Mustafa Kemal's landing in Samsun. Children who grew up celebrating the 23rd of April in their elementary school years also celebrated the 19th of May in their youth. And 29 October, Republic Day, celebrating the birth of the Republic and the accomplishments of the nation on the anniversaries of the proclamation of the Republic, was omnipresent throughout their childhood, school years, and adulthood.

As Hobsbawm has observed, rites of passage are usually not marked in invented traditions of nations because these traditions emphasize the "eternal and unchanging character" of the nation, but political regimes try to find equivalents for traditional rites of passage.[56] The three major national holidays in Turkey functioned as rites of passage for the nation and the citizen in a number of ways. The 23rd of April and the 19th of May corresponded to critical moments in the nation's recent history as well as crucial stages of childhood and youth in the life of an individual, hence serving as rites of passage for the nation and the individual simultaneously. In the lives of individual citizens, the passage from Children's Day in elementary school to Youth and Sports Day in high school served as an important rite of passage marking the transition from childhood into youth. Both 23 April and 29 October signified the birth of the nation. As Öztürkmen has noted, celebrations on the anniversaries of the proclamation of the Republic served as rites of passage for the Republic, as expressed in statements such as "our Republic has become ten years old," and "it's finally fifteen years old."[57] Each anniversary celebration marked another stage in the successful evolution of the Republic into a consolidated regime.

Because the legitimacy of these national holidays derived from the participation of the people in the celebrations, even if not all groups enjoyed equal access to them, these holidays were generally inclusive and open to participation, and in combination with the education system they helped produce a generation of urban, educated Turkish citizens in the 1930s who shared elements of a common Republican national culture. All citizens, regardless of their ethnic or religious backgrounds, were invited to join national holidays provided they adhered to the nationalist content and messages of these programs. Hence, national holidays allowed some room for the inclusion of non-Muslim and non-Turkish citizens in the national community even as they revealed the tension between the civic nationalist ideals and the ethnolinguistic assimilationist tendencies of Turkish nationalism.

In addition to the major national holidays and local liberation days that were celebrated annually, children and youth who attended school also took part in the much smaller-scale, yet routine, ritual of ceremonies marking the beginning and the end of the school week. These ceremonies contained some of the basic elements of the major national celebrations, such as the singing of the National Anthem (*İstiklal Marşı*) and the raising and lowering of the flag—acts that reminded students of their collective national identity. Furthermore, texts such as the lyrics of *İstiklal Marşı* and the *Gençliğe Hitabe*, Mustafa Kemal's address to the Turkish youth at the end of his famous speech, the *Nutuk*, were included in reading and literature textbooks from elementary through high school. Students recited, analyzed, and discussed the meaning of these texts in the classroom, further reminding them of their national history, identity, and duties. In elementary schools, students started the day with a collective recitation of *Andımız*, the pledge of the Turkish children to the nation, written by Reşid Galib, the Minister of Education from 1932–1933:[58]

> I am a Turk, hardworking and true.
> My principal is to protect those younger than myself,
> To respect those older than myself.
> To love my country and my nation more than myself.
> My ideal is to rise higher and to move forward.
> O Great Atatürk!
> I take an oath to walk unceasingly, along the path you have opened,
> Toward the goal you have shown.
> May my existence be a gift to the Turkish existence.
> "How happy is the one who says '"I am a Turk.'"

Celebrations of national days were closely associated with the school and the academic calendar, yet children's socialization into the culture of national celebrations began even before they reached school age. As spectators at nationalist celebrations, and imitating their older siblings or other school children who performed in the ceremonies, small children began to learn about the messages of these celebrations even before starting elementary school. E. Önhan recalled the joys of national days from her childhood years spent in the small town of Patnos in Eastern Anatolia. When she was about three years old, her family moved from Kars to the district of Patnos, in Ağrı province, in 1970. On national holidays, she and her friends would make flags using sticks and paper, and march around their yards singing songs praising the state and its founder. They were clearly imitating their older siblings who participated in the ceremonies as school children. Although she could not remember any of the lyrics to these songs or the specific slogans, she knew they were words in praise of the Republic, very much like the poems, the slogans, and the "we want . . ." signs of children from the 1930s celebrations. Ironically, all the singing and slogans of Önhan and her friends were in Kurdish. Most of the local children in Patnos were of Kurdish origin and spoke Kurdish only; hence, she naturally learned Kurdish from her friends. Despite her mother's prohibiting her from speaking Kurdish, with the fear that she would forget Turkish altogether, Önhan continued to speak Kurdish, probably because that was the only language her friends could speak. After the family moved back from Patnos to Kars when she was about six, she gradually lost most of the Kurdish she had learned as a child.[59]

This story of the children from Patnos suggests that national holidays continued to serve as an instrument of socialization into the national culture as late as the 1970s, starting from preschool years of childhood and reinforced through the school years, even (perhaps especially) in towns where Turkish was not the spoken language of the majority. The children's story also reveals a rather mixed record of the Republican state's reach to the remote and especially non-Turkish-speaking regions of Anatolia. It appears that in this small town in Eastern Anatolia, for the majority of the population the spoken language continued to be Kurdish. Children learned Turkish, the official national language, largely after they started school. Literacy and access to public education lagged significantly behind the national averages in Ağrı and the majority of the Eastern Anatolian provinces. The literacy rate in Ağrı was 6.3 percent in 1935 (10.9 percent for men and particularly low for women, only 1.5 percent) for the population above age seven, when the overall literacy rate for Turkey for the same age group was 20.4 percent. By 1945 the literacy rate in Ağrı improved to 13.9 percent (23.5 percent for men and only 3.6 percent for women), a rate significantly lower than the 30.2 percent for the total population of Turkey.[60] During the RPP era, the state's presence in the province was mainly through the military and the Office of Inspectors General.[61] Many of the regime's usual instruments and institutions of nation-building and modernization, such as the education system, the print media, national celebrations, party organization, and People's Houses, had either no presence or only limited access to the remote and "unruly" provinces of Eastern Anatolia. Nor did the regime have the local social support base in these provinces of the educated urban middle- and upper-middle-classes that supported the regime in other parts of the country. By the 1970s, provinces such as Ağrı were perhaps finally experiencing a process of gradual incorporation into the national culture that other parts of the county had gone through several decades earlier. The Patnos example also suggests a compromise solution between the state's modernist, nationalist goals and the local population's culture, identities, and demands. State institutions such as schools coexisted with a certain degree of expression of local culture and identities, such as the persistence of Kurdish as the spoken language of the local population. The state tolerated the persistence of spoken Kurdish (perhaps in part because it could not eliminate it), and the local population tolerated the presence of state institutions such as schools (perhaps in part because access to public education opened up opportunities for employment and a better life for the younger generation).

National Holidays as Metaphor for an Inclusive Nation

Distant Towns and Dispossessed Citizens Celebrating National Holidays

In principle, all members of the nation were intended to share the joy of national celebrations, at least as spectators. In practice, material differences, urban/rural, and regional differences played an important role in determining if and to what extent one would be included in national celebrations. For the majority of the nation's children, the celebration of the Children's Day took place in conditions of extreme poverty and deprivation. A key function of the national holidays, including the 23rd of April, was to create a sense (and perhaps the illusion) of inclusion and belonging, even and especially to those whose material circumstances suggested that they might not belong to this national community, since they were not getting their fair share of the country's resources, or that the state and the nation did not take care of them as members of the nation. Peasant children, for example, many of them undernourished and poorly clad, celebrated the 23rd of April in their village schools with their teachers and classmates by decorating their schools, reciting poetry, performing folk dances, and parading through their village singing nationalist marches.[62] Others, such as orphans or children whose families could not afford to send them to school, were either left out of celebrating Children's Day, or were included only as objects of charity. National holidays were occasions for the RPP officials, the Children's Protection Society, and the People's Houses to help poor children and their families. RPP officials from the provinces sent photographs of the children dressed or fed by the Children's Protection Society on the occasion of a national holiday to the RPP headquarters. Villagers in areas without People's Houses, People's Rooms, or schools had very limited access to national celebrations. In the less integrated parts of the country where the RPP or the People's Houses did not have any presence or did not receive much local support, national holidays did not have the same significance they had in other parts of the country. The letter below gives a sense of national celebrations in the remote areas of Eastern Anatolia.

Ali Genç, an army officer stationed in Siirt province, told his sister how he spent Victory Day in Siirt in 1942:[63]

> Let me tell you how we spent the 30th of August here. I participated in the official parade with the regiment. The ceremony ended at the regimental headquarters following a mounted procession behind the headquarters. Of course, in a place like Siirt, even this was a lot. Anyway, in the evening there was a ball, and we went. The ball was so-so. The ball here was a far cry from the merriment in the Bomonti beer park [in İstanbul]. In the end, after spending [the 30th of August] like that, life went back to normal.

The lack of public enthusiasm implied in the letter may have had to do with the dire economic and psychological circumstances of the World War II years. (Genç complained in the same letter about the high cost of living and the challenges of making ends meet.) But his letter suggests a perception of a want of public spirit that existed for reasons apart from the adverse effects of the war. Institutions and mediators such as the schools and teachers, the RPP, People's Houses, and other semi-autonomous associations that were essential for the socialization of the local communities into the national culture through education, national holidays, and other cultural projects, were largely lacking in many of the eastern Anatolian provinces. Throughout the early decades of the Republic, the village and tribal populations of the Eastern provinces remained to a considerable degree outside the state's reformist cultural project. In the 1930s, in some of the Eastern Anatolian provinces more than 90 percent of the village children had no access to primary education. In a few of those provinces, that rate was as high as 99 percent.[64] The small but growing middle class of professionals and others such as teachers, lawyers, doctors, journalists, businessmen, and high school and university students who identified with (at least with aspects of) the cultural project of the Republican regime and supported it in the urban centers, was much smaller or essentially missing in many of the remote eastern towns.

Republic Balls

Celebration programs in the cities, especially on Republic Days, but usually on the other major national holidays as well, ended with a ball in the evening. Often the balls had a social and charity function, such as those organized by the Children's Protection Society during Children's Week to generate income for the child welfare services of the Society. A central purpose of these balls, in addition to any charity functions, was to socialize Turkish men and women into new, "modern" forms of sociability and public entertainment. Unlike traditional forms and places of sociability, such as coffeehouses, bars, and mosques that were gender segregated, the Republic balls involved male and female guests eating, drinking, conversing, and dancing together. By the end of the nineteenth century, as a result of the long process of cultural Westernization and secularization, a degree of gender-desegregated forms of sociability had already entered the urban culture of İstanbul and İzmir, and, to a more limited degree, of a few other port cities such as Mersin and Trabzon. As Duben and Behar have observed, by the 1920s and 1930s, it was not uncommon for wives and husbands from middle-class İstanbul families to socialize as couples.[65] Mixed gender socialization was not yet common among the lower-class families of İstanbul, and the idea of an urban Muslim couple attending a public event together was likely a relatively new idea in many parts of the country in the 1920s and 1930s. Local RPP officials were encouraged to attend these balls with their wives in order to set an example of modern Turkish couples.

In contrast to the festivities that took place during the day that were generally more inclusive, these balls tended to be more exclusionary events.

Attendance may have been by invitation only, or any requirement to purchase a dinner ticket would have prevented a great majority from attending. Perhaps as important as the economic and class factors were the cultural implications of going to a ball. Attending such an event would have implied willingness to follow, or at least to exhibit or tolerate, certain cultural norms such as dressing in a modern way, husbands and wives socializing as a couple at a gender-desegregated public event and perhaps listening to Western music and dancing Western style. E. W. F. Tomlin drew a colorful depiction of Republic balls based on his personal observations of such events, presumably in Ankara and İstanbul and a few other cities. Tomlin wrote:

> This is always a very gay affair, and will often last until very late. The modern Turk is a keen and usually a very good dancer; and he has taken to jazz and swing music with great enthusiasm. The women wear tasteful evening dresses and the men dinner jackets or "tails." The atmosphere is completely European. Food is provided in abundance; and a great deal of raki, vodka, beer, and local cognac (*kanyak*) is drunk, especially by the men.[66]

Tomlin's description suggests that these were somewhat exclusive events that appealed mainly to the Westernized upper classes. Interestingly, while Tomlin described these events as entirely European in character, he also noted that as the night advanced and the atmosphere became more relaxed, guests might perform "Turkish dances," such as the *zeybek* of the Aegean and the *horon* of the Eastern Black Sea regions. Even if Tomlin's depiction of the balls includes a certain degree of exaggeration, it nevertheless speaks to the presence of a core group who actively participated in these events and tried to reconcile their aspirations for a European identity and culture with their local and national habits and identities by opening the night with Western dances and ending it with the *zeybek*. The striking contrast between Tomlin's account and the evidence from provincial towns points to the unevenness of the emerging national culture along regional, economic, class, and urban versus rural lines.

While these balls had some genuine supporters, and were not openly opposed or contested, evidence from provincial towns suggests that segments of the urban society, perhaps including some who actually attended these events (voluntarily or because they felt they had to attend), resented and criticized them on cultural grounds. A case from Antep attests to the cultural tensions over the meaning of the balls and similar social events. The Republic Ball held in Antep in 1935 appears to have caused a confrontation between the RPP vice-chairman of the town, *Doktor* Abdülkadir, and a local bureaucrat. This bureaucrat apparently invited Abdülkadir (and his wife)[67] to the stage to join the provincial governor, the military commander, and others, in dancing. Presumably this was a European style dance performed by couples, involving husbands and wives performing together in public, wives in close physical proximity to their husbands and possibly to other men. It was probably the prospect of his wife's dancing in public that annoyed and embarrassed the RPP vice-chairman. This set off a minor crisis between the two men, and mutual accusations that were taken to the local newspaper and the RPP headquarters. Such disputes, no doubt, at least in part had to do with petty rivalries and conflicts of personal interest among local elites and government officials; they are nevertheless telling indicators of the cultural conflicts and contestations in the provincial towns of Anatolia in the 1930s. The bureaucrat argued that it was a "modern and social need to dance," and that the RPP vice-chairman should have joined the dance even if he did not know how to dance. He accused Abdülkadir of having a reactionary mentality and disrespecting the revolution.[68] Dr. Abdülkadir, on the other hand, used the local paper to accuse the bureaucrat, and men like him, of failing to understand the true spirit of the revolution, of being a "*kozmopolit züppe*" who was harmful to the well-being of the society.[69] The reference to the *züppe*, the quintessential symbol of excessive Westernization in the nineteenth century critique of Ottoman modernization, placed this minor dispute that unfolded at a Republic ball in the context of broader, unresolved cultural debates over Turkish culture and modernity.[70]

It is also evident from People's Houses publications of the 1930s that in some Anatolian towns there was only limited popular interest in the evening balls and other cultural activities promoted by a reformist elite and their emerging middle class supporters in those towns. For example, according to *Yeni Tokat*, the publication of the Tokat Halkevi, in 1934 the Women's branch of the Air Association (*Tayyare Cemiyeti*) in Tokat organized a ball for the benefit of the Association, but had to cancel it due to a lack of public interest.

Yeni Tokat again reported that the local residents of the Turhal district failed to attend a play staged "by the youth" in cooperation with the Tokat Halkevi for the benefit of poor children in town.[71] The balls were arguably among the less effective aspects of the national holidays. Some of the other evening activities in towns during national celebrations, such as lighting up of the streets with lanterns and the outdoor concerts and screening of films, created a more festival-like atmosphere and appealed to a greater number of people.

Women

A small segment of educated and urban women actively participated in the making of national celebrations in their capacity as public orators, People's House members, members of associations such as the Children's Protection Society and the Red Crescent, and especially as teachers. Governors, *kaymakam*s, and most mayors were men. Men also controlled key political and social positions, such as local RPP and People's House presidencies. The RPP encouraged women's membership in the party and their active participation, especially through People's Houses. Celebration reports and contemporary press coverage indicate that women, especially female teachers, took part in different stages of the celebration, including organization, giving speeches, and acting in plays. With less interference from state authorities, women as village teachers probably had the best chance of adding their own vision and creativity in celebrating Children's Day with villagers and their children.

Photographs taken at Children's Day, such as the one below taken in Aydın in 1934 (Figure 24),[72] show that while most women could not at the time expect to be active participants in these celebrations, they could be, and were, a part of the celebrating public as spectators, even if they did not fit the image of the new Turkish woman promoted by the state. This photograph captured a moment of the children's parade through the streets of Aydın on the morning of the 23rd of April 1934. In front, in the middle of the street, is an ox cart decorated with branches and flowers (even the faces of the oxen are decorated) and with a bust of Atatürk in the middle. There is a little girl on the cart who appears to sit on Atatürk's lap. School children are marching, following the cart. There are flags hanging outside buildings. Two men in fedora style hats are walking on either side of the cart, and a villager in baggy pants and a cap is in front of the cart. There are spectators on both sides of the road, women, men, and children. The men are in hats and caps. Women are all covered in *peştemals*.

Photographs from a number of other towns also show women as spectators in the 23rd of April celebrations. The photograph in Figure 25, taken in the town of Muğla in the Aegean region during Children's Day celebrations in 1934, shows Muğla Middle School and the guest Milas Middle School playing a volleyball match.[73] There are women among the spectators, most of them in *çarşafs*. They are not mixed in with the circle of male spectators surrounding the field; they are in the background and segregated.

The state encouraged women's public appearance and participation in public life, but as "civilized" women in modern dress. National holidays provided an opportunity for reminding the citizens of their responsibilities toward the nation, which included ensuring that their appearance was in conformity with the requirements of modernity. It was at this point in 1934 that the governor of Aydın issued a declaration to the women of Aydın (discussed in chapter 2) inviting them to leave behind the *peştemal*, "this backward and ugly piece of clothing that lowers the civilizational level of

24. Celebrating Children's Day in Aydın, 1934. An original of this photograph, taken on 23 April 1934 in Aydın, is deposited at BCA 490.01/13.67.1.

25. Celebrating Children's Day in Muğla, 1934. This photograph, taken on 23 April 1934 in Muğla, has been reproduced from an original deposited at BCA 490.01/13.67.1.

this town."[74] During the same 23rd of April celebrations in Aydın, a student from the 7 Eylül School delivered a speech addressing (among other issues) the question of *peştemal*s. He called on the mothers and sisters in the crowd, on behalf of the Turkish youth, to abandon the *peştemal* and to put on the *manto*. Echoing the governor's statement, the student encouraged women to observe this change to elevate the nation's civilizational level and for the sake of the nation's image in foreign countries.[75] It is not clear if the student himself wrote the speech, or if a teacher, a party official, or another adult penned it, but there is evidence from other regions, including very small towns, to suggest that at least some RPP officials and Peoples Houses viewed national holidays as times to intensify the regime's propaganda efforts to enforce the reforms. For example, in the Ulubey district of Ordu province, in the eastern Black Sea region, during the preparations for the 1937 23rd of April celebrations the district governor met with the village heads from the nearby villages to discuss with them the importance of the issue of *peçe*s, *çarşaf*s, and *peştemal*s, and to remind them of the local decrees pertaining to such articles of clothing. As the governor advised the village heads to encourage women to attend the Children's Day ceremonies free from the *peçe, çarşaf,* and *peştemal,* the district sent "131 intellectuals" to the villages in the area to participate in the village celebrations of the 23rd of April by delivering lectures on topics including the revolution and women's dress.[76]

It appears that while these celebrations were generally open to all men and women as spectators, in some instances local administrators or program committees may have restricted participation, even as spectators. The city of Antalya had a detailed program for Children's Week celebrations in 1935 put out by the Children's Protection Society. The program included activities such as plays, athletic events, a ball, a robust-child contest and an excursion. The program specified that "women who have not yet taken off their *çarşaf*s and *peçe*s should not come to these events."[77] This appears to be an extension of local governments' dress regulations to include celebrations. If such restrictions as Antalya's were enforced, they may have limited women's participation in celebrations, which clearly contradicted the purpose behind those decrees.

In the long run, perhaps the most important aspect of the national days for women's inclusion in the national culture as equal citizens was their full participation in those celebrations as children and young women alongside their male classmates year after year. Their active involvement in these public events through marching, reciting poetry, performing in plays, and taking part in athletic events and exhibitions helped legitimize women's place in public life as adult citizens, by preparing their families and the larger society for women's participation in social life.

Commemorating Ertuğrul Gazi, Re-Imagining the Turkish Nation

Unlike French conservatives, who for a very long time refused to celebrate the Republic, preferring instead to commemorate the birth and death dates of the Bourbon kings, and the French peasants who until World War I refused to exchange local memory for the national,[78] it does not appear that Turkish peasants and town residents refused to participate in Republican celebrations. For a vast majority of Turkey's population the slogan "Long Live the Sultan" ("*Padişahım Çok Yaşa*") successfully transformed into "Long Live the Gazi" ("*Yaşasın Gazi/Yaşasın Mustafa Kemal Paşa*") and "Long Live the Republic" ("*Yaşasın Cumhuriyet*" and "*Yaşasın Türk Milleti*") as the figure of Atatürk effectively replaced the figure of the Sultan as the symbol of the idealized form of the state in the popular imagination. However, by the late 1940s, there emerged signs of a public desire to commemorate events and individuals associated with the Ottoman past of the nation. One such case was the commemoration of Ertuğrul Gazi in Söğüt, in northwest Anatolia in Bilecik province. Ertuğrul Gazi was the father of Osman, the founder of the Ottoman dynasty,[79] who along with other *gazi* warriors and dervishes led the Turcoman tribesmen in settling in the area of Söğüt in the late thirteenth century, from whence emerged the Ottoman state, expanding into Anatolia and the Balkans. In the fall of 1950, two residents of Söğüt wrote to president Celal Bayar on behalf of an "Ertuğrul Gazi Commemoration Committee," inviting the president to the upcoming Ertuğrul Gazi Commemoration to be held on October 1. The celebration program[80] (attached to the invitation) is quite telling, concerning how the organizers envisioned and reconciled their local, national, and historical identities. According to the program, all citizens (presumably of Söğüt and the nearby towns and villages) were welcome at the ceremony in their "national costumes," but at the center of the ceremony was a mounted regiment. "Following custom," the elderly [men] would constitute the first division, the middle-aged the second division, and the youth the third division. There would be one *yiğitbaşı* or section leader for each division. There would also be a *sancak* (banner or flag) at the head of each division, and two guards armed with swords. There would be young men with helmets and shields at the head of the regiment. A mounted committee representing the people of Söğüt would meet up with the regiment, and together they would march to the town's sports field. The entire procession then would parade through the main street in Söğüt to the City Hall (*Hükümet Konağı*) at the Republic Square. Following the collective singing of the National Anthem, a wreath of flowers would be placed at the Atatürk memorial. After three minutes of silence and a welcome speech by the *kaymakam* (or someone he designated), the procession would proceed to the tomb of Ertuğrul Gazi. At the tomb, after three minutes of silence and a speech commemorating Ertuğrul Gazi's life and services, two young men would put a wreath on the Gazi's tomb. Following a traditional feast of pilaf, young men would play jereed (*cirid*[81]) and engage in horse races and other equestrian games. Toward the evening, the procession would return to Söğüt in the same order. (The evening celebration program was less specific: There would be local and national music and dances and entertaining "village" plays.) The commemoration would come to an end with the guests leaving Söğüt the next day, after the enjoyment of a feast hosted by the people of Söğüt.

As the modernist nationalism of the early Republic was in large part premised upon a narrative of difference from the Ottoman past, and as the Republican leaders were trying to distance and liberate Turkey from this past, the commemoration of the Ottoman sultans or their ancestors was not a part of the commemorative calendar of the early Republic. (The Ertuğrul Gazi commemorative invitation to the President came just as some of the restrictions on visits to religious shrines and tombs were lifted in 1950.) Suspicious of the intentions of the organizers of a major commemorative event for an ancestor of the Ottoman dynasty outside of any government supervision, the Minister of the Interior asked the governor of Bilecik to investigate and report on why such an event was being organized.[82] The governor justified the commemoration by placing it in the context of the Ottoman-Turkish commemorative tradition and presenting it as the revival of an old Turkish tradition, rather than a recent invention, outside the state's control, of a commemorative tradition for an Ottoman personality.[83] The governor explained that the commemoration of Ertuğrul Gazi was in fact not new: it was an old tradition abandoned after 1908.[84] That tradition had been revitalized since 1946 with the initiative of the Söğüt People's House and the approval of the RPP. He reassured the ministry that the remembrance of Ertuğrul Gazi had nothing to do with his being an ancestor of the Ottoman dynasty, but was due to his role in pioneering the settlement of the Turks in Söğüt and Anatolia. The governor's defense of the organizers of the commemoration is an indication that he, as the highest government official representing the state in the province, agreed with the organizers in commemorating Ertuğrul Gazi as a Turkish hero, or at least that he did not perceive any threat in such an event.

How should we make sense of this resurgence, or re-invention, of a commemorative tradition in 1950? It may be read as a sign that the public no longer associated the Ottoman era with defeat; that enough time had passed since the defeats and scars of the wars early in the century, and the public wanted to remember a national past that went deeper than the post-1918 period provided. The resurgent interest in commemorating the Ottoman founders can also be interpreted as a public desire to celebrate its Ottoman-Turkish origins emerging into the open as the fear of government suppression receded with the transition to a multiparty political system in 1945. This commemoration was also an indication of an alternative imagination of the nation, of an attempt at a new reconciliation or synthesis of the local, national, and historical identities in a ceremony whose form and content were not determined by the central government. The commemoration program suggests an internalization of elements of national celebrations and the national culture it represented, as well as important shifts and deviations in the sites, content, and focus of early Republican national celebrations, including a continuation of the core elements of the Abdülhamid era Ertuğrul Gazi commemorations. This was to be an entirely secular ceremony that identified Ertuğrul Gazi as a founder of the Turkish nation (not as a founder of the Ottoman state) and connected him with Atatürk and other symbols of modern Turkish nationalism. The ceremony included elements of national celebrations such as the gathering at the Republic square, the singing of the National Anthem, and paying respects to Atatürk through a moment of silence and placing a wreath at his memorial. But then the focus of the commemorative events shifted to Ertuğrul Gazi's tomb. The participants paid their respects to Ertuğrul Gazi in exactly the same way they remembered Atatürk (who was also popularly known and referred to as "the Gazi," especially before the Parliament bestowed on him the surname Atatürk with the adoption of family names), through a moment of silence and placing a wreath on his tomb. In that way, the commemoration symbolically elevated Ertuğrul Gazi to the status of an (or the) original founder of the nation, in a line of great leaders extending to Atatürk in the recent past. Like the Liberation Day in the Of district in Trabzon province that placed the local resistance against Russian occupation in World War I, and the role of the *aghas* and *hocas* in that resistance, at the center of Turkish nationalist history and consciousness, the Ertuğrul Gazi commemoration put Söğüt and Ertuğrul Gazi at the center of Turkish nationalist history.[85]

Compared to the national celebrations, the commemoration of Ertuğrul Gazi involved less official presence. In that way it had a more civilian and democratic potential, but the composition of the parade by mounted men, young and old, and guards with helmet and shield suggest a more military-oriented ceremony, and an exclusively male, hierarchical national order. Activities such as the *cirid* games and horseback riding competitions took the place of the recitation of nationalist poetry by children on the 23rd of April, or the formalized athletic performances by young men and women on the 19th of May. In fact, the mounted parade at the tomb, the *cirid* game, and other equestrian events were elements completely borrowed from the Abdülhamid era Ertuğrul Gazi commemorations. In those annual commemorations, the members of the Karakeçili tribe, identified as the "original Ottoman tribe," would march to Söğüt dressed in their Central Asian nomadic costumes, and would perform a mounted parade at the Ertuğrul Gazi memorial, followed by a *cirid* game and other riding shows.[86]

The Ertuğrul Gazi commemoration program suggests an attempt at reordering national memory by remembering the Ottoman-Turkish origins of the nation and the role or place of the local in that process. The program appears to have envisioned in some ways a more liberating (less state-controlled) national ideal that had its own hierarchies and exclusions. This commemoration imagined youth as a male whose place in the national community was determined by the hierarchy of age. Children did not occupy the central place they had in the Republican nationalist imagination and national holidays. The brave young man with helmet and shield replaced the poetry-reading robust child of the early Republican national celebrations. Women and children were either absent or at most present as spectators only. (On the Liberation Day in Of, Meeker noted that women were on rooftops and on balconies.) Meeker has argued, on the basis of his ethnographic research in Of, that by the 1950s and 1960s, "Kemalist representations of the nation-state and nation-people were increasingly challenged by other representations. In the instance of Liberation Day in the district of Of, officials, military forces, school teachers, and classrooms were going out of focus. Local elites, the descendants of aghas and hodjas, were coming into focus."[87] As Meeker's analysis of the Liberation Days in Of and Sürmene (and the Ertuğrul Gazi commemoration) reveals, such celebrations contested aspects of the official nationalist narrative and ideals, but they did not reject the Republican nationalist project in its entirety, instead modifying it and re-imagining it in ways that reflected the local and provincial culture and interests, which in the case of Of was dominated by the interests of the old elites. The process of defining and redefining the nation through celebrations and commemorations continued in the 1950s and 1960s, even as at times it took the form of, to use Meeker's words, "the colonization of the new republic, based on official hierarchy and authoritarianism, by the old republic, based on social hierarchy and authoritarianism. . . ."[88] Because of the close association between the state, the RPP, and the People's Houses in the 1930s, the question emerged after 1946 as to whose holidays some of these celebrations were. Several of the national holidays that evolved in the 1930s and 1940s were either closely related to the RPP or the People's Houses, or had limited audiences from the beginning and failed to survive the transition to multiparty politics. The People's House Festival, for example, disappeared with the closing of the People's Houses in 1951.[89] The disappearance of the People's Houses and the RPP's fall from government limited the personnel, financial, and other resources dedicated to celebrations of holidays. Schools and the education system (and the army for the 30 August Victory Day, which fell outside the school calendar) became even more crucial after 1950 for the preservation of a culture of national holidays. Several of these national celebrations (including the 19th of May Youth, Sports, and Commemoration of Atatürk Day; the 23rd of April National Sovereignty and Children's Day; and the 29 October Republic Day) were institutionalized and have continued to influence generations of Turkish citizens to this day. The form and the content (perceived meanings and messages) of these holidays have changed, and public interest in them has fluctuated, over the decades. Keeping the collective memory of the War of Liberation and the founding years of the Republic alive through national holidays had become less urgent by the post RPP decades.

More recently, however, as the meaning of the secular republic came to be more openly contested (in the 1990s) while the ethnic-based Kurdish nationalist claims continued to violently challenge Turkish nationalism, remembering the foundational period of the nation through Republic Day celebrations gained a new urgency and meaning for segments of Turkish society. The seventy-fifth anniversary of the proclamation of the Republic in 1998 witnessed an unprecedented (although in some ways comparable to the tenth anniversary celebrations) festival-like civil society celebration, in addition to the official celebrations in Ankara and elsewhere, with massive public participation and the crowds singing the Tenth Anniversary March.[90] As the aging Republic approaches its centennial, the meanings of "the republic" and "the nation" continue to be contested and negotiated, among other sites, through the culture of national holidays.

Conclusion

Turkish historians continue to debate exactly when the Turkish nation came into being, or when the Turkish nation-building process finalized—not in the sense of state-building, but in terms of when the various members of the national community finally identified themselves with the nation. While many scholars have identified the 1950s or 1960s as the period when greater numbers of the nation's members, and their divergent ideas about the identity of the nation, finally entered into this nation-building process through the liberalization of the press, democratization of the political system, industrialization, improvements in communications and transportation, and urbanization, this work has shown that the process of fostering an emotional attachment to a national community was already under way during the 1920s, 1930s, and into the 1940s.

This book contributes to these ongoing debates by exploring the implementation and experiences of several specific reforms of the early Republican period. As we saw most directly in the discussion of national celebrations, the experience and memories of the recent wars were crucial for those legislating reforms (and introducing new linguistic, sartorial, or ceremonial practices), as well as for those receiving them. The wars affected communities, families, and individuals in many different ways. Whether they actually participated in the wars; lost a father, husband, or son to the wars; became refugees during or after the wars; or lost their Greek and Armenian neighbors (whose departure left a social, economic, and psychological void, as well as welcome opportunities), the effects of the wars hung over the shoulders of an entire population, altering people's perceptions and expectations, preparing the ground for a fresh start. This, the two decades after 1922, was a period of slow recovery and reconstruction—socially, economically, and psychologically—during which time individual and local memories of the war years were reinforced, recollected, and re-ordered in building a collective historical memory and national consciousness.

Recent scholarship has criticized Turkish historiography for its undue emphasis on the figure of Mustafa Kemal Atatürk: for writing Republican Turkish history not only in a state-centric, but also in a Mustafa Kemal-centered perspective that fails to capture the complexity of modern Turkey from a critical perspective that can maintain a degree of distance and objectivity. While such criticism no doubt makes a valid point, and Turkish historians would be well advised to take such critique into account, here I would like to underscore that the Mustafa Kemal-centered history writing itself has been a very important and largely successful part of the Turkish nation-building process. I have in this book made a conscious choice not to focus on the figure of Mustafa Kemal, not because I did not consider his role relevant, but because one of my main goals has been to shift the emphasis away from the state and leaders to the society in order to understand the people's own experiences of the process of nationalist reforms. The research and writing of this book, especially the oral historical research I conducted, have convinced me that the figure and the myth of Mustafa Kemal have indeed been key elements of the Turkish nation building process. It was in part, and still is, through identification with the figure of Mustafa Kemal as liberator of the nation that members of the nation-in-making came to identify themselves with a Turkish nation. The sentimental attachment to the national community was achieved in part through identification with Mustafa Kemal. In the collective memory of first-generation Republican citizens, the figure of Atatürk holds a prominent place. His role in national history is recollected as an intimate connection between the individual citizen and Mustafa Kemal. Although I intentionally avoided asking my informants any questions about Atatürk, their recollections not only of the specific reforms but also of their own childhood and youth were replete with references to Mustafa Kemal. They proudly shared with me their memories of chance encounters with Mustafa Kemal in different towns and at different times: a quick glance at Mustafa Kemal and Latife Hanım when they got off the boat in Trabzon, a quick glance during his visit to a school in Mersin, a quick glimpse of Mustafa Kemal and Reza Shah in Bankalar Street in İstanbul, a brief conversation during his visit to an elementary school in

Bursa. As Zürcher and others have noted, the institutionalization of the regime (through the RPP, the military, the People's Houses, and the legal and educational systems) was crucial for the survival of the Republican nationalist project after 1938 and after 1945—even if some of these institutions, such as the People's Houses, did not survive the transition to multi-party politics. In the meantime, the figure and later the myth of Mustafa Kemal provided a powerful national symbol to which individual citizens felt emotionally attached. The distinction citizens frequently made between the benevolent state represented by Atatürk and the coercive application of state power at the local level facilitated continued allegiance to the nation-state, despite the excesses of the exercise of state power at the local level.

While I wish to acknowledge Mustafa Kemal's symbolic role in this process, I have argued in this book that the exclusive focus on the state and its institutions, political elites, and organized political movements, and on organized resistance or rebellion, is of limited use in understanding how the process of Kemalist reforms was in fact experienced by individual citizens, families, and communities in their everyday lives. Drawing on a wide range of primary sources, including new archival and oral historical evidence, this study has shown how abstract legislation and ideals acquired meaning for citizens through their actual encounters and interactions with a number of mediating institutions and individuals in four specific sites of the state's attempts to transform the society and culture. Issues fundamental to understanding the social, political, and cultural processes of making and becoming a modern Turkish nation recur throughout the book in the examination of all four areas of reform. These issues include a consideration of the broad range of responses to the modernist nationalist reforms (from active support and promotion to everyday forms of individual and collective resistance), and the recognition of the category of social and culture change at a personal level that may fall outside of ideologically or politically oriented forms of opposition and resistance. Among these individual factors are the importance of childhood and youth and the related phenomenon of generations (whether in abandoning established linguistic or sartorial habits or in learning a new script or language). I have shown that elderly citizens, including those who were ardent supporters of the Republican nationalist project, found it difficult to adapt themselves to some of the reforms that required changes in established habits. On the other hand, the generation that was born at the end of the Empire, and experienced the war years or the 1920s as children, overall developed a very powerful emotional attachment to the nation, even when they disagreed with aspects of the Republican reforms. I have considered religion not only as an element of identity and ideological source of resistance, but also as an instrument of secular nation building. I have emphasized the role of women and gender, the role of class, and urban/rural and regional differences. I have highlighted the importance of individual and collective memory, particularly in the creation of a collective historical consciousness and a new national identity.

I have taken into account the different levels of the state's involvement in the everyday lives of Turkish citizens (from the Republican People's Party central government to governors, *kaymakams*, and the gendarmerie, from the Directorate of Religous Affairs to the teachers). The state operated not only through government bureaucrats and officials, but also through the press, schools and teachers, prayer leaders, and even through individual citizens who actively supported and promoted the state-initiated measures. I have shown in several specific cases that there was not always consensus within the different branches of the RPP government, and that different branches of the government and different officials interpreted reforms, and especially the implementation of reforms, in different ways. I have also argued that the government reaction to noncompliance varied, and was often more compromising and pragmatic than has been assumed, depending on how the authorities interpreted the specific action or case in hand.

In the state's attempts to reorder the society, modernist, secularist and nation-building goals often coexisted side by side. The common view in the field of the Hat Law as a secularizing measure, for example, is an incomplete assessment, since the Law targeted not only the fez, seen at the time as men's Islamic headgear, but also any headgear that could be viewed as not Turkish or not civilized. Hence it was intended as a homogenizing, unifying and nationalizing, and civilizing measure as much as a secularizing process. The overemphasis on the secular versus religious aspect of the reforms hinders our understanding of other issues involved with these measures.

I have also emphasized that the reforms affected citizens in different ways. For example, the alphabet reform meant learning a Latin-based alphabet for the first time, switching from French to the new Turkish letters, or, through the simultaneous literacy campaign, learning to read and write for the first time. Reactions to the reforms also varied depending not only on one's political and religious position, but also on one's social, economic, educational, and family circumstances, one's gender, and one's established habits. I have highlighted the possibilities of individual action open to citizens—of ways of coping with change—through measures such as everyday forms of resistance, distinguishing between public and private spheres, and letter writing or petitioning. Of the new instruments of socialization, the new national holidays particularly found strong support among the public, in part because the public was involved in the emergence of these holidays, and also because the messages of these holidays resonated deeply with the recent experiences of war and the current needs and aspirations of society. It is precisely because many of the reforms were grounded in the ongoing social changes and cultural debates of the late Ottoman era and were implemented with a significant degree of popular participation that the Turkish model has lasted longer than any of its contemporaries. At the same time, as I have stressed throughout the book, the experiences of the reform processes were diverse, uneven, and incomplete.

This study expands our understanding of a critical period of Turkish history. It sheds light on the lived experiences of the Kemalist reforms to help us understand how and to what degree Kemalist authoritarian modernization really worked, and what it meant for its mediators and recipients. It underscores the benefits to be gained from further research combining archival, ethnographic, and sociological methods and approaches. As Turkish historians continue to search for new historical evidence, written and oral, we also need to read the archival evidence, particularly government documents, in a new light for the doors such sources open into the voices of those who have been excluded from or marginalized in the historical narrative. While local history remains an area with rich possibilities, we need to move from isolated local histories (often undertaken by amateur historians) to studies that place the local practices and understandings of the reforms in the broader national historical contexts without erasing the specificities of the local and regional experiences. Equally importantly, we also need further studies on the post-RPP years. Brockett's recent work on the provincial press (*How Happy to Call*

Oneself a Turk) provides a notable effort in that direction. The processes set in motion in the 1920s, from dress reforms to the celebration of national days, did not come to a complete end by the late 1940s, but they continued to evolve at the junction of politics, ideology, culture, and consumption in the subsequent years and decades.

While the primary focus of this book is the Turkish case, I have acknowledged the comparative dimensions of the Kemalist reforms and located the Turkish experience in the larger regional context of the modernist, nationalist, and revolutionary experiences of the early twentieth century. This book aspires to shed light on similar processes in other contexts as well, particularly in the larger Middle East and Central Asia. It also highlights the potential for comparative scholarship: we would benefit considerably from comparing the lived experiences of reform processes in early Republican Turkey (again from dress to the culture of celebrations to alphabet changes) with those especially in other Middle Eastern and Muslim contexts. The impact of many of the changes introduced in the 1920s and 1930s proved to be more permanent in Turkey than in other cases such as Iran and Uzbekistan, although even in the Turkish case the meaning of the nation and its secular modernity continues to be passionately contested to this day.

Notes

References

Index

Notes

Introduction

1. Joel Migdal, "Finding the Meeting Ground of Fact and Fiction: Some Reflections on Turkish Modernization," in *Rethinking Modernity and National Identity in Turkey*, ed. Sibel Bozdoğan and Reşat Kasaba (Seattle: University of Washington Press, 1997), 252–60; Joel Migdal, *State in Society: Studying How States and Societies Transform and Constitute One Another* (Cambridge: Cambridge University Press, 2001).

2. Some of the notable titles on Turkish nationalism include Ziya Gökalp, *The Principles of Turkism*, trans. Robert Devereux (1923; reprint, Leiden: E. J. Brill, 1968); Ziya Gökalp, *Turkish Nationalism and Western Civilization: Selected Essays of Ziya Gökalp*, ed. and trans. Niyazi Berkes (London: George Allen and Unwin, 1959); François Georgeon, *Türk Milliyetçiliğinin Kökenleri: Yusuf Akçura (1876–1935)*, trans. Alev Er (Istanbul: Tarih Vakfı Yurt Yayınları, 1986); A. Holly Shissler, *Between Two Empires: Ahmet Ağaoğlu and the New Turkey* (London: I. B. Tauris, 2003); Günay Göksu Özdoğan, *"Turan"dan "Bozkurt"a Tek Parti Döneminde Türkçülük (1931–1946)*, trans. İsmail Kaplan (Istanbul: İletişim Yayınları, 2001); Ahmet Yıldız, *"Ne Mutlu Türküm Diyebilene" Türk Ulusal Kimliğinin Etno-Seküler Sınırları (1919–1938)* (Istanbul: İletişim Yayınları, 2001); Baskın Oran, *Atatürk Milliyetçiliği: Resmi İdeoloji Dışı Bir İnceleme* (Ankara: Bilgi Yayınevi, 1988); and Tanıl Bora, ed., *Modern Türkiye'de Siyasi Düşünce*, vol. 4, *Milliyetçilik* (Istanbul: İletişim Yayınları, 2002).

3. Soner Çağaptay, *Islam, Secularism and Nationalism in Modern Turkey: Who is a Turk?* (London: Routledge, 2006).

4. Bernard Lewis, *The Emergence of Modern Turkey*, 2nd ed. (London: Oxford University Press, 1968). See also Feroz Ahmad, *The Making of Modern Turkey* (London: Routledge, 1993); and Robert E. Ward and Dankwart A. Rustow, eds., *Political Modernization in Japan and Turkey* (Princeton, NJ: Princeton University Press, 1964).

5. See Ahmet Mumcu, *Tarih açısından Türk Devriminin Temelleri ve Gelişmesi* ([Istanbul]: İnkilâp Kitabevi, n.d.); Suna Kili, *The Atatürk Revolution: A Paradigm of Modernization*, trans. Sylvia Zeybekoğlu, (Istanbul: İş Bankası Kültür Yayınları, 2003); and Orhan Koloğlu, *Bir Çağdaşlaşma Örneği Olarak Cumhuriyet'in İlk Onbeş Yılı (1923–1938)*, 2. Basım (2nd printing) (Istanbul: Boyut, 2002).

6. The assumption underlying such attitudes is that the secular republic has not been fully internalized and that its future is not certain. In other contexts, for instance in the case of France, historical debate revolves around the question of when the French became republican. In the case of Turkey the question may still be "Has Turkey become fully republican and will it remain republican?"

7. Erik-Jan Zürcher, *Turkey: A Modern History*, 3rd ed. (London: I. B. Tauris, 2004).

8. Erik-Jan Zürcher, *The Young Turk Legacy and Nation Building: from the Ottoman Empire to Atatürk's Turkey* (London: I. B. Tauris, 2010). While Zürcher's work has delved into social history as well (see, for example, his "Two Young Ottomanists Discover Kemalist Turkey: The Travel Diaries of Robert Anhegger and Andreas Tietze," *Journal of Turkish Studies/ Türklük Bilgisi Araştırmaları* 26, no. 2 [2002]: 359–69), this type of scholarship continues to put the state at the center of the historical analysis.

9. Erik-Jan Zürcher, ed., *Turkey in the Twentieth Century* (Berlin: Klaus Schwarz Verlag, 2008).

10. Samuel P. Huntington, "Revolution and Political Order," in *Revolutions: Theoretical, Comparative, and Historical Studies*, ed. Jack A. Goldstone (San Diego: Harcourt Brace Jovanovich, Publishers, 1986), 39.

11. Şerif Mardin, "Ideology and Religion in the Turkish Revolution," *International Journal of Middle East Studies* 2 (1971): 197–211.

12. The meaning of the word "*inkılâp*" is also ambiguous. *İnkılâp*, of Arabic origin, can convey the meaning of both reform and (nonviolent) revolution. It was, and is still, used in reference to the specific reforms such as the alphabet reform (*harf inkılâbı*) and hat reform (*şapka inkılâbı*), as well as to refer to the overall process of Kemalist reforms. *Redhouse Çağdaş Türkçe-İngilizce Sözlüğü* (Istanbul: Redhouse Yayınevi, 1983) translates it as "(nonviolent) revolution." As Zürcher correctly points out, the Kemalists carefully distinguished between the terms *ihtilâl*, the term used for the French and Russian Revolutions, and *inkılâp*, Republican leaders' preferred term for the Turkish experience. Zürcher interprets this as further evidence that the Kemalists were not really revolutionary. Erik-Jan Zürcher, "Kemalist Düşüncenin Osmanlı Kaynakları," in *Modern Türkiye'de Siyasi Düşünce, Cilt 2, Kemalizm*, ed. Tanıl Bora and Murat Gültekingil, trans. Özgür Gökmen (Istanbul: İletişim Yayınları, 2001), 44–55. Yet at the same time, the new Turkish word for revolution, *devrim*, at least initially referred to both the Turkish experience and the great social revolutions elsewhere.

13. Taha Parla and Andrew Davison, *Corporatist Ideology in Kemalist Turkey. Progress or Order?* (Syracuse, New York: Syracuse University Press, 2004). The authors draw on their earlier works for much of the information and interpretation in this volume. For Parla's earlier works on political ideology in Turkey, see Parla, *Türkiye'de Siyasi Kültürün Resmî Kaynakları*, vol. 1, *Atatürk'ün Nutuk'u*; vol. 2, *Atatürk'ün Söylev ve Demeçleri*; Vol. 3, *Kemalist Tek Parti İdeolojisi ve CHP'nin Altı Ok'u* (Istanbul: İletişim, 1992); and Parla, *The Social and Political Thought of Ziya Gökalp* (Leiden: Brill, 1985). See also Davison's interpretation of secularism in Turkey in his *Türkiye'de Sekülarizm ve Modernlik*, trans. Tuncay Birkan (Istanbul: İletişim, 2002).

14. Zürcher, *Turkey: A Modern History*, 194.

15. Hakkı Uyar, *Tek Parti Dönemi ve Cumhuriyet Halk Partisi*, 2nd ed. (Istanbul: Boyut Kitapları, 1999). Other important works on political opposition in the early Republic include Zürcher, *Political Opposition in the Early Turkish Republic: The Progressive Republican Party* (Leiden: Brill, 1991); and Mete Tunçay, *Türkiye Cumhuriyeti'nde Tek-Parti Yönetimi'nin Kurulması (1923–1931)* (Istanbul: Tarih Vakfı Yurt Yayınları, 1999).

16. *"150'likler"* refers to the 150 Turkish citizens who were exempt from the general amnesty required by the Treaty of Lausanne. They were asked to leave the country on the grounds of treason or opposition to the War of Independence and their citizenship was revoked in 1927. They were eventually pardoned by the Parliament in 1938 and allowed to return to Turkey.

17. Ceylan Tokluoğlu, "The Formation of the Turkish Nation-State and Resistance" (Ph.D. diss., Carleton University, Ottawa, 1995).

18. See, for instance, Robert Olson, *The Emergence of Kurdish Nationalism and the Sheikh Said Rebellion, 1880–1925* (Austin: University of Texas Press, 1989); Martin Van Bruinessen, *Agha, Sheikh and State: The Social and Political Structures of Kurdistan* (London: Zed Books, 1992); Van Bruinessen, *Kurdish Ethno-Nationalism versus Nation-Building States* (Istanbul: ISIS, 2000); and David McDowall, *A Modern History of the Kurds* (London: I. B. Tauris, 1996), chap. 9.

19. Şerif Mardin, "Projects as Methodology: Some Thoughts on Modern Turkish Social Science" in *Rethinking Modernity and National Identity in Turkey*, ed. Sibel Bozdoğan and Reşat Kasaba (Seattle: University of Washington Press, 1997), 66.

20. Mardin, "Projects as Methodology."

21. Mardin, *Religion and Social Change in Modern Turkey: The Case of Bediüzzaman Said Nursi* (Albany, N.Y.: State University of New York Press, 1989).

22. Mardin, *Religion and Social Change*, 13.

23. Mardin, *Religion and Social Change*, 9.

24. Mardin, *Religion and Social Change*, 13.

25. Mardin, "Projects as Methodology," 67.

26. Mardin, Introduction to *Religion, Society, and Modernity in Turkey* (Syracuse: Syracuse University Press, 2006), xvi.

27. See Sibel Bozdoğan, *Modernism and Nation Building: Turkish Architectural Culture in The Early Republic* (Seattle: University of Washington Press, 2001); Gavin Brockett, *How Happy to Call Oneself a Turk: Provincial Newspapers and the Negotiation of a Muslim National Identity* (University of Texas Press, 2011); Kathryn Libal, "National Futures: The Child Question in Early Republican Turkey" (Ph.D. diss., University of Washington, 2001); Arzu Öztürkmen, "Celebrating National Holidays in Turkey: History and Memory," *New Perspectives on Turkey*, no. 25 (Fall 2001): 47–75; and Meltem F. Türköz, "The Social Life of the State's Fantasy: Memories and Documents on Turkey's 1934 Surname Law" (Ph.D. diss., University of Pennsylvania, 2004). For a useful collection of articles representative of this emerging scholarship,

see Gavin D. Brockett, ed., *Towards a Social History of Modern Turkey: Essays in Theory and Practice* (Istanbul: Libra Kitap, 2011).

28. Faith Childress, "Republican Lessons: Education and the Making of Modern Turkey" (Ph.D. diss., University of Utah, 2001).

29. See, for instance, Ahmet Eskicumalı, "Ideology and Education: Reconstructing the Turkish Curriculum for Social and Cultural Change, 1923–1946" (Ph.D. Diss., University of Wisconsin–Madison, 1994); and Jessica Selma Tiregöl, "The Role of Primary Education in Nation–State-Building: The Case of the Early Turkish Republic (1923–1938)" (Ph.D. diss., Princeton University, 1998). For a recent analysis of educational ideas, policies, and textbooks in the Young Turk and early Republican periods from a comparative perspective, see Barak Aharon Salmoni, "Pedagogies of Patriotism: Teaching Socio-Political Community in Twentieth-Century Turkish and Egyptian Education" (Ph.D. diss., Harvard University, 2002).

30. Meltem F. Türköz, "The Social Life of the State's Fantasy."

31. All three scholars mentioned here (Deniz Kandiyoti, Nilüfer Göle, and Yeşim Arat) draw attention to the same gap in the field. See their contributions in Bozdoğan and Kasaba, eds., *Rethinking Modernity*.

32. James C. Scott, *Weapons of the Weak: Everyday Forms of Peasant Resistance* (New Haven: Yale University Press, 1985).

33. The Prime Minister's Archive of the Republic (Başbakanlık Cumhuriyet Arşivi, the BCA) has only been open to researchers since the late 1990s, and works published as late as 1999, such as Hakkı Uyar's *Tek Parti Dönemi ve Cumhuriyet Halk Partisi*, were written without the benefit of the rich documentary evidence deposited at the BCA. The present study joins an evolving body of historical scholarship on modern Turkey that draws on the BCA, and it complements the documentary evidence from the BCA with new data from the Archive of the Ministry of the Interior.

34. Oral history remains a still-underutilized method in the mainstream histories of Turkey. On the state of oral history in Turkey, see Leyla Neyzi, "Oral History and Memory Studies in Turkey," in *Turkey's Engagement with Modernity: Conflict and Change in the Twentieth Century*, ed. Celia Kerslake, Kerem Öktem, and Philip Robins (Oxford: Palgrave Macmillan, 2010), 443–59; and Leyla Neyzi, *"Ben Kimim?" Türkiye'de Sözlü Tarih, Kimlik ve Öznellik* (Istanbul: İletişim Yayınları, 2004).

35. Esra Özyürek, *Nostalgia for the Modern: State Secularism and Everyday Politics in Turkey* (Duke University Press, 2006). Not all narrators remembered the 1920s and 1930s with Kemalist Republican nostalgia. There were some neutral accounts, and some that were critical of aspects of the RPP era. Other narratives associated the period first and foremost with a sense of loss (following the wars) and material deprivation. At the same time, the nostalgia Özyürek located in the memories of the first generation Republicans seems to derive at least in part from the identification of a segment of the urban upper and middle class with the ideals of the new regime. On collective memory in Turkey, see the collection of essays in

Hatırladıkları ve Unuttuklarıyla Türkiye'nin Toplumsal Hafızası, ed. Esra Özyürek (Istanbul: İletişim Yayıncılık, 2001).

36. Marianne Kamp, *The New Woman in Uzbekistan: Islam, Modernity, and Unveiling under Communism* (Seattle: University of Washington Press, 2006).

1. Dressing the Nation's Citizens: Men's Clothing Reforms in the Early Republic

1. For further discussion of the modernization and Westernization processes since the nineteenth century, see Fatma Müge Göçek, *Rise of the Bourgeoisie, Demise of Empire: Ottoman Westernization and Social Change* (New York: Oxford University Press, 1996); Şerif Mardin, *Religion, Society, and Modernity in Turkey* (Syracuse: Syracuse University Press, 2006); Mardin, *Türk Modernleşmesi (Makaleler 4)* (Istanbul: İletişim Yayınları, 1991); Bozdoğan and Kasaba, eds., *Rethinking Modernity;* Carter Vaughn Findley, *Turkey, Islam, Nationalism, and Modernity: A History, 1789–2007* (New Haven: Yale University Press, 2011); and Uygur Kocabaşoğlu, ed., *Modern Türkiye'de Siyasi Düşünce,* vol. 3, *Modernleşme ve Batıcılık* (Istanbul: İletişim Yayınları, 2002).

2. Eric Hobsbawm, "Introduction: Inventing Traditions," in *The Invention of Tradition,* ed. Eric Hobsbawm and Terence Ranger (Cambridge: Cambridge University Press, 1983), 1–14.

3. Donald Quataert, "Clothing Laws, State, and Society in the Ottoman Empire, 1720–1829," *International Journal of Middle East Studies* 29, no. 3 (1997): 403–25.

4. The Sultan may have considered adopting European headgear rather than the fez for his new army. Although it is not entirely clear why he decided against the European hat, one of the explanations cited is the concern that the Ottoman Muslim public may have considered European headgear with a brim un-Islamic. Niyazi Berkes, *The Development of Secularism in Turkey,* with an introduction by Feroz Ahmad (New York: Routledge, 1998), 125. On the other hand, the fez, of north African origin and introduced to the Ottoman capital by the navy, did not carry previous associations with a particular group or interest in the Ottoman context.

5. Quataert, "Clothing Laws," 412–13.

6. Berkes, for example, has argued that "Shoes, pants, coats, [and] shirts did not encounter resistance. The real difficulty arose over the question of headgear. It is difficult to explain why, after so many changes along European lines, this became such a bugbear. The only explanation appears to be religious. . . ." (Berkes, *The Development of Secularism in Turkey,* 124).

7. Quataert, "Clothing Laws," 413–16.

8. A photograph album commissioned by the Ottoman government for display at the 1873 Vienna Exhibition attests to the diversity of ethnic, religious, and regional clothes, including headgear, of Ottoman subjects. See Osman Hamdi Bey and Victor Marie de Launay, *1873 Yılında Türkiye'de Halk Giysileri. Elbise-i Osmaniyye* (Istanbul: Sabancı Üniversitesi, 1999), trans. Erol Üyepazarcı, originally published as *Les Costumes populaires de la Turquie. Elbise-i Osmaniyye* (Istanbul, 1873). See also the studio portraits and street photographs from

the second half of the nineteenth century by the famous photographers, the Abdullah brothers, in Engin Özendes, *Abdullah Frères: Osmanlı Sarayının Fotoğrafçıları* (Istanbul: Yapı Kredi Yayınları, 1998).

9. *Kalpak*, often rendered in English as "calpac," is a brimless hat made of leather, fur, or heavy cloth in the shape of a truncated cone. Like the plain fez it was worn with no wrapping around it. Different types of *kalpak*s were associated with different ethnic groups: there were, for example, the Tatar, Circassian, Azeri, Persian, and Bulgarian *kalpak*s. Şemseddin Sâmi, *Kâmûs-ı Türkî* (Istanbul: Enderun Kitabevi, 1989, originally published in 1317 [1901–1902]), 1079; Reşat Ekrem Koçu, *Türk Giyim, Kuşam ve Süslenme Sözlüğü* (Ankara: Sümerbank Kültür Yayınları, 1967), 142–43; and Ali Püsküllüoğlu, *Arkadaş Türkçe Sözlük* (Ankara: Arkadaş, 1997), 568. (See figure 2 in this chapter for an image.)

10. *Takke* (*takiye*), from the Arabic "*taqiyya*" is a type of skullcap made of thin cloth, worn under other forms of headgear such as the fez and the *külah*, as a protective first layer that kept the fez or other headgear clean by absorbing sweat. Şemsettin Sami, *Kâmûs-ı Türkî*, 867; Koçu, *Türk Giyim Kuşam*, 220. As we will see later in this chapter, the *takke* persisted after the Hat Law. Koçu notes that in his day (i.e. as late as the 1960s), some men continued to wear a *takke* under their hats and caps or alternatively carried a *takke* in their pockets so that they would not have to perform their daily prayers bareheaded upon removing their hats (Sami, *Kâmûs-ı Türkî*).

11. Cevdet Kırpık, "Osmanlı İmparatorluğunda Modernleşme Sancıları: Fes-Şapka Çatışması," *Toplumsal Tarih*, no. 162, September 2007, 14–22.

12. Kırpık, "Osmanlı İmparatorluğunda Modernleşme, 20

13. Kırpık, "Osmanlı İmparatorluğunda Modernleşme, 14.

14. Kırpık, "Osmanlı İmparatorluğunda Modernleşme, 20–21.

15. Y. Doğan Çetinkaya, *1908 Osmanlı Boykotu. Bir Toplumsal Hareketin Analizi* (Istanbul: İletişim Yayınları, 2004). See especially the sections "Fes *versus* Kalpak: Milli Serpuş Arayışı" and "'Milli Serpuş' İcat Önerileri" in chap. 5, 133–72.

16. *Külah* (of Persian etymological origin) is the common name for a variety of typically conical felt hats that were worn, like the fez, with or without a wrap around them. The *külah* was a popular Ottoman headgear particularly among the artisanal classes. Koçu, *Türk Giyim Kuşam*, 162; Şemseddin Sami, *Kâmûs-ı Türkî*, 1175; and Püsküllüoğlu, *Arkadaş Türkçe Sözlük*, 684–85. See Koçu, p. 163, for images of the different types of *külah*s, including the Mevlevi *külah*.

17. Çetinkaya, *1908 Osmanlı Boykotu*.

18. *Türk Silâhlı Kuvvetleri Tarihi* vol. 3, part 6 (1908–1920), book 1 (Ankara: T. C. Genelkurmay Harp Tarihi Başkanlığı Resmi Yayınları, 1971), "Kıyafet," 368–80.

19. The *enveriye* hat, initially also called *kabalak* or *askeri kabalak*, was introduced to the Ottoman army during World War I by Enver Pasha, hence the name. Likely inspired by the Italian sun-helmet, it was constructed by folding the cloth around a light, plaited straw framework. Koçu, *Türk Giyim Kuşam*, 105–6.

20. Niyazi Berkes, *The Development of Secularism in Turkey*, 125.

21. By the final years of the Empire, it was not unusual for upper class Ottoman Muslim men to own a European style hat that they would wear on trips to Europe. Nezih Neyzi gives an interesting example of this in his family memoirs of transition from Empire to Republic. His father Muzaffer Halim, whom Neyzi describes as a "true Ottoman," on his trips to Europe, would get on the train in Sirkeci wearing a fez, but would bring along his European style hat, replacing the fez with the hat on the train. Nezih Neyzi, *Kızıltoprak Hatıraları* (Istanbul: İletişim Yayınları, 1993), 215–16. Neyzi attributes this purely to economic reasons: his father was charged higher prices in Europe as a fez-wearing customer. Regardless of the specific reasons involved, such prior voluntary use of the hat no doubt played a role in how individual citizens responded to the Hat Law. French journalist Paul Gentizon, who spent several years in Turkey in the 1920s, also alluded to the importance of the European-educated Turks' previous familiarity with wearing European style hats in discussing the initial responses to Mustafa Kemal's hat campaign in the fall of 1925. Paul Gentizon, *Mustafa Kemal ve Uyanan Doğu*, trans. Fethi Ülkü (Ankara: Bilgi Yayınevi, 1983), 99.

22. Paul Stirling underscored the importance of the Hat Law as an expression of regime change and the imposition of state authority in the following words: "To change by government fiat clothing that is locally perceived as part of people's main religious identity is plainly remarkable. It was, of course, also a message—a message from the government that the world had indeed changed, that the government meant business. Once again, an astonishing achievement, but also a question mark. By and large, it seems that in public places, the laws were enforced, and people accepted them" (581). Here Stirling followed the conventional assumptions in the field that the fez was a reflection primarily of an individual's religious identity, leaving aside the connection of dress to ethnic, class, tribal, or other group identities. But at the same time he spoke with caution about the assumption that these changes indeed took place as legislated, hinting at the possibility of different forms of responses and incomplete implementation of legislated reforms. Stirling, "Social Change and Social Control in Republican Turkey," *Papers and Discussions. Türkiye İş Bankası International Symposium on Atatürk* (Ankara: Türkiye İş Bankası Cultural Publications, 1984, 565–600).

23. The Law used the word *şapka* to denote the European style hat. The word *şapka* entered into usage in Turkish through Slavic languages, either through Russian or Polish. Some sources, such as Türk Dil Kurumu, *Türkçe Sözlük*, vol. 2 (Ankara: Türk Dil Kurumu Yayınları, 1988), 1371, gives it as a borrowing from Russian. Other authorities, including İsmet Zeki Eyuboğlu, *Türk Dilinin Etimolojik Sözlüğü*, rev. 3rd ed. (Istanbul: Sosyal Yayınlar, 1995), 623, argue that *şapka* entered Turkish through the Polish *czepska*. Most sources do not give a date of earliest usage, but Eyüboğlu has it entering Turkish as early as the 15th century. Hence, the term for the new national headgear was an already familiar word that also had convenient and desirable phonetic similarities to the French *chapeau*. Although the Law specifically mentions the *şapka*, other forms of headgear such as the *kasket* (cloth caps with a brim in front) became acceptable and widely used.

24. For the debates in the Parliament on the Hat Law (Law No. 671) see Mahmut Goloğlu, *Devrimler ve Tepkileri (1924–1930)* (Ankara: Başnur, 1972), 150–56; Burcu Özcan, "Basına Göre Şapka ve Kılık Kıyafet İnkılâbı" (master's thesis, Marmara University, Istanbul, 2008), 57–63.

25. Başbakanlık Cumhuriyet Arşivi (BCA) 030.10.78.518.7 79.7 5.4.1926, Correspondence from Inspector Sami to RPP General Secretariat, 13 March 1926, Van.

26. İçişleri Bakanlığı Emniyet Genel Müdürlüğü Arşivi (EGM)13211-5, "Tokat vilayetinin umumi durumu hakkında . . . ," report to *Emniyet Umum Müdürlüğü*, 1 July 1937.

27. According to the inspector's report there were thirteen foreign nationals, among them German citizens, working for the newly founded sugar factory in Turhal. In addition to these foreign "experts" and their families in Turhal, the inspector mentioned other foreign residents in Tokat of German, Italian, and Hungarian citizenship, presumably engineers and others employed for their technical skills in the railroads and the mining operations in the province. See EGM 13211-5, "Tokat vilayetinin."

28. EGM 13211-5, "Tokat vilayetinin."

29. Ergün Aybars, *İstiklâl Mahkemeleri 1920–1927*, Cilt 1–2 (Izmir: Dokuz Eylül Üniversitesi Atatürk İlkeleri ve İnkilap Tarihi Enstitüsü, 1995), esp. 406–18; Gavin Brockett, "Collective Action and the Turkish Revolution: Towards a Framework for the Social History of the Ataturk Era, 1923–38," in *Turkey Before and After Atatürk*, ed. Sylvia Kedourie (London and Portland: Frank Cass, 1999), 44–66; Ahmet Eyicil, "İstiklâl Mahkemelerinde Yargılanan K. Maraşlılar," *Türk Dünyası Araştırmaları*, no. 102 (June 1996): 13–45; Gentizon, *Mustafa Kemal ve Uyanan Doğu*. In spite of his clear ideological biases, Ahmet Eyicil's findings on the Maraş riot are particularly noteworthy in showing how local and religious identities interacted with anti-colonial sentiment and local historical memories to produce the riot. Eyicil's description of the events in Maraş on 27 November 1925 points to a locally perceived connection between the hat and the French, whose troops had occupied the province in the aftermath of World War I: Following the Friday prayers in the Grand Mosque in Maraş, the İmam of the mosque—who was not on duty on the particular day—gave a sentimental speech against wearing the hat on the basis that it was un-Islamic and similar to the French headgear. Eyicil argues that the crowd, incited by the statements associating the hat with the French headgear, remembered its enmity against the French and set off for the government building with green and red banners, chanting "God is great." The protest would spread quickly, turning into a riot. Protesters shouted that they would not wear the hat, that they would not recognize a government mandating the hat, and that they did not want an infidel to be governor. In the course of the events, the gates of the prison were brought down and 200 prisoners ran away. Eyicil, "İstiklâl Mahkemelerinde," 14. The riot was put down by the government forces and those arrested for participating in the riot were sent before the Independence Tribunals in Ankara. Seven of the accused were given the death sentence on 18 January 1926 and were executed on the same day. Nine others were sentenced to ten years of imprisonment, one person was sentenced to three years, and forty four were found innocent. Eyicil, "İstiklâl Mahkemelerinde," 31. See also Aybars, *İstiklâl Mahkemeleri*, 414–15. Aybars gives slightly different numbers.

30. James C. Scott, *Weapons of the Weak.*

31. James C. Scott, *Weapons of the Weak*, 29.

32. Cihan Aktaş, *Kılık Kıyafet ve İktidar*, vol. 1 (Istanbul: Nehir, 1991), 148. It should be noted that Hamdi Yazır wrote a Turkish language commentary on the Qur'an for the Directorate of Religious Affairs. Hence, it appears that despite his persistent protest against the hat, Yazır was not totally alienated by the new regime and contributed to a government sponsored project. This also shows the ability of the state institutions to co-opt potential opponents.

33. Dönüş Başarır, "Şapka İnkılâbının Konya Basını ve Kamuoyundaki Yankıları" (master's thesis, Selçuk University, Konya, 1995), 37, citing Ramiz Arda, "Burası Anadolu," *Yeni Konya* (9 April 1962): 3; and 12 April 1962, 3.

34. Lilo Linke, *Allah Dethroned: A Journey through Modern Turkey* (New York: Alfred A. Knopf, 1937), 178–80.

35. Linke also wrote that it was in part due to "peasant avarice" that the man decided to wear the hat. "He had paid for it, so he might just as well wear it." (Linke, *Allah Dethroned*, 180.) Linke certainly had her own opinions and biases and should be read with caution, yet overall she was a careful observer and provides an interesting account of life in Anatolia and the transformations it was going through in the mid-1930s.

36. Ahmet Özer, "abdullah eltan'la söyleşi," *Kıyı* (Trabzon), no. 111 (June 1995): 14–16.

37. BCA 490.01.17.88.1, 26 January 1936.

38. Meral Akkent and Gaby Franger, *Das Kopftuch: Başörtü. Ein Stückchen Stoff in Geschichte und Gegenwart. Geçmişte ve Günümüzde Bir Parça Kumaş* (Frankfurt: Dağyeli Verlag, 1987), 106–9.

39. *Setre* pants are European style trousers. *Setre* essentially was a term used for the European style jacket. More specifically, it referred to the *istanbulin*, or *istanbouline*, a nineteenth-century Ottoman adaptation of the European frock coat with a high collar and buttons down the front. The modernizing Ottoman state had required its functionaries to wear not only the fez, but also the European style jacket and trousers. Koçu notes that the *istanbouline*, by fully covering the chest, had eliminated the need for a starched shirt and tie, thus easing the transition into this new jacket. Koçu, *Türk Giyim Kuşam*, 134, 204; Şemseddin Sâmi, *Kâmûs-ı Türkî*, 708. By the end of the nineteenth century, between government encouragement, Westernization, and fashion, upper class urban Ottoman men in İstanbul and other major cities had adopted the Western suit, but as in Maraş, varieties of local and traditional forms of male clothing persisted in rural Anatolia and the provinces well into the 1920s and 1930s. In the case of Trabzon province, where the majority of urban men had already adopted the European style jacket, trousers, and shoes, the majority of the peasants continued to wear local clothes such as *mintan*s and *zıbka*s in the mid-1920s. In December 1926, the Trabzon Provincial Council passed a decision requiring the replacement of these "primitive" *mintan*s and *zıbka*s, which were not national clothes, with modern attire. Furthermore, the municipality of Akçaabat district banned the manufacturing of *zıbka*s with a view to facilitating the adoption of *setre* pants. Mesut Çapa, "Giyim Kuşamda Medeni Kıyafetlerin Benimsenmesi ve Trabzon

Örneği," *Toplumsal Tarih*, no. 30 (1996), 27. Thus, the local governments were trying to effect social change by shifting both demand and supply. Notably, the Trabzon Provincial Council's decree banning the *zıbka* and *mintan* came shortly after a unanimous council decision prohibiting the women's *peçe*, or the face veil.

40. Bengül Bolat, "Atatürk İnkılaplarının Topluma Yansıması: Kırşehir Örneği" (master's thesis, Hacettepe Üniversitesi, Ankara, 2001), 30.

41. Dönüş Başarır, "Şapka İnkılâbı," 46.

42. EGM 13211-16/4, Circular from the Ministry of the Interior to the Provinces, 9 January 1926. For a similar circular about five years later, see EGM 13211-16/4, Circular from the Ministry of the Interior to the Provinces, 5 November 1930.

43. A *kefiye*, from Arabic, is a light shawl traditionally worn as head covering by Arabs. *Redhouse Türkçe-İngilizce Sözlük* (Sev Matbaacılık ve Yayıncılık: Istanbul, 1997), 631. The *agel* is the round, rope-like accessory that holds the *kefiye*. A *maşlah* is a light, loose-fitting, sleeveless outer garment traditionally worn by Arabs. In Madanoğlu's account, the reference is specifically to the male *maşlah*, although in the late nineteenth and early twentieth century, women of İstanbul also wore the *maşlah*. Koçu, *Türk Giyim, Kuşam*, 170–71.

44. Cemal Madanoğlu, *Anılar (1911–1938)*, vol. 1 (Istanbul: Çağdaş Yayınları, 1982): 123.

45. It is also possible that it was due to lack of financial means or the lack of easily accessible supplies that tribesmen did not buy or wear "modern" pants, jacket, hats, or caps. Poverty and access to supplies were sometimes a real cause of the failure to fulfill the state's sartorial demands, yet often economic factors were linked with cultural ones, and they sometimes provided a convenient excuse to maintain established habits and practices.

46. For example, in a short piece addressed to the children and the youth of Mardin, A. Özkan of the recently inaugurated Mardin Halkevi likened Arabic to a virus that threatened the Turkish body and called on the youth to destroy it like an enemy who has attacked the homeland. He particularly assigned the children the task of spreading the pure Turkish throughout the country. *CHF Mardin Halkevi Broşürü*, Mardin Ulus Sesi Basımevi, 28 Şubat (28 February) 1935, 23,24. In the People's Houses publications and generally in state discourse dealing with the region, Arabic served as shorthand to refer to languages other than Turkish. The focus on Arabic perhaps also helped to draw the attention away from the rich ethnic and linguistic diversity of the region, which included Arabic, Armenian, Syriac, Turkish, and Kurdish. On ethnic diversity in post-Ottoman Turkey, see Peter Alford Andrews, *Türkiye'de Etnik Gruplar*, trans. Mustafa Küpüşoğlu (Istanbul: Ant Yayınları Tümzamanlar Yayıncılık, 1992). On the campaigns to promote the use of Turkish as the primary language of verbal communication, see Senem Aslan, "'Citizen, Speak Turkish!': A Nation in the Making," *Nationalism and Ethnic Politics* 13 (2007): 245–72; Rıfat N. Bali, *Cumhuriyet Yıllarında Türkiye Yahudileri: Bir Türkleştirme Serüveni [1923–1945]* (Istanbul: İletişim, 1999); and Rıfat N. Bali, *1934 Trakya Olayları* (Istanbul: Kitabevi, 2008).

47. In December 1954, about two decades after Madanoğlu's observations on the Urfa tribes, the Urfa provincial governor issued a public statement concerning the use of the *agel*

and the *entari*. (The *entari*, like the *maşlah*, is a long, loose fitting dress traditionally worn by women and men. *Agel* and *entari* here correspond to the *agel-kefiye* and the *maşlah* in Madanoğlu's memoirs. Koçu notes that Ottoman men—he was primarily concerned with İstanbul—wore the *entari* as work or everyday street clothes until the dress reforms of Sultan Mahmud II [Koçu, *Türk Giyim, Kuşam*, 102–3]). The governor informed the citizenry that the state authorities would not tolerate the wearing of the *agel* and the *entari* within the municipal boundaries of the provincial center and the other districts, on the grounds that these could not be considered "modern and national Turkish clothes." He cautioned citizens, both town residents and those who might only be visiting the towns, that noncompliance could lead to the *zabıta* (police) tearing off and confiscating articles of one's clothing, and a referral to the courts. The governor's statement attests to the gradual nature of change in clothing habits and to a degree of persistence of regional, tribal, and other forms of clothing in parts of the country well into the 1950s. EGM 13216-10, "İlan" Urfa Valisi Nedim Evliya, 6 December 1954.

48. The Directorate of Religious Affairs was founded on 3 March 1924 (Law No. 429) as a part of key secularizing laws, and was assigned a comprehensive role in secularizing Turkish society. For the history and structure of the Directorate, as well as a critical assessment of the debates on relations between state and religion in Turkey, secularism, and the Directorate, see İştar B. Tarhanlı, *Müslüman Toplum "Laik" Devlet. Türkiye'de Diyanet İşleri Başkanlığı* (Istanbul: Afa, 1993).

49. See Aktaş, *Kılık Kıyafet ve İktidar*, on debates for and against clothing reforms in the late Ottoman era.

50. İskilipli (Iskilipli) Âtıf Efendi, *Frenk Mukallidliği ve Şapka* (n.p.: Nizam Yayınları, n.d.).

51. On trials at the Independence Tribunals see Ahmed Nedim, *Ankara İstiklâl Mahkemesi Zabıtları 1926* (Istanbul: İşaret Yayınları, 1993) and Ergun Aybars, *İstiklâl Mahkemeleri*.

52. The text of the Decree ("İlmiye Sınıfı ve İlmiye Kisvesi Hakkında Kararname") is available in BCA 051.2.6.9 (V 08), 31 December 1925.

53. *Müfti* or *müftü* is the highest ranking government-appointed Islamic authority responsible from the religious affairs of a province (*vilayet, il*) or district (*kaza, ilçe*).

54. See, for instance, the circular from the governor of Artvin to the *müftis* in the province, BCA 051.2.6.10, 25 January 1926.

55. It was not always clear if an imam or preacher was eligible to wear the religious garb, especially in cases where the person had been appointed to his position by pre-Republican Ottoman authorities. See for instance the petitions for permission to wear religious garb by Vaiz Hüseyin Sabri from Kasaba and Müderris İsmail Hakkı from Turgutlu, BCA 051.13.110.21, 27 September 1925; and BCA 051.13.111.41, 19 November 1926.

56. BCA 051.5.45.32, From the *kaymakam* of Ödemiş to the town's *müfti*, 29 July 1928.

57. BCA 051.2.6.12, From the president of the Directorate to the *müfti* of Şavşat, 15 May 1926. BCA 051.3.19.6, 25 May 1926, From the president of the Directorate to the *müfti* of Uzunköprü, 15 May 1926.

58. BCA 030.10.8.45.12, 6.681, 20 May 1926.

59. Çarık is a kind of handmade rawhide moccasin commonly worn by both men and women in the rural areas before the spread of affordable rubber and leather shoes. The timing of the transition from çarıks to shoes must have varied depending on a region's access to markets, contact with the urban areas, and the individuals' ability to purchase. One of my informants, a retired elementary school teacher, related to me that during a national celebration in 1945 in a small town in Kastamonu province, all but one student showed up for celebrations wearing çarıks. Seeing that only one student had shoes on his feet, Özcan, as the headmaster, asked the student to go find a pair of çarıks and put them on: "Ne lan bu? dedim. Git çarık bul giy dedim." Interview with Mehmet Özcan, 5 March 2003, Kastamonu. Obviously, in this instance, most families could not afford to buy shoes for their children, not even for use on special occasions such as the celebration of a national holiday. Ironically, it was only through the removal of the "modern" article of clothing, the lone pair of shoes on the feet of one child, that the teacher could assure a measure of uniformity (and equality) among the gathered crowd of students.

60. BCA 051.2.13.29, 22 July 1926. From the müfti of Ertuğrul [Bilecik] province to the müfti of Söğüd.

61. BCA 030.10.8.47.7, 6.741, 26 April 1927.

62. BCA 051.2.13.20, 17 November 1925.

63. BCA 051.13.108.2, 10 July 1927.

64. For related correspondence from the Ministry of the Interior, see BCA 051.14.119.18, 8 November 1928; BCA 051.3.15.25, 11 October 1928; and BCA 030.10.192.314.14, 229.33, 16 December 1928.

65. A letter from the Minister of the Interior Şükrü Kaya to the Prime Minister suggests that the circular was triggered when Kaya encountered some men wearing turbans and fezzes in İstanbul. He says the men involved were found to be of Iranian citizenship, but the language of the circular suggests that he may have run into some shopkeepers who were also imams. See EGM 13211-16/1, Correspondence from Şükrü Kaya to the Prime Ministry, 22/23 September 1928; and EGM 13211-16/4. Menlas, or mullahs, are Islamic scholars. Seyyids are or claim to be descendants of the Prophet Muhammed.

66. BCA 051.45.13.108.11, 11 November 1928.

67. Law No. 2596, "Bazı kisvelerin giyilemeyeceğine dair kanun," passed on 3 December 1934 and published in the Official Gazette No. 2879, 13 December 1934. Although the main target of this law was the Islamic clergy, the language of the law was not specific to the Islamic clergy and included all religions and sects, not unlike the recent French debates and regulations on religious symbols in public schools, when the core of the issue is Islamic symbols, especially headscarves. An example of the application of this law could be seen in April 1940 when Şem'un oğlu Pıtrıs, a Syriac priest in Elazığ, was taken to the Public Prosecutor's office for wearing his religious clothing in public. See EGM 13211-21/1, From the governor of Elazığ to the 4th Inspectorate General. See Özcan, "Basına Göre Şapka," chap. 3 for responses to this law by the non-Muslim clergy.

68. Accordingly, the Greek patriarch in İstanbul would be authorized to wear the religious garb outside of the church and beyond religious services, as the representative of the Greek Orthodox church in Turkey, to give but one example of this. The permit would be issued for a limited period of time, but could be renewed upon request.

69. BCA 490.01/611.122.1, 2 July 1935, From the Minister of the Interior to the Inspectors General and the Governors.

70. The influence of the Directorate and the imams was clearly limited to the Sunni Muslim majority. Alevis generally supported the secularizing reforms of the Kemalist period as a way of ending the domination of a Sunni dominated state and society. It is not clear whether the Alevi communities reacted to the hat and other clothing regulations significantly differently from the majority Sunni population. On the Alevis in Turkey, see David Shankland, *The Alevis in Turkey: The Emergence of a Secular Islamic Tradition* (Curzon Press, 2003); and T. Olsson, *Alevi Identity: Cultural, Religious and Social Perspectives*, ed. E. Özdalga and C. Raudvere (Istanbul: Swedish Research Institute, 1998).

71. Hence the Parliamentary bill by Ali Sururi Bey on the mundane-sounding issue of installing hooks in mosques for hanging hats. BCA 030.10.192.314.1, 229/20, 4 April 1926. Jaschke observed that after the Hat Law, villagers wore the cap with the brim on the back or on the side, and those wearing hats put a kerchief on their heads before entering a mosque for prayers in order to be able to comply with the ritual requirement of one's forehead touching the ground. See Gotthard Jäschke, *Yeni Türkiye'de İslâmlık*, trans. Hayrullah Örs (Ankara: Bilgi Yayınevi, 1972), 29.

72. BCA 030.10.102.667.6 90/5M, 14 Kanun-i Evvel 1341 (14 December 1925), From the Minister of the Interior to the Prime Minister, 26 Teşrin-i Sani 1341 (26 November 1925).

73. BCA 030.10.102.667.6 90/5M, 14 Kanun-i Evvel 1341.

74. BCA 051.2.13.23, 5 January 1926. Directorate of Religious Affairs circular, 3 January 1926.

75. For sample preacher/*vaiz* reports from the Kocaeli province, including lists of subjects covered in their sermons, see BCA 051.6.49.1, 29 October 1924–12 December 1938. The reporting system appears to have provided some, although not complete, control by the center over the actions of the individual imams. A major problem seems to have been delays in reporting or failure to report altogether. For official correspondence regarding the purpose and the content of such reports as well as the problems involved, see, for instance: BCA 051.4.30.12, 27 December 1945; BCA 051.4.30.12, 27 December 1945; BCA 051.4.30.20, 1 April 1947; and BCA 051.4.31.4, 29 September 1948. For a circular from the President of the Directorate to the *müftis* criticizing the preachers/*vaiz* for failure in their obligation to guide the public, see BCA 051.4.31.5, 30 September 1948. For a claim that a *hatip* in Konya preached a sermon that was not included amongst the sermons he was authorized by the Directorate to use, see BCA 051.12.103.58, 31 August 1945.

76. EGM 13211-16/2, 8 May 1936. From the governor of Bursa to the Ministry of the Interior. I have not had access to the final result of the investigation on the mosque's imam involved in this case.

77. I have not come across any texts of sermons authored by the Directorate specifically on the question of headgear in the mosque. However, given that it was common practice for the Directorate to provide sermons on a wide range of issues, they no doubt existed. For correspondence regarding the imams' encouraging the public to donate to the Turkish Air Association (Tayyare Cemiyeti) in their sermons, see BCA 051.3.17.21, 10 December 1929; for correspondence asking imams to explain to the public the goals of the National Economics and Savings Association (Milli İktisat ve Tasarruf Cemiyeti), see BCA 051.3.17.23, 26 December 1929. For an example of a sermon authored and distributed by the Directorate, see the prayer sample sent in January 1940 by the Directorate for spiritual support to the public following a number of earthquakes and other disasters in EGM 13211-19, 1940. The actual performance of such prayers could at times exceed or run counter to the intentions of the Directorate and the central government. See also the circular by the Ministry of the Interior, 10 November 1940, regarding concerns over the performance of the aforementioned prayers. EGM 13211-19, 1940. Nevertheless, given the low levels of literacy and newspaper readership, mosque sermons provided a potentially effective venue for conveying the regime's message to the masses of observant Muslim citizens.

78. Başarır, "Şapka İnkılâbı," 46, 47; Mesut Çapa, "Giyim Kuşamda," 22–28; Fuad Arun, *Muallim Refik Kırış: Hayatı ve Eserleri, 1868–1945* (Ankara: Başnur Matbaası, 1968), 150–53.

79. Darüşşafaka was a privately founded free boarding school that opened in 1873. Sponsored by the Society for Islamic Education (Cemiyet-i Tedrisiyye-yi Islamiyye), its primary goal was providing education to poor or orphaned Muslim youth. Darüşşafaka evolved into one of the top schools in İstanbul, producing a number of prominent late Ottoman and early Republican intellectuals. Selçuk Akşin Somel, *The Modernization of Public Education in the Ottoman Empire, 1839–1908: Islamization, Autocracy and Discipline* (Leiden: Brill, 2001), 53,54; and Necdet Sakaoğlu, *Osmanlı'dan Günümüze Eğitim Tarihi* (Istanbul: İstanbul Bilgi Üniversitesi Yayınları, 2003), 86–87. Hüseyin Refik's family, who lived in a village in Sinop, had sent him to İstanbul to stay with his uncle Hüseyin Efendi, Sultan Murad V's head tobacconist. According to Arun, Hüseyin Refik was admitted to the Darüşşafaka in 1877 upon completing the palace school for boys (Sarayı Humayun Sıbyan Mektebi) and the lower level (corresponding to middle school) of the Mülkiye, the Civil Service School. He graduated from the Darüşşafaka in 1887. It appears that his uncle's palace connections and social network in İstanbul provided him with access to a good education in modern Ottoman schools (Arun, *Muallim Refik Kırış*, 1–3).

80. Arun, *Muallim Refik Kırış*, 150–51. Fuad Arun, who was sixteen years old at the time, also notes entering the room bare-headed, in defiance of custom, when he brought his father's hat to the room where the guests had gathered. It appears that Fuad's bareheaded appearance in the presence of senior men was to make a statement, and was based on an understanding between father and son. It also appears that this may have been a planned meeting rather than a surprise or casual visit to Hüseyin Refik's home. Unfortunately, Fuad Arun, our primary source on this meeting, does not tell us more about how the meeting originated. The silences

in the only first-hand account available to the historian make it impossible to fully capture the historical moment. Knowing more about this meeting and how it originated would have been useful to help us understand more fully the role of an individual teacher, but also in understanding more broadly the mediating role of local leaders such as *hocas* and teachers in the reception of the Hat Law in provincial cities. This case points to the presence of a public sphere which, although limited, allowed the nationalist reforms to be debated and defended at the local level. Scholars such as Çağdar Keyder have argued that the emergent bourgeois public sphere of the constitutional era was destroyed by a decade of wars and the emigration and expulsion of most of Anatolia's Christian population. Çağlar Keyder, *State and Class in Turkey: A Study in Capitalist Development* (London: Verso, 1987). It seems that the nascent public sphere, while severely damaged, was not totally destroyed. A potentially pro-reform public existed at least in the major cities of Anatolia such as Konya and Trabzon. On Trabzon, see Çapa, "Giyim Kuşamda," 22–28.

81. The four fundamentals of Islamic canonical law are the Qur'an, the hadith (the traditions of the Prophet Muhammad), consensus of the learned, and analogy.

82. For the text of the sermon "Şapka İstimalinde Mahzurı Dini Olmadığına Dair Hutbe" see Başarır, "Şapka İnkılâbı," Appendix III. For the text of this sermon in Latin transcription, see Arun, *Muallim Refik Kırış*, 151–53; and Çapa, "Giyim Kuşamda," 23–24.

83. Başarır, "Şapka İnkılâbı," 47.

84. Arun, *Muallim Refik Kırış*, 123, 124.

85. Arun, *Muallim Refik Kırış*, 129.

86. As we will see in more detail in subsequent chapters, public support for the reforms and their internalization on an individual level were related, yet distinct, processes. It appears that, like many Turks of his generation, Hüseyin Refik continued to use Ottoman letters in his private life, although he was quick to publicly express his enthusiastic support for the new alphabet in 1928. See Arun, *Muallim Refik Kırış*, 172–73. The handwritten note and signature in Ottoman letters on a picture that Hüseyin Refik Kırış gave to his son Fuad in 1932 appears on the frontispiece.

87. On the role of the press in the implementation of the Hat Law, see Başarır, "Şapka İnkilâbı"; and Zeliha Şahin, "Kılık-Kıyafet Devrimi ve Propaganda" (master's thesis, Gazi Üniversitesi, Ankara, 1997).

88. For an original argument on the role of the print media, and particularly of the provincial press, in the formation and consolidation of a Turkish national identity during the decade following the transition to multiparty politics in 1945, see Brockett, *How Happy to Call Oneself a Turk*.

89. There is a rich and growing scholarship on education in Turkey and its connections with Turkish nationalism and modernity. See, for example, İlhan Başgöz and Howard E. Wilson, *Educational Problems in Turkey 1920–1940* (Bloomington: Indiana University Press, 1968); and Andreas M. Kazamias, *Education and the Quest for Modernity in Turkey* (Chicago: University of Chicago Press, 1966), among the earlier works. See also Sakaoğlu,

Osmanlı'dan Günümüze Eğitim Tarihi; İsmail Kaplan, *Türkiye'de Milli Eğitim İdeolojisi ve Siyasal Toplumsallaşma Üzerindeki Etkisi* (Istanbul: İletişim Yayıncılık, 1999); and Necati Eskicumalı, "Ideology and Education."

90. For examples of recent scholarship on education in the late Ottoman Empire, see Benjamin C. Fortna, *Imperial Classroom: Islam, the State, and Education in the Late Ottoman Empire* (Oxford; New York: Oxford University Press, 2002); Somel, *The Modernization of Public Education;* and Emine O. Evered, *Empire and Education under the Ottomans: Politics, Reform and Resistance from the Tanzimat to the Young Turks* (London: I. B. Tauris, 2012).

91. Law number 430 on the Unification of Education (*Tevhid-i Tedrisat Kanunu*), 3 March 1924. Parliament passed two other laws on the same date that were crucial for the creation of a secular national culture: The Law on the Abolition of Religious Orders (Law number 429) and the Law on the Abolition of the Caliphate (Law number 431). For the parliamentary debates on and the full texts of the three laws, see Reşat Genç, *Türkiye'yi Laikleştiren Yasalar: 3 Mart 1924 Meclis Müzakereleri ve Kararları* (Atatürk Kültür, Dil ve Tarih Yüksek Kurumu, Ankara: Atatürk Araştırma Merkezi, 1998).

92. Even at the primary level, the state was only able to reach a limited segment of the population. The overall primary school attendance rate was lower than 40 percent in 1927 and it passed 50 percent only around 1945 (Tiregöl, "The Role of Primary Education," 185). Still, education served as one of the best means available to the republican state for communicating its ideals and ideology to children and the youth.

93. Mitat Sadullah, *Yeni Yurt Bilgisi* (Istanbul: Tefeyyuz Kitaphanesi, 1929), 178, quoted in Henry Elisha Allen, *The Turkish Transformation: A Study in Social and Religious Development* (Chicago: University of Chicago Press, 1935), 110. Here I have followed Allen's translation. *Ketchekula* must be *keçekülah* in the original. The same lines appeared in a reading book for adult literacy courses offered by the Millet Mektepleri (the Nation's Schools). See chap. 3.

94. Faith J. Childress, "Republican Lessons." See chap. 3, esp. 156–58 and 224–29. In her analysis of images in textbooks, Childress discusses the representations of Atatürk in textbooks as "national savior, war hero and founder of the Republic, role model of physical and moral strength, teacher, national father, and political figure". Childress, "Republican Lessons," 225. I would add to this list: role model also for the proper appearance of the modern Turk, with his fine European outfit combined with his stereotypically European physical attributes, especially his blue eyes and blond hair. Images of Atatürk had (and still have) a significant presence in textbooks. She notes that in a recent history textbook, of the eighty-six photographs included, thirty-six were of Atatürk and eight others were also related to Atatürk. Childress, "Republican Lessons," 240, footnote 71 citing Işık Gürleyen, "The Ideology and Textbooks: 'Turkish Republic History of Renovation and Atatürkism' Textbooks (1980–1990)" (master's thesis, Bilkent University, Ankara, 1998), 72.

95. Childress, "Republican Lessons," 157.

96. Tiregöl, "The Role of Primary Education," 114–16; Benjamin C. Fortna, "Reading, Hegemony and Counterhegemony in the Late Ottoman Empire and the Early Turkish

Republic," in *Counterhegemony in the Colony and Postcolony*, ed. John Chalcraft and Yaseen Noorani (Palgrave Macmillan, 2007), 144; and Cüneyd Okay, "İnkılapların Hayata Geçirilmesinde Eğitimin Yeri ve Şapka Kanunu Örneği," *Bilgi ve Bellek* 2, no. 4 (summer 2005): 189–90. See also 192, 193, 201–7 for the publisher's and the author's letters and sample illustrations from the *Kolay Kıraat* series.

97. Okay, "İnkılapların Hayata Geçirilmesinde," 189–90.

98. Başak Ocak, *Bir Yayıncının Portresi: Tüccarzâde İbrahim Hilmi Çığıraçan* (Istanbul: Müteferrika Yayınları, 2003).

99. Başak Ocak, *Bir Yayıncının Portresi*, 39–42.

100. İbrahim Hilmi regarded Islam as a key element of (Ottoman) Turkish identity. In fact, he published Turkish translations of the Qur'an in Ottoman in the 1920s and in the new letters after 1928. He also published the Qur'an in the new alphabet, with a reading guide, so that the Turks, who were no longer learning the Arabic script, could still read the holy text in its original Arabic. He was supportive of the alphabet reform, and continued to support it despite the considerable financial losses his publishing house incurred because of the change. Ocak, *Bir Yayıncının Portresi*, 123–44. (Interestingly, in his private life, İbrahim Hilmi was never married, but had a life-long Greek companion, Sofya Pikeraki. Ocak, *Bir Yayıncının Portresi*, 39.)

101. For illustrations and further discussion of the old vs. new constructs in the early Republican era which intended to mark the distinction between the Ottoman and Republican eras in order to highlight the backwardness of the former and the modernity of the latter, see Bozdoğan, *Modernism and Nation Building*, chap. 2, "Architecture of Revolution"; and Benjamin C. Fortna, *Learning to Read in the Late Ottoman Empire and the Early Turkish Republic* (New York: Palgrave Macmillan, 2011), chap. 3, "Context and Content."

102. For examples of relevant stories and illustrations in textbooks see Childress, *Republican Lessons*, 158–60.

103. Faik Sabri [Duran], *Türkiye Coğrafyası* Lise 3 (Geography of Turkey High School 3). This example was cited in Childress, "Republican Lessons," 174.

104. Faik Sabri [Duran], *Türkiye Coğrafyası* Lise 3, cited in Childress, "Republican Lessons," 174. Childress notes that a similar illustration appeared in Faik Sabri's *Çocuklara Coğrafya Dersleri*, a geography textbook for the fifth grade of primary school. Some of the images and illustrations that depicted Turkey's progress from a traditional to a modern society in textbooks of the early Republican era appeared in other contexts as well, either in identical or similar formats. It appears that a relatively small collection of images and art works circulated from textbooks (both school books and Millet Mektepleri texts for adult education) to People's Houses magazines, and RPP propaganda materials such as books, posters, and postcards. Although she does not deal with arts and artists in textbook production, Bozdoğan's *Modernism and Nation Building* is useful in understanding early Republican artists and architects in the context of Turkish nation-building and modernization. Both authors and illustrators of textbooks deserve further investigation.

105. Tiregöl, "The Role of Primary Education," 94, 95. Antoine de Saint Exupéry's famous 1943 work *The Little Prince* attests to the cultural and symbolic importance of clothes as visible markers of modernity for recognition as equals in European eyes. In this very popular illustrated children's story, a Turkish astronomer had discovered in 1909 the asteroid B-612, the asteroid from which had come the Little Prince of the tale. The astronomer had presented his findings to the International Astronomical Congress, "[b]ut he was in Turkish costume," featuring a fez on his head, "so nobody would believe what he said." Later "a Turkish dictator made a law" forcing his people to change to European costume. "So in 1920 [Exupéry was off by five years, either by mistake or by intent] the astronomer gave his demonstration all over again, dressed with impressive style and elegance. And this time everybody accepted his report" (Antoine de Saint Exupéry, *The Little Prince* (San Diego: Harcourt Brace Jovanovich, Publishers, 1943/1971), translated by Katherine Woods, 15–16). The preoccupation with appearance of Turkish, Iranian, Afghan, and other modernist leaders and intellectuals in the Muslim or colonized parts of the world in the early twentieth century had a lot to do with their desire to change Western perceptions of their countries and cultures as backward and inferior. For a brief comparative overview of the state attempts to modernize and nationalize male headgear in Afghanistan, Iran, Iraq, Syria, and Turkey, see Orhan Koloğlu, *Bir Çağdaşlaşma Örneği Olarak Cumhuriyet'in*, chap. 9, "Kişilik Arayışında Başlık." See also Houchang E. Chehabi, "Staging the Emperor's New Clothes: Dress Codes and Nation-Building under Reza Shah," *Iranian Studies* 26, no. 3-4 (Summer/Fall 1993): 209–33; and Chehabi, "Dress Codes for Men in Turkey and Iran" in *Men of Order: Authoritarian Modernization under Atatürk and Reza Shah*, ed. Touraj Atabaki and Erik-Jan Zürcher (London: I.B. Tauris, 2004), 209-237.

106. Paul Gentizon, *Mustafa Kemal ou L'orient en Marche*, 127. Muallim Hüseyin Refik most likely wrote his hat sermon after Mustafa Kemal's visit to Konya in October. Curiously, Fuad Arun, Hüseyin Refik's son and biographer, does not share with the reader any memories of that high-profile visit.

107. Hikmet Öksüz and Veysel Usta, *Mustafa Reşit Tarakçıoğlu: Hayatı, Hatıratı ve Trabzon'un Yakın Tarihi* (Trabzon: Serander Yayıncılık, 2008), 200–202. The scale and impact of such services were no doubt limited, given the meager human and economic resources of the Turkish Hearths and the Teachers' Union. They nevertheless refer to an awareness that the nation-building process and national progress and modernity required an actual improvement in the living conditions of the people, as much as they demanded cultural, linguistic, or symbolic transformations.

108. İbrahim Karaer, "Türk Ocakları ve İnkılâplar (1912–1931)" (Ph.D. diss., Ankara Üniversitesi, 1989), 128. See Karaer, "Türk Ocakları . . . ," 127-31, for further examples of the Turkish Hearths' activities in promoting modern dress. Organizations such as the Turkish Hearths and the People's Houses promoted the adoption of modern clothes for women as well as men. However, it is worth noting here that, as we will see in the next chapter, the actual act of unveiling or women's removal of the *peçe* and *çarşaf* was generally a private and

individual affair, in stark contrast to the very public men's fez-rending meetings in Turkey and the *paranji*-burning ceremonies in Soviet Uzbekistan.

109. BCA 490.01.849.358.1, Letter from Ismail Engin to the RPP secretary general, 11 July 1935.

110. Justin McCarthy, "Foundations of the Turkish Republic: Social and Economic Change," *Middle Eastern Studies* 19, no. 2 (April 1983): 143–44.

111. Keyder, *State and Class in Turkey*. See especially chap. 4, "Looking for the Missing Bourgeoisie," and chap. 5, "State and Capital."

112. Orhan Pamuk's rich literary works provide some of the best illustrations of the experiences of Turkish modernization through the lives and life styles of the İstanbul bourgeois families that were in part a product of the Young Turk and early Republican era state support for the creation of a national bourgeoisie. See especially Pamuk's *Cevdet Bey ve Oğulları* (Istanbul: İletişim Yayınları, 1982); and *Yeni Hayat* (Istanbul: İletişim Yayınları, 1994).

113. See, for example, a 1925 poem commemorating the adoption of the hat: "Şapkaya Tarih," *Ülker* (Burdur Halkevi Dergisi [Burdur People's House Magazine]), no. 3 (March 1937): 55.

114. Law number 2590, "Efendi, bey, paşa gibi lâkab ve unvanların kaldırıldığına dair kanun," accepted on 26 November 1934 and published in the Official Gazette no. 2867, 29 November 1934.

115. Law number 2525, "Soy adı kanunu" published in the Official Gazette no. 2741, 2 July 1934.

116. Malik Aksel, "Atatürk ve Sanat Anıları," in *Atatürk ve Sanat Sempozyumu [The symposium on Atatürk and art]*, held in İstanbul 26–28 October 1981 (Istanbul: İstanbul Devlet Güzel Sanatlar Akademisi Publication no. 86), 7–8.

117. Sarah D. Shields, *Fezzes in the River: Identity Politics and European Diplomacy in the Middle East on the eve of World War II* (Oxford: Oxford University Press, 2011), 35. Such reports suggest that it was primarily the youth who adopted the European hat, and that age was a factor in shaping pro- and anti-hat positions in the Sanjak. Such reports also imply that women's dress too was a subject of debate in the province, although it appears that the issue of the veil did not become a part of street politics of the 1930s in the way male hats did.

118. EGM 13211-16/3, From the governor's office of Hatay to the Ministry of the Interior, 7 October 1946. In the absence of the court records or any other testimony by these men, one is left with limited evidence in trying to capture their motives in violating the Hat Law. We know that the majority of them were Turkish, Muslim, born in a village, farmers (*çiftçi*), married, with no schooling, and had not done the military service. Some were very old; Murtaza Tırabzon was in his eighties in 1946. When the government authorities called Bostan Tırabzon, another Hatay resident accused of defying the Hat Law, a reactionary who opposed the regime and engaged in anti-regime propaganda, they almost certainly had more information than the accessible documents revealed. While I have not seen the court ruling on the Hatay cases from 1946, I would have expected, based on other court cases concerning the hat

and assuming no additional charges were brought against these men, monetary fines and possibly a short term (a few days) imprisonment.

119. A 1939 police inspector's report commented that the residents of Hatay had not yet liberated themselves from the influence of Arab customs and that few of them spoke Turkish. The inspector noted that "No doubt a great many of those speaking Arabic are Turks and are conscious of their Turkishness. But they cannot bring themselves to stop speaking Arabic." ("Arapça konuşanların ekserisi hiç şüphe yok ki Türktür, Türklüklerini de müdriktirler. Buna rağmen Arapça konuşmaktan kendilerini alamıyorlar.") The inspector nevertheless expressed confidence that the people of Hatay would soon grasp the meaning of their national identity under the compassionate guidance of the Republic. ("Bu insanlar Cumhuriyetin şefkatli eli altında ati'i karipte benliklerini tamamile anlayacaklardır.") EGM 42217-1/C, "Hatay emniyet teşkilatını teftiş eden polis müfettişi Hasan Fehmi Yalın tarafından tanzim edilen teftiş raporundan . . . ," Kanun evvel 1939. The full integration of Hatay province into the national culture would be more gradual than the process of political unification.

120. Mary Neuburger, *The Orient Within: Muslim Minorities and the Negotiation of Nationhood in Modern Bulgaria* (Ithaca: Cornell University Press, 2004); see especially chap. 3.

121. EGM 13211-16/2, From the Ministry of the Interior to the Inspectors General and the Governors, Cipher no. 651, 17 March 1939.

122. EGM 13211-16/2, From the governor of Sinop to the Ministry of the Interior, no. 24, 20 March 1939.

123. EGM 13211-16/2, From the governor of Çorum to the Ministry of the Interior, 22 March 1939.

124. EGM 13211-16/2, From the governor of Kastamonu to the Ministry of the Interior. No. 26, 18 March 1939.

125. On the 27 November 1925 hat incidents in Maraş and the ensuing trials by the Independence Tribunals, see Eyicil, "İstiklâl Mahkemelerinde," 13–45.

126. EGM 13211-16/2, From Maraş governor İ. Sabri Çıtak to the Ministry of the Interior, no. 167.223, 23 March 1939.

127. EGM 13211-16/2, From Mardin governor Cevat Ökmen to the Ministry of the Interior, no. 65, 26 March 1939.

128. BCA 490.01.612.125.2, From the Kars province inspector report by Cemal Karamuğla, 1939.

129. EGM 13211-16/2, From the Balıkesir Governor to the Minister of the Interior, 28 March 1939.

130. EGM 13216-3, From the Çoruh province governor's office to the Ministry of the Interior, 31 January 1938.

131. EGM 13216-5, From the Antalya Governor to the Ministry of the Interior, 24 March 1938.

132. BCA 030.18.01.79.83.19, Council of Ministers Decree, 5 October 1937.

133. Interview with Avni Yurdabayrak (b.1914 d.September 2010), İstanbul, 25 April 2003.

134. Such generational tensions between fathers and sons in the adoption of the new hat arguably were also reflective of the ongoing effects of a broader modernization process that since the nineteenth century had been expanding young men's authority and reinforcing young men's identities as adult men in part by disrupting traditional hierarchies of age. For further discussion of the transformation of male identities (and the accompanying changes in family and gender relations) in late Ottoman and early Republican periods, see Ayşe Durakbaşa, "Cumhuriyet Döneminde Modern Kadın ve Erkek Kimliklerinin Oluşumu: Kemalist Kadın Kimliği ve 'Münevver Erkekler,'" in *75 yılda kadınlar ve erkekler,* ed. Ayşe Berktay Hacımirzaoğlu (Istanbul: Tarih Vakfı Yayınları, 1998), 40–42; and Deniz Kandiyoti, "Patterns of Patriarchy: Notes for an Analysis of Male Dominance in Turkish Society," in *Women in Turkish Society: A Reader,* ed. Şirin Tekeli (London: Zed Books, 1995), 309–10.

135. EGM 13211-16/2 Testimony by Ahmet Tiryaki, 7 March 1939.

136. Avni Yurdabayrak's narratives of civil service as a judge and public prosecutor make it clear that such differences continued into the post-RPP period. Avni Bey recalled at least one instance of having to deal with confiscated *külahs* of villagers during his days of judicial service in Sakarya province. He returned the confiscated *külahs* that had been brought to his office to the villagers. He justified his decision (to me, the historian, and apparently also to a military commander at the time) on the grounds that there was no intent to violate the law; that the men involved had worn these "hats" because they were suitable for work [in the fields, etc.]. Avni Bey thought it had occurred around 1960; from the context of the conversation it appears it might well have been shortly after the 1960 military coup.

137. BCA 030.10.128.923.10, From Kütahya governor Sedat Erim to the Ministry of the Interior, 31 March 1936.

138. BCA 030.10.128.923.10, From Kütahya governor Sedat Erim . . . , 31 March 1936.

139. BCA 030.10.128.923.10, From Interior Minister Şükrü Kaya to the Prime Minister, 1 April 1936.

140. BCA 030.10.128.923.10, From Interior Minister Şükrü Kaya to the Prime Minister, 9 April 1936.

141. Meltem Türköz also observed this during her oral historical research on the acquisition of family names (Türköz, "The Social Life of the State's Fantasy").

142. This was evident in interviews, for example with Yusuf Altınkaya (1904–2009), İstanbul, 2003; Mehmet Baltacı (1910–2006), Kastamonu, 2003; and Avni Yurdabayrak (1914–2010), İstanbul, 2003.

143. Zürcher has emphasized that the army and the gendarmerie allowed the Republican state to extend its control throughout the country to a degree that had never been achieved by its Ottoman predecessor. Zürcher suggests that "it was this establishment of effective control, more than any of the famous Kemalist reforms (clothing, alphabet, calendar), which heralded

the arrival of the modern state in Anatolia." Zürcher, "From Empire to Republic—problems of transition, continuity, and change," in *Turkey in the Twentieth Century*, ed. Erik-Jan Zürcher (Berlin: Klaus Schwarz Verlag, 2008), 25. As we see in this section, the arrival in the small towns and villages of some of the specific measures of the new regime, such as the requirement of the European hat, was indeed closely linked with the establishment of state control through the presence of the gendarmerie as much as it was through the establishment of administrative, political, and cultural institutions of the state.

144. "Korku, jandarma [fesi] yırtar, ceza verirdi. Korkudan giyemezlerdi. [Jandarma] Seni karakol istedi dedi mi, boku yedin, dayak yemeden çıkamazdın." Interview with Recep Göksoy, Kastamonu, 5 March 2003. Narratives of actual physical violence or threat (and fear) of corporal punishment as a frequently employed method of persuasion and punishment emerged in conversations with respondents of village backgrounds as well as from those who had been in positions of power. One respondent spoke frankly about having used violence in his dealings with ordinary citizens during his service in Anatolian towns. (Reflecting on the past at an advanced age, he no longer considered such action appropriate.) In one such instance, during his service in Zonguldak province in the western Black Sea region, a peasant was brought to his office for having sold his wife for a pair of oxen. Appalled by the exchange of a woman for a pair of oxen, our narrator's first response was to slap the villager on the face, which resulted in blood gushing from the man's nose and the town's doctor having to be called in. In the absence of any written or oral evidence for the peasant's side of the story, our understanding of this event comes from the testimony of the more powerful party involved. Nevertheless, this story illustrates how physical violence worked in combination with (or preceded) legal process in government officials' dealings with rural residents of Anatolia. It must, however, be remembered that the state authorities' control over local populations varied considerably by factors such as region, social organization, and class. The ability of government bureaucrats or gendarmes to intervene in local matters was much more constrained in tribal regions or in areas where government officials were outsiders and did not speak the local language. For a similar argument for the Kurdish speaking regions, see Senem Aslan, "Everyday Forms of State Power and the Kurds in the Early Turkish Republic," *International Journal of Middle East Studies* 43 (2011): 75–93. A detailed analysis of the role of violence as a cultural phenomenon is beyond the scope of this work, but it should be noted that the authoritarian nature of the new regime rested in part on a pre-existing political culture that contained violence as an instrument of social control and social change. Despite an early nineteenth-century cultural shift in the Ottoman Empire away from violence, by the end of the Empire violence persisted as an instrument of punishment and control at political, community, and family levels. Not only had the reach of this nineteenth-century "civilizational" trend delegitimizing the use of violence been uneven and incomplete, but also, arguably, the wars and intercommunal fighting in the final decade of the Empire reinforced the culture of violence. See Roger Deal, "War Refugees and Violence in Hamidian Istanbul," *Middle Eastern Studies* 49, no. 2 (March 2013): 179–90.

145. Interview with Mehmet Baltacı, Kastamonu, 4 March 2003.

146. In the narrative of one respondent, it was in fact shoes—the transition from *çarıks* to rubber shoes (*lastik*) and later to leather shoes (*ayakkabı*)—rather than hats that marked the arrival of modern clothing in Anatolia. Interview with Yusuf Altınkaya, İstanbul, 23 April 2003.

147. It should be noted that the leaders of Kurdish nationalist groups, such as the PKK, that have challenged Turkish nationalism since the late 1970s on the grounds of ethnic identity and collective rights, have in fact amply demonstrated their shared identity with the republican Turkish modernity, among other things in the way they appear and the language they speak. The difference between Iraqi Kurdish leader Masud Barzani's appearance and PKK leader Abdullah Öcalan's is not just linked to their tribal, class, and ideological origins, but is a reflection of what kind of a Kurdish nation and Kurdish modernity they envision. Kurdish nationalism in Turkey reveals many of the common values of the twentieth-century Turkish modernist project, even as it continues to bring to the surface the contradictions and shortcomings of that nationalist project and challenges it.

2. Women, Politics, and the Culture of Dress in the Making of a New Turkish Nation

1. See for, example, Beth Baron, *Egypt as a Woman: Nationalism, Gender, and Politics* (Berkeley: University of California Press, 2005); Camron Michael Amin, *The Making of the Modern Iranian Woman: Gender, State Policy, and Popular Culture, 1865–1946* (Gainesville: University Press of Florida, 2002); Jasamin Rostam-Kolayi, "Expanding Agendas for the "New" Iranian Woman: Family Law, Work, and Unveiling" in *The Making of Modern Iran: State and Society under Riza Shah, 1921–1941*, ed. Stephanie Cronin (London; New York: Routledge Curzon, 2003), 164–89; Afsaneh Najmabadi, *Women with Mustaches and Men without Beards: Gender and Sexual Anxieties of Iranian Modernity* (Berkeley: University of California Press, 2005); Ellen L. Fleischmann, *The Nation and Its "New" Women: The Palestinian Women's Movement, 1920–1948* (Berkeley: University of California Press, 2003); Kamp, *The New Woman in Uzbekistan*; and Adrianne Lynn Edgar, *Tribal Nation: The Making of Soviet Turkmenistan* (Princeton: Princeton University Press, 2004), especially chap. 8, "Emancipation of the Unveiled: Turkmen Women under Soviet Rule," 221–60. For images of the new or modern woman in the Middle East, see Sarah Graham-Brown, *The Portrayal of Women in Photography of the Middle East 1860–1950: Images of Women* (New York: Columbia University Press, 1988).

2. Nilüfer Göle, *The Forbidden Modern: Civilization and Veiling* (Ann Arbor: The University of Michigan Press, 1996). See esp. chap. 2 and 3. See also Deniz Kandiyoti, "End of Empire: Islam, Nationalism and Women in Turkey," in *Women, Islam & the State*, ed. Deniz Kandiyoti (Philadelphia: Temple University Press, 1991), 22–47.

3. Yeşim Arat, "Group-Differentiated Rights and the Liberal Democratic State: Rethinking the Headscarf Controversy in Turkey," *New Perspectives on Turkey*, no. 25 (Fall 2001): 36.

4. Deniz Kandiyoti, "Gendering the Modern: On Missing Dimensions in the Study of Turkish Modernity," in Bozdoğan and Kasaba, eds., *Rethinking Modernity and National Identity in Turkey*, 122.

5. See for example Sadık Sarısaman, "Cumhuriyet'in İlk Yıllarında Kadın Kıyafeti Meselesi," *Atatürk Yolu*, no. 21 (May 1998): 97–106; Mesut Çapa, "Giyim Kuşamda;" Hakkı Uyar, "Çarşaf, Peçe ve Kafes Üzerine Bazı Notlar," *Toplumsal Tarih*, no. 33 (Eylül 1996): 6–11; Kemal Yakut, "Tek Parti Döneminde Peçe ve Çarşaf," *Tarih ve Toplum*, no. 220 (April 2002): 23–32.

6. Albert Hourani, "How Should We Write the History of the Middle East?" *International Journal of Middle East Studies* 23, no. 2 (May 1991): 134.

7. See, for example, Hourani, "How Should We Write the History"; and Stirling, "Social Change and Social Control."

8. *Çarşaf*, from the Persian *"châdor-e shab,"* literally "bed sheets," refers to a woman's outdoors clothing consisting of a top piece covering the head and the upper part of the body and a skirt covering the body from the waist to the feet. Koçu in his *Türk Giyim Kuşam ve Süslenme Sözlüğü*, 65–68, includes *peçe*, the face cover, as an integral part of a *çarşaf*. *Çarşaf* was often complemented with a *peçe*, but not always, and in the period covered by this study the two are generally referred to as two related yet separate articles of clothing. See, for instance, Türk Dil Kurumu, *Türkçe Sözlük*, 281.

9. For a similar social practice in Turkmenistan, see Edgar, *Tribal Nation*.

10. *Yaşmak* (yashmak) is a two piece head and face covering that urban Muslim women typically wore with the *ferace*. Unlike the *peçe*, the *yaşmak* did not cover the wearer's entire face. Often made of fine, white muslin cloth, the upper piece of the *yaşmak* covered the head, while the lower piece, which was tied in the back, covered the face below the eyes, hence revealing the eyes. In its more conservative form, the *yaşmak* was made of thicker cloth or worn folded into two layers for better concealment of the wearer's face. In its more liberal, or *"açık yaşmak,"* form, it was made of fine, semi-transparent muslin cloth, the scarf was worn higher above the eyebrows, and the face piece was tied lower below the eyes, revealing more of the face as well as some hair, and barely concealing the woman's mouth. Koçu, *Türk Giyim Kuşam*, 240, 241; Türk Dil Kurumu, *Türkçe Sözlük*, 1605. See fig. 2 in this chapter for an idealized image of the *yaşmak*.

11. Elizabeth Brown Frierson, "Unimagined Communities: State, Press, and Gender in the Hamidian Era" (Ph.D. diss., Princeton University, 1996); and Nancy Micklewright, "Women's Dress in Nineteenth-Century Istanbul: Mirror of a Changing Society" (Ph.D. diss., University of Pennsylvania, 1986).

12. Nora Şeni, "Fashion and Women's Clothing in the Satirical Press of Istanbul at the End of the 19th Century," in *Women in Modern Turkish Society: A Reader*, ed. Şirin Tekeli (London: Zed Books, 1995), 31; Zafer Toprak, "Tesettürden Telebbüse ya da Çarşaf veya Elbise: "Milli Moda" ve Çarşaf," *Tombak*, no. 19 (April 1998): 58.

13. Nora Şeni, "Fashion and Women's Clothing"; Palmira Brummett, *Image and Imperialism in the Ottoman Revolutionary Press, 1908–1911* (Albany: State University of New York Press, 2000), see chaps. 7, 8, and 9.

14. Micklewright, "*Women's Dress in Nineteenth-Century Istanbul.*"

15. For examples of such decrees, see Vahdettin Engin, *Sultan Abdülhamid ve İstanbul'u* (Istanbul: Simurg Yayınları, 2001), 54–55. Nicole A.N.M. Van Os, "Ottoman Women's Reaction to the Economic and Cultural Intrusion of the West: The Quest for a National Dress," in *Dissociation and Appropriation Responses to Globalization in Asia and Africa*, ed. Katja Füllberg-Stolberg et al. (Berlin: Verlag Das Arabische Buch, 1999), 302. As Nora Şeni has noted, Sultan Abdülhamid's concern was not only a moral, but also a security-related one. Obsessed (not without good reason) with threats to his personal safety, the Sultan had forbidden women dressed in *çarşaf* and *peçe* from entering his palace, for fear that inside the loose *çarşaf* might be a man in disguise. Thus, under Abdülhamid's rule women were prohibited from wearing the *çarşaf* in Beşiktaş, the district where the sultan's residence was located. Şeni, "Fashion and Women's Clothing," 31.

16. Van Os, "Ottoman Women's," 302. Such decrees were apparently not confined to the capital city. Çapa and Çiçek note a similar post-1908 provincial ruling in Trabzon in Mesut Çapa and Rahmi Çiçek, *Yirminci Yüzyıl Başlarında Trabzon'da Yaşam* (Trabzon: Serander Yayıncılık, 2004), 248–49. The Republican state's efforts to transform women's dress through decrees and street level enforcement had their origins in late Ottoman practices such as the imperial and local decrees mentioned here and the attempts to enforce them locally through police forces. It should be noted, though, that as this chapter reveals, in the early Republican period administrative decrees constituted only one element of a broader public effort to transform Turkish women's appearance, and the central government was generally not supportive of the use of police and gendarmerie forces for enforcement.

17. Kandiyoti, "End of Empire," 31.

18. Van Os, "Ottoman Women's," 302–3.

19. In the city of Aydın, for example, the town's officials responded to the growing number of incidents after July 1908 of assaults on women and women's public humiliation by prescribing specific measures of punishment for men and women who spoke in public with a member of the opposite sex: a fine of 100 *kuruş* (piastres) for men and falaka bastinado for women. Güzel argues that in the aftermath of the July 1908 coup, the CUP was not able to fully establish its authority and that the "old" administrators found it convenient to ignore the attacks on women or even to ally with the conservatives. M. Şehmus Güzel, "1908 Kadınları," *Tarih ve Toplum* 2, no. 7 (1984): 6. See also Göle, *The Forbidden Modern*, 48. Similarly, in Egypt, where unveiling was also under way in the early twentieth century for reasons similar to those in the Ottoman case, the *ulama*, Islamic scholars, tried to stop Egyptian women from unveiling by recommending that the government imprison unveiled women for a period of two months and issue a fine of twenty pounds. Beth Baron, "Unveiling in Early Twentieth Century Egypt: Practical and Symbolic Considerations," *Middle Eastern Studies* 25, no. 3 (July 1989): 380–81. Such opposition, however, did not deter increasing numbers of Egyptian women from unveiling.

20. Fatma Kılıç Denman, *İkinci Meşrutiyet Döneminde Bir Jön Türk Dergisi: Kadın* (Istanbul: Libra, 2009), 202–3. It would appear that this was primarily, but not exclusively,

a gendered phenomenon. Women too were involved in the street politics of figuring out proper dress and identity for Ottoman women. There were instances of older women verbally harassing and even physically attacking fashionably dressed younger women in the streets of İstanbul. Ebru Boyar and Kate Fleet, *A Social History of Ottoman Istanbul* (Cambridge: Cambridge University Press, 2010), 300–302. Such tensions between older and younger, traditional and Westernized women were also evident in the cartoons of the late Ottoman period. See Şeni, "Fashion and Women's Clothing" and Brummett, *Image and Imperialism*.

21. For a view that identifies the wars as a major cause of the radical changes in women's dress, public visibility, and social position during the Young Turk era, see Zafer Toprak, "The Family, Feminism, and the State during the Young Turk Period, 1908–1918," in *Première Rencontre Internationale sur l'Empire Ottoman et la Turquie Moderne*, ed. Edhem Eldem (Istanbul: ISIS, 1991), 441–52.

22. Later, the War of Liberation required further sacrifices from Anatolian women, culminating in the figure of self-sacrificing Anatolian women as the founders and symbols of the nation. It is worth noting that similar contributions to a nationalist cause, for example Egyptian women's contributions to the post-war nationalist revolt, did not pay off, as women were excluded from full citizenship rights after independence. Similarly, in the case of Syria and Lebanon, Elizabeth Thompson has argued that World War I had the effect of reinforcing patriarchy. See Baron, *Egypt as a Woman;* and Elizabeth Thompson, *Colonial Citizens: Republican Rights, Paternal Privilege, and Gender in French Syria and Lebanon* (Columbia University Press, 2000). Such differences between the Egyptian, Syrian, and Turkish cases post-war underscore the importance of ideology and leadership as well as the role and legacy of colonialism.

23. Kandiyoti, "End of Empire," 31.

24. İkbal Elif Mahir, "Fashion and Women in the İstanbul of the Armistice Period, 1918–1923" (master's thesis, Boğaziçi University, Istanbul, 2005).

25. Mahir, "Fashion and Women," 136.

26. Brummett, *Image and Imperialism*, 247, 253.

27. Mahir, "Fashion and Women," 186; Toprak, "Tesettürden Telebbüse," 63 quoting Zehra Hakkı, "Milli Moda," *İnci*, no. 1 (1 February 1919). "Ya peçe? Diyeceksiniz. Etrafınıza biraz bakarsanız, anlarsınız ki biz onu zaten kaldırdık." Mahir gives the entire text of Zehra Hakkı's article on pp. 183–86.

28. *Peştemal* (or *peştamal*), from the Persian *"pushtmal,"* refers to a long woven cloth used as a *hamam* (bath house) wrapping and towel, as an artisan's apron, or as women's outerwear covering the head and the body. Koçu, *Türk Giyim Kuşam*, 191; Eyüboğlu, *Türk Dilinin*, 555; Türk Dil Kurumu, *Türkçe Sözlük*, 1181. (In contemporary Turkey, one might add the category of beach *peştemals*, as they have been increasingly popular in Aegean and Mediterranean resort towns in the past decade.) The concern of the mayor of Eskişehir, and of the state, was primarily with the *peştemal* as women's outdoor clothing. *Peştemals* were worn over other layers of clothing and they did not necessarily cover the entire body down to the ankles,

like the traditional *çarşaf*. Women wore *peştemals* as capes covering the head and the upper body, as aprons, as a two-piece set of a cape and an apron, or as a single piece outerwear covering the head and the entire body. Whereas the *çarşaf* was traditionally accompanied by a *peçe*, or face veil, *peştemals* were not necessarily worn with a face veil. *Çarşafs* tended to be solid color and were made of silk, sateen, woolen, or cotton fabrics. *Peştemals* were generally striped or patterned, and their colors, patterns, and fabrics reflected local and regional variations in weaving styles and materials. Aydın *peştemals*, for example, differed from Trabzon *peştemals* in their colors, designs, and materials.

29. Mayor Kamil's announcement in *İstiklal*, 7 Kanunevvel (Aralık/December) 1925, as quoted in Mesut Çapa, "Giyim Kuşamda," 24.

30. Kemal Yakut, "Tek Parti Döneminde Peçe ve Çarşaf," 27, 28. Yakut argues, on the basis of anecdotal evidence, that this decision was indeed successfully implemented, especially in the city, by the municipality police who in public places stopped women dressed in the *peçe* and *çarşaf* and warned them that they would be subject to monetary fines. Yakut offers no specifics about his oral evidence, but his claim about police interference in public places follows a common pattern that emerges from archival and interview evidence, as discussed later in this chapter.

31. BCA 030.10.53.346.6, 47.6, 3 January 1927, "Meclis-i Umumi-i Vilayetin 1 Kanun Sâni 927 tarih ve bir numaralı kararı suretidir."

32. *Üstlük* (*üslük*) is a general term used for a variety of head coverings and outdoor garments including *peştemals*. Koçu, *Türk Giyim Kuşam*, 237; Eyuboğlu, *Türk Dilinin*, 701.

33. "*Zeybek* clothes" referred to the traditional costume of the Western Anatolian, particularly Aegean, *zeybek*s or *efe*s: young men who were known for their bravery and often had a reputation as the protectors of the weak against the injustices of the state or any other authority. Thus, although this local decision in Aydın was concerned primarily with women's appearance, the banning of *zeybek* clothes was mainly about nationalizing men's appearance and identities by eliminating the distinctive costume of the *efe* subculture from everyday use. Interestingly, in the same time frame the culture of *zeybek*s was being relegated to and celebrated at the level of folklore.

34. BCA 030.10.53.346.6, 47.6, 3 January 1927, From the Governor of Aydın to Prime Minister İsmet Paşa (İnönü).

35. Aydın provincial council passed a unanimous decision on 9 August 1935 prohibiting the women of Aydın from wearing articles of clothing such as *çarşaf*, *peçe*, *üslük* and *peştemal*. See EGM 13216-7/1, Copy of the text of Aydın provincial council decision number 467, 9 August 1935.

36. Amin, *The Making of the Modern Iranian Woman*, 84, 85; on the Shah's visit to Turkey, see Afshin Marashi, "Performing the Nation: The Shah's official state visit to Kemalist Turkey, June to July 1934," in *The Making of Modern Iran*, ed. Stephanie Cronin (London; New York: Routledge Curzon, 2003), 99–119.

37. Amin, *The Making of the Modern Iranian Woman*, 94; Houchang E. Chehabi, "Banning of the Veil and Its Consequences" in *The Making of Modern Iran*, ed. Stephanie Cronin (London; New York: Routledge Curzon, 2003), 197–98.

38. EGM 13216-7/1, From the Governor of Antalya to the Ministry of the Interior, 17 December 1934.

39. EGM 13216-7/1, From the Minister of the Interior to the Governor of Antalya, 17 December 1934. A handwritten note, most likely by the minister himself, on a copy of the telegram from Antalya read: "This will happen by enlightening our women and their husbands. . . . Police forces should not be used."

40. EGM 13216-7/1, Circular from the Minister of the Interior to all the Governors and Inspectors General, 17 December 1934.

41. My informants mostly recalled the process of their mothers' and grandmothers' transition from the *çarşaf* to the *manto* and their own growing up without the *çarşaf* as experiences that had a long term effect on how they dressed and appeared in public. In a rare narrative of the reverse process (of going back to the *çarşaf*), Ömer Güner recalled how his mother used to wear the *çarşaf* in Trabzon, how she adopted the *manto*, and how later, "when it became free," she reverted to the *çarşaf*. I could not expect Ömer Bey, or any of my other informants, to remember exactly when these shifts occurred, but it seemed (from the flow of the conversation) that Ömer Bey was referring to the post-1950 period as the time when the *çarşaf* became free. He did not reflect on his mother's motives for returning to the *çarşaf*, which of course would only have given us Ömer Bey's view of why she acted in a certain way on the basis of his memory and filtered through his interpretation. It appears, from the narrative context provided by Ömer Bey, that his mother's family, social, and cultural environment neither required nor encouraged the "new dress" or the values associated with it. Notable aspects of her environment included rural origins and immigration to the city as an adult, polygamous marriage to a local merchant, and continued participation in the Nakşibendi order (for which Ömer Bey noted she feared the police, but was quick to note that "she nevertheless liked Atatürk for liberating us from the bandits (eşkıya)." Interview with Ömer Güner, Trabzon, 21 September 2002.

42. EGM 13216-7/1, From Sinop Governor A. Savaş to the Ministry of the Interior, 4 March 1935.

43. For a recent overview, see Zehra F. Kabasakal Arat, "Institutions and Women's Rights: Religion, the State, and Family in Turkey," in *Family, Gender, & Law in a Globalizing Middle East and South Asia*, ed. Kenneth M. Cuno and Manisha Desai (Syracuse: Syracuse University Press, 2009), 79–101. For a critical reassessment of the actual impact of the new Civil Code on the practice of polygamy, see Nicole A. N. M. Van Os, "Polygamy Before and After the Introduction of the Swiss Civil Code in Turkey," in *The State and the Subaltern: Modernization, Society and the State in Turkey and Iran*, ed. Touraj Atabaki (London: I. B. Tauris, 2007), 179–98. For an earlier anthropological study on the impact of the new Civil Code, see Paul J. Magnarella, "The Reception of Swiss Family Law in Turkey," Anthropological Quarterly 46, no. 2 (April 1973): 100–116.

44. About the same time as the *peçe* and *çarşaf* decrees, some towns banned the wooden lattices covering house windows on the grounds of health. In some instances, lattices and the *peçe* and *çarşaf* were banned in a single decision. For instance, *Son Posta* reported that in the town of Sungurlu, "[t]he party and the municipal administrative committees have met with the health committee and decided that the lattices must be abolished and that the *çarşaf* and the *peçe* must not be worn." *Son Posta*, "Sungurluda Kafesler Kalktı" (10 July 1935). One week later (18 July 1935) *Son Posta* reported that "the *peçe* and the lattices have been prohibited in Sungurlu." For similar reports from other towns see, for example, *Son Posta* (25 July 1935), for Mecitözü; and *Son Posta* (17 August 1935), for Kaş.

45. C.H.P., *Dördüncü Büyük Kurultayı Görüşmeleri Tutulgası 9–16 Mayıs 1935* (Ankara: Ulus Basımevi, 1935), 144.

46. C.H.P., *Dördüncü Büyük Kurultayı Görüşmeleri Tutulgası*, 144.

47. C.H.P., *Dördüncü Büyük Kurultayı Görüşmeleri Tutulgası*, 145.

48. C.H.P., *Dördüncü Büyük Kurultayı Görüşmeleri Tutulgası*, 146.

49. For a classic account of the Soviet attempt to use law to bring about a social and cultural revolution in Central Asia, see Gregory T. Massell, "Law as an Instrument of Revolutionary Change in a Traditional Milieu: The Case of Soviet Central Asia," *Law & Society Review* 2, no. 2 (February 1968): 179–228.

50. C.H.P., *Dördüncü Büyük Kurultayı Görüşmeleri Tutulgası*, 146.

51. "*Kadın istemeyor, erkek istemeyor, o halde bu peçe niçin sallanıp duruyor?*" C.H.P., *Dördüncü Büyük Kurultayı Görüşmeleri Tutulgası*, 147.

52. The published records of the Congress list most members of the Congress by their full names; hence, it appears that a majority of the delegates had already taken a surname by the time of this congress, which took place less than a year after the Surname Law. The records also generally refer to the speakers by their full names, although occasionally their names appear without the family name, as in "Dr. Muhtar" for "Muhtar Berker." This could be seen as an omission or minor inconsistency by the typist and editor; more likely it is an unintended example of the process of getting used to identifying people by their family names. Where the surname was omitted, I have given it in parentheses.

53. The *enveriye* hat was a brimless military sun helmet. See chap. 1 for more.

54. Notions of appropriate male-female interaction in public places changed gradually and unevenly across urban-rural, regional, and class lines. Yusuf Duygu's mention of village women's public behaviour brings to mind a childhood memory that attests to the gradual nature of this process. I still recall how my late grandmother, when we went out in her small Black Sea town, upon encountering a man would wait for him to cross the street before we did, even when the man was half my grandmother's age or younger. Men still had the right of way, so to speak. As a child I could not make sense of what must have been a dying practice. I remember the young men, often young teachers or other government officials out for a stroll, telling my grandmother not to wait for them. This was around the late 1970s and early 1980s.

55. "Katiyen olmaz." C.H.P., *Dördüncü Büyük Kurultayı Görüşmeleri Tutulgası*, 149.

56. In the chapter on the regulation of men's clothing, I have discussed in detail the multiple functions of dress codes in nation building through homogenizing appearance, as well as in serving the nation's desire for recognition as a modern nation in the Europeans' eyes. For an insightful analysis of these considerations in reforming men's and women's clothes in Iran under Reza Shah, see Chehabi, "Staging the Emperor's New Clothes."

57. C.H.P. *Dördüncü Büyük Kurultayı Görüşmeleri Tutulgası*, 149.

58. See, for example, Yeşim Arat, "The Project of Modernity and Women in Turkey," in *Rethinking Modernity and National Identity in Turkey*, ed. Sibel Bozdoğan and Reşat Kasaba (Seattle: University of Washington Press, 1997), 100–106.

59. C.H.P., *Dördüncü Büyük Kurultayı Görüşmeleri Tutulgası*, 151.

60. The Us proposal as read by the session chair referred to both the *peçe* and *çarşaf*: "I request the passage of a law on the abolition of *peçe* and *çarşaf*" ("Peçe ve çarşafın kaldırılması üzerinde bir kanun çıkarılmasını dilerim.") C.H.P., *Dördüncü Büyük Kurultayı Görüşmeleri Tutulgası*, 151. From subsequent comments by Us, it appears that his proposal likely referred to the *peçe* only.

61. Kandiyoti, "Emancipated but Unliberated? Reflections on the Turkish Case," *Feminist Studies* 13, no. 2 (Summer, 1987): 317–38. For a recent study that demonstrates how the single party regime did not tolerate the development of autonomous women's associations, see Yaprak Zihnioğlu, *Kadınsız İnkılap: Nezihe Muhiddin, Kadınlar Halk Fırkası, Kadın Birliği* (Istanbul: Metis, 2003).

62. Kandiyoti, "Gendering the Modern," 123; Kandiyoti, "Patterns of Patriarchy," 311.

63. Arat, "The Project of Modernity," 98,99.

64. Latife Hanım dressed in a much more conservative fashion for these public appearances than she would have otherwise, unveiled but always covering her head. Nevertheless, Latife Hanım's public visibility provided an occasion for a conservative campaign against Mustafa Kemal with propaganda leaflets condemning the president for his wife's uncovered face. One such leaflet distributed in 1923, which showed an unveiled Latife sitting cross legged in the company of her husband and his male colleagues, openly attacked Mustafa Kemal for allegedly violating Islamic morality and the nation's honor. It called on good Muslims to act now and "break this hand" that has "intruded into [their] harems," or else to say good-bye to religion and the honor of their wives and daughters forever. İpek Çalışlar, *Latife Hanım* (Istanbul: Doğan Kitap, 2006), 187. Whereas similar conservative backlash in Afghanistan in 1928 led to the dethroning of Amanullah Khan, Mustafa Kemal and Latife Hanım managed the situation much more successfully. Latife Hanım cautiously tried to maintain a balance between projecting a modest or even conservative image acceptable to the broader public and wearing her own style of modern dress. Mustafa Kemal responded to these conservative attacks with the same language of religion by securing the support of religious authorities in the provinces. In Adana, for example, the *müfti* issued a religious opinion confirming that Latife Hanım's attire and her travelling with her husband were in conformity with Islamic teachings. Moreover, even the authors of anti-Mustafa Kemal propaganda leaflets were compelled

to acknowledge the broad popular support Mustafa Kemal commanded as a war hero and the liberator of the country (*Halaskâr Gazi*) when they referred to Mustafa Kemal as "the man you call the Great Liberator." It should also be noted that such angry attacks, drawing on a blending of religious conservatism and patriarchy, did not reflect the much more diverse and potentially moderate positions of a largely rural, war weary Anatolian population caught up in poverty and the problems of everyday existence. In addition, as this book demonstrates, many of the changes promoted by the regime concerning women not only had the support of significant segments of the population, but were at least in part a consequence of the ongoing social and cultural changes. Finally, the coercive means of an authoritarian state prevented such religious conservatism from turning into an effective threat to the regime.

65. Müjgan Cunbur, "Atatürk'ün Türk Giyimi Üzerine Düşünceleri," in *Proceedings of the International Conference on Atatürk held on November 9–13, 1981*, vol.1 (Istanbul, 1981), 1–16.

66. Nermin Abadan Unat, "Türkiye'de Kadın Hareketi-Dün-Bugün," *Bilanço 1923–1998*, vol. 2 (Istanbul: Tarih Vakfı, 1999), 249–50.

67. Ahmed Emin Yalman, *Turkey in my Time* (Norman: University of Oklahoma Press, 1956), 175.

68. Yalman, *Turkey in my Time*, 151,152.

69. Contemporary modernist reformers in other contexts such as Iran and the Soviet Union made similar arguments in justifying their attack on the veil as part of their project of cultural transformation. For Soviet reformers' arguments on the veil as a symbol of backwardness and primitiveness in Uzbekistan see Douglas Northrop, *Veiled Empire: Gender and Power in Stalinist Central Asia* (Ithaca: Cornell University Press, 2004), 58–68.

70. C.H.P. *Dördüncü Büyük Kurultayı Görüşmeleri Tutulgası*, 152.

71. The opening of the Soviet archives after the dissolution of the Soviet Union has allowed historians of Soviet Central Asia to document in some detail secular modernist Soviet policies in Central Asia, including gender policies, and their impact. On the Uzbek case, see Northrop, *Veiled Empire*; and Kamp, *The New Woman in Uzbekistan*. See also Edgar, *Tribal Nation*, especially chap. 8, "Emancipation of the Unveiled: Turkmen Women under Soviet Rule," 221–60; and Shoshana Keller, *To Moscow Not Mecca: The Soviet Campaign Against Islam in Central Asia, 1917–1941* (Westport, CT: Praeger, 2001).

72. Northrop, *Veiled Empire*, 259, 266. Northrop interpreted such acts of violence against the unveiled women in the context of anticolonial resistance to Soviet intervention in Uzbek culture and ways of life. Marianne Kamp, on the other hand, has suggested that Uzbek women's unveiling should be understood not only as an issue of colonialism, but also in the context of struggles over Uzbek identity: Uzbek women unveiled in part because of the modernist Uzbek demand for the New Woman. Kamp argues, then, that violence against unveiled women should be understood not so much as anticolonial resistance, but as a male attempt to defend patriarchy. Kamp notes that the violence against women did not change the course of Soviet policies toward women, nor did it preserve women's seclusion in the long run. Kamp,

The New Woman in Uzbekistan, chap. 7–10; see esp. chap. 8, "The Counter-Hujum: Terror and Veiling."

73. Amanullah Khan's modernization program challenged tribal and religious authorities not only by expanding state power through centralization, but also through the radical legal and cultural changes it introduced concerning Afghan women. The expansion of women's rights in marriage through new laws (for example, outlawing child marriage and limiting polygamy), state support for women's education and for the termination of women's seclusion, and public encouragement for modern dress threatened the patriarchal tribal social order. Amanullah Khan's public support for women's unveiling and Queen Soraya's public unveiling became focal points of the tribal and conservative religious resistance to the Amanullah Khan regime, which culminated in the outbreak of a (second) rebellion in 1928. Amanullah Khan was compelled to abdicate by 1929. Although Turkey was vastly different from Afghanistan in terms of the political and military capacity of the state, the nationalist ideology and movement, political organization, social structure, historical experience, and cultural traditions, Amanullah Khan's failure in Afghanistan still served as a reminder to the Republican regime in Turkey that unveiling was a powerful emotional issue that could trigger undesirable tribal, religious, and patriarchal reactions to the regime. Leon B. Poullada, *Reform and Rebellion in Afghanistan, 1919–1929: King Amanullah's Failure to Modernize a Tribal Society* (Ithaca: Cornell University Press, 1973); Valentine M. Moghadam, *Modernizing Women: Gender and Social Change in the Middle East* (Boulder: Lynne Rienner Publishers, 1993), chap. 7.

74. See for instance the circular sent to all governors and inspectors general by the Ministry of the Interior on 22 July 1935. This document has been printed in *Cumhuriyetin 75. Yıldönümünde Polis Arşiv Belgeleriyle Gerçekler. 150'likler. Kubilay Olayı. Çarşaf-Peçe-Peştemalla Örtünme Sorunu* (TC İçişleri Bakanlığı Emniyet Genel Müdürlüğü. Araştırma Planlama ve Koordinasyon Dairesi Başkanlığı Publication No. 129, Ankara, 1998).

75. A Declaration by Governor Fevzi of the Aydın province, published in the provincial newspaper, nine years after that province had taken specific action. *Aydın*, 26 April 1934.

76. Uyar, *Tek Parti Dönemi*, 261, and chap. 6, n. 94; Uyar, "Çarşaf, Peçe ve Kafes." The work generally cited to support this argument is Bernard Caporal, *Kemalizmde ve Kemalizm Sonrasında Türk Kadını (1919–1970)* (Ankara: Türkiye İş Bankası Kültür Yayınları, 1982). Kemal Yakut's "Tek Parti Döneminde Peçe ve Çarşaf" is one of the few exceptions so far.

77. For a comprehensive study of the governors of the Kemalist era, see Ali Galip Baltaoğlu, *Atatürk Dönemi Valileri (29 Ekim 1923–10 Kasım 1938)* (Ankara: Ocak Yayınları, 1998).

78. Despite the destruction of the war years and the loss of its Greek (*Rum*) and other non-Muslim communities, which disrupted its economic vitality and social and cultural diversity, Trabzon still had an emerging modernist public sphere centered around associations such as the Teachers' Union, the Turkish Hearths, and later the Trabzon People's House. Even if these organizations were not fully autonomous from the ruling RPP, the teachers, journalists, doctors, and others who actively participated in these organizations provided a genuine local support base for the Republican regime and its reformist agenda.

79. The provincial decision prohibiting the *peçe* had called for reforming women's clothing by discarding primitive and foreign (*gayrı milli*) clothing and through the adoption of modern (*medeni*) and national dress. Çapa, "Giyim Kuşamda," 27.

80. When the members of the Trabzon Turkish Hearths decided to wear the hat (*şapka*) in an October 1925 meeting, the membership (which included a small number of women, as well) also decided that women should discard the *peçe* and *çarşaf* and adopt the *manto* (coat) and hat. They further resolved that women should be encouraged to participate in social life. Öksüz and Usta, *Mustafa Reşit Tarakçıoğlu*, 200. Partial mid-1930s membership statistics available for the Trabzon Halkevi, which was established in 1932 after the closing of all Turkish Hearths in 1931, indeed reveal that women were involved in the Trabzon Halkevi as active members. But their small numbers, and the occasional difficulty the organization had in recruiting women to perform in the Halkevi plays, suggest that women's full participation in the social and cultural life of the city was a gradual process. İbrahim Azcan, *Türk Modernleşmesi Sürecinde Trabzon Halkevi (1932–1951)* (Trabzon: Serander Yayınları, 2003): see p. 124 on women's participation in the Halkevi theater, and chap. 4 on membership statistics.

81. As Hakkı Uyar has pointed out, without the minutes of the RPP municipal council meetings, it is difficult to capture the motives of those opposing the decree. Of course, the minutes may not reveal much either, particularly if there was not much debate prior to the vote. Still, we could reasonably argue that this contestation was an indication of a strong conservative male position against Westernization of women's appearance and redefinition of women's morality and public participation. It also suggests a patriarchal resistance of men giving up their authority over women as fathers and husbands to the Westernizing state. How religiously motivated their opposition was remains open to debate.

82. For a recent critique of the scholarly treatment of the RPP as a strong and disciplined, monolithic party, see Murat Metinsoy, "Kemalizmin taşrası: Erken Cumhuriyet taşrasında parti, devlet ve toplum," *Toplum ve Bilim*, no. 118 (2010): 124–64.

83. The list of provinces is from Uyar, *Tek Parti Dönemi*, 235.

84. "Bitliste Çarşaf ve Peçe Kalkıyor," *Son Posta* (2 October 1935).

85. "Siirtte Çarşaflar Atıldı," *Son Posta* (13 October 1935).

86. EGM 13216-7/2, From Hakkari Governor Sadullah Koloğlu to the Ministry of the Interior, 20 November 1938. The decision was taken on the 19th of November, shortly after Atatürk's death on the 10th, and may have been triggered by it.

87. EGM 13216-7/2, From the Minister of the Interior to the Governor of Hakkari, 22 November 1938.

88. EGM 13216-7/2, From the Governor of Hakkari to the Ministry of the Interior, 25 November 1938.

89. *Eşarp*, from the French "*écharpe*," is a women's scarf. Whereas the generic term *baş örtüsü* referred to a broad category of head scarves with potentially religious connotations, the term *eşarp* suggested a European-style, often smaller, scarf worn to cover the hair or around the neck. In the 1920s and 1930s, first *manto* and *eşarp* and later *manto* and hats

emerged as modern alternatives to the women's *çarşaf, peştemal,* and other forms of traditional or regional dress.

90. EGM 13216-7/2, From the Governor of Hakkari, 25 November 1938.

91. This was also the case in Iran. Janet Afary notes that "The new [unveiling] decree became popular among men and women from the upper and new middle classes, composed of teachers, nurses, doctors, and civil servants." Afary, *Sexual Politics in Modern Iran* (Cambridge: Cambridge University Press, 2009), 157.

92. On changes in women's dress and consumption in the late Ottoman era, see Micklewright, *Women's Dress in Nineteenth-Century Istanbul;* and the essays in Donald Quataert, ed., *Consumption Studies and the History of the Ottoman Empire, 1550–1922: An Introduction* (Albany, NY: State University of New York Press, 2000). On the relationships among modernization, fashion, and mentality in the Turkish/Ottoman context, see Fatma Karabıyık Barbarosoğlu, *Modernleşme Sürecinde Moda ve Zihniyet* (Istanbul: İz, 1995); and Şeni, "Fashion and Women's Clothing."

93. Interview with Meliha Tanyeli, İstanbul, August 2003. She related to me an incident on the adoption of the *manto.* One day in Trabzon her grandmother Şükriye Hanım was stopped by a man in the street (by a gentleman, or *"bey"* to use the narrator's exact wording, which may indicate that the man appeared respectable; however, the word choice may also have been a reflection of the narrator's style of polite speech). The gentleman inquired why she was dressed like this [i.e. wearing a *çarşaf*]. Şükriye Hanım told him she was on her way to the tailor for a fitting of her *manto.* It was not clear from Meliha Hanım's narrative if Şükriye Hanım was indeed on her way to the tailor, or said so simply in order to avoid any confrontation on the grounds that she failed to wear the *manto.* It may well have been the second. Either way, with a quick response, Şükriye Hanım was not only explaining away the *çarşaf* on her body at the moment, but was also communicating to this gentleman, perhaps a government official, her willingness and readiness to wear what was perceived as modern dress. A family photograph from the mid-1930s outside Belkıs (Şükriye Hanım's daughter) and Ali Salim Peker's summer house in Soğuksu (just outside the city) indeed shows all the men and women in the family, including Şükriye Hanım, wearing modern clothes. From upper class urban women to peasants visiting a city, Turkish citizens were quick to craft stories of justification for their visible failure to obey the law. However, as we have seen, the manner in which such encounters took place, as well as the consequences of such, varied considerably. It is worth noting that in this instance Şükriye Hanım's encounter with this gentleman was limited to a verbal exchange, with no physical intervention (such as the removal of or an attempt to remove her *çarşaf*) or monetary fines, or landing in a police station or court room. Women of lower classes and village women may have been more vulnerable to direct intervention than, for example, the women of the local notable families whose family networks and class positions would have given them relatively more protection from direct government intervention in public places. The potential of backlash from the family, the tribe, or the local community

varied considerably (across regions and classes), resulting in different levels of constraint on everyday interventions by the police, gendarmes, or other government officials.

94. My access to these family photographs was thanks to the courtesy of the late Meliha Tanyeli.

95. As Elif Ekin Akşit explains in her work on the Girls Institutes, making hats and sewing modern or new clothes for the family, for civil servants and their wives, and for others, became one of the more visible means through which the students and graduates of these Institutes participated in the process of nationalist modernization. The primary task assigned to these Republican Girls, *Cumhuriyet Kızları*, in the modernist republican ideal was in the home: they would participate in the construction of a modern nation by becoming patriotic and knowledgeable mothers, wives, and house managers. Akşit insists on using the term "Kız" (girl, unmarried woman, virgin) to highlight the gendered dimension of their education and their in-between position between childhood and womanhood, which eased the family and social acceptance of their education by delaying their passage into womanhood. See Elif Ekin Akşit, *Kızların Sessizliği: Kız Enstitülerinin Uzun Tarihi* (İletişim Yayınları: İstanbul, 2005).

96. Arzu Öztürkmen, "Remembering through Material Culture: Local Knowledge of Past Communities in a Turkish Black Sea Town," *Middle Eastern Studies* 39, no. 2 (April 2003): 183; and Arzu Öztürkmen, "Rethinking Regionalism: Memory of Change in a Turkish Black Sea Town," *East European Quarterly* 39, no. 1 (March 2005): 50.

97. Tirebolu, a small but vibrant port town active in trade with Russia in the late Ottoman and early Republican eras (within the greater Trabzon province in the Ottoman period and a district of the new Giresun province post-Republic) gradually lost its economic and cultural vitality, hence the elderly residents' reference to their home town as a "fallen town." During the disruptions of the war years the town lost its Greek and Armenian community (fifteen percent and one percent, respectively, of the total population). Öztürkmen, "Remembering through Material Culture," 179. This demographic transformation, the reorientation of the town's economy after the Republic and particularly the closing of trade with the Soviet Union during the Cold War led to a gradual transformation of the town and a (perceived as well as real) decline in the town's social, economic, and cultural life.

98. Meltem Karadağ, "Taşra kentinde yaşam tarzları alanı: Kültür ve ayrım," *Toplum ve Bilim*, no. 118 (2010): 39–58; Ayşe Durakbaşa, "Taşra Burjuvazisinin Tarihsel Kökenleri," *Toplum ve Bilim*, no. 118 (2010): 6–38; Gül Özsan, "Eşraf Ailelerinin Statü Mücadelelerinde Kadınların Rolü," *Toplum ve Bilim, no.* 118 (2010): 59–91; Ayşe Durakbaşa, Gül Özsan, and Meltem Karadağ, "Women's Narratives as Sources for the Study of Eshraf Families," in *Women's Memory: The Problem of Sources*, ed. D. Fatma Türe and Birsen Talay Keşoğlu (Newcastle upon Tyne: Cambridge Scholars Publishing, 2011), 153–68.

99. "Katiyen Trabzon'da çarşaf yoktu." Interview with Meliha Tanyeli. This statement could be seen as a testimony to the rapid changes in the clothing of the women within her own family and social milieu and among her peers, or as an example of the selective work of

memory. Other written, oral, and visual sources indicate a significant decline in the use of the *çarşaf* in Trabzon, but not its total elimination. For urban women of Meliha Hanım's generation, who were children in the 1920s and who had access to education in the 1930s and 1940s, wearing modern dress was much more a product of their education and socialization than a result of decrees banning the *peçe* and *çarşaf*. As Reşat Ekrem Koçu noted, in urban Ottoman Muslim families, a young woman's putting on the *çarşaf* when she reached twelve or thirteen was an important rite of passage, very much like a Muslim boy's circumcision. Koçu, *Türk Giyim Kuşam*, 68. For Meliha Hanım and many other urban Turkish women in her generation, that rite of passage had ceased to exist. Unlike their mothers and grandmothers, these women never got used to the *çarşaf* and *peçe* in the first place.

100. Fortna, *Learning to Read*, 6.

101. As we will see again in discussing elderly citizens' transitioning into the new alphabet, Kitabi Hamdi (Başman) (1862–1948) was the founder of the first (Muslim) publishing house and bookstore in Trabzon. Starting in 1885 and continuing through the Young Turk era and the early Republican years, he published books in a wide range of fields, many of them textbooks but also dictionaries, alphabet books, readers, works on farming and photography, illustrated geographies, and maps. Like other Muslim businesses in the city, Kitabi Hamdi Efendi's store was closed down when Trabzon came under Russian occupation in April 1916, and the family left the province, becoming war refugees. Hamdi Efendi restarted his business after the Russian army withdrew in the aftermath of the Bolshevik Revolution and the family returned to Trabzon after two years of *muhacirlik*. Kitabi Hamdi ve Mahdumları or Kitabi Hamdi et Fils (the name of the business was in Ottoman Turkish and in French on the store windows as well as in the business advertisements) operated as a publisher, bookstore, stationery, and camera and photography shop. As local historians have noted, Kitabi Hamdi Efendi contributed to the creation of a reading public in Trabzon through his publishing and by providing access to books and newspapers from İstanbul for a provincial readership. Çapa and Çiçek, *Yirminci Yüzyıl Başlarında*, 229–31. The principal published source on Kitabi Hamdi Efendi is İhsan Hamamioğlu, *Trabzon'da İlk Kitapçı: Kitabi Hamdi "Efendi" ve Yayınları* (Istanbul: Kemal Matbaası, 1947). Similarly, in the memories of later generations of his family, Kitabi Hamdi Efendi's bookstore emerged as a place that inspired children with its books, paper, ink, and painting supplies, introducing them to the marvelous world of reading and arts. Önder Küçükerman and İlhan Berk, *Ressam Orhan Peker: Hayatı, Eserleri, Görüşleri* (Istanbul: Millî Reasürans T.A.Ş., 1994), 16 & 26. Kitabi Hamdi Efendi appears as an excellent example of the Muslim Ottoman/Turkish entrepreneur whose emergence the Young Turk regime and later the Republican state encouraged in their effort to create a national bourgeoisie. In his public life, Kitabi Hamdi was a successful businessman, a modernist entrepreneur whose bookstore in Trabzon's Uzunsokak his grandson Orhan Peker (Meliha Tanyeli's brother and a painter who is perhaps best known for his portrait of the Anatolian folk poet Aşık Veysel) recollected from his childhood as a place of sociability for poets and writers. Küçükerman and Berk, *Ressam Orhan Peker*, 26. In his private life, Kitabi Hamdi Efendi was a caring father

who was close to his children and cared about their education and upbringing. (See Figure 19, his 1899 photograph with his sons and daughters, in the next chapter.)

102. Rıfat Danışman was the governor of Trabzon at that time, and thus presumably had a fair amount of influence over school officials. Yet in Meliha Hanım's memory he was remembered as a caring father rather than in his role as the provincial governor.

103. Göle, *The Forbidden Modern*, esp. 77–78.

104. Kandiyoti, "Gendering the Modern," 123. See also Ayşe Durakbaşa, "Cumhuriyet Döneminde Modern Kadın," esp. 40–50.

105. The emphasis in the scholarship on the crucial role played by modernist fathers in the emergence of a generation of educated Turkish women should not eclipse the role women, especially mothers, played in the process. Even if mothers may not have had the type or degree of social and political influence men had to support their daughters' participation in public life, they nevertheless were important in women's access to education and employment. The earlier-mentioned research on the 20th century trajectory of local notable families in Anatolian towns, for example, has revealed that respondents often cited their mothers as a source of inspiration and support for their education. See Özsan, "Eşraf Ailelerinin," 59–89. As we will see later in this chapter, fathers played contradictory roles in raising the first generation of republican women. Whereas modernist fathers' support was crucial for the education, public visibility, and employment of their daughters, other fathers insisted on defending their daughters' veiling and seclusion. Beth Baron has similarly noted that in early twentieth-century Egypt, modernist fathers such as Qasim Amin (lawyer and a proponent of women's rights) encouraged their daughters' unveiling, whereas others forced their daughters into veiling and seclusion. Baron, "Unveiling in Early Twentieth Century Egypt," 379.

106. Proponents of co-education such as Hamdullah Suphi Tanrıöver were confronted by ideologically grounded opposition as well as by material and financial constraints such as insufficient schools and teachers. In the first years of the Republic, coeducation was only implemented at the university and elementary school levels, while girls and boys attended separate middle and high schools. Coeducation was introduced in the 1927–1928 school year in middle schools, and in the 1934–1935 school year in high schools. Zehra F. Arat, "Kemalizm ve Türk Kadını," in *75 Yılda Kadınlar ve Erkekler*, ed. Ayşe Berktay Hacımirzaoğlu (Istanbul: Tarih Vakfı Yayınları, 1998), 64. Arat argues that the patriarchal nature of education persisted after the institution of coeducation through gender-biased policies: for instance, through the subjects they studied and the strict controls placed over female students' appearance and public behavior. Ultimately, Arat views this as a consequence of the Kemalist reforms which treated women as "symbols and tools" for its modernist nation-building project. Meliha Hanım's narrative of her youth and schooling in the 1930s Trabzon provides us with a more nuanced appreciation of how the women who experienced the Kemalist reforms first hand made sense of what the reforms concerning gender, education, and dress meant.

107. Hüseyin Albayrak, *Tarih İçinde Trabzon Lisesi* (Trabzon: Trabzon Liselerinden Yetişenler Derneği Yayınları, 1987), 224.

108. Mehmet Emin Yavruoğlu, another graduate of Trabzon High School from the 1930s, remembered a slightly different classroom arrangement involving three classrooms: section A for girls, section B for provincial boys ("taşradan gelenler") from Artvin, Gümüşhane, Rize, Giresun, and Ordu, and section C for local boys. Albayrak, *Tarih İçinde Trabzon Lisesi*, 201. Despite this minor discrepancy in the memory of two Trabzon High School alumni, both narratives point to an initial separation of the local male students from women and from provincial men. It is quite likely that in their attempt to accommodate physical growth and in trying to figure out women's integration into the school, school officials tried various arrangements in the first few years of women's admission and that the oral accounts reflect a memory of different moments from the 1930s.

109. Alan Duben and Cem Behar, *İstanbul Households: Marriage, Family and Fertility, 1880–1940* (Cambridge: Cambridge University Press, 1991), 226–38.

110. The family was indeed on good terms with the Republican state's representatives in town and enjoyed entertaining local bureaucrats, teachers, and school officials as family friends in their Soğuksu home. Küçükerman and Berk, *Ressam Orhan Peker*, 11.

111. Küçükerman and Berk, *Ressam Orhan Peker*, 21.

112. For my discussion here on Antep, I rely heavily on the findings of an oral historical project conducted by Sevil Atauz in Antep in the 1990s. Atauz interviewed twenty-two elderly residents of Antep, the majority of them from the old notable families of the town. The respondents were originally from the towns of Antep, Kilis, and Aleppo (who had migrated to Antep when Aleppo came under allied occupation in World War I), and represented different professions, families, and ideological backgrounds. Many of them came from landowning families. The vast majority of the interviewees were women; thus, the findings of the research were particularly helpful for the present chapter. Sevil Atauz, "Cumhuriyet'in İlk Yıllarında Gaziantep'te Gündelik Yaşamın Dönüşümü: Bir Sözlü Tarih Çalışması," in *Bilanço 1923–1998: "Türkiye Cumhuriyeti'nin 75 Yılına Toplu Bakış" Uluslararası Kongresi*, vol. 2, ed. Zeynep Rona (Istanbul: Tarih Vakfı Yayınları, 1999), 217–29. (Interestingly, in a more recent multi-site sociological research that explored the social processes of the twentieth century transformation of provincial notable families in several cities, including Antep, Ayşe Durakbaşa and her coresearchers had only limited access to the women of some of the families they interviewed, because conservative businessmen blocked the researchers' direct contact with their wives. Durakbaşa, "Taşra Burjuvazisinin Tarihsel Kökenleri," 9.)

113. Given that the majority of Atauz's interviewees were from elite families, their memories may not be reflective of the practices of the city's lower class women. In the case of male attire, though, the narrators were clear about the varying headwear practices of the different classes—the wealthy wearing the fez, artisans wearing the *külah*, and others wearing *terlik/ takke*, with the fez wearers putting on round European hats and others adopting the *kasket* after 1925. We may recall here that in İstanbul, significant numbers of Muslim women had discarded the *peçe* by the end of World War I. As Mesut Çapa has noted, by the War of Liberation years women had begun unveiling in the city of Trabzon as well. Çapa, "Giyim Kuşamda," 25.

Unveiling as a process of social and cultural change had entered different regions at varying degrees when the local authorities throughout the country began passing decrees on the *peçe* and *çarşaf* in the late 1920s and 1930s.

114. Atauz, "Cumhuriyet'in İlk Yıllarında Gaziantep'te," 221.

115. Atauz, "Cumhuriyet'in İlk Yıllarında Gaziantep'te," 220.

116. EGM 13216-7/1, From the Governor of Maraş to the Minister of the Interior, 13 August 1935. Other strategies the governor of Maraş proposed for the women's "awakening" included appointing greater numbers of female teachers to the province, requiring women to unveil in government buildings, and employing the gendarmerie to enforce the unveiling requirement in government buildings. The Minister approved all the proposed measures, including the persuasion of the families of civil servants, but disapproved of the use of the gendarmerie. EGM 13216-7/1, From the Minister of the Interior to the Governor of Maraş, 13 September 1935. In correspondence with other provinces as well, such as Aydın, Kayseri, and Ordu, the ministry was clear that the police forces and the gendarmerie should not be used. This warning was particularly pronounced in correspondence with Ordu, where the governor issued a decree in 1937 prescribing monetary fines for noncompliance with a ban on the *peçe, çarşaf,* and *peştemal* to be enforced with the help of the police and the municipal police (belediye zabıtası). In addition, the Ordu provincial decree proposed that women wearing the prohibited articles of clothing should be denied service in courts and other government offices. EGM 13216-7/1. From the Governor of Ordu, "Peçe, Çarşaf ve Peştemal Yasağı Hakkında Tamim," 5 March 1937. The Ministry disapproved of any such measures on the grounds that there was no legal basis for such policies, and presumably because of a fear of potential backlash. The minister reiterated the need to focus on propaganda and to work through the families of civil servants. EGM 13216-7/1, From the Minister of the Interior to the Governor of Ordu, 14 May 1937.

117. EGM 13216-7/1, From Maraş Governor A. Bayman to the Minister of the Interior, 5 November 1935, reporting a unanimous decision banning the *peçe, çarşaf,* and *karadon.*

118. EGM 13216-7/1, From Maraş "İlbayı" A. Bayman to the Minister of the Interior, 7 November 1935.

119. *Son Posta* (10 November 1935), 4.

120. Atauz, "Cumhuriyet'in İlk Yıllarında Gaziantep'te," 221.

121. Scott, *Weapons of the Weak,* 27.

122. Atauz's respondents from Antep did not mention women's seclusion in their homes as a response to the local decrees on the *peçe* and *çarşaf.* It is possible that such responses simply did not occur within their own families. Such responses may also have had a generational dimension. The oral history respondents had been young women in the 1930s; while they were quite forthcoming about the roles of their fathers and husbands in their transition to modern dress and *asri hayat,* there was much more silence about their mothers.

123. See Chehabi, "The Banning of the Veil," and Chehabi, "Staging the Emperor's New Clothes." See also Amin, *The Making of the Modern Iranian* Woman, 106; and Afary, *Sexual Politics in Iran,* 157. Afary says, "The strongest opposition to unveiling arose within the

old urban middle classes, clerics, merchants, and artisans. In some homes, women decided to remain indoors for years, while some prominent clerics prevented their daughters from attending school."

124. "Kiliste de Çarşaf ve Peçe Kalktı," *Son Posta* (23 September 1935), 1.

125. "Kiliste Şemsiye Modası," *Son Posta* (17 December 1935), 4.

126. The meaning and symbolism of clothes are by no means fixed, and change over time and under different circumstances. The *manto*, an acceptable substitute for the *çarşaf* in the 1930s, has become, in combination with the *türban* headscarf, a strong symbol of Islamist identity and politics since the 1980s. For a discussion of the voluntary adoption of such symbols (especially the headscarf) by the Islamist women in recent decades, See Nilüfer Göle, "The Voluntary Adoption of Islamic Stigma Symbols," *Social Research* 70, no. 3 (Fall 2003): 809–28; and Göle, *The Forbidden Modern*, chap. 4.

127. EGM 13211-16/2, From Maraş governor İ. Sabri Çıtak to the Ministry of the Interior, Cipher no. Emniyet 167.223, 23 March 1939.

128. Interview with Nuriye Güner, Trabzon, 21 September 2002.

129. This must have been sometime after the Ministry of Education sent a circular to schools on 15 January 1924 making it mandatory for female teachers to take off the *peçe* in class (Yakut, "Tek Parti Döneminde Peçe ve Çarşaf," 26/234 gives this information, citing *Cumhuriyet*, 16 January 1341/1925) and around the time of the banning of the *peçe* in Trabzon in November 1926 (Çapa, "Giyim Kuşamda," 27). The banning of the *çarşaf* in Trabzon was in 1936, by which time Nuriye Hanım would have finished school and gotten married.

130. Nuriye Hanım also related to me what appears to have been a compromise solution: she recalled that a girl she knew would wear her *çarşaf* going to school, and would take it off and put it in her bag at the gate. A similar phenomenon of older elementary school students removing their *çarşafs* before entering school appeared in the oral interviews from Antep. Atauz, "Cumhuriyet'in İlk Yıllarında Gaziantep'te," 225.

131. Atauz, "Cumhuriyet'in İlk Yıllarında Gaziantep'te," 224–26.

132. Ceylan Tokluoğlu, for instance, has also argued that there was public pressure against unveiling (as well as public encouragement for it), including open attacks in parts of Anatolia against unveiled women. She does not, however, present evidence to substantiate her claim. See her "The Formation of the Turkish Nation-State and Resistance," 254–55.

133. On the Iranian case, see Najmabadi, *Women with Mustaches*, 153–55; Chehabi, "The Banning of the Veil," 202. On Syria and Lebanon, see Thompson, *Colonial Citizens*, chap. 7. Thompson reports that in Damascus and Beirut there were repeated incidents of men attacking women with acid for not covering themselves sufficiently or for wearing European style clothes. Thompson, *Colonial Citizens*, 136.

134. BCA 030.10.102.668.8, From Minister of the Interior Şükrü Kaya to the Prime Minister, 21 February 1929. An earlier case of assault on women involved an attack on a female teacher in the town of Zile. But in this case I am not certain the attack was specifically linked to the issues of dress. BCA 030.10.101.654.15, 16 November 1925.

135. Afyon *şar kurulu* (the Afyon City Council) banned the *peçe* and the *çarşaf* in August 1935. "Afyonda Peçe Tamamen Kalkıyor," *Son Posta* (24 August 1935).

136. EGM 13216-7/1, From the governor of Afyon to the Ministry of the Interior, 13 November 1935. The report did not specify what it was exactly that Emine was wearing at the time of the attack, but it is clearly suggested that she was not wearing the *peçe* and *çarşaf*, and that was why she was assaulted.

137. EGM 13216-7/1, From the Minister of the Interior to the Governor of Afyon, 28 November 1935. The Minister also requested the result of Ahmed's trial. I did not, however, see the court's decision in the relevant file.

138. EGM 13216-7/1, From the governor of Konya to the Minister of the Interior, 1 November 1935.

139. Michael E. Meeker, *A Nation of Empire: The Ottoman Legacy of Turkish Modernity* (Berkeley: University of California Press, 2002), 387. Meeker does not specify when this incident took place, but it appears to have happened in the mid-1960s.

140. Meeker, *A Nation of Empire*, 386, 387.

141. Consul Knight to Sir G. Clerk, Trebizond, May 12, 1927, in *Turkey, March 1927–December 1929*, ed. Bülent Gökay, Part 2, series B, vol. 31 of *British Documents on Foreign Affairs: Reports and Papers From the Foreign Office Confidential Print*, University Publications of America, 1997, 41–43. Provincial reports too confirm a tendency that the transition from the *çarşafs* to the *manto* was a later and more gradual process than the removal of the *peçe* or *yaşmak*.

142. While the government was directly involved in the supply of hats and caps through a hat factory in Gölcük and through Sümerbank, the promotion of men's and women's hats (and European style clothes more broadly) as symbols of civilized dress created new economic opportunities for an emerging private textile industry in the early decades of the Republic, whose leaders became ardent supporters of the Republican regime's modernist social project. See, for example, the autobiography of Vitali Hakko, the founder of the Vakko textile company and department stores, *My Life: Vakko*, trans. Michael D. McGaha (Istanbul: Libra Kitap, 2011).

143. BCA 030.10.67.447.5, 74/56, Letter from the governor of Rize Derviş Hüsnü Uzgören to the Prime Minister, 13 July 1939.

144. Notably there was no mention of the men's hats in this letter from Rize. Presumably men were wearing caps or other acceptable headgear and the diversity of their clothing was mainly in items of clothing such as their baggy pants and local shirts.

145. When the *çarşaf* question came up in the post-RPP (and post-Democrat Party) period, governors and women activists referred to conservatism, rather than poverty, as the real problem. Writing from Gaziantep, Governor Niyazi Araz and Türkan Gencer of the Committee for the Struggle Against the Çarşaf wrote that efforts such as the provision of *mantos* free of charge, propaganda campaigns through the press, schools, and movie theaters, and propaganda tours to the districts did not pay off. Women were accepting the free *mantos*

(assuming it was a government order), but because conservative men defended the *çarşaf*, rather than wearing their newly acquired *mantos* women were simply putting them away in their trunks or wardrobes. Araz and Gencer argued that particularly in the conservative South East Anatolian provinces the complete elimination of *çarşafs* would only be possible through the passage of a law. Araz wrote that only the institution of monetary fines sanctioned by legislation would solve the *çarşaf* issue. EGM 13216-7/2, From Governor Niyazi Araz to the Ministry of the Interior, Gaziantep, 8 February 1961; From Türkan Gencer to the President Cemal Gürsel, Gaziantep, 26 December 1960. Notably, as they were debating strategies for the complete abolition of the *çarşaf*, there was no mention of the *peçe*; it had nearly disappeared.

146. On the use of petitions in the context of the early Turkish Republic see Yiğit Akın, "Reconsidering State, Party, and Society in early Republican Turkey: Politics of Petitioning," *International Journal of Middle East Studies* 39, no. 3 (2007): 435–57; and Yiğit Akın, "Fazilet Değil Vazife İstiyoruz: Erken Cumhuriyet dönemi sosyal tarihçiliğinde dilekçeler," *Toplum ve Bilim* 99 (Winter 2003/2004): 98–128. On women's petitions, see Hale Yılmaz, "Petitions as a Source in Women's History of the Republican Period," in *Women's Memory: The Problem of Sources from the Ottoman Period to Our Times*, ed. Fatma Türe and Birsen Talay Keşoğlu (Newcastle upon Tyne: Cambridge Scholars Publishing, 2011), 81–93.

147. EGM, 13216-2. Letter sent from Ismail Efe to Hamdi Bey, Ödemiş, 18.12.937. In translating this letter (and the next two), rather than editing and standardizing the language I have closely followed the non-standard, informal Turkish that İsmail Efe used, to give the reader a sense of how the citizens communicated with the highest levels of state officials despite the authoritarian character of the regime. There are ambiguities in the letters which have been replicated in the translation.

148. That the mixing of old and new, and local and Western clothes was not uncommon due to reasons such as efforts to circumvent government regulations and economic hardship is reflected in other sources as well, including governors' reports and travelers' accounts. See, for instance, Linke, *Allah Dethroned*; and Zürcher, "Two Young Ottomanists Discover Kemalist Turkey."

149. EGM 13216-7/1, From Governor of İzmir Fazlı Güleç to Minister of the Interior Şükrü Kaya, 24.11.937.

150. EGM 13216-7/1, From the governor of İzmir to Minister of the Interior Şükrü Kaya, 9.12.1937. "Vilayetimiz çevresinde çarşaf giyen ve peçe takan kadın katiye kalmadığını arz."

151. Lex Heerma van Voss, Introduction to *Petitions in Social History*, International Review of Social History Supplements 9 (Cambridge: Cambridge University Press, 2002), 6.

152. EGM 13216-2.

153. This letter was most likely written to Refik Saydam, Minister of Health at the time of the writing of the letter. He served as Minister of the Interior for a short time after Atatürk's death in November 1938 and was Prime Minister 1939–1942.

154. EGM 13216-2.

155. EGM 13216-2.

156. EGM 13216-2, Cipher from Governor of İzmir Fazlı Güleç to the Ministry of the Interior, 15 January 1938.

157. EGM 13216-2, Cipher from Governor of İzmir Fazlı Güleç to the Ministry of the Interior, 28 January 1938.

158. EGM 13216-2, Cipher from Governor of İzmir Fazli Güleç to the Ministry of the Interior, 2 February 1938.

159. Van Voss, Introduction to *Petitions*, 9. See also Natalie Zemon Davis, *Fiction in the Archives: Pardon Tales and Their Tellers in Sixteenth Century France* (Stanford: Stanford University Press, 1987).

160. EGM 13216-7/1, From ".... Komiser Tahsin" to "Emniyet İşleri Genel Direktörlüğüne," Tosya, 21 August 1935.

161. EGM 13216-7/1, From ".... Komiser Tahsin."

162. Interview with Nuriye Güner. Trabzon, 21 September 2002. She related to me a specific instance of intervention by a government official. A relative of Nuriye Hanım's was stopped by a man in the street in Trabzon one day. The man asked her why she was "dressed like this" and advised her against wearing the *çarşaf*. She ignored the man and continued on her way. She would later find out that this man was the governor of Trabzon. I cannot tell for sure if the man referred to in this account was indeed the governor of Trabzon. Given that this encounter became so memorable, he was probably an important government official, though not necessarily the governor himself. What this account indicates, however, is that the administrative officials themselves took the propaganda effort to the streets. Note that unlike the instances of Ödemiş and Tire in the Aegean and Tosya in Kastamonu province, where policemen, gendarmes, or other government officials reportedly removed *peçes* and *çarşafs* from women's faces and bodies in the streets, in this instance from Trabzon the intervention was limited to a verbal warning.

163. See C.H.P. *Dördüncü Büyük Kurultayı Görüşmeleri Tutulgası*.

164. EGM 13216-2, From Emniyet U. Müdürü to Millî Em. H. Reisliği, 17 February 1938.

165. EGM 13216-2, From M. Em. H. Bşk. Y. to Em. U. Md., Ankara, 19 July 1938.

166. This is also very interesting from the point of view of surname adoptions after the Surname Law of 1934.

167. For more on *efes* and *eşkıyas* see Sabri Yetkin, *Ege'de Eşkıyalar* (Istanbul: Tarih Vakfı Yurt Yayınları, 1996); and Halil Dural, *19. ve 20. Yüzyılda Ege'de Efeler* (Istanbul: Tarih Vakfı Yurt Yayınları, 1999).

168. Celal Bayar, *Ben de Yazdım: Milli Mücalele'ye Giriş*, vol. 6 (Istanbul: Baha Matbaası, 1968). See esp. 1909.

169. It is very likely that the İsmail Efe mentioned and photographed in *Bize Derler Çakırca* and *15 Yılda Aydın* is the same İsmail Efe who wrote these petitions. If so, we have a citizen fully integrated into the new system: first in *Bize Derler Çakırca,* posing with a group of Boy Scouts of the Republic (295); and in the other photograph, posing with the students of a mandolin class sometime in the mid-1930s.

170. EGM 13216-2, Cipher from Governor Fazlı Güleç to the Ministry of the Interior, 21 October 1938.

171. EGM 13216-7/1, "Aydın Şar Kurulunun 9/8/935 tarih ve 467 sayılı kararı örneğidir," Aydın Vilayeti Emniyet Müdürlüğü, 17 August 1935. See also "Aydında Çarşaf ve Peçe Kalktı," *Son Posta*, (11 August 1935).

172. EGM 13216-7/1, From Aydın Governor S. Günday to Minister of the Interior Şükrü Kaya, Aydın, 26 August 1935.

173. EGM 13216-7/1, From Dokumacı Ahmet Şevki to Gazi Mustafa Kamal [sic] Atatürk, Aydın, 16 August 1935. The governor noted that this was not the first time Dokumacı Şevki petitioned Atatürk, the prime minister, or other high level government officials.

174. This was often an unintended consequence of petitions. See Akın, "Reconsidering State, Party, and Society" for a similar observation.

175. EGM 13216-7/1, From the Governor of Aydın S. Günday to Minister of the Interior Şükrü Kaya, Aydın, 26 August 1935 and 2 September 1925.

176. EGM 13216-7/2, From the governor of Aydın İ. S. Çıtak to the subordinate provincial offices, Aydın, 8 April 1940.

3. Language: A New Turkish Script for a New and Literate Turkish Nation

1. See Geoffrey Lewis, *The Turkish Language Reform: A Catastrophic Success* (Oxford: Oxford University Press, 1999); Uriel Heyd, *Language Reform in Modern Turkey*, Oriental Notes and Studies no. 5 (Jerusalem: The Israel Oriental Society, 1954); Charles F. Gallagher, "Language Reform and Social Modernization in Turkey," in *Can Language Be Planned? Sociolinguistic Theory and Practice for Developing Nations*, ed. Joan Rubin and Björn H. Jernudd ([Honolulu]: University Press of Hawaii, 1971), 159–78; John R. Perry, "Language Reform in Turkey and Iran," *International Journal of Middle East Studies* 17, no. 3 (August 1985): 295–311; Bernt Brendemoen, "The Turkish Language Reform and Language Policy in Turkey," in *Handbuch Der Türkischen Sprachwissenschaft*, Part 1, ed. György Hazai (Wiesbaden: Otto Harrassowitz, 1990), 454–93; Kemal H. Karpat, "A Language in Search of a Nation: Turkish in the Nation-State," in *Studies on Turkish Politics and Society: Selected Articles and Essays* (Leiden: Brill, 2004), 435–65; İlker Aytürk, "The First Episode of Language Reform in Republican Turkey: The Language Council from 1926 to 1931," *Journal of the Royal Asiatic Society* (3rd series) 18, no. 3 (2008): 275–93.

2. See Senem Aslan, "'Citizen, Speak Turkish!'"; Bali, *Cumhuriyet Yıllarında Türkiye Yahudileri*; Bali, *1934 Trakya Olayları*; Tekin Alp, *Türkleştirme* (Ankara: T.C. Kültür Bakanlığı Kültür Eserleri Dizisi 326, 2001); and Avram Galanti, *Vatandaş Türkçe Konuş!* Çevrimyazı Ömer Türkoğlu (Transliterated by Ömer Türkoğlu), (Ankara: Kebikeç Yayınları, 2000).

3. Meltem Türköz, "Surname Narratives and the State-Society Boundary: Memories of Turkey's Family Name Law of 1934," *Middle Eastern Studies* 43, no. 6 (November 2007): 893–908; Türköz, "The Social Life of the State's Fantasy"; Temuçin F. Ertan, "Cumhuriyet Kimliği

Tartışmasının Bir Boyutu: Soyadı Kanunu," *Kebikeç*, no. 10 (2000): 255–72; and Necati Gökalp, "Türk Basınında Soyadı Kanunu" (master's thesis, İstanbul Üniversitesi, 1996).

4. Ayhan Yüksel, "Trabzon Vilâyetinde Yer Adlarını ve İdarî Yapıyı Değiştirme Teşebbüsleri," *Trabzon Tarihi Sempozyumu 6–8 Kasım 1998 Bildiriler* (Trabzon: Trabzon Belediyesi Kültür Yayınları, 1999), 201–22; and Murat Koraltürk, "Milliyetçi Bir Refleks: Yer Adlarının Türkçeleştirilmesi," *Toplumsal Tarih*, no. 117 (September 2003): 98, 99.

5. Birol Caymaz and Emmanuel Szurek, "La révolution au pied de la lettre. 'l'alphabet turc,'" *European Journal of Turkish Studies* [Online], 6 (2007).

6. For a detailed account of the alphabet debates from the Tanzimat era to the passing of the Alphabet Law see Agâh Sırrı Levend, *Türk Dilinde Gelişme ve Sadeleşme Evreleri*, 3rd ed. (Ankara: Türk Dil Kurumu Yayınları, 1972); Hüseyin Sadoğlu, *Türkiye'de Ulusçuluk ve Dil Politikaları* (Istanbul: İstanbul Bilgi Üniversitesi Yayınları, 2003); Bilâl N. Şimşir, *Türk Yazı Devrimi* (Ankara: Türk Tarih Kurumu Yayınları, 1992); Sadettin Buluç, "Osmanlılar Devrinde Alfabe Tartışmaları," *Harf Devriminin 50. Yılı Sempozyumu* (Ankara: Türk Tarih Kurumu Yayınları, 1991), 45–48; Yavuz Uğur Özdemir, "Türk Yazı Devrimi ve İlk Uygulamalar" (master's thesis, Dokuz Eylül Üniversitesi, İzmir, 2001); and Ali Dikici, "Early Republican Reforms from the Perspective of Elite vs. the People, with Particular Reference to the Alphabet and Language Reforms" (master's thesis, Boğaziçi University, Istanbul, 1996).

7. Sultan Abdülhamid II himself used this argument in suggesting that it might be best to switch to Latin characters. Sultan Abdülhamit, *Siyasî Hatıratım* (Istanbul: Dergâh Yayınları, 1999), 143.

8. For further discussion of the connections between literacy, reading, and the alphabet, see Benjamin Fortna, "Learning to Read in the Late Ottoman Empire and Early Turkish Republic," *Comparative Studies of South Asia, Africa and the Middle East* 21 (2001): 33–41; and Johann Strauss, "Literacy and the Development of the Primary and Secondary Educational System: The Role of the Alphabet and Language Reforms," in *Turkey in the Twentieth Century*, ed. Erik-Jan Zürcher (Berlin: Klaus Schwarz Verlag, 2008), 479–516.

9. On the relationship between the Latin-based Albanian alphabet of Şemseddin Sami and the Turkish alphabet reform, see Frances Trix, "The Stamboul Alphabet of Shemseddin Sami Bey: Precursor to Turkish Script Reform," *International Journal of Middle East Studies* 31, no. 2 (May 1999): 255–72.

10. Sadoğlu, *Türkiye'de Ulusçuluk ve Dil Politikaları*, 218–19; and Şimşir, *Türk Yazı Devrimi*, 23–27.

11. Betül Aslan, "Sovyet Rusya Hâkimiyetindeki Türk Halklarının 'Birleştirilmiş Türk Alfabesi'ne Geçişi ve Bu Olayda Azerbaycan'ın Rolü," *Uluslararası Karadeniz İncelemeleri Dergisi. International Journal of Black Sea Studies* 3, no. 6 (Spring 2009): 81–111.

12. Alfred Kuhne, *Mesleki Terbiyenin İnkişafına Dair Rapor*, (Istanbul: 1939), 9, as cited in Başgöz and Wilson, *Educational Problems in Turkey*, 85. In 1926 the Republican government initially invited the renowned German educator Kerschensteiner. Due to an illness Kerschensteiner sent one of his assistants, Dr. Kuhne, to Turkey. (Among Kuhne's other

recommendations were the expansion of education for girls and the expansion and improvement of vocational schools.) While the opinions of foreign educational experts were taken seriously, some of their recommendations did not take into account Turkey's specific conditions and needs and were unrealistic, and Turkey did not have the financial means to implement many of the suggested measures. Tiregöl, "The Role of Primary Education," 59–60; and Arslan Kaynardağ, "Eğitimle İlgili Üç Rapor ve Atatürk İş Üniversitesi," *International Conference on Atatürk, November 9–13, 1981: Proceedings* vol. 2 (Istanbul: Boğaziçi Üniversitesi, 1981), 5–6.

13. In this chapter I focus on his involvement in the alphabet reform only. Atatürk continued to participate personally in other aspects of language reform, such as the purification of Turkish and the creation of new Turkish words. As an example of this kind of work he undertook, see the geometry book he wrote in 1936–1937 in which he invented Turkish equivalents for many terms in geometry. *Geometri*, 3rd ed. (Ankara: Türk Dil Kurumu Yayınları, 1991).

14. The original text used the word "*cehalet*," which carries the meaning of both "illiteracy" and "ignorance."

15. M. Şakir Ülkütaşır, *Atatürk ve Harf Devrimi* (Ankara: Türk Dil Kurumu Yayınları, 1981), 77.

16. Ülkütaşır, *Atatürk ve Harf Devrimi*, 77.

17. Law No. 4353 "Türk Harflerinin kabul ve tatbiki hakkında kanun" published in the Official Gazette on 3 November 1928. See the text in the original Ottoman and the Latin transcription in Türkiye Büyük Millet Meclisi Arşivi, "İnkılâp Kanunları Dosyası." For a concise account of the alphabet reform, see Zürcher, *Turkey: A Modern History*, 188–90.

18. Interview with Meliha Tanyeli. İstanbul, August 2003. Another source cited Tanyeli as saying that Lütfi Bey would come to their home to teach her father the new Turkish alphabet. See Hüseyin Albayrak, *Kuruluşunun 100. Yılında Cudibey İlkokulu* (Trabzon, 1988), 111. Given the rest of my conversation with Tanyeli, I believe her mother was included in these private informal lessons.

19. Governor of a *sancak* administrative unit in the Ottoman Empire.

20. Tûba Çandar, *Hitit Güneşi. Mualla Eyuboğlu Anhegger* (Istanbul: Doğan Kitap, 2003), 15–20.

21. Çandar, *Hitit Güneşi. Mualla Eyuboğlu Anhegger*, 28.

22. *İstatistik Yıllığı: Annuaire Statistique* 2 (1929), 33. The difficulty of learning the Arabic letters was invoked in explaining the high levels of illiteracy and in justifying the adoption of a modified Latin alphabet. It is true that Arabic letters were not particularly suitable to render Turkish sounds and not easy to master, and that the Turkish reformers indeed hoped to facilitate literacy through the adoption of Latin letters, but the prevailing rates of illiteracy had more to do with the historical circumstances than the difficulty of the Arabic alphabet, per se. The literacy rate in Turkey in 1927 represents a significant decline from the literacy rate in the Ottoman Empire in the last decade of the nineteenth century. Karpat gives an illiteracy rate of 34.3 percent in the Ottoman Empire in 1894/5 for individuals over the age of ten. When children are included, Karpat estimates that 46 percent of the total Ottoman population was

illiterate. See Kemal H. Karpat, *Ottoman Population 1830–1914: Demographic and Social Characteristics* (Madison, Wisconsin: University of Wisconsin Press, 1985), 221. Despite questions of reliability of the census figures for either period, the estimated figures reveal a substantial decline in literacy in the final two decades of the Ottoman Empire. This decline was the result of a combination of factors, such as higher rates of mortality among the adult population, especially the male population, during the decade of wars from the Balkan wars through the War of Liberation; the disruption of public, private, and missionary educational institutions (hence, lower rates of access to education for the younger population); and population movements during the war years. In his assessment of late Ottoman literacy rates, François Georgeon suggests that Karpat's estimates of Ottoman literacy are too high. Still, even Georgeon's estimated rate of 10–15 percent Ottoman literacy on the eve of World War I also reveals a clear decline in literacy rates between 1914 and the foundation of the Republic. François Georgeon, "Lire et écrire à la fin de l'Empire ottoman: quelques remarques introductives,» in *Oral et écrit dans le monde turc-ottoman*, Nicolas Vatin, ed., *Revue de monde musulman et de la Méditerranée*, 75–76 (1995): 171–73.

23. On Millet Mektepleri, see İsmail Arar, "Gazi Alfabesi," in *Harf Devriminin 50. Yılı Sempozyumu* (Ankara: Türk Tarih Kurumu Yayınları, 1991), 147–68; Rauf İnan, "Yazı Değişimi" in *Harf Devriminin 50. Yılı Sempozyumu*, 169–86; and Ufuk Ataş, "Millet Mektepleri (1928–1935)" (master's thesis, Anadolu Üniversitesi, Eskişehir, 2003).

24. Walter Weiker, *The Modernization of Turkey: From Atatürk to the Present Day* (New York and London: Holmes & Meyer, 1981), 154.

25. "Millet Mektebi teşkilâtı Talimatnamesi," published in the Official Gazette on 24 December 1928. I have consulted this document as printed in *Jandarma Emirleri Mecmuası*, no. 286, 15 December 1928, 501–9. Şimşir gives a very detailed summary of the *Talimatname* in his *Türk Yazı Devrimi*, 237–41.

26. Although attendance was in principle mandatory, in practice enforcement efforts varied considerably and were overall quite limited.

27. The caption to this image reads: "The alphabet reform is among the greatest victories of the Turkish nation. The one who achieved this victory is the Great Liberator and the Guide, His Excellency Gazi Mustafa Kemal. Today 900,000 Turks, women and men, are learning to read and write in the Nation's Schools which were opened on his orders." *Halk*, 11 February 1929.

28. Interview with Mehmet Baltacı. Kastamonu, 4 March 2003.

29. One striking element of Baltacı's memories of the Millet Mektepleri and his primary school education in his rural village was the centrality in his narrative of *yokluk (poverty)*, the scarcity or the lack of teachers, books, and other reading and writing supplies. In Baltacı's words, "We did not have teachers. We did not have books. Ten kids would share one textbook." Baltacı considered himself fortunate for having access to his cousins' used textbooks from Ayancık, in neighboring Sinop province. Baltacı's portrayal of the lack of books in a larger context of *yokluk* or *yoksulluk* is noteworthy because it is commonplace for scholars, whose opinions are generally formed by the more urban and upper class developments, to discuss a

communications revolution and the emergence of a culture of reading and writing as though a majority of the citizens had access to books, newspapers, or other reading materials. This account is a reminder that in rural Anatolia of the 1920s, not only was literacy rare, but literacy did not necessarily lead to (regular) reading. In fact, as we will see in another case, the lack of reinforcement after the initial acquisition of reading skills could lead to a relapse into illiteracy. In the case of Mehmet Baltacı, having received some elementary education and having learned the new letters proved useful for gaining employment first in a forestry company in Ayancık, a small Black Sea port town in Sinop, and later in İstanbul when he moved there in the mid-1930s. (Immigration to the big city for employment and with aspirations for a better life was not a common phenomenon before the 1950s. In this instance, eloping with the daughter of the *muhtar* of a neighboring village, Baltacı found himself forced to run away from the village, and board the ferry with her from Ayancık to İstanbul. He thus ended up moving to İstanbul in 1936, at the age of 26, several decades before many of his fellow villagers immigrated to urban centers in the process of large scale rural-to-urban migration.) In İstanbul, he first completed and received an elementary school diploma as he worked whatever job he could find, perhaps out of a personal interest in learning, but also to secure better employment. He landed a public sector job in the State Maritime Enterprises (*Denizcilik İşletmeleri*) in 1940, after which he also completed middle school, which ensured his promotion to a *memur* (civil servant) status. His regular employment enabled him to support the education of all three of his children, including his daughter. As was quite typical in the life narratives of first generation Republicans, in Mehmet Baltacı's reconstruction of the past, family history was framed through and merged with national history. The war years (World War I and the War of Liberation) and the family's contributions to the war effort marked the beginning of the narrative, while education and urbanization registered the family's entrance into national modernity.

30. Interview with Mehmet Baltacı.

31. Şimşir, *Türk Yazı Devrimi*

32. Şimşir, *Türk Yazı Devrimi*, 243.

33. See Çağaptay, *Islam, Secularism, and Nationalism*; and Aslan, "'Citizen, Speak Turkish!'"

34. Ülkütaşır, *Atatürk ve Harf Devrimi*, 70–71.

35. Acara or Acar (or Gurian) is a dialect of Georgian spoken by Acars (Adzhars), descendants of Georgians who converted to Islam under the Ottoman rule between the sixteenth and seventeenth centuries. Historically they lived in Batum in Western Georgia. Following the Ottoman defeat in the 1877–78 Russo-Ottoman war the Muslim Acars left Russian-controlled Batum and emigrated to Ottoman territories. Andrews, *Türkiye'de Etnik Gruplar*, 246–49. According to the 1935 census, the number of Turkish citizens who spoke Georgian as their native tongue was 57,325. Census figures did not differentiate between different dialects of Georgian: hence, this number includes both Acar speakers and the small numbers of Christian Georgians. By 1945 the number of native speakers of Georgian in Turkey declined to

40,076. *İstatistik Yıllığı: Annuaire Statistique 1951*, vol. 19 (Ankara: Başbakanlık İstatistik Genel Müdürlüğü, [1952]), 109.

36. Çağaptay, *Islam, Secularism, and Nationalism*, 157. In a recent work, Senem Aslan argues that the state's ability to teach Turkish to its sizeable Kurdish population in Eastern Anatolia and Southeastern Anatolia was in fact rather limited. Aslan, "Everyday Forms of State Power."

37. See Benedict Anderson, *Imagined Communities: Reflections on the Origin and Spread of Nationalism*, rev. ed. (London: Verso, 1991).

38. Şimşir, *Türk Yazı Devrimi*, 180–83.

39. See, for example, "Yazı" in the "Benim Kıraatim" section, *Cumhuriyet*, 6 Teşrinievvel 1928.

40. Nuri İnuğur, *Türk Basın Tarihi* (Istanbul: Gazeteciler Cemiyeti, 1992), 63, 82, 86–87.

41. See Şimşir, *Türk Yazı Devrimi*, 226–28, for further discussion and statistics on the temporary decline of newspaper readership and the limited government subsidies to the press.

42. For a recent work on the role of the military and of compulsory military service in Turkish nation and state building, and especially in the formation of a particular understanding of the Turkish nation, see Ayşe Gül Altınay, *The Myth of the Military-Nation: Militarism, Gender, and Education in Turkey* (New York: Palgrave Macmillan, 2004).

43. For an elaboration of the Republican state's view of the army as a school, see A. Âfetinan, *Medenî Bilgiler ve M. Kemal Atatürk'ün El Yazıları*, Üçüncü Baskı (Ankara: Türk Tarih Kurumu Yayınları, 1998), 122–23.

44. İhsan Sungu, "Harf İnkılabı ve Millî Şef İsmet İnönü," *Tarih Vesikaları* 1, no. 1 (June 1941): 10–19.

45. Ülkütaşır, *Atatürk ve Harf Devrimi*, 92.

46. Because women were exempt from military service, the direct literacy and educational benefits of the mandatory service applied to male citizens exclusively, inadvertently contributing to the disparity between male and female literacy rates. According to Necdet Sakaoğlu, the literacy rate among the conscripts at the end of their military service was 17 percent in 1926. He says the literacy rate among the conscripts went up after the alphabet campaign to 25 percent for those completing their military service in 1931 and to 75 percent for those completing their service in 1936. Sakaoğlu, *Osmanlı'dan Günümüze Eğitim Tarihi*, 192. In her recent work on the role of the military and of compulsory military service in Turkish nation and state building, Altınay briefly discusses the function of the military in teaching Turkish language and literacy to common soldiers in the context of the military's "civilizing mission." See Altınay, *The Myth of the Military-Nation*, 71–72. Başgöz and Wilson tied the mandatory literacy classes for conscripts to the need to teach the soldiers how to use the modern weapons. They noted that the army rewarded the peasant conscripts who made the best progress in learning literacy by making them noncommissioned officers who then had the responsibility of providing military training for the new conscripts. Başgöz and Wilson also discuss other

(failed) attempts at using the army and the conscripts for agricultural development and adult education. Başgöz and Wilson, *Educational Problems in Turkey*, 123–25.

47. "Tartışmalar ve Açıklamalar," *Harf Devrimi'nin 50. Yılı Sempozyumu* (1981; reprint, Ankara: Türk Tarih Kurumu Yayınları, 1991), 132.

48. One skill he maintained from his literacy class was his ability to read numbers, which proved useful in the weekly market in the nearby town, especially during his transactions as a peasant tradesman buying and selling animals to supplement his modest rural income. Perhaps he maintained his ability to read numbers because he had to deal with the market. Later his limited literacy of the numbers also proved useful when telephone technology entered the country. He did not have to depend on others to make a phone call (at least with the few numbers that he could memorize or numbers that he had written down for him). The first elementary school in his village opened several years after his return from the army. However, neither the presence of the school nor the eventual migration to the big city and living in İstanbul for several decades reversed his illiteracy. Personal conversations with Mustafa Bayındırlı, İstanbul, 2003, 2010. Notably, his narrative of losing his ability to read and write was not framed as a loss as such, perhaps because it was not that crucial to be literate in the village and he had not expected to maintain his newly gained partial literacy in the first place. I should also note that for the respondent, learning to read and write in the military was not one of the most memorable, exciting, or important moments of his military service. He spoke of learning to read in the military because I, the researcher, was interested in the connection between military service and literacy. More prominent in my grandfather's memories of military service were the playful moments of defying authority and the lasting friendships he established with other conscripts. Despite the scholarly emphasis on the more disciplinary and ideological aspects of compulsory military service, for young village men, simply travelling to other parts of Anatolia and making friendships with fellow citizens from other regions and backgrounds must have been just as important in fostering a sense of patriotism and belonging to a larger national community. The immediate importance and value of literacy during military service was closely tied with staying in touch with one's family. If one could read and write, then one would not have to depend on others to read the letters from home (which, of course, were oftentimes penned by a literate acquaintance).

49. Zürcher, *Turkey: A Modern History*, 194. Başgöz and Wilson suggest that the "educators" project was rooted in a process already underway: Tonguç himself and his educational inspectors had observed during their village visits that in many villages the sergeants and corporals returning home after the completion of their military service "had already taken the initiative by teaching others reading and writing, as well as the new ideas they had learned in the army." Başgöz and Wilson, *Educational Problems in Turkey*, 143. Tonguç's choice of the term educator rather than teacher for these men is indicative that teaching was only a small part of their expected task. (That this was an exclusively male group of educators likely had implications for who had access to their services.) The *eğitmen* campaign would be followed by a more comprehensive education project in the form of Village Institutes (*Köy Enstitüleri*).

Young men and women from rural areas were trained in these boarding schools as elementary school teachers and appointed to their villages after graduation with the expectation that these teachers would go beyond the task of teaching children at school and help transform the countryside by introducing villagers to modern science, technology and ideas at a practical level. These schools were closed down in 1950. On Village Institutes, see Fay Kirby's classic work *Türkiye'de Köy Enstitüleri* (Ankara: İmece Yayınları, 1962). For a revisionist interpretation of the Village İnstitutes see M. Asım Karaömerlioğlu, "The Village Institutes Experience in Turkey," *British Journal of Middle Eastern Studies* 25, no. 1 (May 1998): 47–73; and M. Asım Karaömerlioğlu, *Orada Bir Köy Var Uzakta: Erken Cumhuriyet Döneminde Köycü Söylem* (Istanbul: İletişim Yayınları, 2006).

50. See Şimşir, *Türk Yazı Devrimi*, Chap. 5; and Şimşir, "Türk Harf Devrimi'nin Türkiye Dışına Yayılması: Bulgaristan Türkleri Örneği" in *Harf Devriminin 50. Yılı Sempozyumu* (Ankara: Türk Tarih Kurumu Yayınları, 1991), 187–206.

51. Georgeon, "Lire et écrire à la fin de l'Empire," 169–79. On the connections between reading, children's education, and modernity in the late Ottoman and early Republican periods, see Fortna, *Learning to Read*.

52. Norbert Elias, *The Civilizing Process: Sociogenetic and Psychogenetic Investigations*, rev. ed., trans. Edmund Jephcott (1939; reprint, Malden, MA: Blackwell, 2000).

53. Georgeon, "Lire et écrire à la fin de l'Empire," 170. Works such as Mahmut Makal's *Bizim Köy: A Village in Anatolia* (Istanbul: Literatür, 2008, originally published Istanbul: Varlık, 1950) attest to the persistence of skeptical attitudes toward the Latin alphabet and education, especially women's education, in rural Anatolia. Makal, a graduate of the Village Institutes (and later a member of the "Village Literature" current in modern Turkish literature) wrote critically of his experiences and observations as a village teacher in his widely read *Bizim Köy*, published in 1950. Makal wrote that he was able to get only four girls to register for school, none of whom actually attended school, in this village of nearly 700 people in Niğde province in central Anatolia. Mahmud Makal, *Bizim Köy*, 113–15. Bernard Caporal's research detailed the uneven development of access to literacy and education along regional and gender lines during the RPP era, Democrat Party years, and up to the 1970s. His research showed that women's access to education in Southeast Anatolian provinces continued to lag behind the rest of the country, with the exception of a couple of provinces. Caporal, *Kemalizmde ve Kemalizm Sonrasında*, part 2, chap. 3. Caporal noted that considering the question of literacy in a regional and global context, Turkey performed better than its Middle Eastern neighbors such as Iran and Syria, but worse than its neigbors in the Balkans. While Turkey and the Soviet Union had embarked on ambitious mass literacy and education campaigns around the same time, by 1970 the Soviet Union had nearly eradicated illiteracy (0.3 percent female, and 0.2 percent male illiteracy). In Turkey, on the other hand, 66.4 percent of the women and 30.0 percent of the men were still illiterate. It was also notable that in all the countries included in Caporal's comparison, with the exception of the Soviet Union, women's literacy rates lagged significantly behind male literacy rates (Caporal, *Kemalizmde*

ve Kemalizm Sonrasında, 343). Recent initiatives organized by civil society organizations, such as the *Baba Beni Okula Gönder* (Father Send Me To School) campaigns for the education of young women mainly in Eastern Anatolia, suggest that even today gender, regional, and economic differences continue to influence attitudes toward literacy and education. In 2000, 19.36 percent of the women above age six, as opposed to 6.14 percent of the men of the same age group, were illiterate. These figures reflect a significant improvement for both genders compared to the 1975 figures: 23.79 percent for men and 49.99 percent for women; yet the improvement is much more pronounced for men. *İstatistik Göstergeler Statistical Indicators 1923–2008* (Ankara: Türkiye İstatistik Kurumu, 2009), online pdf ed., 21, http://www.tuik .gov.tr/Kitap.do?metod=KitapDetay&KT_ID=0&KITAP_ID=158, accessed 9 October 2010. According to the 2008 census results, 13.09 percent of the women and 3.30 percent of the men in Turkey above age six could not read and write. *İstatistiklerle Türkiye, 2009 (Turkey in Statistics, 2009)* (Ankara: Turkish Statistical İnstitute, 2009), online pdf ed., 13, http://www .turkstat.gov.tr/IcerikGetir.do?istab_id=5, accessed 10 October 2010. The current rates of primary school attendance, over 98 percent for both genders for 2009, suggest further improvement in literacy, but also that it will take more time to reach the goal of complete elimination of illiteracy. *Türkiye İstatistik Yıllığı, Turkey's Statistical Yearbook 2009* (Ankara: Türkiye İstatistik Kurumu, 2010), online pdf ed., 116. http://www.tuik.gov.tr/yillik/yillik.pdf, accessed 10 October 2010.

54. Fortna, "Reading, Hegemony," 141–54; Fortna, "Learning to Read," 33–41; and Fortna, *Learning to Read*.

55. Brockett, *How Happy to Call Oneself a Turk*.

56. Bolat, *Atatürk İnkılaplarının Topluma Yansıması*, 41.

57. BCA 030.10.12.73.4, 21 June 1929. Telegram from Şükrü Kaya to Prime Minister İsmet Paşa (İnönü).

58. For example, Ekrem Üçyiğit mentioned at a 1978 symposium on the fiftieth anniversary of the alphabet reform the continued use of the old letters as an occasional practice of his own generation, a generation on the brink of extinction. "Tartışmalar ve Açıklamalar," *Harf Devriminin 50. Yılı Sempozyumu*, 135. François Georgeon wrote in the 1990s that it was not uncommon to see elderly Turks who had learned to write in the old letters still use those letters for their personal notes or in their private correspondence. Georgeon, "Des Caractères Arabes a l'alphabet Latin: un pas vers l'Occident?" in *Des Ottomans aux Turcs: Naissance d'une Nation*, ed. François Georgeon (Istanbul: ISIS, 1995), 214.

59. I use the terms "functional illiteracy" and "partial literacy" in the absence of a better term to describe the situation these people found themselves after 1928. Obviously, they did not become illiterate in a general sense, but the practical use of their literacy was significantly confined.

60. Interview with Meliha Tanyeli, İstanbul, August 2003.

61. For a complete list and annotated bibliography of Kitabi Hamdi Efendi's publications, see Hamamioğlu, *Trabzon'da İlk Kitapçı*, 17–26.

62. Hamamioğlu, *Trabzon'da İlk Kitapçı*, 12.

63. Küçükerman and Berk, *Ressam Orhan Peker*, 16, 26.

64. This photograph has been reproduced in Albayrak, *Kuruluşunun 100. Yılında Cudibey İlkokulu*, 67.

65. Kitabi Hamdi Efendi's 1899 picture (see Figure 19) with his young children is also quite informative about the Westernization of the upper class Ottoman families in Anatolian cities. Both the sons and the daughters, who were, like Hamdi Efendi, dressed in European style clothes, stood close to the father, an indication of a close relationship between father and children. This picture from Trabzon is quite similar to the family portraits from İstanbul in the late nineteenth and early twentieth century. (See examples of this in Duben and Behar, *Istanbul Households*.) It appears that segments of upper and upper-middle class urban (Muslim) families in Anatolian cities, at least in port cities with connections to İstanbul and other parts of the world, such as İzmir and Trabzon, were emulating the new ways of life of İstanbul families. As was usually the case in pre–World War I family photographs of elite İstanbul families, the mother is absent from the picture.

66. İsmet İnönü, *Hatıralar*, 2. Kitap (vol. 2) (Ankara: Bilgi Yayınevi, 1987), 222.

67. Avni Bey remembered vividly the moment when his brother, black *kalpak* on his head, declared his decision to join the movement as the family was reading the news of the rise of the resistance in Anatolia in their Bursa home. No doubt the remembrances of the family's participation in the war effort are part of a perhaps unconscious effort to demonstrate the family's contribution to the nationalist cause. However, both the family's experiences of war and the recollection of those experiences within the context of national history contributed to the process of individual citizens' and families' sense of belonging to and identification with the nation. The experiences and the memories of the recent wars were also crucial in shaping how individuals and families received and reacted to the Kemalist reforms. (Citizens did not necessarily respond to all the reforms in the same ways. The reforms affected different segments of society in different ways and some of the reforms lent themselves more easily than others to the participation of individual citizens in the unfolding of the reform, allowing individuals to actively locate their family histories within national history and thus imagine themselves as a part of a Turkish nation.) The response of Avni Bey's family to the 1934 Surname Law provides an excellent example of how some of the reforms allowed telling family history as national history, thus helping to build a common historical consciousness. When the new Surname Law required all citizens to adopt a family name, Avni Bey's family responded in a way that highlighted the family's services to the nation, not only in its recent past (in the War of Liberation), but also during its Ottoman and Caucasian pasts. Upon the passage of the law, family members (the father and the sons, according to Avni Bey's narrative) debated among themselves what name to take. Avni Bey recalled that he and his father wanted to take a variation of the name Bayraktar. Not only had his father Molla Ahmet volunteered in his youth as a *bayraktar* (standard bearer) in the 1893 Ottoman-Greek War (*1313 Yunan seferi*), but also a family ancestor, an Apti Bayraktar, had fought in one of the Ottoman-Russian wars, planting the flag on the Azak castle. Avni

Bey recalled that they could not take *bayraktar* or *bayrakdar* because when the Surname Law was first adopted, names containing Arabic elements could not be registered as family names. (Bayrakdar, of course, contains a Persian suffix, not Arabic, but the narrator was right about the requirement of the Law that only Turkish names could be registered as permanent family names.) As Avni Bey and his father were debating possible Turkish alternatives such as "bayrak-tutan," "bayrakçeken," and "bayraktaşıyan," they received a letter from his older brother Abdullah suggesting that they take the name "yurdabayrak." The brother, a military officer in Urfa who had fought in the War of Liberation, had been named Abdullah after the great grandfather Apti Bayraktar mentioned above. He was, apparently, making sense of the Surname Law, like his father and brother, in a way that recognized the family's positive contributions to the nation. Upon receiving Abdullah's letter, Avni Bey and his father decided Abdullah's suggestion "yurdabayrak" sounded better. Molla Ahmet went to the population office in Bursa and successfully registered the name "yurdabayrak" as a family name, which would be a permanent marker of the family's patriotism. No doubt Avni Bey's memories of surname registration were in part shaped by living most of his life through a process of nation building. What he could remember and how he remembered it was also shaped by factors such as the passage of time and his ideological and political persuasions. Nevertheless, his narrative of surname taking, despite all the incomplete and perhaps sometime incorrect details, attests to a process of a family making sense of a reform decree in a way that allowed them to honor their family by integrating their family history with national history. This also allowed them, at least as individuals and as a family, to imagine a national past that comfortably extended deep into the Ottoman era. Moreover, by choosing their own family name (although within the constraints of the law that mandated a Turkish name), rather than being given one, they (at least the adult males in the family) were actively participating in the process of making and becoming a Turkish nation.

68. Interview with Avni Yurdabayrak, İstanbul, 25 April 2003.

69. Victoria Clement, "Alphabet Changes in Turkmenistan, 1904–2004," in *Everyday Life in Central Asia: Past and Present*, ed. Jeff Sahadeo and Russell Zanca (Bloomington: Indiana University Press, 2007), 278.

70. Martha C. Howell and Walter Prevenier, *From Reliable Sources: An Introduction to Historical Methods* (Ithaca: Cornell University Press, 2001), 134.

71. In her anthropological work on public memory and the recent nostalgia for the modernity of the Kemalist era, Esra Özyürek aptly calls this generation the "elderly children of the Republic." Özyürek, *Nostalgia for the Modern*. See especially chap.1 and 2.

72. Leyla Neyzi, "Object or Subject? The Paradox of 'Youth' in Turkey," *International Journal of Middle Eastern Studies* 33, no. 3 (August 2001): 411–32.

73. Most of the text of this letter (transliterated by Vedat Günyol), written on 7 and 9 April 1929, has been printed in Çandar, *Hitit Güneşi. Mualla Eyuboğlu Anhegger*, 23–25.

74. For more on the life and journalism of Cemal Rıza Osmanpaşaoğlu, see the published interviews by Hüseyin Albayrak, "Trabzon Kültüründe İz Bırakanlar," *Kuzey Haber* (Trabzon), 19 May 1984–28 May 1984.

75. Interview with Hayrünnisa Osmanpaşaoğlu, Trabzon, 22 September 2002.

76. For a discussion of changes from surnames taken at the time of the Surname Law to older family names, see Türköz, "The Social Life of the State's Fantasy."

77. BCA 030.10.144.32.10, 147/10; Correspondence from the Minister of the Interior Şükrü Kaya to the Prime Ministry, 25 April 1931.

78. On Menteşe, see İbrahim Alâettin Gövsa, *Türk Meşhurları Ansiklopedisi. Edebiyatta, Sanatta, İlimde, Harpta, Politikada ve her sahada şöhret kazanmış olan Türklerin Hayatları Eserleri* (Istanbul: Yedigün, [194?]), 253.

79. BCA 030.10.1.2.20, 1/45, 17 April 1931, Letter from "Esbak meb'usan reisi Halil" to "Reisi Cumhur Gazi Mustafa Kemal Hazretleri."

80. İsmet İnönü made that point explicitly: "The letters that we have adopted are not the French letters. They are Turkish letters, it's a Turkish alphabet." The quote is as translated in Strauss, "Literacy," 491.

81. BCA 030.10.15.84.2, Circular from the Prime Minister to ministries and government offices, 9 July 1934.

82. BCA 030.10.15.84.2, Text of telegram from the Prime Minister's Office to the Anatolian News Agency, 9 July 1934. Another announcement along the same lines was sent to the Anatolian Agency on 28 November 1934, also in BCA 030.10.15.84.2.

83. Bengü (1900–1953) was a writer of plays, romance, and detective novels and the translator of a number of novels from the French.

84. BCA 490.01.875.440.1, Vedat Ürfi Bengü, "Halkevleri . . . Kültür Evleri . . . 'Notlar,'" 1943.

85. Although he does not offer any specific examples or explanations of this practice, Johann Strauss too has noted that "many authors continued to submit their manuscripts to the editor in Arabic script. They were subsequently transcribed by those proficient in the new script. This practice continued for a long time." Strauss, "Literacy," 513.

86. The Menemen incident has been a highly contested subject in early Republican Turkish history. The orthodox version of the Menemen incident identifies it as a major example of the threat posed by Islamic reactionaries to the secular state. The opposing version, on the other hand, argues that the trials afterwards were unjust and that the incident was in fact concocted by the state to provide a pretext to eliminate opposition, including the Nakşibendi Islamic order. There has been renewed interest in this case in recent years, with suggestions of new interpretations. See, for instance, Eyüp Öz, *Menemen Olayı ve Türkiye'de Mehdicilik* (Istanbul: 47 Numara Yayıncılık, 2007); Umut Azak, "A Reaction to Authoritarian Modernization in Turkey: The Menemen Incident and the Creation and Contestation of a Myth, 1930–31," in *The State and the Subaltern: Modernization, Society and the State in Turkey and Iran*, ed. Touraj Atabaki (London: I. B. Tauris, 2007), 143–58; Nurşen Mazıcı, "Menemen Olayı'nın sosyo-kültürel ve sosyo-ekonomik analizi," *Toplum ve Bilim* 90, Fall 2001, 131–46; Gavin Brockett, "Collective Action and the Turkish Revolution," 44–66; and David Shankland, "Old Ideas in New Forms: The Mehti in Modern Turkey," in *The Coming Deliverer: Millenial themes*

in world religions, ed. Fiona Bowie and Christopher Decay (Cardiff: University of Wales Press, 1997), 224–37.

87. BCA 030.10.144.32.9, 12 January 1930.

88. BCA 030.10.144.32.14, Copy of circular from Minister of the Interior Şükrü Kaya, 28 November 1932.

89. BCA 030.10.192.315.18, Copy of telegram from Elaziz Vakıflar Memurluğu to Vakıflar Umum Müdürlüğü, 12 December 1935.

90. BCA 030.10.192.315.18, Correspondence from Vakıflar Umum Müdürü to Başvekalet, 13 December 1935.

91. BCA 030.10.192.315.18, Correspondence from the Prime Minister to the Governor of Elaziz, 17 December 1935.

92. See, for example, the handwritten notes in Ottoman in response to requests (*dilekler*) sent to the Prime Minister Şemsettin Günaltay from a number of Aegean towns in 1949. BCA 030.01.2.13.3, 10 November 1949.

93. See BCA 030.01.50.304.15.

94. "Osmanlıca başladılar, Türkçe bitirdiler: 'Tedrisat'tan 'Öğretim'e," *NTV Tarih*, no. 21 (October 2010): 33.

4. Celebrating National Holidays

1. The most significant work so far on the celebrations of the Republican period is by Öztürkmen, "Celebrating National Holidays in Turkey," 47–75; Öztürkmen, "Milli Bayramlar: Şekli ve Hatırası-I," *Toplumsal Tarih* 5, no. 28 (April 1996): 29–35; and Öztürkmen, "Milli Bayramlar: Şekli ve Hatırası-II," *Toplumsal Tarih* 5, no. 29 (May 1996): 6–12. See also the mostly descriptive but very informative work of Nezahat Demirhan on the celebration of the tenth anniversary of the Republic: Nezahat Demirhan, *Cumhuriyetin Onuncu Yılının Türk İnkılâp Tarihinde Yeri ve Önemi* (Ankara: AKDTYK Atatürk Araştırma Merkezi, 1999); and Kathryn Libal's careful examination of the Children's Week celebrations in the context of the broader "child question" in the early Republican period: Libal, "National Futures; and Libal, "The Children's Protection Society: Nationalizing Child Welfare in Early Republican Turkey," *New Perspectives on Turkey*, no. 23 (Fall 2000): 53–78.

2. Of course, folklore itself has been put at the service of nationalist ideologies. For connections between the evolution of Turkish nationalism and Turkish folklore see Arzu Öztürkmen, *Türkiye'de Folklor ve Milliyetçilik* (Istanbul: İletişim Yayınları, 2001).

3. Eric Hobsbawm, "Introduction: Inventing Traditions." Here I follow Hobsbawm's definition of "invented tradition" as "a set of practices, normally governed by overtly or tacitly accepted rules and of a ritual or symbolic nature, which seek to inculcate certain values and norm of behavior by repetition, which automatically implies continuity with the past."

4. In a comparative analysis of Republic Day celebrations in India and Turkey, Srirupa Roy too has observed the crucial role played by public participation in such rituals, but her

study does not address the historical processes by which such commemorations have contributed to the creation of an Indian or Turkish collective historical consciousness and national identity. Srirupa Roy, "Seeing a State: National Commemorations and the Public Sphere in India and Turkey," *Comparative Studies in Society and History* 48, no. 1 (2006): 200–32.

5. For a comprehensive study of ceremonies in the last century of the Ottoman Empire and their political and ideological functions, see Hakan T. Karateke, *Padişahım Çok Yaşa! Osmanlı Devletinin Son Yüzyılında Merasimler* (Istanbul: Kitap Yayınevi, 2004). See also Selim Deringil, *The Well-Protected Domains: Ideology and the Legitimation of Power in the Ottoman Empire, 1876–1909* (London: I. B. Tauris, 1998).

6. Öztürkmen, "Celebrating National Holidays in Turkey."

7. Yael Zerubavel, *Recovered Roots: Collective Memory and the Making of Israeli National Tradition* (Chicago: University of Chicago Press, 1995). Arieh Saposnik extends Zerubavel's argument to the pre-Mandate era. He asserts that the process of the cultivation of a Hebrew national culture within the Jewish community of Ottoman Palestine was well under way in the years preceding the outbreak of World War I in 1914 through a multitude of means and institutions including language, education, arts, and holidays. The emergence of a culture of Jewish national holidays involved adding new content to old holiday traditions such as Passover and Hanukkah, as well as the creation of new holiday and commemorative traditions such as Herzl Day and the Flower Day which celebrated "the renewal of the Jewish bond with nature and the landscape of Palestine." Arieh Bruce Saposnik, *Becoming Hebrew: The Creation of a Jewish National Culture in Ottoman Palestine* (Oxford: Oxford University Press, 2008), 221. James Gelvin makes an insightful argument on the role of the competing cultures of ceremonies and invented traditions (such as public holidays, theater, and demonstrations) in the emergence of Syrian nationalism and of mass politics in Syria during the months of Faysal's rule preceding the imposition of the French mandate. James L. Gelvin, *Divided Loyalties: Nationalism and Mass Politics in Syria at the Close of Empire* (Berkeley: University of California Press, 1998).

8. Afshin Marashi, *Nationalizing Iran: Culture, Power, and the State, 1870–1940* (Seattle: University of Washington Press, 2008), 110–32. It is interesting to note a major difference here between Turkish and Iranian national celebrations in the 1930s. Both states used public celebrations and commemorations as a part of their nation-building process, but the two states' conceptions of the nation differed in a significant way, which was reflected in what the two regimes chose to celebrate as a nation. Whereas Iran as a constitutional monarchy celebrated the birth of the Shah, in Turkey three of the major national days (Republic Day, Youth and Sports Day, and National Sovereignty and Children's Day) symbolically celebrated the birth of the nation. As I have discussed in the previous chapters, Atatürk's charismatic leadership played an important role in the introduction and public acceptance of a number of the key reforms and in the overall process of Turkish nation building. In fact, it would not be unreasonable to argue that in the popular consciousness the figure of Mustafa Kemal took the place of the Ottoman Sultan. As contemporary observers such as Donald Webster have emphasized, Atatürk remained immensely popular as a war hero despite misgivings about some of the

state's secularizing policies. That none of the new national holidays celebrated the person of the immensely popular leader (during his lifetime) is quite telling about the nature of the Turkish state and the nation-building process, especially in a regional context.

9. Turkey retained İstanbul and a small number of other provinces of the European territories of the Ottoman Empire, but Anatolia became synonymous with the homeland (*vatan*) in the new nationalist rhetoric. This was in part a reflection of the actual physical boundaries (the small size of the European provinces compared to the size of the Asian territories) and the experience of the War of Liberation as a war fought in and for Anatolia. It was also about the desire to separate the nation from its Ottoman past, as well as about elevating the status of Anatolia, in the eyes of the intellectuals and the nation overall, to the beloved homeland to replace Rumelia, which had been the social, geographic, and economic heartland of the Empire before its gradual loss in the course of the nineteenth and early twentieth centuries. For an interesting recent study on the place of Rumelia in Turkish and Ottoman history see Ebru Boyar, *Ottomans, Turks and the Balkans: Empire Lost, Relations Altered* (London: Tauris Academic Studies, 2007). In the early decades of the Republic, Anatolia gained a special place in Turkish national consciousness not only through the sheer reality of Turkey's physical boundaries and through official discourses but also through a re-writing of national history, archeology, museums, schools and textbooks, literature (short stories, novels, and especially poetry), music, folklore, and national holidays. In modern Turkish literature, the Anatolianism or *Anadoluculuk* current, as best exemplified by the popular works of Halikarnas Balıkçısı (Cevat Şakir Kabaağaç), contributed enormously to that process.

The naming of two of the major state banks as Etibank (Hittite Bank) and Sümerbank (Sumerian Bank) and the borrowing of the Hittite sun disk for the city emblem of Ankara, the new capital city, were symbolic acts of establishing historical continuity between the nation and its homeland and of imagining the Turkish nation as heir to the ancient civilizations of Anatolia. Ironically, Etibank and Sümerbank no longer exist and the city emblem of Ankara is now a mosque: indications of the liberal economic policies in the last two decades and of the current contestations over the ideological content of Turkish nationalism and the secular character of the Republic.

10. Anderson, *Imagined Communities*.

11. John R. Gillis, "Memory and Identity: The History of a Relationship," in *Commemorations: The Politics of National Identity*, ed. John R. Gillis (Princeton: Princeton University Press, 1994), 8.

12. Hobsbawm, "Introduction: Inventing Traditions," 2.

13. Pierre Nora, "Between Memory and History: Les Lieux de Mémoire," *Representations*, no. 26 (Spring 1989): 7–25.

14. For a recent revisionist perspective on the War of Liberation see Ryan Gingeras, *Sorrowful Shores: Violence, Ethnicity, and the End of the Ottoman Empire, 1912–1923* (Oxford: Oxford University Press, 2009).

15. Officially, it was much later, after the 1980 coup that the definition of 19 May was expanded to include the "commemoration of Atatürk." Süleyman İnan, "19 Mayıs Gününün Bayramlaşması," *Bilgi ve Bellek* 2, no. 3 (Kış 2005): 65.

16. Law No. 2739, passed on 27 May 1935. The same law recognized as "general holidays" 30 August Victory Day, 23 April National Sovereignty Day, 1 May Spring Holiday, 1 January New Year's Day, three days of *Şeker Bayramı* at the end of Ramazan, and four days of *Kurban Bayramı* (Sacrifice holiday). The law also accepted Sunday as the weekly day of rest to replace Friday. Minister of the Interior Şükrü Kaya and three other parliamentarians argued that the change of the day of rest had nothing to do with religion, but was a social and economic requirement resulting from Turkey's determination to be a part of the Western world. See Mahmut Goloğlu, *Tek Partili Cumhuriyet (1931–1938)* (Ankara: Goloğlu Yayınları, 1974), 159, 160.

17. As Michael Meeker has noted, in some towns Liberation Days in fact commemorated events that predated the War of Independence. The Russian army had occupied the eastern Black Sea coastal region in 1916, but withdrew in 1918 after the Bolshevik Revolution. Hence, Liberation Days in the eastern Black Sea commemorate events that had taken place before the beginning of the War of Liberation. Meeker explains how the citizens of the town of Of in Trabzon province tried to make sense of their town's liberation in the context of the new national history, and how this process allowed the local elites to incorporate local *hoca*s and *agha*s in the nationalist history as founders of the nation. See Meeker, *A Nation of Empire*, 285–317.

18. By the end of the 1930s the invention of national days essentially came to an end, and a period of consolidation or dying out would begin. In the post RPP decades, one attempt to add a new national holiday was the failed effort in the early 1960s to institute a 27 May Day in celebration of the 1960 "Revolution." Unlike the reference events of the major early Republican holidays associated with the liberation of the nation, the coup commemorated by the 27 May Day did not have the broad public support necessary for its survival, nor was it being instituted under a single-party rule. See Paul J. Magnarella's brief discussion on the 27 May Day celebrations in the town of Susurluk in Balıkesir province near İstanbul in his *Tradition and Change in a Turkish Town* (Cambridge, MA: Schenkman; New York: John Wiley and Sons, 1974), 138–40. On the 1960 coup and the politics in the 1960s and early 1970s see Feroz Ahmad, *The Turkish Experiment in Democracy 1950–1975* (Boulder, CO: Westview Press, 1977).

19. From RPP Secretary General N. Kansu to the Presidency of the People's Houses, 490.01/6.29.44, 6 June 1946.

20. Nazlı Öktem, "Ölümsüz Bir Ölüm, Sonsuz Bir Yas: Türkiye'de 10 Kasım," in *Hatırladıkları ve Unuttuklarıyla Türkiye'nin Toplumsal Hafızası*, ed. Esra Özyürek (Istanbul: İletişim, 2001), 325–46. Anıtkabir, the Atatürk Memorial Tomb in Ankara, has provided a permanent location for the everyday official and unofficial commemorations of the founder of the Republic since its completion in 1953. For a critical assessment of the functions of Anıtkabir see Michael Meeker, "Once There Was, Once There Wasn't: National Monuments and Interpersonal Exchange," in Bozdoğan and Kasaba. eds., *Rethinking Modernity*, 157–91.

21. The continuity in the culture of celebrations is evident in the ambivalent yet comprehensive and inclusive meanings of the term "*bayram*," which best translates as "holiday," "festival," or "celebration." When I asked my elderly respondents about *bayram*s in their childhood and youth, some of them began telling me immediately about the Ramazan or the Sacrifice holidays; from others, my questions elicited personal memories of national days during their school years; and yet others responded by asking me if I wanted to hear about the religious or the national holidays. Their initial responses were in part shaped by my presence and the context of our conversation. They were also reflective of their own background and individual identity as a deeply devout or a secular person. On the other hand, the ease with which our conversations traveled back and forth between the two types of holidays reveals that both religious and secular national holidays have become integral parts of the national culture. The coexistence of religious and national holidays, with religious holidays at times taking on secular meanings and secular holidays at times maintaining traditional forms or content, were also apparent to foreign residents of Turkey in the early decades of the Republic. Writing about "festivals" in Turkey, E. W. F. Tomlin begins with an overview of the two major religious holidays and continues with a discussion of the celebration of the new national days. From the perspective of an optimistic Western observer of Turkey's experimentation with secular modernization, Tomlin may have exaggerated the overall secularization of the culture and the new secular meanings of the religious holidays. Still, his descriptions reveal a vibrant culture of both religious and secular national holidays. E. W. F. Tomlin, *Life in Modern Turkey* (London: Thomas Nelson and Sons Ltd., 1946), chap. 4, "Festivals," 27–34. A good example of Islamic holidays taking on secular national and political dimensions in the early years of the Republic was Mustafa Kemal's reception of *Ramazan Bayramı* guests (*tebrikler*) at the National Assembly in his capacity as the president. (See a relevant announcement from the office of the president on 11 April 1926 at BCA 030.10.197.351.16. 233/15.)

22. Veysi Akın, *Bir Devrin Cemiyet Adamı Doktor Fuad Umay (1885-1963)* (Ankara: AKDTYK Atatürk Araştırma Merkezi, 2000), 103, 104.

23. "Ulusal Bayram ve genel tatiller hakkında kanun," Law no. 2739, 27 May 1935, *Düstur*, Tertip 3, vol. 16, 550.

24. Duben and Behar, *Istanbul Households*, chap. 7.

25. Cüneyd Okay, "War and Child in the Second Constitutional Period," in *Enfance et jeunesse dans le monde musulman. Childhood and Youth in the Muslim World*, ed. François Georgeon and Klaus Kreiser (Paris: Maisonneuve et Larose, 2007), 220.

26. Duben and Behar, *Istanbul Households*, 228, quoting Şerif Mardin.

27. Okay, "War and Child," 230.

28. Libal, "National Futures," 145.

29. Kathryn Libal, "Realizing Modernity Through the Robust Turkish Child, 1923-1938," in Daniel Thomas Cook, ed., *Symbolic Childhood* (New York: Peter Lang Publishing, 2002), 109-30.

30. Libal notes that at the establishment of the Republic "200,000 children had been orphaned, abandoned, or otherwise separated from their families." Libal, "National Futures," 157. For an in-depth treatment of children's problems and child welfare in the 1920s and 1930s, see also Libal, "The Child Question: The Politics of Child Welfare in Early Republican Turkey," in *Poverty and Charity in Middle Eastern Contexts*, ed. Michael Bonner, Mine Ener, and Amy Singer (Albany: State University of New York Press, 2003), 255–72.

31. İffet Aslan, "Dünyanın İlk Çocuk Bayramı 23 Nisan ve Uluslararası Çocuk Yılı," (Türk Tarih Kurumu) *Belleten* 46, no. 183 (Temmuz 1982): 567–93.

32. Veysi Akın, *Bir Devrin Cemiyet Adamı*, 104–6.

33. See, for example, a letter from the RPP Secretary General to the People's Houses, governors, RPP chairmen, and Inspector Generals asking them to support the Children's Protection Society in the upcoming celebration of 23 April, "a national as well as a social and cultural holiday of our country," with activities such as conferences, contests, plays, and publications focusing on children. BCA 490.01.4.20.10, 9 April 1939.

34. For a detailed account see Süleyman İnan, "19 Mayıs Gününün Bayramlaşması."

35. İnan, "19 Mayıs Gününün Bayramlaşması."

36. Yiğit Akın, *"Gürbüz ve Yavuz Evlatlar" Erken Cumhuriyet'te Beden Terbiyesi ve Spor* (Istanbul: İletişim Yayınları, 2004); Sefa Şimşek, *Bir İdeolojik Seferberlik Deneyimi: Halkevleri 1932-1951* (Istanbul: Boğaziçi Üniversitesi Yayınevi, 2002), chap. 10; Parla and Davison, *Corporatist Ideology in Kemalist Turkey*, 248, 253–54.

37. BCA 490.01/15.80.1, "23 Nisan 935 Ulus egemenliği ve Çocuk bayramı raporudur," Boyabat CHP Kaza Kurum Başkanlığı, 16 May 1935.

38. BCA 490.01/15.80.1, Report from Sandıklı People's House to the RPP Secretary General, 4 May 1935.

39. The photograph was taken in Maraş on 23 April 1936.

40. Libal, "National Futures."

41. Interview with Meliha Tanyeli, İstanbul, August 2003. As we saw in chap. 2, Meliha Hanım was among the very first group of girls to attend Trabzon High School when it began admitting female students in the mid-1930s. The personal memory of the national celebrations as public performance may be more pronounced for women narrators since it was probably a more special occasion for a young woman to participate in a major public event, especially in a leadership position. Women's public performance was not entirely new, but was still much less common than men's in the 1930s.

42. Interview with the late Recep Göksoy. Kastamonu, 5 March 2003. Göksoy passed away in spring 2006. I have not been able to find a full published version of this poem. The translation here follows the version remembered by Göksoy, which may be slightly different from the original.

43. Subutay Hikmet, *Anılar. Birinci Bölüm (1929-1941)* (Istanbul: Şiir Dergisi Yayınları, n.d. [ca. 1976 or 1977]), 76.

44. See "Unutma," http://web.inonu.edu.tr/~mkilic/babamin_siirleri.html, accessed on 23 August 2010. Yaşar Yıldırım also gives a similar version of the same poem as remembered by İlyas Karpuz from his elementary school years in the town of Kozanlı, Konya, in the early 1930s. See "Unutma" http://www.antoloji.com/unutma-92-siiri/, accessed 23 August 2010.

45. In fact, Baltacı's recollections of growing up in wartime included accompanying his mother in collecting wheat and transporting it to İnebolu on ox-carts for the troops. Such experiences formed the basis of one of the most powerful myths and lasting images of the War of Liberation: the heroic peasant woman and her children transporting food and weapons to the front on ox-carts. War monuments such as the Şerife Bacı memorials in Kastamonu province have incorporated women in the memories of the War of Liberation and serve as daily reminders of women's role in the nationalist struggle. The Şerife Bacı memorials commemorate the life of legendary Şerife Bacı, a peasant woman from Kastamonu, who froze to death while carrying ammunition from İnebolu with her child in the winter of 1921. The iconography of the War of Liberation portrays women and children as active contributors to the nationalist struggle. A number of the paintings exhibited at the Museum of the Revolution in Atatürk's masoleum in Ankara also depict women's involvement in the war, reminding visitors of women's role in the nation's liberation. Such efforts to include women in the collective memory of the nation in early Republican Turkey stand in contrast to the early twentieth century commemorative culture in Europe, where most war memorials, especially World War I monuments, were dedicated to men.

46. It was quite common for my elderly informants who were born in the final decades of the Empire or in the first few years of the Republic to use the *Rumi* calendar when referring to the events of their childhood. (Turkey adopted the Western [Gregorian] calendar in 1925. The *Rumi* [or *Mali*] calendar, the Ottoman fiscal calendar, is a modified Julian calendar, dated [like the Islamic lunar calendar] from the Prophet Muhammad's flight from Mecca in AD 622. Due to the difference in the length of the year, *Hicri* and *Rumi* years did not necessarily match.) While official history, the media, and the education system led to the collective remembrance of major events in the final years of the Empire and the first few years of the Republic in the Western calendar, dates relating to personal and family history often continued to be remembered in the *Rumi* calendar. This was particularly the case for birth dates. Hence, it was quite normal to first hear from a male narrator that he was born in the 1330s and to hear a few minutes later that he went to school in the 1930s or did his military service in the 1940s. The change of calendar in 1925 created a symbolic and mental break between the new national time and the old imperial era. Elderly men and women continue to remember their birthdays in the *Rumi* calendar, but *Rumi* dates became unintelligible to the later generations and even to the generation who still remembers its own birthdates in the *Rumi* calendar. In her ethnographic research on Kemalism and the nostalgia for the early Republican era, Esra Özyürek has also noted the parallel uses of the old and new calendars by the first generation Republican women and men she interviewed. Özyürek emphasizes that the first generation Republicans chose to use one or the other calendar to connect or separate aspects of their life stories from

important dates in the nationalist history of the early Republic. See her discussion of the uses of a dual-calendar time frame by the first generation Republicans in Özyürek, *Nostalgia for the Modern*, 82–89.

47. Justin McCarthy, *Muslims and Minorities: The Population of Ottoman Anatolia and the End of the Empire* (New York: New York University Press, 1983), 120. (The estimate did not include figures for Eastern Anatolia, where the war mortality rate was higher.)

48. Turkey stayed out of World War II thanks in large part to the İnönü regime's carefully managed policy of allied-friendly neutrality, but during the war years it was not at all clear that Turkey could avoid involvement in a second world war. On Turkish foreign policy during World War II, see Selim Deringil, *Turkish Foreign Policy During the Second World War: An "Active" Neutrality* (Cambridge: Cambridge University Press, 1988). For a detailed analysis of the wartime foreign and domestic policies of the Turkish governments, see Cemil Koçak, *Türkiye'de Milli Şef Dönemi (1938-1945) Dönemin iç ve dış politikası üzerine bir araştırma*, 2 vols. (Istanbul: İletişim Yayınları, 1996).

49. BCA 490.01/5.24.8, Circular from the RPP Secretary General, 21 May 1941.

50. Quoted in Allen, *The Turkish Transformation*, 108.

51. Date is Allen's addition.

52. Quoted in Allen, *The Turkish Transformation*, 112.

53. Tiregöl, "The Role of Primary Education," 105–6. Textbook writers and publishers revised textbook content to reflect the evolving vision of the Republican regime. Textbook depictions of *bayrams* also changed following the various reforms. In an example of this type, illustrations accompanying a poem titled "Bayram" changed from the 1925 to the 1927–1928 edition of a second grade reader. The poem itself remained the same, referring to the *bayram* of Ramazan, a religious holiday, but the illustration changed to reflect the modernization efforts of the Republic through dress codes and the place of children in the nation-building project of the new Republic. The drawing in the 1925 illustration shows a *bayram* procession led by a couple of men in traditional clothes, a turbaned drummer and another turbaned man holding "a traditional staff of the Ottoman military bands." In the next edition, the drummer appears in a modern uniform wearing a hat on his head and standing in front of a boy and a girl dressed in Western clothes. The children are no longer in the background led by traditional men, but they are at the center of the image, symbolic of the place assigned to them in the new nation. This illustration, drawn from Seraceddin, *Kolay Kıraat II* (Istanbul: İbrahim Hilmi, 1925) and Seraceddin, *Kolay Kıraat II* (Istanbul: İbrahim Hilmi, 1927–1928), was cited in Tiregöl, "The Role of Primary Education," 115, 116.

54. "Neler Yaptık?" *Birinci Sınıf Dergisi*, no. 11 (23 Nisan 1939): 15.

55. Fortna's argument about reading as an activity with a counter-hegemonic potential may not generally apply to magazines such as *Birinci Sınıf Dergisi*—publications that were intended for classroom use and therefore had to have the approval of the Ministry of Education.

56. Hobsbawm, "Introduction: Inventing Traditions," 10.

57. Öztürkmen, "Celebrating National Holidays in Turkey," 58, 59.

58. Children first recited the oath during the Children's Day celebrations in 1933. The recitation of the oath at schools was required by a decision of the Board of Education and Instruction (*Talim ve Terbiye Kurulu*) on 10 May 1933. Tiregöl, "The Role of Primary Education," 102. For discussion of *Andımız*, see also Tiregöl, 102–3; Leyla Neyzi, "Object or Subject? The Paradox of 'Youth' in Turkey," 417; and Childress, "Republican Lessons," 156.

59. Personal communication with E. Önhan, Boston, November 2009, and e-mail from E. Önhan, 10 and 13 May 2010.

60. *İstatistik Yıllığı Annuaire Statistique 1951*, 100, 102.

61. On the inspectors general administration in the eastern and southeastern provinces see Cemil Koçak, *Umumi Müfettişlikler (1927–1952)* (Istanbul: İletişim Yayınları, 2003).

62. We may recall here (from chap. 1) Mehmet Özcan's poorly clad students celebrating a national holiday in rural Kastamonu with *çarık*s (rawhide moccasins) on their feet.

63. Letter from Ali Genç to Neriman Genç, Siirt, 3 September 1942. I thank Neriman and Sema Tanyolaç for allowing me to use this letter.

64. Başgöz and Wilson, *Educational Problems in Turkey*, 127–31.

65. Duben and Behar, *İstanbul Households*, 223.

66. Tomlin, *Life in Modern Turkey*, 32–33.

67. The documents read almost as if Abdülkadir's wife were not present, except for one passing mention.

68. BCA 490.01.42.176.2, Letter from "Tekıtler G. Antep Baş Müdürü," 24 November 1935, and copy of letter from the same to "Doktor Abdülkadır," 14 November 1935.

69. "Züppe Tipi ve Devrim," *Gaziantep* (22 İkinci Teşrin [22 November], 1935).

70. On the anti-cosmopolitan nature of the critique of excessive Westernization since the late Ottoman era, see Şerif Mardin, "Super-Westernization in Urban Life in the Ottoman Empire in the Last Quarter of the Nineteenth Century," in Mardin, *Religion, Society, and Modernity in Turkey*, 135–63. Scholars such as Kandiyoti and Najmabadi have noted that while the nineteenth century symbol of excessive Westernization was a male figure, in the twentieth century, in both Turkish and Iranian national contexts, such criticisms increasingly focused on the Westernized woman, to such an extent that in the Iranian case, the figure of the *gharbzadeh*, or "[W]estoxicated," woman came to embody all the ill effects of Iranian Westernization by the 1960s and 1970s. The image of the Westernized woman went from being a symbol of Iranian modernity in the early twentieth century nation-building process to a symbol of the loss of Iranian authenticity, turning her into a main target of the Islamic revolutionaries. Afsaneh Najmabadi, "Hazards of Modernity and Morality: Women, State and Ideology in Contemporary Iran," in *Women, Islam & the State*, ed. Deniz Kandiyoti (Philadelphia: Temple University Press, 1991), 64–66. In the Antep example discussed here, the primary target of the "*kozmopolit züppe*" criticism was a male, but in Turkey, too, the Westernized woman increasingly became the main target of such criticisms, although in the Turkish case, the meaning of the image of the Westernized woman continues to be contested.

71. Sabri Zengin, "Türk İnkılabının Tokat'taki Yansımaları," http://idak.gop.edu.tr/szengin/makaleler/seminer.doc, citing *Yeni Tokat*, no 14 (15 March 1934); no. 15 (1 April 1934); and no. 16 (15 April 1934). Zengin suggests that in the 1930s, a segment of the population in Tokat revealed its reaction to the overall Kemalist reform process (among other things) through indifference toward social functions such as balls and plays.

72. An original of this photograph, taken on 23 April 1934 in Aydın, is deposited at BCA 490.01.13.67.1.

73. This photograph taken on 23 April 1934 in Muğla has been reproduced from an original deposited at 490.01/13.67.1.

74. *Aydın* (26 April 1934).

75. "7 Eylûl Mektebi talebesinden Feridun efendinin sözleri," *Aydın* (25 April 1934).

76. *Güzelordu* (19 Nisan 1937 and 3 Mayıs 1937). It appears that the district governor (*kamunbay/nahiye müdürü*) was quite concerned with having a modern-looking crowd for the guest RPP officials who would be coming from the provincial center to attend the town's 23 April ceremonies. As I discussed in chap. 2, such propaganda efforts by themselves had limited results in changing women's clothing habits.

77. BCA 490.01/15.80.1, Antalya Çocuk Esirgeme Kurumu Başkanlığı, "1935 Çocuk Yedi Gününün Porgramı [*sic*]."

78. Gillis, "Memory and Identity," 8–9.

79. In his critical assessment of the historiography on the emergence of the Ottoman state (wherein he advanced a revised version of Paul Wittek's *gaza* thesis), Kafadar considers Ertuğrul Gazi to be an actual historical figure, and indeed Osman's father, although reliable evidence on many of the details of his life is nonexistent. Cemal Kafadar, *Between Two Worlds: The Construction of the Ottoman State* (Berkeley: University of California Press, 1995).

80. EGM 13211-14, "Örnek" Ertuğrul Gazi İhtifali (Proğram) (n.d., ca. 1950).

81. Jereed (*cirid*) is a traditional mounted game in which blunt spears are thrown at the opposing players. For Turkish nationalism in the twentieth century it came to represent an element of the authentic Turkish culture found in the nation's nomadic Central Asian origins and early Ottoman past.

82. EGM 13211-14, From the Ministry of the Interior to the Governor of Bilecik, draft letter (n.d.).

83. EGM 13211-14, "Sayın Bakanın yüksek buyrukları üzerine bu ihtifâlin sebep ve gayesi hakkında Bilecik valisinin telefonla yazdırdığı not:" (n.d., ca. 1950).

84. The invention of the annual Ertuğrul Gazi commemoration took place during the reign of Sultan Abdülhamid II. As a part of the effort to bolster his legitimacy through monuments and ceremonies, Abdülhamid II promoted Söğüt as the heartland of the Ottoman Empire and had a commemorative mausoleum built there for the legendary Ertuğrul Gazi. In addition to having Ertuğrul Gazi's tomb and mosque rebuilt in 1886, he had Osman's first tomb restored (even though Osman had been reburied in Bursa), as well as the graves of

twenty-five of Ertuğrul Gazi's fellow warriors. The Sultan also had a tomb reputedly belonging to Ertuğrul's wife rebuilt. He later had the nearby buildings demolished to create a ceremonial space where an annual Ertuğrul Gazi commemoration took place during his reign. Selim Deringil, *The Well-Protected Domains*, 31, 32; and Caroline Finkel, *Osman's Dream: The Story of the Ottoman Empire 1300–1923* (New York: Basic Books, 2005), 11–12. The governor's claim that the annual Ertuğrul Gazi commemoration was abandoned during the Young Turk era, if true, was probably in part due to the identification of the Ertuğrul Gazi memorial and commemoration with Sultan Abdülhamid. It also attests to one of the cultural transformations of the late Ottoman period as well as to the continuity between the Young Turk and early Republican eras: the source of the legitimacy of the state was already moving away from the dynasty to the nation. That process culminated in the more explicit recognition of the principal of national sovereignty in 1922–24.

85. Meeker wrote, "The Liberation Day celebration, attended and enjoyed by a significant fraction of the district population, was an impressive demonstration of the public spirit of the Oflus. On an occasion that commemorated a local episode in a struggle that led to a national awakening, they were able to imagine themselves as something more than mountaineers living in remote and isolated hamlets. . . . Despite a mishmash of local customs, an unacceptable Turkish dialect, an embarrassing non-Turkic language, and country manners, the Oflus did not consider themselves bystanders in world history." Meeker, *A Nation of Empire*, 376. Similarly, Söğüt was also a backwater in early Republican Anatolia, without a special place in the present or the recent history of the nation. The reinvention of the Ertuğrul Gazi commemorative tradition assigned Söğüt a distinct place in nationalist consciousness as the birth place of Ertuğrul Gazi, hence of the Turkish nation in its current homeland, reassuring the people of Söğüt that they indeed played a crucial role in the nation's long history.

86. The parade would be accompanied by the singing of a march whose refrain was "We are soldiers of the Ertuğrul Regiment. . . ." "We are ready to die for our Sultan Abdülhamid." Deringil, *The Well-Protected Domains*, 32.

87. Meeker, *A Nation of Empire*, 378.

88. Meeker, *A Nation of Empire*, 378.

89. On the closing of the People's Houses, see Şimşek, *Bir İdeolojik Seferberlik Deneyimi*, 204–14; and Anıl Çeçen, *Atatürk'ün Kültür Kurumu Halkevleri*, rev. 2nd ed. (Istanbul: Cumhuriyet Kitap Kulübü, 2000), 195–214.

90. For an analysis of the seventy-fifth anniversary celebrations see Özyürek, *Nostalgia for the Modern*, chap. 4.

References

Primary Sources

Archives

Başbakanlık Cumhuriyet Arşivi (BCA) [The Prime Minister's Archive of the Republic], Ankara
  Cumhuriyet Halk Partisi Kataloğu [Republican People's Party Catalogue]
  Başbakanlık Muamelat İşleri Kataloğu [Transactions of the Prime Minister's Office Catalogue]
  Diyanet İşleri Başkanlığı Kataloğu [Directorate of Religious Affairs Catalogue]
İçişleri Bakanlığı Emniyet Genel Müdürlüğü Arşivi (EGM) [The Archive of the Ministry of the Interior], Ankara
Türkiye Büyük Millet Meclisi Arşivi [Turkish Grand National Assembly Archive], Ankara
  İnkılâp Kanunları Dosyası [Dossier on the Revolutionary Laws]

Newspapers, Magazines, and Yearbooks

15 Yılda Aydın
Aydın (Aydin)
Birinci Sınıf Dergisi (Istanbul)
Cumhuriyet (Istanbul)
Düstur [Code of Laws] (Ankara)
Güzelordu (Ordu)
Halk (Ankara)
İstatistik Yıllığı: Annuaire Statistique. Vol. 2, 1929. Ankara: Baş Vekalet İstatistik Umum Müdürlüğü, 1929.

İstatistik Yıllığı: Annuaire Statistique. Vol. 19, 1951. Ankara: Başbakanlık İstatistik Genel Müdürlüğü, 1952.

İstatistik Göstergeler [Statistical indicators] 1923–2008. Ankara: Türkiye İstatistik Kurumu, 2009. Online pdf edition, p. 21. http://www.tuik.gov.tr/Kitap.do?metod =KitapDetay&KT_ID=0&KITAP_ID=158. Accessed 9 October 2010.

İstatistiklerle Türkiye, 2009: Turkey in statistics, 2009. Ankara: Turkish Statistical Institute, 2009. Online pdf edition. http://www.turkstat.gov.tr/IcerikGetir.do ?istab_id=5. Accessed 10 October 2010.

Son Posta (Istanbul)

Tarih Vesikaları [Historical documents] (Ankara).

Türkiye İstatistik Yıllığı [Turkey's statistical yearbook], 2009. Ankara: Türkiye İstatistik Kurumu, 2010. Online pdf edition. http://www.tuik.gov.tr/yillik/yillik .pdf. Accessed 10 October 2010.

Cited Interviews and Unpublished Personal Documents

Interview with Yusuf Altınkaya. Istanbul, 23 April 2003.

Interview with Mehmet Baltacı. Kastamonu, 4 March 2003.

Interview with Mustafa Bayındırlı. Istanbul, 2003, July 2010.

Interview with Recep Göksoy. Kastamonu, 5 March 2003.

Interview with Nuriye Güner. Trabzon, 21 September 2002.

Interview with Ömer Güner. Trabzon, 21 September 2002.

Interview with Hayrünnisa Osmanpaşaoğlu. Trabzon, 22 September 2002.

Interview with E. Önhan, Boston, MA, November 2009.

Interview with Mehmet Özcan, Kastamonu, 5 March 2003.

Interview with Meliha Tanyeli. Istanbul, August 2003.

Interview with Avni Yurdabayrak. Istanbul, 25 April 2003.

Letter from Ali Genç to Neriman Genç. Siirt, 3 September 1942.

Photograph album of Meliha Tanyeli.

Photograph album of Neriman Tanyolaç.

Other Primary Sources

Arun, Fuad. *Muallim Refik Kırış: Hayatı ve Eserleri, 1868–1945.* Ankara: Başnur Matbaası, 1968.

(Sultan) Abdülhamit [II]. *Siyasî Hatıratım.* Istanbul: Dergâh Yayınları, 1999.

Alp, Tekin. *Türkleştirme*. T.C. Kültür Bakanlığı Kültür Eserleri Dizisi, no. 326. Günümüz yazı ve diline aktaran Özer Ozankaya [Transliterated and rendered into modern Turkish by Özer Ozankaya]. Ankara, 2001. Originally published as a pamphlet (Istanbul, 1928).

Âfetinan, A. *Medenî Bilgiler ve M. Kemal Atatürk'ün El Yazıları*. Üçüncü Baskı [third printing]. Ankara: Türk Tarih Kurumu, 1998.

Atatürk, Mustafa Kemal. *Geometri*. Third Edition. Ankara: Türk Dil Kurumu Yayınları, 1991.

(İskilipli) Âtıf Efendi. *Frenk Mukallidliği ve Şapka*. Nizam Yayınları, n.d. Sadeleştiren Ömer Faruk. [Rendered into modern Turkish by Ömer Faruk]. Includes reprint in Turkish characters as well as the 1924 original text. [Istanbul]: Nizam Yayınları, 1994. Originally published in 1924.

Bayar, Celal. *Ben de Yazdım: Milli Mücalele'ye Giriş*. Vol. 6. Istanbul: Baha Matbaası, 1968.

CHF (Cumhuriyet Halk Fırkası [Republican People's Party]) *Mardin Halkevi Broşürü*. Mardin Ulus Sesi Basımevi, Mardin, 28 February 1935.

C.H.P. (Cumhuriyet Halk Partisi [Republican People's Party]). *Dördüncü Büyük Kurultayı Görüşmeleri Tutulgası 9–16 Mayıs 1935*. Ankara: Ulus Basımevi, 1935.

Cumhuriyetin 75. Yıldönümünde Polis Arşiv Belgeleriyle Gerçekler. 150'likler. Kubilay Olayı. Çarşaf-Peçe-Peştemalla Örtünme Sorunu. TC İçişleri Bakanlığı Emniyet Genel Müdürlüğü. Araştırma Planlama ve Koordinasyon Dairesi Başkanlığı Yayın No: 129. Ankara, 1998.

Eyuboğlu, İsmet Zeki. *Türk Dilinin Etimolojik Sözlüğü*. Revised Third Ed. Istanbul: Sosyal Yayınlar, 1995.

Galanti, Avram. *Vatandaş Türkçe Konuş!* Çevrimyazı [Transliterated by] Ömer Türkoğlu. Ankara: Kebikeç Yayınları, 2000.

Gentizon, Paul. *Mustafa Kemal ve Uyanan Doğu*. Translated by Fethi Ülkü. Ankara: Bilgi Yayınevi, 1983.

Gentizon, Paul. *Mustapha Kemal ou L'orient en Marche*. Paris: éditions Bossard, 1929.

Gökalp, Ziya. *The Principles of Turkism*. Translated by Robert Devereux. Leiden: E. J. Brill, 1968 [1923].

Gökalp, Ziya. *Turkish Nationalism and Western Civilization: Selected Essays of Ziya Gökalp*. Edited and translated by Niyazi Berkes. London: George Allen and Unwin, 1959.

Gökay, Bülent, ed. *Turkey, March 1927–December 1929*. Part 2, series B, vol. 31 of *British Documents on Foreign Affairs: Reports and Papers from the Foreign Office Confidential Print*. [Frederick, MD]: University Publications of America, 1997.

Gövsa, İbrahim Alâettin. *Türk Meşhurları Ansiklopedisi. Edebiyatta, Sanatta, İlimde, Harpta, Politikada ve her sahada şöhret kazanmış olan Türklerin Hayatları Eserleri*. Istanbul: Yedigün, [194?].

Hamamioğlu, İhsan. *Trabzonda İlk Kitapçı: Kitabi Hamdi "Efendi" ve Yayınları*. Istanbul: Kemal Matbaası, 1947.

Hikmet, Subutay. *Anılar Birinci Bölüm (1929–1941)*. Istanbul: Şiir Dergisi Yayınları, n.d.

Histoire de la Republique Turque. Redige par la Societe pour l'etude de l'histoire Turque. Istanbul: Devlet Basımevi, 1935.

İleri, Celal Nuri. *Türk İnkılâbı*. Transliterated and edited by Recep Duymaz. Ankara: Atatürk Kültür Merkezi Başkanlığı, 2000.

İnönü, İsmet. *Hatıralar*. 2. Kitap [Vol. 2]. Ankara: Bilgi Yayınevi, 1987.

Koçu, Reşad Ekrem. *Türk Giyim Kuşam ve Süslenme Sözlüğü*. Ankara: Sümerbank Kültür Yayınları, 1967.

Linke, Lilo. *Allah Dethroned: A Journey through Modern Turkey*. New York: Alfred A. Knopf, 1937.

Madanoğlu, Cemal. *Anılar (1911–1938)*, vol. 1. Istanbul: Çağdaş Yayınları, 1982.

Nedim, Ahmed. *Ankara İstiklâl Mahkemesi Zabıtları 1926*. Istanbul: İşaret Yayınları, 1993.

Neyzi, Nezih. *Kızıltoprak Hatıraları*. Istanbul: İletişim Yayınları, 1993.

Osman Hamdi Bey and Victor Marie de Launay, *1873 Yılında Türkiye'de Halk Giysileri: Elbise-i Osmaniyye*. Translated by Erol Üyepazarcı. Istanbul: Sabancı Üniversitesi, 1999. Originally published as *Les Costumes populaires de la Turquie: Elbise-i Osmaniyye*. Istanbul, 1873.

Özendes, Engin. *Abdullah Frères: Osmanlı Sarayının Fotoğrafçıları*. Istanbul: Yapı Kredi Yayınları, 1998.

Peker, Recep. *İnkılâp Dersleri*. Istanbul: İletişim Yayınları, 1984.

Püsküllüoğlu, Ali. *Arkadaş Türkçe Sözlük*. Ankara: Arkadaş, 1997.

Redhouse Türkçe-İngilizce Sözlük. Istanbul: Sev Yayıncılık, 1997.

De Saint Exupéry, Antoine. *The Little Prince*. Translated by Katherine Woods. San Diego: Harcourt Brace Jovanovich, 1971. First published in 1943 by Reynal and Hitchcock, New York.

Safa, Peyami. *Türk İnkılâbına Bakışlar*. Ankara: Atatürk Kültür, Dil ve Tarih Yüksek Kurumu Atatürk Araştırma Merkezi, 1996.

Sami, Şemseddin. *Kâmûs-ı Türkî*. Istanbul: Enderun Kitabevi, 1989. Originally published in 1317 [1901–1902].

"Şapkaya Tarih." *Ülker* (Burdur Halkevi Dergisi [Burdur People's House Magazine]) no. 3 (March 1937): 55.

Tomlin, E. W. F. *Life in Modern Turkey*. London: Thomas Nelson and Sons Ltd., 1946.

Türk Dil Kurumu. *Türkçe Sözlük*. 2 vols. Ankara: Türk Dil Kurumu Yayınları, 1988.

Secondary Sources

Afary, Janet. *Sexual Politics in Modern Iran*. Cambridge: Cambridge University Press, 2009.

Ahmad, Feroz. *The Making of Modern Turkey*. London: Routledge, 1993.

———. *The Turkish Experiment in Democracy: 1950–1975*. Boulder, CO: Westview Press, 1977.

Akın, Veysi. *Bir Devrin Cemiyet Adamı Doktor Fuad Umay (1885–1963)*. Ankara: AKDTYK Atatürk Araştırma Merkezi, 2000.

Akın, Yiğit. "Reconsidering State, Party, and Society in Early Republican Turkey: Politics of Petitioning." *International Journal of Middle East Studies* 39, no. 3 (2007): 435–57.

———. "Fazilet Değil Vazife İstiyoruz: Erken Cumhuriyet dönemi sosyal tarihçiliğinde dilekçeler." *Toplum ve Bilim* 99 (Winter 2003/2004): 98–128.

———. "Gürbüz ve Yavuz Evlatlar" Erken Cumhuriyet'te Beden Terbiyesi ve Spor. Istanbul: İletişim Yayınları, 2004.

Akkent, Meral, and Gaby Franger. *Das Kopftuch: Başörtü. Ein Stückchen Stoff in Geschichte und Gegenwart. Geçmişte ve Günümüzde Bir Parça Kumaş*. Frankfurt: Dağyeli Verlag, 1987.

Aksel, Malik. "Atatürk ve Sanat Anıları." *Atatürk ve Sanat Sempozyumu: The symposium of Atatürk and Art, 26–28 October 1981*, İstanbul. İstanbul Devlet Güzel Sanatlar Akademisi Publication no. 86: 7, 8.

Akşit, Elif Ekin. *Kızların Sessizliği: Kız Enstitülerinin Uzun Tarihi*. Istanbul: İletişim Yayınları, 2005.

Aktaş, Cihan. *Kılık Kıyafet ve İktidar*, Vol. 1. Istanbul: Nehir, 1991.

Albayrak, Hüseyin. *Kuruluşunun 100. Yılında Cudibey İlkokulu*. N.p.: Trabzon, 1988.

———. *Tarih İçinde Trabzon Lisesi*. Trabzon: Trabzon Liselerinden Yetişenler Derneği Yayınları, 1987.

———. "Trabzon Kültüründe İz Bırakanlar." *Kuzey Haber* (Trabzon). 19 May–28 May 1984.

Allen, Henry Elisha. *The Turkish Transformation: A Study in Social and Religious Development*. Chicago: University of Chicago Press, 1935.

Altınay, Ayşe Gül. *The Myth of the Military-Nation: Militarism, Gender, and Education in Turkey*. New York: Palgrave Macmillan, 2004.

Amin, Camron Michael. *The Making of the Modern Iranian Woman: Gender, State Policy, and Popular Culture, 1865–1946*. Gainesville: University Press of Florida, 2002.

Anderson, Benedict. *Imagined Communities: Reflections on the Origin and Spread of Nationalism*. Revised edition. London: Verso, 2002.

Andrews, Peter Alford. *Türkiye'de Etnik Gruplar*. Translated by Mustafa Küpüşoğlu. Istanbul: Ant Yayınları; Istanbul: Tümzamanlar Yayıncılık, 1992. (Originally published as *Ethnic Groups in the Republic of Turkey*. Wiesbaden: Ludwig Reichert, 1989.)

Arar, İsmail. "Gazi Alfabesi." In *Harf Devriminin 50. Yılı Sempozyumu*, 147–68. Ankara: Türk Tarih Kurumu Yayınları, 1991.

Arat, Yeşim. "Group-Differentiated Rights and the Liberal Democratic State: Rethinking the Headscarf Controversy in Turkey." *New Perspectives on Turkey*, no. 25 (Fall 2001): 31–46.

———. "The Project of Modernity and Women in Turkey." In *Rethinking Modernity and National Identity in Turkey*, edited by Sibel Bozdoğan and Reşat Kasaba, 100–106. Seattle: University of Washington Press, 1997.

Arat, Zehra F. Kabasakal. "Institutions and Women's Rights: Religion, the State, and Family in Turkey." In *Family, Gender, & Law in a Globalizing Middle East and South Asia*, edited by Kenneth M. Cuno and Manisha Desai, 79–101. Syracuse: Syracuse University Press, 2009.

Arat, Zehra F. "Kemalizm ve Türk Kadını." In *75 Yılda Kadınlar ve Erkekler*, edited by Ayşe Berktay Hacımirzaoğlu, 51–70. Istanbul: Tarih Vakfı Yayınları, 1998.

Aslan, Betül. "Sovyet Rusya Hâkimiyetindeki Türk Halklarının 'Birleştirilmiş Türk Alfabesi'ne Geçişi ve Bu Olayda Azerbaycan'ın Rolü." *Uluslararası Karadeniz İncelemeleri Dergisi. International Journal of Black Sea Studies* 3, no. 6 (Spring 2009): 81–111.

Aslan, İffet. "Dünyanın İlk Çocuk Bayramı 23 Nisan ve Uluslararası Çocuk Yılı." *Belleten* (a journal of Türk Tarih Kurumu [Turkish Historical Association]) 46, no. 183. (Temmuz [July] 1982): 567–93.

Aslan, Senem. "Everyday Forms of State Power and the Kurds in the Early Turkish Republic." *International Journal of Middle East Studies* 43 (2011): 75–93.

———. "'Citizen, Speak Turkish!': A Nation in the Making." *Nationalism and Ethnic Politics* 13 (2007): 245–72.

Atabaki, Touraj and Erik-Jan Zürcher. "Introduction." In *Men of Order: Authoritarian Modernization under Atatürk and Reza Shah*, edited by Touraj Atabaki and Erik-Jan Zürcher, 1–12. London: I.B. Tauris, 2004.

Ataş, Ufuk. "Millet Mektepleri (1928–1935)." Master's thesis, Anadolu Üniversitesi, Eskişehir, 2003.

Atauz, Sevil. "Cumhuriyet'in İlk Yıllarında Gaziantep'te Gündelik Yaşamın Dönüşümü: Bir Sözlü Tarih Çalışması." in *Bilanço 1923–1998: "Türkiye Cumhuriyeti'nin 75 Yılına Toplu Bakış" Uluslararası Kongresi*, vol. 2, edited by Zeynep Rona, 217–29. Istanbul: Tarih Vakfı Yayınları, 1999.

Aybars, Ergün. *İstiklâl Mahkemeleri 1920–1927 Cilt 1–2 1920–1927*. Izmir: Dokuz Eylül Üniversitesi Atatürk İlkeleri ve İnkılap Tarihi Enstitüsü, 1995.

Aytürk, İlker. "The First Episode of Language Reform in Republican Turkey: The Language Council from 1926 to 1931." *Journal of the Royal Asiatic Society* Third Series 18, no. 3 (2008): 275–93.

Azak, Umut. "A Reaction to Authoritarian Modernization in Turkey: The Menemen Incident and the Creation and Contestation of a Myth, 1930–31." In *The State and the Subaltern: Modernization, Society and the State in Turkey and Iran*, edited by Touraj Atabaki, 143–58. London: I. B. Tauris, 2007.

Azcan, İbrahim. *Türk Modernleşmesi Sürecinde Trabzon Halkevi (1932–1951)*. Trabzon: Serander Yayınları, 2003.

Bali, Rıfat N. *1934 Trakya Olayları*. Istanbul: Kitabevi, 2008.

———. *Cumhuriyet Yıllarında Türkiye Yahudileri: Bir Türkleştirme Serüveni [1923–1945]*. Istanbul: İletişim, 1999.

Baltaoğlu, Ali Galip. *Atatürk Dönemi Valileri (29 Ekim 1923–10 Kasım 1938)*. Ankara: Ocak Yayınları, 1998.

Barbarosoğlu, Fatma Karabıyık. *Modernleşme Sürecinde Moda ve Zihniyet*. Istanbul: İz, 1995.

Baron, Beth. *Egypt as a Woman: Nationalism, Gender, and Politics*. Berkeley and Los Angeles: University of California Press, 2005.

———. "Unveiling in Early Twentieth Century Egypt: Practical and Symbolic Considerations," *Middle Eastern Studies* 25, no. 3 (July 1989): 370–86.

Başarır, Dönüş. "Şapka İnkılâbının Konya Basını ve Kamuoyundaki Yankıları." Master's thesis, Selçuk University, Konya, 1995.

Başgöz, Ilhan and Howard E. Wilson, *Educational Problems in Turkey, 1920–1940*. Bloomington: Indiana University Publications, 1968.

Berkes, Niyazi. *The Development of Secularism in Turkey*. Introduction by Feroz Ahmad. New York: Routledge, 1998.

Bolat, Bengül. "Atatürk İnkılaplarının Topluma Yansıması: Kırşehir Örneği." Master's thesis, Hacettepe Üniversitesi, Ankara, 2001.

Bora, Tanıl, ed. *Modern Türkiye'de Siyasi Düşünce*. Vol. 4, *Milliyetçilik*. Istanbul: İletişim Yayınları, 2002.

Boyar, Ebru. *Ottomans, Turks and the Balkans: Empire Lost, Relations Altered*. London: Tauris Academic Studies, 2007.

Boyar, Ebru, and Kate Fleet. *A Social History of Ottoman Istanbul*. Cambridge: Cambridge University Press, 2010.

Bozdoğan, Sibel. *Modernism and Nation Building: Turkish Architectural Culture in the Early Republic*. Seattle: University of Washington Press, 2001.

Bozdoğan, Sibel, and Reşat Kasaba, eds. *Rethinking Modernity and National Identity in Turkey*. Seattle: University of Washington Press, 1997.

Brendemoen, Bernt. "The Turkish Language Reform and Language Policy in Turkey." In *Handbuch Der Türkischen Sprachwissenschaft*, edited by György Hazai. Part 1, 454–93. Wiesbaden: Otto Harrassowitz, 1990.

Brockett, Gavin. "Betwixt and Between: Turkish Print Culture in the Emergence of a National Identity (1945–1954)." Ph.D. dissertation, University of Chicago, 2003.

———. "Collective Action and the Turkish Revolution: Towards a Framework for the Social History of the Ataturk Era, 1923–38." In *Turkey Before and After Atatürk*, edited by Sylvia Kedourie, 44–66. London and Portland: Frank Cass, 1999.

———. *How Happy to Call Oneself A Turk: Provincial Newspapers and the Negotiation of a Muslim National Identity*. Austin: University of Texas Press, 2011.

———, ed. *Towards a Social History of Modern Turkey: Essays in Theory and Practice*. Istanbul: Libra Kitap, 2011.

Brummett, Palmira. *Image and Imperialism in the Ottoman Revolutionary Press, 1908–1911*. Albany: State University of New York Press, 2000.

Van Bruinessen, Martin. *Agha, Sheikh and State: The Social and Political Structures of Kurdistan*. London: Zed Books, 1992.

———. *Kurdish Ethno-Nationalism versus Nation-Building States*. Istanbul: ISIS, 2000.

Buluç, Sadettin. "Osmanlılar Devrinde Alfabe Tartışmaları." In *Harf Devriminin 50. Yılı Sempozyumu*. Ankara: Türk Tarih Kurumu Yayınları, 1991: 45–48.

Caporal, Bernard. *Kemalizmde ve Kemalizm Sonrasında Türk Kadını (1919–1970)*. Ankara: Türkiye İş Bankası Kültür Yayınları, 1982.

Caymaz, Birol and Emmanuel Szurek, "La révolution au pied de la lettre. 'l'alphabet turc.'" *European Journal of Turkish Studies* [Online], 6 (2007).

Chehabi, Houchang E. "The Banning of the Veil and Its Consequences." In *The Making of Modern Iran: State and Society under Riza Shah, 1921–1941*, edited by Stephanie Cronin, 193–210. London: Routledge Curzon, 2003.

———. "Dress Codes for Men in Turkey and Iran." In *Men of Order: Authoritarian Modernization under Atatürk and Reza Shah*, edited by Touraj Atabaki and Erik J. Zürcher, 209–37. London: I.B. Tauris, 2004.

———. "Staging the Emperor's New Clothes: Dress Codes and Nation-Building under Reza Shah." *Iranian Studies* 26, no. 3–4 (Summer/Fall 1993): 209–33.

Childress, Faith J. "Republican Lessons: Education and the Making of Modern Turkey." Ph.D. dissertation, University of Utah, 2001.

Clement, Victoria. "Alphabet Changes in Turkmenistan, 1904–2004." In *Everyday Life in Central Asia: Past and Present*, edited by Jeff Sahadeo and Russell Zanca, 266–80. Bloomington: Indiana University Press, 2007.

Cunbur, Müjgan. "Atatürk'ün Türk Giyimi Üzerine Düşünceleri." In *Proceedings of the International Conference on Atatürk, Istanbul, November 9–13, 1981*, vol. 1, 1–16.

Cagaptay [Çağaptay], Soner. *Islam, Secularism, and Nationalism in Turkey: Who is a Turk?* London: Routledge, 2006.

Çalışlar, İpek. *Latife Hanım.* Istanbul: Doğan Kitap, 2006.

Çandar, Tûba. *Hitit Güneşi. Mualla Eyuboğlu Anhegger.* Istanbul: Doğan Kitap, 2003.

Çapa, Mesut. "Giyim Kuşamda Medeni Kıyafetlerin Benimsenmesi ve Trabzon Örneği." *Toplumsal Tarih*, no. 30 (1996): 22–28.

Çapa, Mesut, and Rahmi Çiçek. *Yirminci Yüzyıl Başlarında Trabzon'da Yaşam.* Trabzon: Serander Yayıncılık, 2004.

Çeçen, Anıl. *Atatürk'ün Kültür Kurumu Halkevleri.* Revised second edition. Istanbul: Cumhuriyet Kitap Kulübü, 2000.

Çetinkaya, Y. Doğan. *1908 Osmanlı Boykotu. Bir Toplumsal Hareketin Analizi.* Istanbul: İletişim Yayınları, 2004.

Davis, Natalie Zemon. *Fiction in the Archives: Pardon Tales and Their Tellers in Sixteenth Century France.* Stanford: Stanford University Press, 1987.

Davison, Andrew. *Türkiye'de Sekülarizm ve Modernlik.* Translated by Tuncay Birkan. Istanbul: İletişim, 2002.

Deal, Roger. "War Refugees and Violence in Hamidian Istanbul." *Middle Eastern Studies*, 49, no. 2 (March 2013): 179–90.

Demirhan, Nezahat. *Cumhuriyetin Onuncu Yılının Türk İnkılâp Tarihinde Yeri ve Önemi.* Ankara: AKDTYK Atatürk Araştırma Merkezi, 1999.

Denman, Fatma Kılıç. *İkinci Meşrutiyet Döneminde Bir Jön Türk Dergisi: Kadın.* Istanbul: Libra, 2009.

Deringil, Selim. *Turkish Foreign Policy During the Second World War: An "Active" Neutrality.* Cambridge: Cambridge University Press, 1988.

————. *The Well-Protected Domains: Ideology and the Legitimation of Power in the Ottoman Empire, 1876–1909.* London: I. B. Tauris, 1998.

Dikici, Ali. "Early Republican Reforms from the Perspective of Elite vs. the People, with Particular Reference to the Alphabet and Language Reforms." Master's thesis, Boğaziçi University. Istanbul: 1996.

Duben, Alan, and Cem Behar. *Istanbul Households: Marriage, Family and Fertility, 1880–1940.* Cambridge: Cambridge University Press, 1991.

Durakbaşa, Ayşe. "Cumhuriyet Döneminde Modern Kadın ve Erkek Kimliklerinin Oluşumu: Kemalist Kadın Kimliği ve 'Münevver Erkekler'." In *75 yılda kadınlar ve erkekler,* edited by Ayşe Berktay Hacımirzaoğlu, 29–50. Istanbul: Tarih Vakfı Yayınları, 1998.

————. "Taşra Burjuvazisinin Tarihsel Kökenleri." *Toplum ve Bilim,* no. 118 (2010): 6–38.

Durakbaşa, Ayşe, Gül Özsan, and Meltem Karadağ. "Women's Narratives as Sources for the Study of Eshraf Families." In *Women's Memory: The Problem of Sources,* edited by D. Fatma Türe and Birsen Talay Keşoğlu, 153–68. Newcastle upon Tyne: Cambridge Scholars Publishing, 2011.

Dural, Halil. *19. ve 20. Yüzyılda Ege'de Efeler.* Edited by Sabri Yetkin. Istanbul: Tarih Vakfı Yurt Yayınları, 1999.

Edgar, Adrianne Lynn. *Tribal Nation: The Making of Soviet Turkmenistan.* Princeton: Princeton University Press, 2004.

Elias, Norbert. *The Civilizing Process: Sociogenetic and Psychogenetic Investigations.* Revised edition, translated by Edmund Jephcott Malden. Boston: Blackwell, 2000 [1939].

Engin, Vahdettin. *Sultan Abdülhamid ve İstanbul'u.* Istanbul: Simurg Yayınları, 2001.

Ertan, Temuçin F. "Cumhuriyet Kimliği Tartışmasının Bir Boyutu: Soyadı Kanunu." *Kebikeç,* no. 10 (2000): 255–72.

Eskicumalı, Ahmet. "Ideology and Education: Reconstructing the Turkish Curriculum for Social and Cultural Change, 1923–1946." Ph.D. dissertation, University of Wisconsin–Madison, 1994.

Evered, Emine O. *Empire and Education under the Ottomans: Politics, Reform and Resistance from the Tanzimat to the Young Turks.* London: I. B. Tauris, 2012.

Eyicil, Ahmet. "İstiklâl Mahkemelerinde Yargılanan K. Maraşlılar." *Türk Dünyası Araştırmaları*, no. 102 (June 1996): 13–45.

Findley, Carter Vaughn. *Turkey, Islam, Nationalism, and Modernity: A History.* New Haven: Yale University Press, 2011.

Finkel, Caroline. *Osman's Dream: The Story of the Ottoman Empire 1300–1923.* New York: Basic Books, 2005.

Fleischmann, Ellen L. *The Nation and Its "New" Women: The Palestinian Women's Movement, 1920–1948.* Berkeley: University of California Press, 2003.

Fortna, Benjamin C. *Imperial Classroom: Islam, the State, and Education in the Late Ottoman Empire.* Oxford: Oxford University Press, 2002.

———. *Learning to Read in the Late Ottoman Empire and the Early Turkish Republic.* New York: Palgrave Macmillan, 2011.

———. "Learning to Read in the Late Ottoman Empire and Early Turkish Republic." *Comparative Studies of South Asia, Africa and the Middle East* 21, no. 1 (2001): 33–41.

———. "Reading, Hegemony and Counterhegemony in the Late Ottoman Empire and the Early Turkish Republic." In *Counterhegemony in the Colony and Postcolony*, edited by John Chalcraft and Yaseen Noorani, 141–54. New York: Palgrave Macmillan, 2007.

Frierson, Elizabeth Brown. "Unimagined Communities: State, Press, and Gender in the Hamidian Era." Ph.D. dissertation, Princeton University, 1996.

Gallagher, Charles F. "Language Reform and Social Modernization in Turkey." In *Can Language Be Planned? Sociolinguistic Theory and Practice for Developing Nations*, edited by Joan Rubin and Björn H. Jernudd, 159–78. Honolulu: University Press of Hawaii, 1971.

Genç, Reşat. *Türkiye'yi Laikleştiren Yasalar: 3 Mart 1924 Tarihli Meclis Müzakereleri ve Kararları.* Ankara: Atatürk Kültür, Dil ve Tarih Yüksek Kurumu Atatürk Araştırma Merkezi, 1998.

Georgeon, François. "Des Caractères Arabes à l'alphabet Latin: un pas vers l'Occident?" In *Des Ottomans aux Turcs: Naissance d'une Nation*, edited by François Georgeon, 199–221. Istanbul: ISIS, 1995.

———. "Lire et écrire à la fin de l'Empire ottoman: quelques remarques introductives." In *Oral et écrit dans le monde turc-ottoman, Revue de monde musulman et de la Méditerranée*, edited by Nicolas Vatin, 75–76 (1995): 171–73.

———. *Türk Milliyetçiliğinin Kökenleri: Yusuf Akçura (1876–1935).* Translated by Alev Er. Istanbul: Tarih Vakfı Yurt Yayınları, 1986.

Gelvin, James L. *Divided Loyalties: Nationalism and Mass Politics in Syria at the Close of Empire*. Berkeley: University of California Press, 1998.

Gillis, John R. "Memory and Identity: The History of a Relationship." In *Commemorations: The Politics of National Identity*, edited by John R. Gillis, 3–24. Princeton: Princeton University Press, 1994.

Gingeras, Ryan. *Sorrowful Shores: Violence, Ethnicity, and the End of the Ottoman Empire, 1912–1923*. Oxford: Oxford University Press, 2009.

Goloğlu, Mahmut. *Devrimler ve Tepkileri (1924–1930)*. Ankara: Başnur, 1972.

———. *Tek Partili Cumhuriyet (1931–1938)*. Ankara: Goloğlu Yayınları, 1974.

Göçek, Fatma Müge. *Rise of the Bourgeoisie, Demise of Empire: Ottoman Westernization and Social Change* (New York: Oxford University Press, 1996).

Gökalp, Necati. "Türk Basınında Soyadı Kanunu." Master's thesis, İstanbul Üniversitesi, 1996.

Göle, Nilüfer. *The Forbidden Modern: Civilization and Veiling*. Ann Arbor: The University of Michigan Press, 1996 (1999 printing. Originally published in Turkish as *Modern Mahrem*. Istanbul: Metis Yayınları, 1991).

———. "The Voluntary Adoption of Islamic Stigma Symbols." *Social Research* 70, no. 3 (Fall 2003): 809–28.

Graham-Brown, Sarah. *The Portrayal of Women in Photography of the Middle East 1860–1950: Images of Women*. New York: Columbia University Press, 1988.

Güzel, Mehmet Şehmus. "1908 Kadınları." *Tarih ve Toplum* 2, no. 7 (1984): 6–12.

Hakko, Vitali. *My Life: Vakko*. Translated by Michael D. McGaha. Istanbul: Libra Kitap, 2011.

Hobsbawm, Eric. Introduction: "Inventing Traditions." In *The Invention of Tradition*, edited by Eric Hobsbawm and Terence Ranger, 1–14. Cambridge: Cambridge University Press, 1983.

Harf Devriminin 50. Yılı Sempozyumu. (First printing 1981.) Ankara: Türk Tarih Kurumu Yayınları, 1991.

Heyd, Uriel. *Language Reform in Modern Turkey*. Oriental Notes and Studies no. 5. Jerusalem: The Israel Oriental Society, 1954.

Hourani, Albert. "How Should We Write the History of the Middle East?" *International Journal of Middle East Studies* 23, no. 2 (May 1991): 125–36.

Howell, Martha C. and Walter Prevenier. *From Reliable Sources: An Introduction to Historical Methods*. Ithaca: Cornell University Press, 2001.

Huntington, Samuel P. "Revolution and Political Order." In *Revolutions: Theoretical, Comparative, and Historical Studies*, edited by Jack A. Goldstone. San Diego: Harcourt Brace Jovanovich, 1986.

İnan, Rauf. "Yazı Değişimi." In *Harf Devriminin 50. Yılı Sempozyumu.* (First printing 1981), 169–86. Ankara: Türk Tarih Kurumu Yayınları, 1991.

İnan, Süleyman. "19 Mayıs Gününün Bayramlaşması." *Bilgi ve Bellek* 2, no. 3 (Kış 2005): 45–66.

İnuğur, Nuri. *Türk Basın Tarihi.* Istanbul: Gazeteciler Cemiyeti, 1992.

Jäschke, Gotthard. *Yeni Türkiye'de İslâmlık.* Translated by Hayrullah Örs. Ankara: Bilgi Yayınevi, 1972.

Kafadar, Cemal. *Between Two Worlds: The Construction of the Ottoman State.* Berkeley: University of California Press, 1995.

Kamp, Marianne. *The New Woman in Uzbekistan: Islam, Modernity, and Unveiling under Communism.* Seattle: University of Washington Press, 2006.

Kandiyoti, Deniz. "Emancipated but Unliberated? Reflections on the Turkish Case." *Feminist Studies* 13, no. 2 (Summer, 1987): 317–38.

———. "End of Empire: Islam, Nationalism and Women in Turkey." In *Women, Islam & the State,* edited by Deniz Kandiyoti, 22–47. Philadelphia: Temple University Press, 1991.

———. "Gendering the Modern: On Missing Dimensions in the Study of Turkish Modernity." In *Rethinking Modernity and National Identity in Turkey,* edited by Sibel Bozdoğan and Reşat Kasaba, 113–32. Seattle: University of Washington Press, 1997.

———. "Patterns of Patriarchy: Notes for an Analysis of Male Dominance in Turkish Society." In *Women in Turkish Society: A Reader,* edited by Şirin Tekeli, 306–18. London: Zed Books, 1995.

Kaplan, İsmail. *Türkiye'de Milli Eğitim İdeolojisi ve Siyasal Toplumsallaşma Üzerindeki Etkisi.* Istanbul: İletişim Yayıncılık, 1999.

Karadağ, Meltem. "Taşra kentlerinde yaşam tarzları alanı: Kültür ve ayrım." *Toplum ve Bilim,* no. 118 (2010): 39–58.

Karaer, İbrahim. "Türk Ocakları ve İnkılâplar (1912–1931)." Ph.D. dissertation, Ankara Üniversitesi, 1989.

Karaömerlioğlu, Asım. *Orada Bir Köy Var Uzakta: Erken Cumhuriyet Döneminde Köycü Söylem.* Istanbul: İletişim Yayınları, 2006.

———. "The Village Institutes Experience in Turkey." *British Journal of Middle Eastern Studies* 25, no. 1 (May 1998): 47–73.

Karateke, Hakan T. *Padişahım Çok Yaşa! Osmanlı Devletinin Son Yüzyılında Merasimler.* Istanbul: Kitap Yayınevi, 2004.

Karpat, Kemal H. "A Language in Search of a Nation: Turkish in the Nation-State." *Studies on Turkish Politics and Society: Selected Articles and Essays,* edited by

Kemal Karpat, 435–65. Leiden: Brill, 2004. Originally published in *The Emergence of National Languages*, edited by Aldo Scarglione, Ravenna: Longo Editore, 1984.

———. *Ottoman Population 1830–1914: Demographic and Social Characteristics*. Madison: University of Wisconsin Press, 1985.

Kaynardağ, Arslan. "Eğitimle İlgili Üç Rapor ve Atatürk İş Üniversitesi." *International Conference on Atatürk, November 9–13, 1981: Proceedings*, vol. 2 [*Tebliğler Cilt 2*]: 1–13. Istanbul: Boğaziçi Üniversitesi, 1981.

Kazamias, Andreas M. *Education and the Quest for Modernity in Turkey*. Chicago: University of Chicago Press, 1966.

Keller, Shoshana. *To Moscow Not Mecca: The Soviet Campaign Against Islam in Central Asia, 1917–1941*. Westport, CT: Praeger, 2001.

Keyder, Çağlar. *State and Class in Turkey: A Study in Capitalist Development*. London: Verso, 1987.

Kırpık, Cevdet. "Osmanlı İmparatorluğunda Modernleşme Sancıları: Fes-Şapka Çatışması." *Toplumsal Tarih*, no. 162 (September 2007): 14–22.

Kili, Suna. *The Atatürk Revolution: A Paradigm of Modernization*. Translated by Sylvia Zeybekoğlu. Istanbul: İş Bankası Kültür Yayınları, 2003.

Kirby, Fay. *Türkiye'de Köy Enstitüleri*. Ankara: İmece Yayınları, 1962.

Kocabaşoğlu, Uygur, ed., *Modern Türkiye'de Siyasi Düşünce*, Vol. 3, *Modernleşme ve Batıcılık*. Istanbul: İletişim Yayınları, 2002.

Koçak, Cemil. *Türkiye'de Milli Şef Dönemi (1938–1945) Dönemin iç ve dış politikası üzerine bir araştırma*. 2 vols. Istanbul: İletişim Yayınları, 1996.

———. *Umumi Müfettişlikler (1927–1952)*. Istanbul: İletişim Yayınları, 2003.

Koloğlu, Orhan. *Bir Çağdaşlaşma Örneği Olarak Cumhuriyet'in İlk Onbeş Yılı (1923–1938)*. 2. Basım [2nd printing]. Istanbul: Boyut Yayıncılık, 2002.

Koraltürk, Murat. "Milliyetçi Bir Refleks: Yer Adlarının Türkçeleştirilmesi." *Toplumsal Tarih*, no. 117 (September 2003): 98–99.

Kuhne, Alfred. *Mesleki Terbiyenin İnkişafına Dair Rapor* (Istanbul: 1939). In *Educational Problems in Turkey 1920–1940*, edited by İlhan Başgöz and Howard E. Wilson, 85. Bloomington: Indiana University Press, 1968.

Küçükerman, Önder and İlhan Berk, *Ressam Orhan Peker: Hayatı, Eserleri, Görüşleri*. Istanbul: Millî Reasürans T.A.Ş., 1994.

Levend, Agâh Sırrı. *Türk Dilinde Gelişme ve Sadeleşme Evreleri*. 3rd ed. Ankara: Türk Dil Kurumu Yayınları, 1972.

Lewis, Bernard. *The Emergence of Modern Turkey*. 2nd ed. London: Oxford University Press, 1968.

Lewis, Geoffrey. *The Turkish Language Reform: A Catastrophic Success*. Oxford: Oxford University Press, 1999.

Libal, Kathryn. "The Child Question: The Politics of Child Welfare in Early Republican Turkey." In *Poverty and Charity in Middle Eastern Contexts*, edited by Michael Bonner, Mine Ener, and Amy Singer, 255–72. Albany: State University of New York Press, 2003.

———. "The Children's Protection Society: Nationalizing Child Welfare in Early Republican Turkey." *New Perspectives on Turkey*, no. 23 (Fall 2000): 53–78.

———. "National Futures: The Child Question in Early Republican Turkey." Ph.D. dissertation, University of Washington, 2001.

———. "Realizing Modernity Through the Robust Turkish Child, 1923–1938." In *Symbolic Childhood*, edited by Daniel Thomas Cook, 109–30. New York: Peter Lang Publishing, 2002.

Magnarella, Paul J. "The Reception of Swiss Family Law in Turkey." *Anthropological Quarterly* 46, no. 2 (April 1973): 100–116.

———. *Tradition and Change in a Turkish Town*. Cambridge, MA: Schenkman; New York: John Wiley and Sons, 1974.

Mahir, İkbal Elif. "Fashion and Women in the İstanbul of the Armistice Period, 1918–1923." Master's thesis, Boğaziçi University, Istanbul, 2005.

Makal, Mahmut. *Bizim Köy*. Istanbul: Literatür Yayınları, 2008. Originally published Istanbul: Varlık, 1950.

Marashi, Afshin. *Nationalizing Iran: Culture, Power, and the State, 1870–1940*. Seattle: University of Washington Press, 2008.

———. "Performing the Nation: The Shah's Official State Visit to Kemalist Turkey, June to July 1934." In *The Making of Modern Iran: State and Society under Riza Shah, 1921–1941*, edited by Stephanie Cronin, 99–119. London: Routledge Curzon, 2003.

Mardin, Şerif. "Ideology and Religion in the Turkish Revolution." *International Journal of Middle East Studies* 2 (1971): 197–211.

———. Introduction to *Religion, Society, and Modernity*, xiii–xvi.

———. "Projects as Methodology: Some Thoughts on Modern Turkish Social Science." In *Rethinking Modernity and National Identity in Turkey* edited by Sibel Bozdoğan and Reşat Kasaba, 64–80. Seattle and London: University of Washington Press, 1997.

———. *Religion and Social Change in Modern Turkey: The Case of Bediüzzaman Said Nursi*. Albany, N.Y.: State University of New York Press, 1989.

———. *Religion, Society, and Modernity in Turkey*. Syracuse: Syracuse University Press, 2006.

———. "Super-Westernization in Urban Life in the Ottoman Empire in the Last Quarter of the Nineteenth Century." In Mardin, *Religion, Society, and Modernity, 135–63.*

———. *Türk Modernleşmesi (Makaleler 4).* Istanbul: İletişim Yayınları, 1991.

Massell, Gregory T. "Law as an Instrument of Revolutionary Change in a Traditional Milieu: The Case of Soviet Central Asia." *Law & Society Review* 2, no. 2 (February 1968): 179–228.

Mazıcı, Nurşen. "Menemen Olayı'nın sosyo-kültürel ve sosyo-ekonomik analizi." *Toplum ve Bilim* 90 (Fall 2001): 131–46.

McCarthy, Justin. "Foundations of the Turkish Republic: Social and Economic Change." *Middle Eastern Studies* 19, no. 2 (April 1983): 139–51.

———. *Muslims and Minorities: The Population of Ottoman Anatolia and the End of the Empire.* New York: New York University Press, 1983.

McDowall, David. *A Modern History of the Kurds.* London: I. B. Tauris, 1996.

Meeker, Michael E. *A Nation of Empire: The Ottoman Legacy of Turkish Modernity.* Berkeley and Los Angeles: University of California Press, 2002.

———. "Once There Was, Once There Wasn't: National Monuments and Interpersonal Exchange." In *Rethinking Modernity and National Identity in Turkey,* edited by Sibel Bozdoğan and Reşat Kasaba, 157–91. Seattle: University of Washington Press, 1997.

Metinsoy, Murat. "Kemalizmin taşrası: Erken Cumhuriyet taşrasında parti, devlet ve toplum." *Toplum ve Bilim,* no. 118 (2010): 124–64.

Micklewright, Nancy. "Women's Dress in Nineteenth-Century Istanbul: Mirror of a Changing Society." Ph.D. dissertation, University of Pennsylvania, 1986.

Migdal, Joel. *State in Society: Studying How States and Societies Transform and Constitute One Another.* Cambridge: Cambridge University Press, 2001.

———. "Finding the Meeting Ground of Fact and Fiction: Some Reflections on Turkish Modernization." In *Rethinking Modernity and National Identity in Turkey,* edited by Sibel Bozdoğan and Reşat Kasaba, 252–60. Seattle: University of Washington Press, 1997.

Moghadam, Valentine M. *Modernizing Women: Gender and Social Change in the Middle East.* Boulder: Lynne Rienner Publishers, 1993.

Mumcu, Ahmet. *Tarih açısından Türk Devriminin Temelleri ve Gelişmesi.* [Istanbul]: İnkilâp Kitabevi, *n.d.*

Najmabadi, Afsaneh. "Hazards of Modernity and Morality: Women, State and Ideology in Contemporary Iran." In *Women, Islam & the State,* edited by Deniz Kandiyoti, 48–76. Philadelphia: Temple University Press, 1991.

——. *Women with Mustaches and Men without Beards: Gender and Sexual Anxieties of Iranian Modernity.* Berkeley: University of California Press, 2005.

Neuburger, Mary. *The Orient Within: Muslim Minorities and the Negotiation of Nationhood in Modern Bulgaria.* Ithaca, NY: Cornell University Press, 2004.

Neyzi, Leyla. *"Ben Kimim?" Türkiye'de Sözlü Tarih, Kimlik ve Öznellik.* Istanbul: İletişim Yayınları, 2004.

——. "Object or Subject? The Paradox of 'Youth' in Turkey." *International Journal of Middle East Studies* 33, no. 3 (August 2001): 411–32.

——. "Oral History and Memory Studies in Turkey." In *Turkey's Engagement with Modernity: Conflict and Change in the Twentieth Century,* edited by Celia Kerslake, Kerem Öktem, and Philip Robins, 443–59. Oxford: Palgrave Macmillan, 2010.

Nora, Pierre. "Between Memory and History: Les Lieux de Mémoire." *Representations,* no. 26 (Spring 1989): 7–25.

Northrop, Douglas. *Veiled Empire: Gender and Power in Stalinist Central Asia.* Ithaca, NY: Cornell University Press, 2004.

Ocak, Başak. *Bir Yayıncının Portresi: Tüccarzâde İbrahim Hilmi Çığıraçan.* Istanbul: Müteferrika Yayınları, 2003.

Okay, Cüneyd. "İnkılapların Hayata Geçirilmesinde Eğitimin Yeri ve Şapka Kanunu Örneği," *Bilgi ve Bellek* 2, no. 4 (summer 2005): 186–207.

——. "War and Child in the Second Constitutional Period." In *Enfance et jeunesse dans le monde musulman. Childhood and Youth in the Muslim World,* edited by François Georgeon and Klaus Kreiser, 219–32. Paris: Maisonneuve et Larose, 2007.

Olson, Robert. *The Emergence of Kurdish Nationalism and the Sheikh Said Rebellion, 1880–1925.* Austin: University of Texas Press, 1989.

Olsson, T. *Alevi Identity: Cultural, Religious and Social Perspectives.* Edited by E. Özdalga and C. Raudvere. Istanbul: Swedish Research Institute in Istanbul (SRII), 1998.

Oran, Baskın. *Atatürk Milliyetçiliği: Resmi İdeoloji Dışı Bir İnceleme.* Ankara: Bilgi Yayınevi, 1988.

"Osmanlıca başladılar, Türkçe bitirdiler: 'Tedrisat'tan 'Öğretim'e." *NTV Tarih,* no. 21 (October 2010): 32–33.

Öksüz, Hikmet and Veysel Usta. *Mustafa Reşit Tarakçıoğlu: Hayatı, Hatıratı ve Trabzon'un Yakın Tarihi.* Trabzon: Serander Yayıncılık, 2008.

Öktem, Nazlı. "Ölümsüz Bir Ölüm, Sonsuz Bir Yas: Türkiye'de 10 Kasım." In *Hatırladıkları ve Unuttuklarıyla Türkiye'nin Toplumsal Hafızası,* edited by Esra Özyürek, 325–46. Istanbul: İletişim Yayınları, 2001.

Öz, Esat. *Otoriterizm ve siyaset: Türkiye'de tek-parti rejimi ve siyasal katılma, 1923–1945.* Ankara: Yetkin Basın Yayın ve Dağıtım, 1996.

Öz, Eyüp. *Menemen Olayı ve Türkiye'de Mehdicilik.* Istanbul: 47 Numara Yayıncılık, 2007.

Özcan, Burcu. "Basına Göre Şapka ve Kılık Kıyafet İnkılâbı." Master's thesis, Marmara University, Istanbul, 2008.

Özdemir, Yavuz Uğur. "Türk Yazı Devrimi ve İlk Uygulamalar." Master's thesis, Dokuz Eylül Üniversitesi, İzmir, 2001.

Özdoğan, Günay Göksu. *"Turan"dan "Bozkurt"a Tek Parti Döneminde Türkçülük (1931–1946).* Translated by İsmail Kaplan. Istanbul: İletişim Yayınları, 2001.

Özer, Ahmet. "abdullah eltan'la söyleşi." *Kıyı* (Trabzon), no. 111 (June 1995): 14–16.

Özsan, Gül. "Eşraf Ailelerinin Statü Mücadelelerinde Kadınların Rolü." *Toplum ve Bilim*, no. 118 (2010): 59–91.

Öztürkmen, Arzu. "Celebrating National Holidays in Turkey: History and Memory." *New Perspectives on Turkey*, no. 25 (Fall 2001): 47–75.

———. "Milli Bayramlar: Şekli ve Hatırası-I." *Toplumsal Tarih* 5, no. 28 (April 1996): 29–35.

———. "Milli Bayramlar: Şekli ve Hatırası-II." *Toplumsal Tarih* 5, no. 29 (May 1996): 6–12.

———. "Remembering through Material Culture: Local Knowledge of Past Communities in a Turkish Black Sea Town," *Middle Eastern Studies* 39, no. 2 (April 2003): 179–93.

———. "Rethinking Regionalism: Memory of Change in a Turkish Black Sea Town." *East European Quarterly* 39, no. 1 (March 2005): 47–62.

———. *Türkiye'de Folklor ve Milliyetçilik.* Istanbul: İletişim Yayınları, 2001.

Özyürek, Esra, ed. *Hatırladıkları ve Unuttuklarıyla Türkiye'nin Toplumsal Hafızası.* Istanbul: İletişim Yayıncılık, 2001.

———. *Nostalgia for the Modern: State Secularism and Everyday Politics in Turkey.* Durham, N.C.: Duke University Press, 2006.

Pamuk, Orhan. *Cevdet Bey ve Oğulları.* Istanbul: İletişim Yayınları, 1982.

———. *Yeni Hayat.* Istanbul: İletişim Yayınları, 1994.

Parla, Taha. *The Social and Political Thought of Ziya Gökalp.* Leiden: Brill, 1985.

———. *Türkiye'de Siyasi Kültürün Resmî Kaynakları.* Vol. 1, *Atatürk'ün Nutuk'u*; Vol. 2, *Atatürk'ün Söylev ve Demeçleri*; Vol. 3, *Kemalist Tek Parti İdeolojisi ve CHP'nin Altı Ok'u.* Istanbul: İletişim, 1992.

Parla, Taha and Andrew Davison. *Corporatist Ideology in Kemalist Turkey: Progress or Order?* Syracuse, New York: Syracuse University Press, 2004.

Perry, John R. "Language Reform in Turkey and Iran." *International Journal of Middle East Studies* 17, no. 3 (August 1985): 295–311.

Poullada, Leon B. *Reform and Rebellion in Afghanistan, 1919–1929: King Amanullah's Failure to Modernize a Tribal Society*. Ithaca: Cornell University Press, 1973.

Quataert, Donald. "Clothing Laws, State, and Society in the Ottoman Empire, 1720–1829." *International Journal of Middle East Studies* 29, no. 3 (1997): 403–25.

———, ed. *Consumption Studies and the History of the Ottoman Empire, 1550–1922. An Introduction*. Albany, NY: State University of New York Press, 2000.

Rostam-Kolayi, Jasamin. "Expanding Agendas for the "New" Iranian Woman: Family Law, Work, and Unveiling." In *The Making of Modern Iran: State and Society under Riza Shah, 1921–1941*, edited by Stephanie Cronin, 164–89. London; New York: Routledge Curzon, 2003.

Roy, Srirupa. "Seeing a State: National Commemorations and the Public Sphere in India and Turkey." *Comparative Studies in Society and History* 48, no. 1 (2006): 200–232.

Sadoğlu, Hasan. *Türkiye'de Ulusçuluk ve Dil Politikaları*. Istanbul: İstanbul Bilgi Üniversitesi Yayınları, 2003.

Sadullah, Mitat. *Yeni Yurt Bilgisi*. Istanbul: Tefeyyuz Kitaphanesi, 1929. Quoted in Henry Elisha Allen, *The Turkish Transformation: A Study in Social and Religious Development*, 110. Chicago: University of Chicago Press, 1935.

Sakaoğlu, Necdet. *Osmanlı'dan Günümüze Eğitim Tarihi*. Istanbul: İstanbul Bilgi Üniversitesi Yayınları, 2003.

Salmoni, Barak Aharon. "Pedagogies of Patriotism: Teaching Socio-Political Community in Twentieth-Century Turkish and Egyptian Education." Ph.D. dissertation, Harvard University, 2002.

Saposnik, Arieh Bruce. *Becoming Hebrew: The Creation of a Jewish National Culture in Ottoman Palestine*. Oxford: Oxford University Press, 2008.

Sarısaman, Sadık. "Cumhuriyet'in İlk Yıllarında Kadın Kıyafeti Meselesi." *Atatürk Yolu*, no. 21 (May 1998): 97–106.

Scott, James C. *Weapons of the Weak: Everyday Forms of Peasant Resistance*. New Haven: Yale University Press, 1985.

Shankland, David. *The Alevis in Turkey: The Emergence of a Secular Islamic Tradition*. London: RoutledgeCurzon, 2003.

———. "Old Ideas in New Forms: The Mehti in Modern Turkey" in *The Coming Deliverer: Millenial Themes in World Religions*, edited by Fiona Bowie and Christopher Decay. Cardiff: University of Wales Press, 1997.

Shields, Sarah D. *Fezzes in the River: Identity Politics and European Diplomacy in the Middle East on the Eve of World War II.* Oxford and New York: Oxford University Press, 2011.

Shissler, A. Holly. *Between Two Empires: Ahmet Ağaoğlu and the New Turkey.* London: I. B. Tauris, 2003.

Somel, Selçuk Akşin. *The Modernization of Public Education in the Ottoman Empire, 1839–1908: Islamization, Autocracy and Discipline.* Leiden: Brill, 2011.

Stirling, Paul. "Social Change and Social Control in Republican Turkey." *Papers and Discussions. Türkiye İş Bankası International Symposium on Atatürk*, 565–600. Ankara: Türkiye İş Bankası Cultural Publications, 1984.

Strauss, Johann. "Literacy and the Development of the Primary and Secondary Educational System: The Role of the Alphabet and Language Reforms." In *Turkey in the Twentieth Century*, edited by Erik-Jan Zürcher, 479–516. Berlin: Klaus Schwarz Verlag, 2008.

Sungu, İhsan. "Harf İnkılabı ve Millî Şef İsmet İnönü." *Tarih Vesikaları* 1, no. 1 (June 1941): 10–19.

Şahin, Zeliha. "Kılık-Kıyafet Devrimi ve Propaganda." Master's thesis, Gazi Üniversitesi, Ankara, 1997.

Şeni, Nora. "Fashion and Women's Clothing in the Satirical Press of Istanbul at the End of the 19th Century." In *Women in Modern Turkish Society: A Reader*, edited by Şirin Tekeli, 25–45. London: Zed Books, 1995.

Şimşek, Sefa. *Bir İdeolojik Seferberlik Deneyimi: Halkevleri 1932–1951.* Istanbul: Boğaziçi Üniversitesi Yayınevi, 2002.

Şimşir, Bilâl N. "Türk Harf Devrimi'nin Türkiye Dışına Yayılması: Bulgaristan Türkleri Örneği." In *Harf Devriminin 50. Yılı Sempozyumu*, 187–206. Ankara: Türk Tarih Kurumu Yayınları, 1991.

———. *Türk Yazı Devrimi.* Ankara: Türk Tarih Kurumu Yayınları, 1992.

Tarhanlı, İştar B. *Müslüman Toplum "Laik" Devlet: Türkiye'de Diyanet İşleri Başkanlığı.* Istanbul: Afa, 1993.

"Tartışmalar ve Açıklamalar." *Harf Devrimi'nin 50. Yılı Sempozyumu*, 128–46. Reprint. Ankara: Türk Tarih Kurumu Yayınları, 1991. First printed in 1981.

Thompson, Elizabeth. *Colonial Citizens: Republican Rights, Paternal Privilege, and Gender in French Syria and Lebanon.* New York: Columbia University Press, 2000.

Tiregöl, Jessica Selma. "The Role of Primary Education in Nation–State-Building: The Case of the Early Turkish Republic (1923–1938)." Ph.D. dissertation, Princeton University, 1998.

Tokluoğlu, Ceylan. "The Formation of the Turkish Nation-State and Resistance." Ph.D. dissertation, Carleton University, Ottawa, 1995.

Toprak, Zafer. "The Family, Feminism, and the State during the Young Turk Period, 1908–1918." In *Première Rencontre Internationale sur l'Empire Ottoman et la Turquie Moderne*, edited by Edhem Eldem, 441–52. Istanbul: ISIS, 1991.

———. "Tesettürden Telebbüse ya da Çarşaf veya Elbise: 'Milli Moda' ve Çarşaf." *Tombak*, no. 19 (April 1998): 52–63.

Trix, Frances. "The Stamboul Alphabet of Shemseddin Sami Bey: Precursor to Turkish Script Reform." *International Journal of Middle East Studies* 31, no. 2 (May 1999): 255–72.

Tunçay, Mete. *Türkiye Cumhuriyeti'nde Tek-Parti Yönetimi'nin Kurulması (1923–1931)*. Istanbul: Tarih Vakfı Yurt Yayınları, 1999.

Türk Silâhlı Kuvvetleri Tarihi Vol. 3, part 6 (1908–1920), book 1. Ankara: T. C. Genelkurmay Harp Tarihi Başkanlığı Resmi Yayınları, 1971.

Türköz, Meltem. "Surname Narratives and the State-Society Boundary: Memories of Turkey's Family Name Law of 1934." *Middle Eastern Studies* 43, no. 6 (November 2007): 893–908.

Türköz, Meltem F. "The Social Life of the State's Fantasy: Memories and Documents on Turkey's 1934 Surname Law." Ph.D. dissertation, University of Pennsylvania, 2004.

Ülkütaşır, M. Şakir. *Atatürk ve Harf Devrimi*. Ankara: Türk Dil Kurumu Yayınları, 1981.

Unat, Nermin Abadan. "Türkiye'de Kadın Hareketi-Dün-Bugün." In *Bilanço 1923–1998*, edited by Zeynep Rona, vol. 2, 247–66. Istanbul: Tarih Vakfı, 1999.

"Unutma." http://web.inonu.edu.tr/~mkilic/babamin_siirleri.html. Accessed on 23 August 2010.

"Unutma." http://www.antoloji.com/unutma-92-siiri/. Accessed on 23 August 2010.

Uyar, Hakkı. "Çarşaf, Peçe ve Kafes Üzerine Bazı Notlar." *Toplumsal Tarih*, no.33 (Eylül [September] 1996): 6–11.

———. *Tek Parti Dönemi ve Cumhuriyet Halk Partisi*. Istanbul: Boyut Kitapları, 1999.

Van Os, Nicole A. N. M. "Polygamy Before and After the Introduction of the Swiss Civil Code in Turkey." In *The State and the Subaltern: Modernization, Society and the State in Turkey and Iran*, edited by Touraj Atabaki, 179–98. London: I. B. Tauris, 2007.

———. "Ottoman Women's Reaction to the Economic and Cultural Intrusion of the West: The Quest for a National Dress." In *Dissociation and Appropriation*

Responses to Globalization in Asia and Africa, edited by Katja Füllberg-Stolberg, et al., 291–308. Berlin: Verlag Das Arabische Buch, 1999.

Van Voss, Lex Heerma. "Introduction." In *Petitions in Social History* (International Review of Social History Supplement 9), edited by Lex Heerma van Voss, 1–10. Cambridge: Cambridge University Press, 2002.

Ward, Robert E. and Dankwart A. Rustow, eds. *Political Modernization in Japan and Turkey*. Princeton, NJ.: Princeton University Press, 1964.

Weiker, Walter. *The Modernization of Turkey: From Atatürk to the Present Day*. New York: Holmes & Meyer, 1981.

Yakut, Kemal, "Tek Parti Döneminde Peçe ve Çarşaf." *Tarih ve Toplum*, no. 220 (April 2002): 23–32.

Yalman, Ahmed Emin. *Turkey in my Time*. Norman: University of Oklahoma Press, 1956.

Yetkin, Sabri. *Ege'de Eşkıyalar*. Istanbul: Tarih Vakfı Yurt Yayınları, 1996.

Yıldız, Ahmet. *"Ne Mutlu Türküm Diyebilene" Türk Ulusal Kimliğinin Etno-Seküler Sınırları (1919–1938)*. Istanbul: İletişim Yayınları, 2001.

Yılmaz, Hale. "Petitions as a Source in Women's History of the Republican Period." In *Women's Memory: The Problem of Sources from the Ottoman Period to Our Times*, edited by Fatma Türe and Birsen Talay Keşoğlu, 81–93. Newcastle upon Tyne: Cambridge Scholars Publishing, 2011.

Yüksel, Ayhan. "Trabzon Vilâyetinde Yer Adlarını ve İdarî Yapıyı Değiştirme Teşebbüsleri." *Trabzon Tarihi Sempozyumu 6–8 Kasım 1998 Bildiriler*, 201–22. Trabzon: Trabzon Belediyesi Kültür Yayınları, 1999.

Zengin, Sabri. "Türk İnkılabının Tokat'taki Yansımaları." http://idak.gop.edu.tr /szengin/makaleler/seminer.doc.

Zerubavel, Yael. *Recovered Roots: Collective Memory and the Making of Israeli National Tradition*. Chicago: University of Chicago Press, 1995.

Zihnioğlu, Yaprak. *Kadınsız İnkılap: Nezihe Muhiddin, Kadınlar Halk Fırkası, Kadın Birliği*. Istanbul: Metis Yayınları, 2003.

Zürcher, Erik-Jan. "From Empire to Republic—problems of transition, continuity and change." In *Turkey in the Twentieth Century*, edited by Erik-Jan Zürcher. Berlin: Klaus Schwarz Verlag, 2008.

———. "Institution Building in the Kemalist Republic: The Role of the People's Party." In *Men of Order: Authoritarian Modernization under Atatürk and Reza Shah*, edited by Touraj Atabaki and Erik-Jan Zürcher, 98–112. London: I.B. Tauris, 2004.

——. "Kemalist Düşüncenin Osmanlı Kaynakları." In *Modern Türkiye'de Siyasi Düşünce, Cilt 2, Kemalizm*, edited by Tanıl Bora and Murat Gültekingil and translated by Özgür Gökmen, 44–55. Istanbul: İletişim Yayınları, 2001.

——. *Political Opposition in the Early Turkish Republic: The Progressive Republican Party*. Leiden: Brill, 1991.

——. *Turkey: A Modern History*. Third Edition. London: I. B. Tauris, 2004.

——. *Turkey in the Twentieth Century*. Edited by Erik-Jan Zürcher. Berlin: Klaus Schwarz Verlag, 2008.

——. "Two Young Ottomanists Discover Kemalist Turkey: The Travel Diaries of Robert Anhegger and Andreas Tietze." *Journal of Turkish Studies/Türklük Bilgisi Araştırmaları* 26, no. 2 (2002): 359–69.

——. *The Young Turk Legacy and Nation Building: from the Ottoman Empire to Atatürk's Turkey*. London: I. B. Tauris, 2010.

Index

HALE YILMAZ earned a Ph.D. in History from the University of Utah and is currently Assistant Professor of Middle East and Islamic History at Southern Illinois University, Carbondale.

.